PRAISE FOR
INSIDE INTEL

"A keyhole view of the company's history, laced with remarkable detail and sometimes shocking revelations. Anybody interested in a juicy tale of high-tech empire building will find this book fascinating—and a little disturbing."

—*Business Week*

"Lively . . . fascinating narratives."

—*New York Times*

"It's all here . . . the monumental egos, screaming matches, fast foreign cars, alcohol, insanity. . . . Jackson dishes the dirt and comes up with a few surprises."

—*Information Week*

"A lively, accessible, and informative overview of Intel Corp. First-rate."

—*Kirkus Reviews*

TIM JACKSON, a columnist for the *Financial Times*, has worked as a foreign correspondent in Japan and Belgium. He is the author of two previous books, *Turning Japanese*, a study of the conflict between U.S. and Japanese businesses in the European market, and *Virgin King*, a biography of Richard Branson, founder of the billion-dollar Virgin airline conglomerate. Tim Jackson lives in London.

INSIDE INTEL

Andy Grove and the Rise of the World's Most Powerful Chip Company

TIM JACKSON

With a New Preface by the Author

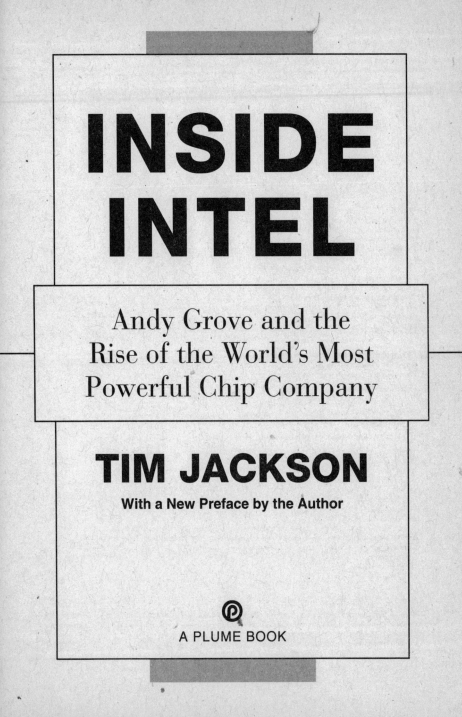

A PLUME BOOK

PLUME
Published by the Penguin Group
Penguin Putnam Inc., 375 Hudson Street,
New York, New York 10014, U.S.A.
Penguin Books Ltd, 27 Wrights Lane,
London W8 5TZ, England
Penguin Books Australia Ltd, Ringwood,
Victoria, Australia
Penguin Books Canada Ltd, 10 Alcorn Avenue,
Toronto, Ontario, Canada M4V 3B2
Penguin Books (N.Z.) Ltd, 182–190 Wairau Road,
Auckland 10, New Zealand

Penguin Books Ltd, Registered Offices:
Harmondsworth, Middlesex, England

First published by Plume, an imprint of Dutton NAL,
a member of Penguin Putnam Inc.
Previously published in a Dutton edition.

First Plume Printing, October, 1998
10 9 8 7 6 5 4 3 2 1

Ⓟ REGISTERED TRADEMARK—MARCA REGISTRADA

The Library of Congress had catalogued the Dutton edition as follows:
Jackson, Tim.
Inside Intel : Andy Grove and the rise of the world's most
powerful chip company / Tim Jackson.
p. cm.
Includes index.
ISBN 0-525-94141-X (hc.)
ISBN 0-452-27643-8 (pbk.)
1. Intel Corporation.   2. Semiconductor industry—United States.   3. Grove, Andrew S.
4. High technology industries—United States—Management.   5. Technological innovations—
Economic aspects—United States.   6. Corporations—United States.   7. Chief executive officers—
United States.   I. Title.
HD9696.S44I585   1997
338.7'621395'0973—dc21   97-4394
                                                                CIP

Printed in the United States of America

CONTENTS

PREFACE TO THE PLUME EDITION

In late 1997, when the first edition of this book came out, the business career of Andy Grove appeared to be drawing to a triumphant conclusion. During his three decades at Intel, Grove had gradually transformed himself from backroom operations chief to media personality and technology guru. By December 1997, that transformation was proven complete: *Time* magazine lauded him with a lengthy cover story designating him its Man of the Year. Earlier in the year, Grove won a quieter but perhaps still more prestigious recognition from the world's business leaders and politicians. He was invited to deliver a keynote address at the exclusive World Economic Forum in Davos, Switzerland, where prime ministers and presidents from around the world rub shoulders with international financiers and economists.

With public recognition had also come financial reward. In 1997 alone, Grove made $52.6 million from his involvement with Intel. (Typically of the company that he had built, less than $500,000 of that sum came from salary alone. Apart from nearly $3 million in cash bonuses, the bulk of the money came from stock options whose value was a direct result of the work that Grove had put into the business.) His total rewards from a career inside Intel added up to more than $300 million—not bad for someone who had arrived in the United States from Hungary a teenage refugee with nothing. To be fair, Grove's millions seemed almost modest by comparison with the $7 billion that Intel's two founders had made—but then Grove had been an employee rather than a founding investor, and had not put cash into the business thirty years earlier.

In early 1998, Intel's bruising patent dispute with Digital Equipment Corporation was also drawing to a conclusion. After a year of hostilities, in which Digital had accused Intel of copying the patented technology inside its Alpha range of processors and Intel had made its own counterclaims against Digital, Grove could now claim an unequivocal victory. Digital, under pressure as a result of the Intel dispute, was sold to Compaq, the world's largest PC manufacturer. As part of the deal Intel bought up its former rival's chip manufacturing facilities for $625 million. A battle that had shown every sign of lasting for years was settled more swiftly than anyone imagined possible.

With these achievements to his name, Grove could now quit while he was ahead. He was in a strong enough position to pass on the chief executive officer's mantle to Craig Barrett, the successor he had been grooming for almost a decade. To most people in Silicon Valley, Grove's elevation to the chairmanship of Intel, which was announced in March 1998 and took effect a couple of months later, was clearly the end of an era. But nobody who knew the driven, high-pressure genius of the man could expect him to retire to his garden. Grove would continue to work at Intel five days a week, often late into the evening. The difference was that his efforts would now be devoted to strategy rather than to day-to-day concerns.

Grove picked the right time to retire. After barrelling through his 50s as though he expected to be immortal, the Intel chief had received the jolt of his life when he was diagnosed with prostate cancer. Now, at 62, he needed to calm the pace a little. Although a bout of radiation-seed therapy seemed to have driven the disease into remission, Grove took no chances. He refined his already healthy eating habits to give himself the best life expectancy so much so that *Time* joked in its profile that "eating with Grove most days is like a trip to a vegan commune—tofu, veggies, five servings of fruit a day, a palmful of antioxidant pills."

But what kind of legacy did Andy Grove leave behind? Within months of his departure from the CEO's chair, problems facing Intel that had helped depress its stock price during the past half year suddenly began to look more forbidding. The company found itself at the wrong end of an antitrust action from the Federal Trade Commission. It faced problems at the bottom end of the market, with rising demand for cheap PCs threatening to eat away at its famously high margins. And it faced problems at the top end of its market, with a delay in the delivery of its upcoming bet-the-company Merced processor.

The FTC lawsuit was the result of repeated investigation and scrutiny of Intel by the trust busters over a number of years and hit the presses shortly after the U.S. Department of Justice launched a matching case against Microsoft. The existence of the two cases was a potent reminder that the market position often referred to as the "Wintel duopoly" wasn't any such thing. Microsoft and Intel each operated separate monopolies, cooperating where possible but competing where necessary in order to secure the largest possible share of the dollars paid by consumers for computers.

Microsoft's case, however, was very different from that of Intel. While the trust busters at Justice had launched an assault on the very core of the software company's future strategy—the integation of its web browser into the PC's operating system—their counterparts at the FTC had found only the narrowest ledge from which to attack Intel. The focus of the FTC's case was on the alleged misuse of confidential information. According to the FTC, Intel had taken unfair advantage of its position in the market by withholding technical information from companies that did not do what Intel wanted.

Intel's standard practice for many years was to release technical specifications, information, and samples of products to a large number of partners in the computer industry before they became public, but tó release them only under strict confidentiality agreements. This practice made sense for both sides. It allowed the PC industry to implement new Intel technologies swiftly after their release, and it helped Intel get products out into the market quickly. But the agreements governing the release of this information were tightly drawn. Intel could pull back its technical information whenever it wanted, and because the company's market power was so great, this could be damaging to its partner. Without access to Intel specifications and samples, it would become impossible to develop new PC products and bring them to market in good time. And it might even be difficult to solve technical problems with products already on the market.

Three specific cases had been cited, and in all three the behavior Intel was accused of was similar: using the threat of withholding access to this confidential information as a negotiating lever to bring a difficult partner into line. One of the cases was Digital itself: after Digital complained that Intel was infringing its Alpha patents, Intel had swiftly closed down the information channel Digital needed to build new Intel-equipped computers. More aggressively still, argued the FTC, Intel had arranged for a Digital employee to be ostentatiously expelled from a large industry gathering at which Intel technical information was being presented. This created a very public humiliation for Digital that raised fears in the industry that its Intel-based business was in danger of grinding to an immediate halt.

Coincidentally, the second case involved Compaq, the company to which Digital was eventually sold. Here the FTC charged that Compaq had sued Packard Bell, a rival PC manufacturer, claiming that an Intel component in Packard Bell machines infringed Compaq's own patents and that Intel, which was required to take up the cudgels on Packard Bell's behalf, used its own technical data to put the frighteners on Compaq. In an attempt to persuade the Houston-based PC maker to back down from its complaint, the FTC claimed, Intel had cut off technical information needed to design systems based on Intel's newest chips.

The third case was more blatant still, for it involved Intergraph Corporation, a small business based in Alabama specializing in high-end workstations. According to the FTC, Intergraph found itself in an unfavorable position with regard to Intel's technical information policy for one reason and one reason alone: the chip manufacturer wanted free-of-charge rights to a piece of Intergraph technology and tried to use its technical information as a lever to extort them.

In all three cases, the FTC complained, Intel's behavior was "not reasonably necessary to service any legitimate, procompetitive purpose," and in each case, Intel had "no reasonable belief" that the company whose access to technical secrets it was denying "had misused, could misuse, or would misuse" that information.

Intel's response to the FTC was very different from Microsoft's way of addressing the antitrust case from Justice. Microsoft had gone forth with all guns blazing, deriding the Justice department as anti-capitalist and anti-success. Bill Gates joked that Justice's demand that Microsoft Windows should give the Netscape browser the same access as its own Explorer product made no more sense than requiring Coca-Cola to include "three cans of Pepsi in every six-pack."

Intel, by contrast, was fairly passive in its response. It made no effort to take the battle to the American public. And instead of arguing over the details, Intel readily acknowledged the facts of the three cases. Where it differed from the trust busters, Intel said, was in the meaning of the law. According to Intel, it had no obligation to give anyone access to its technical secrets, and it believed there was nothing in U.S. antitrust law that forbade it from withdrawing technical cooperation from businesses it was on bad terms with.

One final point distinguished the two cases. For Microsoft, the Justice case threatened the company's very future. It was clearly an antitrust case on the same scale as that launched against IBM twenty years earlier. And Bill Gates, Microsoft's take-no-prisoners chairman, was determined not to lose it. The Intel case was a different matter. Even if the company lost the case completely—something that was by no means certain, since its lawyers had a track record of doing their homework carefully and the point of law was at least open to debate—Intel had little to lose. It would do little harm to Intel's competitive position to be forced by the government to stop using technical information as a negotiating tool.

If the antitrust case offered little cause for alarm, more fundamental changes in the wider computer industry did look worrying. The year 1997 saw the emergence for the first time of a mass market for "cheap PCs," machines priced at below $1,000. Although there had been various manufacturers offering sub-$1,000 PCs for years, this bottom end of the market was given dramatic legitimacy when Compaq brought its Presario consumer range below the magic price point. By August 1997, one leading industry survey was showing that 40 percent of all the retail computer sales in the United States were in this segment of the market.

For Intel, the change raised big strategic issues. The company's success had for more than a decade been built on a model of selling processors at prices far, far higher than their manufacturing cost. If the price of PCs were to fall closer to $500, then the minimal cost of the other components in the box would leave too little money left for Intel to continue its existing business model. Other makers, such as Cyrix, the company that had made a big hit with its low-margin, low-cost MediaGX processor, would be in a position where they could eat Intel's lunch.

The Intel marketing team at Santa Clara responded with a double-pronged attack. First, they accelerated the company's Inside Intel branding campaign and moved it over to the Web, so that PCs sold through the burgeoning Internet channel would be subject to the same barrage of Intel marketing messages as PCs advertising in the paper computer press. The campaign worked by Intel offering to pay part of the cost of PC ads where the ads gave prominence to the Intel brand and product. On the Web, the company added a further kicker: advertisers could claim a larger contribution from Intel if they advertised on processor-intensive websites that encouraged users to use high-end Pentium II chips. This raised some hackles in the Internet business, because some website owners complained that Intel was trying to exert editorial control over their content.

The increase in brand spending was only part of the strategy. The other prong was the launch of a new processor brand, Celeron. This name, more evocative of a space-age salad vegetable than of a piece of technology, was destined to be the low-end competition killer that would help Intel maintain its position at the bottom of the market.

In 1998, analysts in the industry were unable to predict with certainty how important the new market for cheap PCs would be. The optimists, among them the writers at the influential *Microprocessor Report* newsletter, argued that cheap PCs might well be a flash in the pan, doomed to be extinguished by a new generation of power-hungry software applications like video-conferencing and voice recognition that would once again push consumers towards the high end of Intel's product range.

But the more likely outcome seemed that consumers would become used to the idea of paying less than $1,000 for a PC—and would then be hard to steer back to the more expensive models. And whatever the behavior of American computer buyers, the case seemed stronger still in the new markets of the world. In China, in India, and elsewhere in the developing world, cheap PCs raised the prospect of increasing the size of the market by hundreds of millions of units a year. The danger facing Intel is that if it fails to participate at this end of the market, it may find itself in the 2000s retreating to high-priced niches in the same way as the competitors that it drove out of the workstation processor market in the 1990s.

If Grove leaves one enduring legacy at Intel, it is his self-styled paranoia, his obsessive concern for problems ahead that could put the company into difficulties. This trait, born of the dark years in the mid-1980s when the combined pressure of inefficient manufacturing and Japanese competition forced Intel to withdraw from the market for memory chips, is likely to be useful to Craig Barrett after taking over the reins. For the Merced project is the riskiest departure from Intel's core business that it has taken in twenty years.

The move from processing information 32 bits at a time to 64 is no less inevitable than the move from 8 to 16 or the move from 16 to 32. But the Merced chip, slated for introduction in mid 2000, represents a revolutionary rather than evolutionary step. For it will be the first time since the 1970s that Intel introduces a new instruction set for its mainstream product. The company's current "x86" instruction set—slightly enlarged but otherwise barely changed since the first x86 chip was architected in a ten-week burst twenty years ago—is the company's most precious barrier to entry. It is the key ensuring that thousands of software products used by tens of millions of people run on Intel processors and only those of competitors who devote great effort to cloning the functionality of Intel processors. Once Intel gives up this legacy instruction set, its processors must compete in the market more on technical merit—a criterion that has not always been kind to the company in the past, since it is marketing and industry muscle that has made Intel's chips victorious over faster products from competitors.

The preparations for the transfer to the new 64-bit Intel architecture, known as IA-64, have been under way since 1993. In December of that year, a group of Intel engineers began holding regular secret meetings in Palo Alto, forty minutes' drive north of Intel's Santa Clara headquarters, with their archcompetitors from Hewlett-Packard, the company whose own RISC processors were once one of Intel's most daunting high-end competitors. Since then, Intel and HP have developed the Merced chip together, and the other key players at the high end of the microprocessor business have stepped out of the way of this juggernaut combination.

Silicon Graphics, whose MIPS products were once feared in Santa Clara, has indicated that it will build computers around the Merced processor. Digital's Alpha business is now in Intel's hands, after the 1998 sale to Compaq. Sun will develop a version of its Solaris operating system for Merced, leaving in doubt its long-term commitment to maintaining its SPARC processor platform as a competitor to Intel chips. Only IBM stands out as a high-end computer processing company that has resisted the siren call of Merced.

But convincing the competition that Merced will succeed is not the same as convincing the customers. Over the coming two years, Intel will have a daunting sales job to perform, persuading PC manufacturers and software developers to put their energies behind the new architecture. Matters have not been helped by a "change in schedule"—Intel-speak for a delay—announced in May 1998, in which the launch of Merced has been pushed back from 1999 to the middle of the following year. The company attributes the delay to technical considerations that have emerged during the development. "At this point," said a company spokesman in a press release announcing the change, "we have more precise schedule and product data, which allows us to better understand the scope of the product development."

The reasons are probably not only technical. At a time when the pressure is on to compete at the low end of the market, Intel needs to be as sure as it possibly can be of the success of Merced before it fixes the chip's introduction date. The move to 2000, one of the company's first key decisions under Craig Barrett's tenure as CEO, represents a caution born of Grove-style paranoia. And if this caution helps Intel to maintain its preeminent position, then Gove will be able to claim it as his legacy.

PROLOGUE

A Half-Billion-Dollar Mistake

Arthur Rock was probably standing staring out of the floor-to-ceiling windows, gazing at the evening lights of the December city skyline, when the call came in.

His office suite, on the twelfth floor of a tall tower in San Francisco's financial district, had a group of comfortable sofas at one end dominated by a collection of bold modern pictures. But Rock, who suffered a bout of polio as a child, liked to take calls standing up. Next to his desk stood a light-colored wooden reading lectern, which allowed him to work on his feet—like a clerk in a nineteenth-century government office.

It was hard, though, to imagine anyone further removed from the nineteenth century. Rock was a billionaire venture capitalist, who had made his money by investing in some of the most successful technology companies in history. He saw his job as doing more than simply picking winners and then sitting back to watch them get on with it. When Arthur Rock invested money in a company, he sat on its board of directors and helped guide its strategy. In times of crisis, when his investments might be at risk, he was ready if needed to step in with firm advice on how the company should recover its correct course.

The incoming phone call gave no clue that today might be one of those occasions. As Rock's secretary put the call through to his speakerphone, he heard the soft-spoken voice of Gordon Moore, chairman of Intel Corporation, opening the proceedings with his customary calm. Ever methodical, Moore would often start Intel's board meetings by checking that all the participants had received the appropriate papers from Jean Jones, his trusted secretary for nearly thirty years.

Rock didn't need to be told why the Intel directors were holding today's board meeting by conference call instead of at the company's headquarters in Santa Clara, just over an hour's drive south of the city. Like the other Intel directors, he had read all about the crisis in the *New York Times* and the *Wall Street Journal.*

Intel's heavily advertised flagship product, its new Pentium microprocessor, was flawed. The company had known about the flaw for some months and kept quiet about it, believing that only a tiny fraction of the millions of users of the chip across the world would ever be inconvenienced by the problem. But the flaw had been discovered by a mathematics professor, whose data had been posted on the Internet. Intel's attempt to play down the issue had angered customers, worried investors, and ultimately provoked a storm of criticism in the media, culminating in a damaging report on CNN.

As the problem escalated, Intel's response had been doggedly consistent. The company had kept repeating that the flaw was unimportant and insisting that it required no corrective action from most owners of computers equipped with a Pentium chip. Intel had admitted that a small number of specialized users, mostly scientists or mathematicians, might need their Pentiums replaced. But Andy Grove, the company's combative chief executive officer, insisted that the people best equipped to decide who was in this category were Intel's own engineers. As a result, customers who wanted to return a flawed Pentium would have to call Intel and convince the company that they really needed a replacement.

Intel's approach to the issue had the support of the computer industry. The last thing that makers and retailers of PCs wanted was to be put in a position where they had to open up hundreds of thousands or even millions of PCs already in the distribution channel on their way to end users, and go through the time-consuming and expensive business of replacing each processor with a new one. So the industry, which understood from experience that no microprocessor was ever perfect on first launch, stood staunchly behind its leading chip manufacturer. Company after company issued press releases telling customers that the Pentium flaw was nothing to worry about and that Intel's approach to the problem was just fine.

But that wasn't how the general public saw the issue. Inflamed by critical comments on the Internet, newspaper readers and TV viewers couldn't understand why a maker of microprocessors should be any different from the rest of industry. If you were in any other business, and discovered a major problem with one of your products, you offered customers a free exchange, no questions asked. It was as simple as that. You didn't screw them around by telling them the problem probably wouldn't affect them and forcing them to call you and jump through hoops before they could get a replacement. Yet that was what Intel seemed to be doing—and its attitude seemed to be brazenly arrogant, since the problem with its new chip, advertised as the latest and greatest in computer technology, was a simple one: It couldn't do long division properly.

For a few uneasy weeks, the alliance of expert insiders had succeeded in defying the instincts of the less well informed outsiders. It had looked as though Andy Grove's boldness and willingness to take criticism and unpopularity would eventually triumph. The chorus of complaints against Intel had begun to die down, and consumers had seemed to be getting the message that the Pentium flaw wasn't such a big deal after all.

But the situation was precarious. It depended on the giants of the computer business maintaining complete unanimity. If just one major vendor changed sides, then it would no longer be possible for Intel to convince its customers that all the experts agreed there was no problem.

That change had now happened. IBM, the computer giant that had unwittingly helped Intel rise to dominance of the industry, had broken ranks. Disputing Intel's claim that most Pentium users would never come across the problem, the company had issued an announcement saying that it was putting shipments of new machines equipped with Pentium chips on hold until the issue was resolved.

The result was pandemonium as Intel's customer-support lines were flooded with anxious callers. A new round of criticism was unleashed in the media. Finally, the company was forced to face one of the toughest decisions in its history. Should it guarantee to exchange all the flawed chips—even for customers who used their computers for nothing but playing games—and face up to wasting a half billion dollars on an unnecessary returns program? Or should Intel stick to its guns? Should it save some money in the short term but run the risk of throwing the computer industry into turmoil and causing long-term damage to the value of its brand?

This, Gordon Moore explained, was the question that Intel's board now had to decide.

Maybe Arthur Rock should sit down after all.

The decision the Intel board took that day was undoubtedly the right one. Reversing completely its former position, the company announced that it would now offer a no-questions-asked exchange to anyone who owned a flawed Pentium. Andy Grove issued a groveling public apology for the irritation that his previous stance had caused, and the company set up an emergency call center to handle the expected rush of customers dialing in to take up the offer. To cover the costs of the incident, the company set aside $475 million—more than half its earnings during the last quarter of 1994, when the board meeting took its decision—and turned one million of the world's most advanced microprocessors into nothing more than ornamental tie pins and key chains.

Once Intel had backed down, the bad publicity went away almost instantly. Within weeks, public confidence in the corrected Pentium chip began to return. Within months, the two class-action lawsuits that had been filed against the company as a result of the Pentium flaw began to move to settlement. And Intel, scarred and chastened by the experience, began to return to the business it knew best: building microprocessors for personal computers.

Today, three years later, the incident has been forgotten by most people other than specialists in the microprocessor industry. Intel's brand is stronger than ever, and its share price has nearly quadrupled since that telephone board meeting. In retrospect, the Pentium incident now looks like an aberration, a buying opportunity, a hiccup in the otherwise irresistible rise of one of America's most powerful and successful companies.

But was it an aberration? Or did the Pentium scandal reveal something important about Andy Grove and the company he ran?

Intel Corporation, founded in 1968, can claim credit for inventing some of the most important technologies of the modern electronics industry and bringing them successfully to the mass market. Towering among its achievements is the microprocessor, which has brought the power of computing to the desks of hundreds of millions of people all over the world and has changed the world around us by putting intelligence into appliances ranging from vacuum cleaners to cell phones, from toys to cars.

The conditions that gave rise to this extraordinary spike of scientific innovation were put in place by two men, Robert Noyce and Gordon Moore, both leading figures in California's electronics industry long before the San Francisco Bay area even became known as Silicon Valley. It was their charisma, their leadership, their contacts, and their reputation that brought together a group of the most talented engineers in the world and established the framework that allowed scientific creativity to flow.

But it was only for a short time that innovation was the most significant thing that Intel did. When it released the world's first microprocessor to the market, Intel was just two years old and had been a public company for only one month. It did not yet stand out far from the crowd of other start-up companies trying to make money from the uncertain new technology of integrated electronics.

So Intel changed. From being just an innovator, it became a company whose slogan was to *deliver*—to make sure its good ideas were turned into practical products that customers could use, that arrived on schedule and at prices that fell consistently year by year. This transformation was no mean feat. It forced Intel to become rigorously organized and focused, and to find a balance that allowed it to keep firm control over its operations without jeopardizing the creativity of the scientists who were its greatest asset.

The result of this transformation was that Intel rose to domination of its industry. Its memory chips, the products that generated most of its sales, swept the mainframe computer industry by storm, and its microprocessors became the standard on which the entirely new industry of the personal computer was built. It wasn't the intrinsic merits of Intel's products that brought about this domination. Instead, it was more apparently banal things like distribution, customer support, product range, documentation, and technical development tools.

The process was by no means smooth. Nearly nine years after Intel created the microprocessor, the company found itself running last in a three-way race for market share. Yet the company refused to give up. In a matter of days, it created a campaign to convince its employees that regaining leadership of the microprocessor industry, and crushing its leading competitor, was a matter of survival. The campaign, called Operation Crush, worked like a dream. Intel's microprocessor, acknowledged even by its own engineers as technically inferior to the competition, became the industry standard. Almost by accident, a later version of it was chosen by IBM as the basis for its personal computer.

As the PC began to change the face of the computer industry in the 1980s, Intel once again went through a transformation. Now that it was the industry leader, the company no longer needed to focus on delivering ground-breaking new products or using marketing campaigns to overthrow a more powerful rival. Instead, the key to its continued success was to keep challengers at bay and to attack any threat to its high profit margins. So Intel planned and carried out a ruthlessly brilliant program to change the rules of the chip industry. Instead of authorizing other companies to base their products on its designs—a practice, known as "second sourcing," which was accepted as the only way to give customers security of supply—Intel resolved secretly that it would become the monopoly supplier of its chip designs. To achieve this goal, the company had to disentangle itself from a long-term technology agreement with a key partner. But the stakes were too high for this to be an obstacle.

So lucrative was Intel's monopoly, though, that the company began to face the problem that plagues all successful technology businesses: how to stop others from setting up new companies that threatened its position. Here Intel responded in a style that would have earned the respect of any general on the battlefield. It launched a string of long-running lawsuits against competing chip design teams, former employees, semiconductor manufacturing plants, venture capitalists, and at one stage the computer companies that were its customers. Intel's legal department spent hundreds of millions of dollars. At one point, the general counsel who headed it was told that one of the targets he would have to meet in order to get a good performance appraisal was a fixed number of new lawsuits to start each quarter. The strategy of suing everyone in sight wasn't likely to win many friends, and Intel lost or settled more cases than it won. But the policy of filing writs first and asking questions later helped Intel to hold on to its monopoly profits for longer.

The other focus of this "exclusion" phase of Intel's history was branding. After years of giving its products only part numbers instead of names, and marketing to engineers in the computer business instead of to end-users, the company realized at the end of the 1980s that the ultimate way to keep competitors out was to make consumers associate the Intel name with high quality and reliability. So the company ran a succession of programs encouraging PC buyers to concentrate on the processor inside, not the name on the box. First came the "Red X" campaign, in which a big red X was spray-painted over the name of an outdated Intel chip that the company wanted to supersede. Then came "Intel Inside," in which the company subsidized the cost of PC manufacturers' advertisements if they included the right slogan and logo in their copy. Finally, in a move that made it dramatically harder for competitors to attract the attention of customers, the company switched from numbering its processors to giving them names.

The campaign was brilliantly successful at excluding competitors, but it had a side effect. It infuriated many of the most powerful players in the PC industry. They saw Intel's promotion of its brand as a direct threat to their own brands and a move that would tilt the balance of power against them in favor of low-cost, no-name companies that would now have the credibility of Intel's backing. In one startling moment, the CEO of Compaq Computer went public with a withering attack on Intel's strategy.

Though the issue continues to rumble on, it has partly been overtaken by events. Intel's domination of the microprocessor industry is now so complete that the company has little to gain from making life harder for rivals building processors that conform to the Intel instruction set, or chip makers promoting entirely different standards. In the late 1990s, Intel is in the position of a gardener who has marked out a plot and removed all the weeds. Its job now is cultivation. In this fourth and latest phase of the company's history, the objectives are to make sure that every time a consumer walks out of a computer store with a PC in a cardboard box, more of the total selling price of that machine falls straight to Intel's bottom line; to persuade consumers to replace their PCs more often, or as a second best to keep their old machines but upgrade the Intel processors inside them; and to make the PC as a whole a more attractive product so that people choosing between buying a new TV and a new computer will make the choice that brings in profits for Intel.

This new "cultivation" phase puts Intel in the position of being less a competitor to other companies than a leader for an entire industry. It has given the company an incentive to devise new technologies not because it hopes to make money from them directly but because they can increase overall demand for computers. For instance, Intel developed a piece of software letting people make telephone calls over the Internet—and gave it away, inviting people to download it for free from its Web site. No matter that other companies were trying to sell such software, or that Intel's new package might threaten an existing line of conferencing products that the company had developed. The point was simply that the new software package gave customers without a PC a new reason to buy one.

With booming sales and profits, fewer threats on the horizon than for many years, and tens of thousands of employees whose loyalty is assured by the hundreds of thousands of dollars they stand to make from Intel stock options, the company seems almost unassailable. But it has its weaknesses—and they, like its strengths, are intimately tied to the personality of one man. To a greater degree than most outsiders realize, Intel is the personal creation of its chief executive, Andy Grove.

A Hungarian refugee who anglicized his name after arriving in the United States by boat in 1956, Andy Grove is one of the most extraordinary figures in American business. He is brilliantly intelligent and articulate, driven, obsessive, neat, and disciplined. Intel has been built in his image. The values taught in the company's private "university"—directness in confronting problems and extreme rationality in approaching management questions—are an extension of Grove's own personality.

Andy Grove's slogan—some have called it "Grove's law"—is "only the paranoid survive." Daily life inside Intel follows this maxim to the full. By comparison with Microsoft, the company is almost obsessively secretive. The house joke is that its photocopiers are fed with paper that is already marked "Intel Confidential" at the top of every page. The company also operates a security department whose job is surveillance not only of competitors or thieves who might harm Intel's interests but also of the company's own employees. This department has several times crossed the boundaries of what is considered proper behavior in U.S. corporate life.

In a recent book, Grove claims to have elevated paranoia to a tool of management. He argues that it helps companies to watch out for dramatic changes in the business environment that faces them— changes that he calls "10x forces" because they are ten times more powerful than the forces normally encountered—and to respond quickly to them. Yet the irony is that Intel's own record here is patchy at best. The first 10x force facing Intel in its history was the replacement of old-fashioned core memory devices in the computer business with smaller, cheaper, faster integrated circuits. The company responded brilliantly; it recognized the trend, led the change, and grew to become a significant industry player as a reward for its vision.

But later 10x forces have been recognized more slowly. A case in point is the microprocessor. Although it was Intel that sold the world's first microprocessor, the company was very slow to see the potential of its creation—taking it seriously only when two of its best engineers left to set up in competition. It viewed the device for years as a component to be used primarily in industrial controls rather than in computers, and it turned down an early suggestion by a team of its own scientists to build the world's first "desktop computer" The company also refused a gift from inventor Gary Kildall of the operating system that could have taken the place of Microsoft's MS-DOS. Despite these mistakes, Intel came to dominate the PC microprocessor business—so little harm was done by its lack of vision.

The same cannot be said for the third 10x force that faced Intel. Toward the end of the 1970s, Japanese semiconductor makers started to pose a serious threat to the memory chip business, which had always been Intel's cash cow. The issue was complicated by roller-coaster market conditions that prompted the Japanese firms to "dump" their products on the American market, selling them not only below the prices they charged in their home market but also well below their manufacturing cost. But the underlying problem, which Grove and Moore refused to face up to until it was too late, was that Japanese chip companies paid more attention to quality and spent more effort trying to perfect their manufacturing processes than Intel did.

The result was that Intel began to fall behind in the memory chip business that it had created—and by the middle of the 1980s, the company's refusal to accept that it needed to go back to school was threatening its very survival. Only when Andy Grove and Gordon Moore asked themselves what they would do if they were a new management team brought in to clear up the mess did the solution emerge. Intel pulled out of memory chips, savagely cut back its workforce, and refocused its firepower on microprocessors. This decision, analyzed exhaustively in business-school case studies and magazine articles, has been hailed as one of the company's finest moments. But the praise begs the question of whether Intel could have solved the problem earlier at lower cost. Had Grove responded to the 10x force of Japan more quickly, might Intel today be twice as big and profitable as it is?

In 1997, it is the Internet that Grove identifies as the most powerful 10x force facing Intel, along with the rest of the computer industry. So far, few fundamental changes to the company and its operations have seemed necessary. While Microsoft has made extensive changes to its applications products and operating systems, basing them on a new vision of working in which almost all information from daily calendars to reports is published and exchanged over computer networks, Intel's response seems to have been more muted. The company has issued an extension to the instruction set of its processors, called MMX, which allows computers to process sound and pictures more efficiently. It has made some astute venture capital investments in a number of the more interesting Internet start-ups. It has helped push the PC industry toward building computers that cost less and are easier to install and maintain.

But Intel would look very different in a networked world in which individual users had less computing horsepower and fewer bloated software packages on their desks, relying instead on smaller, simpler, and faster pieces of software downloaded across the Internet as needed. In such a world, the extensive installed base of software that is compatible with Intel technical standards would be much less of an advantage. Yet the company's response so far has been to do little more than point out, with some justification, all the shortcomings and flaws in this vision, and to pour cold water on the much-hyped Network Computer promoted by Oracle's Larry Ellison. It is all too tempting to wonder whether the moment when Intel's triumph appears sweetest might—like the moment when IBM's mainframes seemed secure in their domination of the computer business—be the beginning of its downfall.

As it faces the challenges ahead, Intel has a number of strengths. Its management team, developed almost entirely internally, is extremely strong. Its corporate culture allows the company to set objectives, communicate them swiftly to its workforce, and make a good attempt at achieving them. Its compensation system, which rewards hard work and loyalty with stock options worth millions but checks under-performance with regular reviews and "corrective action" programs, is highly successful in motivating Intel people to give their best. And its lack of hierarchy makes it easier for the company to respond swiftly to change and to make rational decisions.

But the Intel that Andy Grove has created also has its weaknesses. The company has been plagued by arrogance since its earliest years. It has frequently taken a high-handed approach to its customers, and suffers from the "not-invented-here" syndrome as badly as many technology companies. Most alarmingly, the company has found it increasingly hard to accept outsiders into its senior ranks. Like transplanted organs, managers brought into Intel from outside have more often been rejected than absorbed by the patient.

These weaknesses are likely to come into renewed focus when Andy Grove departs from the scene. To many insiders, a post-Grove Intel is still unimaginable. After managing the company's operations for two decades, and more recently guiding its strategy too, Grove has become almost synonymous with Intel. But he has already passed his sixty-second birthday and had a narrow escape from prostate cancer in 1996. Not even his closest lieutenants believe that Grove is immortal.

In theory, the succession is settled. Craig Barrett, Intel's president, now officially handles the company's day-to-day business and has been publicly groomed as the man who will succeed Grove on his retirement. But it is unclear whether a less forceful, less driven personality than Grove will be able to lead the company with the same success.

And people, not technologies or strategies, are the focus of this book. My aim is to offer an account of Intel's story as seen through the eyes of dozens of different employees, from the most junior to the most senior. The lives of these people don't add up to a comprehensive history of the company. Since the company has always refused to cooperate with outsiders attempting to tell its story from an independent standpoint, such a history is unlikely to see the light of day for many years. Instead, the intention here is to give a view of life inside Andy Grove's Intel—and to identify some of the features that have made Intel one of the most extraordinary and most ruthlessly successful businesses in history.

PART ONE

INNOVATION

"We are really the revolutionaries in the world today—not the kids with the long hair and beards who were wrecking the schools a few years ago."

—Gordon Moore, Intel founder,
quoted in *Fortune* magazine, 1973

1

The Odds-on Favorite

You probably think you can skip this chapter.

The scene may already be in your mind. It's late at night, and the garage is entirely dark except for the pool of light cast on the workbench by a low-cost anglepoise lamp. The future billionaire is hunched over the computer, oblivious to the clutter of empty pizza boxes around him, absorbed in his work. His hair is unwashed, and he's been wearing the same grimy T-shirt almost every day since he dropped out of college. He has few contacts and no backers. His only assets are his technical skills and the brilliant powers of persuasion and negotiation that will blossom over the years to come.

There's probably no single company that conforms to every one of these stereotypes. But most of America's most successful technology companies display at least some of them: modest beginnings, fighting against the odds, brilliant ideas that go against conventional wisdom, founders who are outsiders and have nothing to lose if they fail. Look at Steve Jobs and Apple, or Bill Gates and Microsoft. These are the models that we've come to think of as the ways to start a successful high-tech company.

The creation of Intel Corporation in 1968 includes none of these ingredients.

Instead of being young and rebellious, its two founders were middle-aged and respectable. Instead of being poor and isolated, they were prosperous and known already as leading figures in their industry. Instead of laboring for months or even years to find a backer for their venture, they rounded up $2.3 million of funding in an afternoon, on the basis of a couple of sheets of paper containing one of the sketchiest business plans ever financed.

The two most important words of the business plan were *Robert Noyce*. Forty years old, Noyce was the general manager of Fairchild Semiconductor, one of the most prominent businesses in the Bay Area to the south of San Francisco. But he was more than that: He was one of the creators of the integrated circuit.

To understand the significance of this, you have to remember that the earliest computers used vacuum tubes as the basic elements of their circuits. Vacuum tubes, working like small lightbulbs, were bulky and unreliable—and since they had to be heated before they could work properly, they were also gluttonous consumers of electricity. A large computer could easily be big enough to require its own little power station—and its vacuum tubes pumped out enough heat to turn a massive room into an oven.

The building block of today's electronics industry is a miniature switch that takes advantage of the fact that certain crystals, such as silicon, sometimes conduct electricity and sometimes don't. This switch, dubbed a "transistor," earned a Nobel Prize for the three physicists at Bell Labs who discovered it in 1948. The early transistors were smaller than vacuum tubes and needed no heating element to make them work. Also, they didn't need to be changed like a lightbulb every so often. But they shared one of the drawbacks of the vacuum tube: to build a computer, you had to connect them one by one into electrical circuits.

Bob Noyce's claim to fame was making it possible to put more than one transistor on the same fragment of silicon. The circuits built using this technique became known as "integrated circuits." Coincidentally, two different teams in different companies two thousand miles apart conceived the integrated circuit almost simultaneously in 1959. The winner of the first integrated-circuit patent was Jack Kilby, an engineer at Texas Instruments. But it was Noyce and his colleagues at Fairchild Semiconductor who succeeded in turning the integrated circuit from a laboratory prototype into a product that could be mass-produced in ever-increasing numbers and ever-falling prices, and it was Noyce who made it possible for engineers to dream of a myriad of new products that had never before been possible.

Noyce did not fit the stereotype of the inventor. He was gregarious, charming, athletic, and handsome. Brought up in Grinnell, a small town in Iowa where his father was a Congregational minister, he was a Boy Scout who went to Sunday school every week and graduated valedictorian at the local high school. His entry in the school's yearbook described him as the Quiz Kid, "the guy who has the answers to all the questions," who played in the school band, sang in its chorus, was a leading light of the Latin and Science clubs, and acted in six plays. At college, he was the swimming team's best diver and took the lead in a radio soap opera. The sole cloud over his exemplary youth, which formed the centerpiece of a profile of Noyce that Tom Wolfe wrote for *Esquire* in 1983, was an incident at college when he and a fellow student stole a twenty-five-pound suckling pig for a Hawaiian barbecue on campus. People took pigs seriously in the Iowa farm belt. But it was a sign of the charmed life that Noyce seemed to lead that not even an offense of this gravity could spoil his career. An admiring physics teacher talked the college authorities out of expelling him. Instead, he was sent off to work at an insurance company for a few months, and then after his graduation to the Massachusetts Institute of Technology, where he earned his Ph.D.

More than two decades later, Bob Noyce had become general manager at Fairchild and chairman of the board of trustees of his old college in Iowa—but he was still everybody's best friend. He had a way of looking at you that made it clear that he took what you said very, very seriously, and a way of talking in his gravelly, deep voice, usually waiting until everyone else had weighed in first, that made you take what he said more seriously still. He had what Wolfe described as the "halo effect." ("People who have it seem to know just what they are doing; they make you see their halo.") He was not only a born leader; he was also an inspiration.

Gordon Moore, reporting to Noyce at Fairchild Semiconductor as head of research and development, was a very different personality. While Noyce was five foot eight and dark-haired, Moore was over six feet and balding. While Noyce would be the life and soul of every party—drinking, singing, playing tricks, and accepting every dare offered to him—Moore would sit with a few close friends, quietly talking around a table. His temperament was a model of equanimity, and his two great passions were fishing and messing around in boats. He had been born in the small coastal town of Pescadero, just thirty miles south of San Francisco, where his father was deputy sheriff of the county. If you bumped into him walking out of his local hardware store on a Saturday morning, which people often did, you'd find him in a pair of worn overalls, almost peering down at his solid work boots through his wire-framed glasses. You might easily have mistaken him for a modestly prosperous orchard farmer, out in his pickup to buy something he needed to fix a leaking pipe or to put up a swing for the kids on the apple tree in the backyard.

But Moore was every bit as great an engineer as Noyce. His Ph.D., in chemical engineering, was from Caltech, the prestigious California Institute of Technology near Pasadena. He was the winner of a number of important patents. And he had an uncanny knack for solving technical problems. If you took a problem that looked as though it had five or six routes to a possible solution, most engineers would waste a lot of time exploring and then ruling out the ones that didn't work. Not Moore: For some reason that neither he nor anyone else could explain, the one avenue of inquiry that he would choose would often be the one that yielded the best results.

Moore was legendary for sitting down at the lunch table in the company cafeteria with a group of engineers who had been battling with a problem for several months and suggesting, very quietly, that they might like to take a look at this or try that. More often than you would expect, they would go away and take his advice—and discover that fifteen minutes of Gordon Moore had brought them closer to a solution than months of unaided work. Moore was also a gifted listener and judge of character. Slow to anger, he would hear everyone out. Only in the presence of people who went on for too long, repeating themselves far beyond the point of boredom, would Moore's self-control slip and his anger become visible.

When a local paper asked Moore in 1968 why he and Noyce had decided to set up a new company, his answer was that the two men wanted to experience once again the thrill of working in a small, fast-growing company. Not for the first time, he might have added. Noyce and he had been involved in start-ups twice already. In 1956, they had helped William Shockley, the leader of the team at Bell Laboratories that developed the transistor, set up his own laboratory. A year later, the pair had been among a group of eight who walked out on Shockley to start their own transistor company under the banner of Fairchild.

The mass defection from Shockley Laboratories had been provoked by the old man's irascibility and paranoia, and his insistence on ignoring their advice in a technical dispute over which area of research they should concentrate on. To raise funding for the new company, the "Traitorous Eight" struck a deal with Sherman Fairchild, an inventor on the East Coast whose father had been one of IBM's earliest investors. Fairchild had advanced $1.5 million to them in 1957, on the understanding that they would create a subsidiary of his Fairchild Camera and Instrument Corporation specializing in the manufacture of semiconductors. If the venture failed, Fairchild would pick up the tab. If it was a success, the company would have the right to buy them out for $300,000 apiece.

It was a success. Two years later, Fairchild's company exercised its option and made them all rich men. The eight founders were left in place at Fairchild Semiconductor—but they no longer had any real control over the business or any great stake in its success. Noyce was promoted from general manager to group vice-president of the parent company, and was held in the highest respect by its owner; but everyone knew that the big decisions were always made by the accountants back in Syosset, New York.

For a while, the problems remained invisible. As the 1960s wore on, however, members of the original team became bored and drifted out of the company to set up on their own. Fairchild Semiconductor became the electronics industry's equivalent of a sycamore tree with its winged seeds: Every season, seeds from Fairchild would spin away gently in the wind, land somewhere nearby, and burst into growth as new saplings. Meanwhile, as Fairchild's growth began to slow, the moneymen from New York began to come up with strange compensation schemes, in which the general manager of each part of the division was paid a bonus linked to the current profits of the business he was responsible for. This turned cooperation into rivalry and made the managers reluctant to put into effect the technologies developed by Moore and his team. New technologies might make money in the long term, but not in the short—and in the fast-moving environment of Silicon Valley, who could tell where you'd be working by the time the payoff came?

The bell tolled for Fairchild Semiconductor in 1967, when Charlie Sporck, the company's famed manufacturing genius, set up in competition at National Semiconductor and hired away busloads of his former colleagues. It required no great insight to tell that Fairchild was irreparably injured and that the best Noyce and Moore could do would be to slow, rather than stanch, the flow of blood. A year later, the two men were the last of the eight founders left.

The decisive moment was a conversation between the two men on a sunny weekend afternoon while Noyce was mowing his front lawn—which led to a partnership between them. Moore, as head of Fairchild Semiconductor's research and development (R&D) department, would start work on the products the new business would develop. Noyce, who had led the negotiations with Sherman Fairchild eleven years earlier that created the company they were now planning to leave, would raise the money.

It took Noyce just one phone call. The deal with Fairchild a decade earlier had been brokered by an investment banker from New York called Arthur Rock. Rock had come out to California to see the Traitorous Eight; he had helped them draw up a list of potential backers; and he had shopped their idea to thirty-five different companies before getting a yes from Sherman Fairchild. Since then, Rock's life had become intertwined with the Fairchild founders. He had moved to California and set up a new investment bank of his own in San Francisco, specializing in the financing of new companies. (Today, this business is known as "venture capital"; the phrase was invented by Rock himself.) Rock felt bound by loyalty to Fairchild to avoid taking any active steps that would hasten the breakup of Fairchild Semiconductor. But he had already helped two of the founders of the business set up on their own, and Bob Noyce was his best friend among the remaining six. The two men used to take hiking and camping holidays together.

"Bob just called me on the phone," Rock related later. "We'd been friends for a long time. . . . Documents? There was practically nothing. Noyce's reputation was good enough. We put out a page-and-a-half little circular, but I'd raised the money even before people saw it. If you tried to do it today, it would probably be a two-inch stack of papers. The lawyers wouldn't let you raise money without telling people what the risks are."

Rock made fifteen phone calls that afternoon and received fifteen acceptances. His goal was not simply to raise the money for Noyce and Moore: With their track record and his contacts, that would be a snap. Instead, Rock wanted to find investors who could offer some expertise that would be useful to the new business. Partly out of a wish to prevent any single shareholder from becoming too powerful, he decided to scale back the contributions offered by his fifteen contacts. One of the new company's founding shareholders was Grinnell College of Iowa, Robert Noyce's alma mater. By now, the pig incident had long been forgotten. With Noyce now chairman of the college's board of trustees, the success of Fairchild made it seem only natural to sell his old college a $300,000 slice of the new venture. The board was happy with the idea; its resident investment guru, Warren Buffett of Omaha, Nebraska, had no objection, and so the investment went ahead. Noyce and Moore had already each put up $250,000; Rock himself came in for $300,000. The backers' investment in Noyce and Moore would be the best deal they ever made.

It took only a few weeks to choose a business name. The pair started out calling themselves "NM Electronics," but it was agreed on all sides that this sounded kind of old-fashioned. After discarding more than a dozen other ideas, Moore finally came up with "Integrated Electronics." Noyce admitted that it captured just what the new business was about, but suggested that they should contract the name to a single word: Intel. Arthur Rock, whose work in raising the company's start-up capital had earned him the job of Intel's first chairman, had no objection. The pair discovered too late, shortly after the incorporation papers were drawn up on July 16, 1968, that there was already a company in existence called Intelco. By then, the word was already out about their new venture, and the easiest way to head off any lawsuits was to pay $15,000 for the right to use the Intel name.

Two weeks later, in August 1968, the local *Palo Alto Times* got wind of the story and called up Gordon Moore for an interview. The resulting story, which ran across the top of an entire page of the paper, helpfully included both men's home addresses. Within days, they began to receive résumés, calls, and letters of application from talented engineers all over the industry who knew of Noyce's work on the integrated circuit or of Moore's achievements at Fairchild. Finding good employees willing to join a start-up—usually one of the hardest tasks facing most entrepreneurs—was clearly not going to be a problem for the two.

2

Two Thousand
Starts a Week

Great changes were happening in the world during the long, hot summer of 1968. In Paris, students set up barricades against their college professors and the government. In Chicago, demonstrations against the war in Vietnam turned into riots that marred the Democratic National Convention. But the foundation of Intel, which has had a bigger effect on the lives of people in the world than either of these, took place without being noticed outside the narrow confines of the Bay Area's electronics industry.

That was just how Gordon Moore liked it. The very opposite of a self-publicist, he instinctively avoided talking about his achievements until they were complete.

When Moore was asked by one of the local papers at the beginning of August what kind of devices he and Robert Noyce intended to build at their new company, his response was about as uninformative as could be.

"We particularly are interested in the product areas that none of the manufacturers are supplying," he said.

Come on, Gordon, that's hardly news. You wouldn't be setting up a new company just to copy something already on the market, would you?

When asked to elaborate, Moore would offer only two further thoughts. First, the new company would avoid direct government business. Second, the company would keep to the industrial end of the business rather than trying to develop products for end consumers.

From anyone else, this apparent vagueness might have indicated indecisiveness. But Moore hadn't spent nine years at the helm of Fairchild's extensive R&D operation for nothing. His principle was straightforward: There was no need to give away any information, however trivial, to potential competitors. If the people who had backed him and Noyce to the tune of several hundred thousand dollars each could do without detailed information on their technical plans, then so could the rest of the world.

This was no surprise to people who had known him at Fairchild. Moore was always hard to pin down on technical detail, even when he was giving a speech in public. When he was once sitting on a panel at a technical conference devoted to semiconductor materials, someone in the audience raised a question about the silicon nitride layers that Moore's technical team were rumored to have been experimenting with. What had the results been?

"We got exactly what we were predicting," he answered. There was just one piece of crucial information he withheld from the audience. The engineering team had come to the conclusion that silicon nitride deposits would have no useful technical effect, and some careful tests had proved them right. But Moore thought that if it had taken his own researchers weeks to discover that the technology was a dead end, there was no reason to tell the world. Let the competition waste some time, too.

Behind the veil of vagueness, however, Noyce and Moore knew exactly what business they were going into. They would build memory devices. Across America, companies were buying mainframe computers to manage their accounting systems or payroll or medical records. In every case the computer needed a place where programs and data from work in progress could be stored, and then retrieved at high speed. Yet while integrated circuits were increasingly being used in the logic devices that carried out the calculations themselves, memory storage was stuck in the pretransistor age. The cheapest form of computer memory was "magnetic core," a tiny magnetic doughnut that stored information in the form of ones and zeroes depending on the way it was magnetized. If only a way could be found to integrate memory cells with the circuits that Noyce had pioneered, then computer memory could become far more compact and speedier to operate. Once one computer company began to use integrated-circuit memory, the rest would follow suit. Then an accelerating trend of increasing volumes and falling costs would follow, ending up with the complete replacement of core memory with the new semiconductor devices. The potential market was millions upon millions of units a year.

A good reason for keeping so quiet about Intel's plans was that Moore and Noyce were not alone in seeing this potential. The idea that core memory was eventually going to be replaced by semiconductors wasn't a wild-eyed obsession held only by eccentrics. It was the received wisdom inside the industry. Route 101, the highway that ran south from San Francisco through the Valley and then onward to Los Angeles, was dotted with laboratories racing to be the first to develop semiconductor memory devices.

Gordon Moore, though, had a head start. Shortly before his departure from Fairchild, a gifted young Italian semiconductor scientist in his department named Federico Faggin had invented a new variation on the standard integrated-circuit manufacturing process, known as metal oxide on silicon. By 1968, the new technique, called "silicon gate," was working stably in the laboratory. But with $2 million in the bank and a team of good engineers behind them, Moore knew that he and Noyce could make as good a stab as anyone else in the world at developing this technology to the point where memory devices could be mass-produced at low cost.

But silicon gate MOS was only one of three promising approaches to the problem of building integrated-memory circuits. Another was to build multichip memory modules; a third was to use a process known as Schottky bipolar. Moore and Noyce decided that they would pursue all three simultaneously—and sell whichever they were able to mass-produce first. (Since Schottky proved easily replicable by competitors and multichip modules too hard even for Intel, Moore came to refer to the decision to pursue three lines of research simultaneously as the "Goldilocks" strategy. Like the bowls of porridge left by the bears, only one—silicon gate—turned out just right.)

The scientists left behind at Fairchild after the departure of Noyce and Moore would later respond with hurt pride to the news that their former boss and his new company were trying to commercialize an invention made in their laboratory. They put up a large placard, visible to all comers to the R&D department, emblazoned with the words "Silicon Gate Was Invented Here." One former employee of both companies, looking back, put the accusation baldly:

"Intel was *founded* to steal the silicon gate process from Fairchild."
Another was more forgiving. "What [we] brought with us was the
knowledge that [we] had seen some built, and the knowledge of
the device physics. . . . We didn't bring with us recipes, mask sets,
device designs, that sort of stuff. . . . What we brought was a lot of
knowledge."

In any case, Fairchild Semiconductor had only itself to blame for
losing one of its key secrets to a new competitor. For a couple of years
now, the best technologies developed in its research labs in Palo Alto
never seemed to get put into practice at Fairchild's Mountain View
manufacturing facility. Instead, they seemed to be attracted by some
osmotic principle to Charlie Sporck's manufacturing aces at National
Semiconductor.

This was partly because the rules were different in the 1960s. The
days had not yet arrived when technology companies would use
patents, trade secrets, and other forms of intellectual property as
commercial weapons. Scientists were happy to assign to their employer the rights in any patents they earned in return for a token dollar and a framed copy of the first page of the patent. Why should
they be any less generous when it came to scientists in other companies? After all, these were exciting times. Trying to hold back
the spread of information at a time when things were moving ahead
so fast was not only self-defeating, since any competing technol-
ogist worth his salt could design his way around a patent, it also felt
unsporting.

Every Friday night, engineers from different companies would
assemble at the Wagon Wheel, a local watering hole, to exchange
gossip. Not just who was sleeping with whom but also who was working on what and who was having which problems with which designs
and which processes. Prominently displayed on the wall of the bar
was a huge enlargement of the innards of an integrated circuit, created by "popping the top" of the circuit's packaging and using an
industrial-strength camera to record the secrets inside. The image
served almost as a religious icon, looking down with approval as scientists threw their employers' secrets across the table as casually as
they would pay for a round of drinks.

The selection process Noyce and Moore used in assembling their
team was simple. The pair asked everyone they respected, particularly in the electronic engineering departments of universities, for the
names of the brightest research scientists they knew. Noyce or Moore

would make contact with a phone call, and the candidate would be invited over for a chat—either at Noyce's house or at some modest local restaurant like the International House of Pancakes. They would chat over a lunch or a breakfast, the candidate sitting on one plastic banquette, the Intel founders sitting opposite on the other, and then Noyce and Moore would make their decision. In addition to being a brilliant engineer, you had to pass two tests to get a job at Intel. You had to be willing to come to work for Bob and Gordon for no more than your current salary with your existing employer—and sometimes, if they thought you were overpaid, for 10 percent less. In return, you'd be promised stock options, which you would have to trust would be adequate compensation for a pay raise forgone. Also, you had to be willing to take a demotion. If Intel was going to grow as fast as its founders hoped, its first round of hires would soon be responsible for running much larger teams of people. In the meantime, they would have to spend a few months doing work that was actually more junior than the job they had come from. An engineer currently running an entire division with five thousand staff to order about and sales of $25 million a year would find himself at Intel once again managing a single fabrication plant, or "fab," where the big issue of his day might be a maladjustment of a single machine.

The consolation was the strong sense that things would not stay this way for long. Ted Hoff, a brilliant postdoctoral researcher at Stanford who was recommended to Noyce by a professor in his department, reminded the Intel founder during his interview that more than half a dozen other new companies were already in the market trying to develop semiconductor memory. Was there any need for another semiconductor company? What were the chances of success?

Noyce's reply exuded quiet confidence. "Even if we don't succeed," he said, "the founders will probably end up OK."

Intel's new hires found that his confidence was shared by people outside the company. Gene Flath, a product group general manager hired in from Fairchild to a senior job in the fledgling company's manufacturing operation, decided to spend the week's holiday he was owed by his former employer down in Los Angeles looking over new chip-manufacturing equipment at a trade show on behalf of Intel. When a couple of pieces took his fancy, it seemed only natural to put in an order for the equipment then and there. And it seemed equally natural that the vendors, hearing that Flath had signed up with Noyce and Moore, were willing to give him immediate credit. *Noyce and Moore? That's OK. They'll have the money.*

There was something infectious in the evident confidence of Noyce and Moore. As their first working space, they chose an old Union Carbide plant, seventeen thousand square feet, on Middlefield Road in the town of Mountain View, an hour south of San Francisco. When the deal was signed, Union Carbide hadn't quite moved out. Intel got the front office of the building immediately, with the right to hang a big sign outside bearing its logo—the company name, printed in blue all in lowercase Helvetica letters, with the *e* dropped so that its crossbar was level with the line. The idea was that the lower-case letters showed that Intel was a modern, go-ahead company for the 1970s; the dropped *e* was a reminder to its customers that its name was a contraction of "integrated electronics." Some employees, but not all, took that *e* to mean that the word Intel should be pronounced with the emphasis on the second syllable.

Over the succeeding weeks, Union Carbide cleared more equipment from the back of the building and Intel brought more people into the front, until one day late in the fall of 1968, Intel Corporation found itself at last the sole occupant of a large industrial shell, ready plumbed for the heavy-duty power, water, and gases that were essential to the process of making semiconductors.

Fabricating silicon chips was the modern world's answer to medieval alchemy, the turning of base metals into gold. Except here, the raw material was sand, which was turned into crystalline silicon that arrived at the fab molded into a long sausage, two inches in diameter. The silicon would then be sliced into thin "wafers" a fraction of an inch thick. By a series of secret, almost magical processes, each wafer would be coated with scores of identical miniature circuits, neatly stepped in rows and columns. Then the wafers would be scored with a diamond-cutter, and the individual chips would be sawn away from their neighbors and wired individually into black ceramic packages, often with a line of metal pins down each side. When one engineer showed the completed chips in their packaging to his kids, they referred to them as "Barbie combs." But if you were in the industry, you knew that each one could sell for a dollar, or ten dollars, or even more, depending on what was inside.

It was the guy given the job of laying out the floor design for manufacturing who was the first to realize the scale of the ambitions of Intel's two founders. When he asked what capacity the fab should plan for, the figure he was given was two thousand wafer starts a week. Two thousand clear silicon wafers, each one starting its way through the production process. Each one etched with one hundred or more circuits on its surface. Two hundred thousand circuits a week; ten million a year. Of course in those days you'd be lucky if 10 percent of them came out right. But for a start-up, which had not yet developed either a circuit design or a process to build it with, such investment in capacity was unheard of. Even Fairchild, which had become the world's leading semiconductor manufacturer, could handle only five times as much. Who did Noyce and Moore think they were?

3

The Third and Fourth Men

One of the first decisions that Noyce and Moore had to take was to choose a director of operations for their new company. "Director Ops," as the title was commonly abbreviated, was the job that carried responsibility for getting products designed on time and built to cost. Only sales and marketing, and the big-picture strategy decisions, were beyond its remit. Picking the right director ops was one of the most important decisions that any new electronics company had to make—and the success of Charlie Sporck at National Semiconductor was proof of how successful a company could be if it got its manufacturing operations right.

With their reputation in the industry, Noyce and Moore could have hired just about anyone they wanted within fifty miles. Yet the choice they made was so bizarre that it mystified most of the people who were watching their new business take shape. They offered the director ops job to a guy who had no manufacturing experience at all—who was more a physicist than an engineer, more a teacher than a business executive, more a foreigner than an American. They offered the job to Andy Grove.

Grove was born in Hungary in 1936 with the name András Gróf. As a Jew, he was forced to go into hiding when German tanks rolled into Hungary, and to stay hidden for the duration of World War II. The defeat of the Nazis brought only a slight improvement in the hardships suffered by the members of the Gróf family who survived the Holocaust—for Hungary became a satellite state of the USSR, ruled with totalitarian oppression. Like many other Hungarians, the young Gróf was forced to struggle simply to achieve the basics of getting enough food to eat and fuel to stay warm—and his teenage years in 1950s Budapest were bleak.

By 1956, after Soviet tanks crushed a reforming Hungarian government and replaced it with a puppet regime willing to answer to Moscow, Gróf became a politically conscious university student. It was clear that young people who had thrown Molotov cocktails at the tanks didn't have much of a future in Budapest—and that his life might be no more at risk if he tried to escape to the West than if he stayed where he was. The Austrian border beckoned, a gateway to a better life in the capitalist world.

Some weeks later, Gróf arrived in America aboard a rusty old ship that had carried U.S. troops during the war. The journey fell far short of the dream nurtured by so many aspiring immigrants to America. Instead of admiring the New York City skyline as the ship made its way into harbor, Grove did not get so much as a glimpse of the Statue of Liberty. He and his fellow passengers were transferred through the Holland Tunnel by bus to Camp Kilmer in New Jersey, a former prisoner-of-war camp. Gróf's first impression of the grim dormitories was not favorable—in fact, he wondered whether the claims made by the Communist propaganda machine that conditions were no better in the West might actually be true.

Soon, however, things began to look up. Andrew Grove, as the new immigrant now called himself, moved in with an uncle in the Bronx and enrolled in a course in chemical engineering at the City College of New York. He began to make a life for himself, waiting tables at restaurants to help pay for his tuition. He hated New York, but worked hard and graduated top of his class, with honors that would give him the right to choose where to continue with his studies. When the moment came to decide, the weather was the deciding factor. To get away from the bitter winters of the Northeast, Grove enrolled at the University of California at Berkeley, an idyllically sunny town a few miles north of San Francisco. By then, the young scientist was no longer alone. Working as a busboy in a resort hotel in the Catskill Mountains near New York, Grove had met a young Hungarian woman named Eva who became his wife. In 1963, shortly after winning his Ph.D., Grove got a job at Fairchild Semiconductor, where he worked for the next five years in the R&D department while continuing to lecture at UC Berkeley.

As he grew older, Grove seemed to make a deliberate attempt to blot out the first twenty years of his life. Although he and Eva had a number of Hungarian friends, and his mother had come to California to join them, Grove rarely discussed his East European background with his colleagues at work. He was also extremely reticent about being a Jew; he did not attend any of the local synagogues or participate in the Jewish community. Only to his closest confidants would he drop an occasional clue about his former life. To one, he revealed that he would regularly wake up at night, shaken out of his sleep by a dream that he was being chased by a pack of barking dogs. To another, he explained that the most appalling experience of his childhood was not the privations he suffered while hiding from the Nazis but the humiliation of being told by some of his childhood Hungarian friends immediately after the war that their fathers had forbidden them to play with a Jew. To a third, he said that he had hesitated before buying a dog for his two little girls because he knew his mother would associate the dog with the German shepherds the Nazis used to herd minorities and political opponents onto the trains that would take them to the death camps.

Yet for all Grove's attempts to remake himself as a regular American and to turn his back on his former life, it was plain to anyone who met him in 1968 that he was something exotic and out of the ordinary. Grove spoke English with an accent that was almost incomprehensible. Over his head, he wore an awkward hearing-aid device that looked like a product of East European engineering. His attitude to work was like that of Stakhanov, the legendary Russian miner whose long hours of labor and tons of output for the greater glory of the proletariat were celebrated by Soviet propagandists. And his manner? Well, put it like this: Andy Grove had an approach to discipline and control that made you wonder how much he had been unwittingly influenced by the totalitarian regime he had been so keen to escape.

But that wouldn't emerge until later. In 1968, people who met Grove for the first time usually noticed three things. One was that he was very bright, very good at explaining things—particularly semiconductor devices, whose physical behavior he had written a book about. Another was that he was very organized and seemed to know exactly what he wanted and how he was going to achieve it. A third was that he was very keen to make an impression, to justify his position. Grove knew that Noyce and Moore had taken a risk by giving him the job of director of operations, and he was determined to prove that they had made no mistake.

Glancing through the various corporate histories that Intel has published, a casual reader might get the impression that Andy Grove was the very first outsider Noyce and Moore spoke to after deciding to set up in business together. This impression is heightened by Bob Noyce's frequent references to the company as a "three-headed monster," and also by the fact that Grove is described in some company publications as one of Intel's three founders.

In fact, a fourth man was present at the company's birth, but he left the company a few years after its foundation. Although he pursued a highly successful business career afterward, he became a nonperson from the company's point of view, like a disgraced member of the Politburo whose photo has been airbrushed out of the Kremlin balcony photographs. His name is Bob Graham.

Graham was one of Fairchild's star marketing men. Joining Fairchild a couple of years after its creation in 1957, he soon came to Bob Noyce's attention by winning Fairchild its first ever million-dollar contract. The distinction was double-edged; although the deal was the company's largest ever, it gave Fairchild the lowest price per unit it had ever received—$1.09 per transistor for a one million lot. Only later, when Gordon Moore's research would uncover the workings of the economics of the chip business, did it became widely accepted that falling prices and rising volumes were trends that semiconductor makers had to embrace if they were to thrive.

Graham had been one of the earlier departures from Fairchild, leaving in 1965 to take a job in Florida running the whole of sales and marketing for a competing semiconductor company. But Noyce hadn't forgotten him. When he began the search for a leader to oversee the marketing effort of his new company, it was Graham that Noyce called first.

"I thought it over for about a microsecond," recalls Graham, "and then said 'Sure.' "

He concluded terms with Noyce and Moore on June 5, 1968, the night that Robert Kennedy was shot. On the strength of a handshake, Graham then went straight back to Florida, resigned his job, and called in the house movers so he and his wife could return to California.

Graham made an important contribution to the new company right away. Over a series of phone conversations with Noyce and Moore, he pressed the case for building bipolar circuits as well as those based on metal oxide on silicon technology. His reasoning was straightforward. Memory circuits based on MOS would still require peripheral devices, known as "drivers," to allow them to work properly with the computer. Those drivers would have to be bipolar. If Intel did not develop its own bipolar processes, it would be forced to rely on other companies to build them—yet the bipolar companies, terrified that MOS would put them out of business, would have no incentive to cooperate with Intel. Even if MOS were a sure bet—which it wasn't yet by any means—Graham was convinced that Intel needed a bipolar division too to ensure its survival.

Bob Graham's contract in Florida required him to give ninety days' notice, so Andy Grove was already on board when Graham reappeared in California ready to do business. This had two significant effects on Graham's career with Intel. One was that he had no hand in hiring many of the first wave of staff people; instead, dozens of engineers and managers made their first contact with Grove, and to him they established their first loyalty. The other effect of Graham's delayed arrival was that Grove took on more responsibility than he otherwise might have done. Who does what is always vague in a start-up; an intelligent, energetic person with an eye for detail who is willing to do things that others have left behind can become considerably more powerful than his job title would suggest. And Andy Grove was the ultimate details guy.

4

Into the Potato Patch

Sometime in the fall of 1968, when Intel's research into semiconductor memory was already in full flow, one of the company's first hires grabbed Bob Noyce in a corridor.

"Bob," he said, "there's something I need to ask you. I've been here for three days already, and I'm not really clear on the reporting structure of this outfit. Can you just draw me a quick organization chart?"

Noyce smiled and turned into an open doorway. Walking to the blackboard, he picked up a piece of chalk and drew a small X. Around it, he swept a circle, and along the circle he added six or seven more Xs. Then he drew a spoke connecting each of the Xs outside the circle to the X in the center.

He pointed to the X in the center.

"That's you," he said. "And these"—he tapped the outside Xs one by one, the clack of the chalk echoing against the linoleum floor— "these are me, Gordon, Andy, Les, Bob, Gene, and the other people you'll be dealing with. That's what our organization chart looks like."

Noyce's point was more than mere rhetoric. At Fairchild Semiconductor, the East Coast owners of the business had been very strong on hierarchies and on reporting. They believed in clear lines of command. They thought employees should be like officers in an army, communicating only with their immediate superiors and immediate inferiors. And like soldiers, they considered it the height of disloyalty for an employee to raise an issue with someone higher up if he was dissatisfied with the response his immediate superior gave him.

Visionaries before their time, Noyce and Moore saw that in a fast-moving industry where speed of response to change was all-important, and where information had to flow as swiftly as possible if the company was to make the right decisions, this approach did not make sense. Instead, they wanted to encourage anyone who had a good idea to speak up, anyone who had a question to ask it. Staff meetings were to be open to anyone who thought they could contribute something by attending; no manager, no matter how senior, should refuse a request for help or information from another employee.

The prestige of Intel's stars was never in doubt—the PA system kept drumming it in, day after day, as announcements went out every few minutes for *Doctor* Noyce, *Doctor* Moore, *Doctor* Grove. But they were very visible, lending a hand where needed. If a circuit layout needed to be checked, Bob Noyce would be ready to lend a hand. If a process designer needed to know something about the behavior of transistors under specific temperature ranges, Andy Grove would be ready to pull down from the shelf the textbook he had written on semiconductor physics, identify the key equations that predicted how a substance would behave, and help turn the equations into statements in the FORTRAN programming language. If a piece of complex machinery didn't work, the man who unscrewed the casing and took a look inside might well be Gordon Moore.

Inevitably, this led to some tensions within a matter of months. Gene Flath, who had been hired to run the company's first fabrication line, began to find that engineers he had asked to go off and deal with a process problem would come back and announce that they had done something completely different. When he asked them why, the answer would always be the same: "Grove told me to do it." When Flath confronted Grove—and confrontations inside Intel would often be with both parties screaming at the top of their lungs, in front of other people—Grove would deny that he'd given the errant engineers any direct orders. It took some time for Flath to convey to Grove that as director of operations, he had more power than he realized. To the average engineer, a "suggestion" from Grove was something to be acted on immediately. If Flath was expected to deliver on commitments he had made, this would have to stop. The philosophy inside the company that anyone could talk to anyone else was fine, Flath believed—but it had its drawbacks.

"It's very desirable, because you get a lot of good ideas. But it's not OK to change the batting order without anybody decreeing that this is what would happen."

The company's first year was punctuated with intermittent stand-up screaming matches while issues such as this one were gradually sorted out. But broadly, Intel people felt a refreshing sense of freedom. Instead of having to fight the bureaucracy of a purchasing department, every engineer had the authority to sign on behalf of the company for equipment costing up to $100,000. The company parking lot had no preassigned spaces for senior management; instead, the rule was simply that those who arrived earliest for work got the spaces closest to the front door. And as the research continued, there was a feeling that you were part of an elite corps, an assembly of the brightest, hardest-working people, a world-beating team. Of course there was a risk of failure. But everyone knew that a talented engineer could easily find work elsewhere if things didn't work out. There was no fear of long-term unemployment to discourage risk taking.

"They offered me the job at the end of breakfast," said one of Intel's very first engineering hires. "I called my wife, and told her that I'd just accepted a job with a pay cut of one-third, working for an unknown start-up. The good news, I said, was that there were some big names running it. And if it proved a mistake, I could always go and pump gas someplace."

Of the three memory technologies that Moore wanted to investigate, one swiftly ruled itself out. An early look at multichip memory modules suggested that they were too far from becoming a commercial product to be worth devoting effort to. That left the bipolar route and the MOS route. By the fall, Intel's engineering effort was clearly organized into two teams, each led by a former Fairchild research engineer, to follow these up separately. The MOS team was led by Les Vadasz, a balding, short-tempered engineer who shared Andy Grove's Hungarian background; the bipolar team came under the control of a brilliant but equally short-tempered engineer named Dick Bohn.

From the very first, there was friendly rivalry between the two teams to see who could deliver a manufacturable product and a stable process first. The bipolar team had an early psychological boost when Phil Spiegel arrived from Honeywell, an East Coast computer company that was one of the "seven dwarfs" competing against IBM to sell mainframe computers. Spiegel explained that Honeywell wanted to steal a march on its competitors by being the first computer manufacturer to build a machine that used semiconductor memory instead of magnetic core. He knew that Fairchild had come very close to developing a bipolar memory circuit with 16 cells, or bits. Yet Fairchild had never quite managed it because somehow one of the cells was always a dud. Insiders used to joke that Fairchild's R&D people had built a great 15-bit memory chip.

Spiegel explained to the people at Intel that Honeywell wanted to be able to ship a new line of computers in 1969 or 1970 that would contain a 64-bit scratchpad memory, big enough to store an eight-letter English word. The company was inviting a number of firms in the electronics business to try to build some working prototypes to this testing specification. Intel was new and untried, but Noyce and Moore's pedigrees were impressive. If Honeywell could give Intel a down payment of $10,000 to help fund its research work, was the company interested in trying to beat the other six companies that had already started on the problem?

The offer was less crazy than it sounded. Whichever company came up with a mass-produced chip first was likely to win an order from Honeywell for ten thousand units at $100 apiece. So the up-front fee, although crucially important for a start-up that had to keep an eye on its bank balance, represented a bet that only represented 1 percent of what Honeywell was expecting the finished chips to cost. Since it was by no means clear that *anyone* could build a 64-bit semiconductor memory circuit, the $10,000 was a small price to pay for adding one more talented team to the field already competing for the prize. Anyway, one of Intel's engineers had impressed Spiegel and his colleagues as particularly committed and reassuring: H. T. Chua, a Stanford graduate of Chinese ancestry who had emigrated to the United States from Singapore. Chua was a quiet, thoughtful man, but he had an air of unmistakable quiet confidence about him that seemed to exude the message: *We'll build your chip for you, and we'll beat everyone else too.*

Chua kept his promise. When Spiegel returned to California in spring 1969, Chua met him at the factory door with a sample chip in his hand. The chip designed for Honeywell therefore became the new company's first commercial product. It was a symptom of Intel's target market that the new chip wasn't even given a name. Instead, it was referred to only by a part number, 3101. Intel's potential customers were engineers inside computer companies, who thought of themselves as rational decision makers choosing between one part and another strictly on technical merit, quality, and price. A catchy name wouldn't increase sales; on the contrary, it might excite suspicion that there was a shortage of engineering talent to cover up for. A simple part number, preferably a number that meant something, was what Intel needed to go for.

Bob Graham, Intel's marketing chief, realized the success of the 3101 could be of enormous value to Intel. The industry was littered with companies that made grand promises they failed to fulfil. Cynics used to joke that National Semiconductor, in particular, used to send around a specification for a new chip to customers, and then wait to see what reaction it got before deciding whether to start designing it. Graham wanted Intel to earn the opposite reputation, so he coined the slogan *Intel Delivers*. It became almost an unbreakable rule inside Intel never to announce a product in advance, just in case something went wrong 'twixt cup and lip. Instead, he resolved that the company would wait until chips were already on distributors' shelves before going out to customers to spread the word about a new device.

This early triumph from the bipolar team cranked up the pressure on the competing MOS team to deliver. At one point, Vadasz and his colleagues became convinced that they were almost there. The test production line they had set up yielded one device that worked perfectly. The MOS team immediately toasted its arrival with champagne in the cramped company cafeteria—but it was to be many months before they were able to build a second working MOS circuit.

Part of the trouble was that the manufacturing process itself was so rudimentary. Everyone understood that particles in the air could contaminate a semiconductor production line; defense industries did their most sensitive assembly work inside giant sealed "clean rooms," where the air was filtered to remove the tiny specks that could spoil a circuit. But Intel had no such luxury. Its fab area, recalled Andy Grove, "looked like Willy Wonka's factory, with hoses and wires and contraptions chugging along. . . . It was state-of-the-art manufacturing at the time, but by today's standards it was unbelievably crude."

No matter how hard they tried to clean up the fab area, the MOS engineers still couldn't make circuits that worked. At one late-night meeting, almost in desperation, Andy Grove finally lost patience. Why was the company bothering with silicon gate MOS technology at all, he asked. Why not go back to a simpler, less tricky metal gate technology where this problem would not arise?

It was Gordon Moore—quiet, thoughtful, Gordon—who broke in on Grove's tirade.

"I want to see every wafer that comes off the line for the next thirty days," he said slowly. "Then we'll make a decision on what to do."

Over the coming days and weeks, the engineers of the group brought the faulty wafers to Moore one by one. They watched him check the devices under a microscope and test them with the makeshift equipment they had developed. Before the thirty days were up, Moore told them what he thought the problem was. When a memory chip was being built, he reminded them, it had to be repeatedly heated up and cooled during different stages of the production process. The temperature change was not abnormal for the electronics industry, but this circuit was particularly sensitive. Because the design had sharp corners where the metal oxide and the silicon met, one would expand more quickly than the other, and a crack would appear that broke the circuit and rendered it useless.

Moore came up with a solution to the problem that was brilliant in its simplicity. He told the engineers to "dope" the oxide with impurities so that its melting-point would fall. This would reduce the brittleness of the chip's edges and allow the oxide to flow evenly around the rough corners like melting ice cream. To their astonishment, the MOS team soon discovered that Moore was right. Working almost as an armchair engineer, he had solved the problem that had eluded them for months.

There was a long debate inside Intel as to whether the company should patent the "reflow" process that Moore had invented. The issue was not whether the process could be patented; it clearly satisfied all the legal requirements for a patent. The bigger question was whether the patent would be self-defeating, because the information Intel would have to publish would set competitors on the right track toward similar solutions. In the end, the team chose a halfway house. The process was patented in Moore's name (and a framed copy of the patent was hung in his office as a reward); but once the chip was in production, the exact nature of the reflow process was kept secret from the hourly workers who had been hired to carry out the chip fabrication and packaging. On the long list of processes that the silicon wafer had to undergo before it could be scored and sliced up into dozens of finished memory chips, the reflow process was referred to only using "anneal," a word used to mean heating glass and cooling it slowly. That way, the risk was reduced that a line worker would be offered a dollar more per hour by a competitor and walk out of Intel's door with the fledgling company's most valuable trade secret.

Until there were products to sell, Bob Graham had little to do. The company did not have enough spare cash to hire salesmen to sit around and wait for the engineers to do their job. So Graham identified a candidate who could serve as his second-in-command in the sales and marketing division when the time came—and in the meantime, he amused himself fishing.

Setting his alarm clock to wake him several hours before dawn, Graham would tiptoe out of his modest house in Saratoga to avoid waking his wife. Then he would climb into the old Ford Mustang that he had bought from Bob Noyce and roar up a deserted Highway 101 all the way to San Francisco, where he would park as close as possible to the Golden Gate Bridge. There, waiting under a streetlamp, he would find Gordon Moore in his overalls and work boots. With the motor engine burbling softly beneath the dark wash, the two men would ease Moore's fishing boat out under the bridge and toward the grounds beyond the Bay where salmon were plentiful.

For a scientist, Moore seemed to show scant interest in the state of repair of his craft. Sometimes he had to scrape the rust off the spark plugs with his pocketknife. Other times, the boat's rudimentary radio would break down, leaving the fishermen cut off from the outside world. But on one occasion, a more serious problem arose. The part of the expedition that required the most skill was traversing what the local fishermen called the Potato Patch, a narrow channel bordered with rocks just beyond the bridge that led to the fishing grounds beyond. One morning, just as they were halfway through the Potato Patch, Graham noticed water slopping around in the bilges of the boat.

"Oh," said Moore absentmindedly, "I must have forgotten to switch the bilge pump on." He disappeared for a few seconds, and Graham began to hear the sound of the electric pump groaning into action. Thirty seconds later, however, the water level was still rising.

"The pump!" yelled Graham. "It's not working!"

Frantically, he and Moore grabbed whatever receptacles were closest to hand and began to throw bucketfuls of water overboard. Yet as fast as they bailed water out, more seemed to come in. While Graham continued to empty the buckets as fast as he could—*splash, splash, splash, splash, splash*—Moore went to inspect the drain fittings.

Ten minutes later, the problem was solved. The hole in the boat that Moore had discovered was plugged with an old oily rag, and the two friends lay back, exhausted by their efforts. As the sun rose over the city behind them, they celebrated their survival into a new day with an early-morning beer.

5

A Savior from Bucks County

Bob Graham's appointment as Intel's sales director had an unintended consequence. It led indirectly to the creation of another electronics company that for the next two decades would intermittently be Intel's greatest ally and its most bitter enemy.

Here's how it happened.

Soon after Bob Noyce had left Fairchild Semiconductor to set up Intel with Gordon Moore, the management of the Fairchild parent company on the East Coast began the search for Noyce's replacement as general manager. C. Lester Hogan, the feared and admired head of Motorola, got the job—but the terms he demanded hardly showed confidence in the state of the company. Hogan was to receive $1 million in salary over three years, plus Fairchild stock options worth over $500,000, and a loan of a further $5 million to buy more stock with. He also secured guarantees that he would be able to run the semiconductor operation as an independent business, free from interference by the accountants back east that had so plagued Bob Noyce.

The new general manager's first move once he was installed at Fairchild was to fire most of the top executives left in the company and bring in his own band of hard men, later known as Hogan's Heroes. Only one senior manager stayed on: Jerry Sanders, the company's sales and marketing director.

Flamboyant, clever, fast-talking and handsome, Sanders satisfied every cliché of what a businessman in California headed for the high-tech 1970s ought to look like. But behind the Italian suits and the perfectly bouffant hairstyle, the marketing chief was not what he seemed. Sanders had been born the son of a dissolute traffic-signal repairman in Chicago's dangerous South Side, and had been brought up by his grandparents after spending his earliest years with his mother in a succession of dingy low-rent apartments while his father went on periodic drinking binges. Like many poor boys before him, Sanders had hoped to parlay his good looks into a career in the movies. But his chances were set back just one semester into a two-year course at the University of Illinois. A gang of local toughs set on him after a football game, fractured his jaw, skull, and ribs, carved up his face with a can opener, and dumped him, bleeding, in a trash can. A friend carried him in the trunk of a car to the local hospital, where he was rushed into the emergency room.

Once recovered and with his rearranged profile, Sanders realized he would have to give up his ambition to be a matinee idol. Instead, he resolved to put his electrical engineering training to practical use and joined the Douglas Aircraft Company as a designer of air-conditioning systems. It took him only a few years to discover that if he wanted a company car, a good salary, and an expense account, he was in the wrong job. In the electronics industry, salesmen made better money than engineers.

Sanders made the switch and rose swiftly through the ranks. He made a spectacular success of running Fairchild Semiconductor's regional office in Los Angeles, and then landed the company's top marketing slot back in Silicon Valley. With a large house in the Hollywood hills, an attractive wife, a black Cadillac, and a taste for Dom Pérignon champagne, he lived more like a movie mogul than an electronics guy. Yet Sanders knew the electronics industry inside out—and behind the glitz and ostentation was a determined and hard worker.

Sanders was always something of a favorite with Bob Noyce—perhaps because he reminded the older man of the showmanship and extroversion that was part of his own character. The young marketing star was much less kindly looked on by the more conservative Gordon Moore, who had a full dose of the disdain that many engineers have for salesmen. He viewed them as a necessary evil, but no better than that. Moore knew that the old saying "Build a better mousetrap, and the world will beat a path to your door" wasn't true.

But he wished it were. Perhaps this was why Bob Graham got the new sales and marketing job at Intel, while Jerry Sanders was left at Fairchild Semiconductor.

Whether this was the reason or not, Sanders knew his position at Fairchild was precarious. He felt like a courtier left over from a discredited régime after the arrival of a new king. Within a matter of weeks, the agony ended. Hogan called Sanders into his office and told him point-blank that he was surplus to requirements. The only consolation was that while many other Fairchild loyalists had been fired after years of service with no more than a couple of weeks' notice, Sanders was able to extract a year's salary in compensation— allowing him to rent a beach house in Malibu where he could sit in the sun and ponder his next move.

Six weeks later, early in 1969, Sanders called an old pal—Ed Turney, one of Fairchild's best salesmen. Sanders had given Turney the job of running Fairchild's Los Angeles region, and the two men had become friends. By this time, Turney had been fired too and was holed up in a cabin in a nearby ski resort.

"How'd you like to start a company?" Sanders asked.

"What, making records?" Turney still believed that Sanders had secret showbiz ambitions.

"No, making semiconductors."

Sanders explained that he had been approached by a group of four other Fairchild employees who were looking for someone of presidential caliber to help them raise finance. Sanders had agreed to lead them, on two conditions. He thought the future was in the kind of digital circuits Intel was making, not the old-fashioned analog circuits they had set their heart on. So he wanted the new company to make both classes of product. Also, he wanted to nominate some of his own people. If Turney was ready to join the start-up, Sanders promised, a seat would be kept warm for him.

Within a few weeks, Sanders had assembled an eight-man team. To the four members of the analog group, he added himself and another former Fairchild colleague, plus Turney, who was offered the sales and marketing job but also wanted to control purchasing. The top engineering job for the digital operation went to Sven Simonsen, a Danish-born engineer still on the Fairchild payroll.

Three weeks later, Jerry Sanders was ready to talk to potential investors about his plans. Capital Group Companies, a leading investment firm in Los Angeles, agreed to arrange introductions—and its chairman wrote a personal check for $50,000 to pay the living expenses of the team members who had lost their jobs and been less successful than Sanders in securing a payoff.

Sanders's first port of call was Arthur Rock, the man who had raised $2.3 million for Bob Noyce and Gordon Moore in a single afternoon.

The diminutive venture capitalist looked up from the seventy-page document before him and sighed. Bristling with technical terms, process details, and price curves, the plan set forth a powerful case for the view that demand for integrated circuits would explode in the 1970s. It detailed which products the company would build and how, estimated the prices these products would sell for, outlined the backgrounds of all eight founders, and predicted profitability after seven quarters and positive cash flow after ten. But Rock didn't like it.

"It's too late," he said.

Sanders began to expostulate.

Rock was polite, but firm. His belief, he said, was that with dozens of other companies already in the market, it was now too late to start up a broad-based semiconductor company. Before the master salesman could begin to put his wiles to work, Rock added a second point for good measure. Of all the investments he had ever made, said the venture capitalist as he looked Sanders coldly in the eye, the only ones that ever lost money had been run by marketing men.

The meeting was an omen. As Sanders continued on his road show, he found that potential investors fell into two categories: those who knew so little about the industry that they plagued him with ill-informed questions; and those who knew enough about it to doubt seriously whether, with all the new companies that had been set up over recent years, the semiconductor industry was still young enough for another entrant. Neither category yielded any investors.

As the weeks turned into months, Sanders found himself as far as ever from the $1.75 million target that had been set for the company's initial funding, and facing the first rumblings of discontent from his impatient team. One or two of the five members who were still on the Fairchild payroll began to wonder whether it might be wise to stay put for the moment. Meanwhile, Turney and Carey began to chafe at the idea of working full-time on the project unpaid while others were still sitting on the sidelines, hedging their bets by hanging on to their day jobs.

Sanders realized that it was time to take charge. He called a meeting of the team members at his house and presented those who were still at Fairchild with draft resignation letters for them to submit so that they could be ready for work on May 1, 1969. He arranged to have the company formally incorporated on the same date—in Delaware, he said, so as to give investors on the East Coast a warm feeling that proper attention was being paid to minimize directors' liabilities. And he committed himself to raising the money they would need by the end of July.

When one member of the team asked him whether this was realistic, Sanders's reply was immediate and confident: "We're absolutely going to get the money. *We're absolutely going to get the money.*" It was a mantra that he would find himself repeating again and again over the coming weeks.

Some weeks later, Bob Noyce received an unexpected visitor at Intel. The man who walked into his office was Tom Skornia, a young lawyer who had recently started out in private practice.

"I'm here to represent Jerry Sanders," said Skornia as he sat down.

"I'm glad to hear it," replied Noyce. Sanders had asked him for advice in finding a good lawyer to serve as general counsel for his new business. On Noyce's recommendation, Sanders and his colleagues had interviewed three different law firms, but had settled on Skornia's in the belief that a sole practitioner who was just starting out would be likely to give them higher priority than a bigger firm with dozens of associates to delegate work to. One other point had been in Skornia's favor: He was the only lawyer they met who could talk as fast as Ed Turney.

"And I'm here to ask for money," continued Skornia.

He handed Noyce the Sanders business plan and explained that the company, initially known as Sanders Associates, had now been incorporated in Delaware under the name of Advanced Micro Devices. Like Noyce and Moore, Sanders and his colleagues had run through a long list of possible names before they found one that was still free in the state registry.

As Noyce flipped through the business plan, a bemused expression began to play across his face. He knew the industry inside out. He knew the products that Sanders was proposing to build. Reading between the lines of the limited biographical details that the plan included, he could even identify all the people involved. If anyone could see that the proposed company was stronger in marketing and sales than in the core discipline of inventing and building new products, it was Noyce.

"You mean they're actually going to *make* the stuff?" he asked.

The two men looked at each other and burst into laughter. Skornia knew that the ice was broken. There was no point trying to gloss over the shortcomings of the proposed business with Noyce. But equally, there was no need to explain Sanders's qualities. Noyce had always recognized the steel inside his brash young marketing manager, and he was willing to back it. Yes, AMD could soon be in direct competition with his own company. Yes, its top management was drawn from people Noyce himself had turned down for Intel. But Bob Noyce would become one of AMD's founding investors all the same. Why not? It was a gamble, but Noyce loved taking risks.

The decision of Intel's founder to back Sanders was a strong psychological boost in the struggle to raise funding for AMD. Sanders, Turney, and Skornia flew down to the Capital Group's Los Angeles offices to tally the checks and wire transfers that had come in from investors in the new company. It was June 20, 1969, and their plan was to confirm that AMD's investors had contributed the minimum agreed sum of $1.55 million, then fly straight back to Silicon Valley to start work. But their timing was unlucky. The New York stock market had fallen sharply that morning and the institutions were playing it safe. Instead of celebrating the successful funding of the project, the founders were forced to hang around, imprisoned in the office by the sultry summer heat, waiting for more money to come in and canvasing every potential investor they could think of in an attempt to reach the threshold before the 5:00 P.M. deadline.

By 4:30 P.M., the total stood at $1,480,000, and no number of recounts could make it any higher. For the next twenty minutes, the three men and their two Capital Group advisers sat in sickened silence, staring at each other. At 4:55 P.M., a messenger arrived with an envelope. Inside was a check for $25,000 from a private investor in Bucks County, Pennsylvania. With five minutes and $5,000 to spare, AMD was in business.

6

The Rebels

While Intel was developing its first memory chips, the American people were entranced by the drama of the space race with the Soviet Union. The company's founders relaxed an early rule forbidding radios in the lab so Intel engineers could listen while they worked to Neil Armstrong's live broadcast from the surface of the moon in July 1969. But neither Noyce, Moore, nor Grove had much time for the Beatles, hippies, marijuana, or any of the other enthusiasms that had gripped so many young Americans. For student activism or demonstrations against the war in Vietnam they had still less time. Interviewed by *Fortune* in 1973, Moore said: "We are really the revolutionaries in the world today—not the kids with the long hair and beards who were wrecking the schools a few years ago."

But political radicalism was not dead inside Intel. Its leading exponent was a gifted young circuit designer by the name of Joel Karp. With bell-bottoms and long hair, Karp was willing to risk the consternation of his employers by carrying anti-Vietnam petitions around Intel parties—and he was not even slightly put off when Grove and Les Vadasz, with the excess patriotism of the naturalized citizen, refused with stony faces to sign.

Karp displayed a wonderful ability to wind up his more conventional colleagues. On one occasion, a new sales executive Bob Graham hired bumped into him as he was about to leave the office for a technical meeting with a client. The shocked sales chief took one look at Karp's shoulder-length hair and ordered him to get it cut before attending the meeting. The following day, Karp reappeared in the office with his hair blow-dried and styled with great skill, but only one-eighth of an inch shorter than the day before. There was silence from his colleagues as Karp walked down the lab, informed the sales chief with a smile that he was going to claim the haircut as a business expense, and presented him with a receipt for the then astounding sum of $25.

"What about taking a bath?" the VP replied acidly. "Will you charge that to the company too?"

Since he had been handing out leaflets arguing against the Vietnam war, Karp was the most natural suspect when a group of peace protesters assembled a picket in front of Intel's offices to protest what they mistakenly believed to be a company that was engaged in military contracting. For once, even Bob Noyce displayed a flash of anger. "Get those fucking Berkeley friends of yours outta here," he told Karp through gritted teeth.

But beneath his long hair, Karp had a rare aptitude for circuit design. A graduate of MIT, he had taught the subject to scientists at NASA, and had spent some time designing Polaris nuclear missile systems. Intel found him at a competing electronics company and brought him in to do crucial parts of the work on the design for the Intel's first MOS memory chip. He was also the principal designer of a new MOS chip commissioned by Honeywell to follow the bipolar 3101 project that H. T. Chua had worked on, and he played a big part in bringing into the daylight a later product that would make Intel's fortune.

Another highly visible young member of the Intel crew was Bruce MacKay, who had the double distinction of being both the company's youngest professional staffer and its only professional without a university degree. Born in Britain, he had learned the ropes of electronics at Texas Instruments' local facility there before moving to Bell Telephone in Canada.

"It's lucky that you're over twenty-five," Andy Grove told MacKay one day, "because we don't hire anyone under twenty-five." The young engineer, who was part of the team responsible for taking memory chips off the wafer lines and sending them through assembly and test, refrained tactfully from giving Grove his date of birth there and then.

MacKay drew attention to himself by becoming the first engineer to try to resign from Intel. A call came in from AMD, and MacKay was invited over to meet Jerry Sanders in Sunnyvale, where he was subjected to the full power of the Sanders sales pitch. He was told that he would be working with a group of real people instead of a bunch of weirdos; he would have the same responsibilities but more money; and he would be given an outright grant of company stock instead of options. Intel's stock option scheme was arranged so that only a quarter of the options that employees were granted could be exercised in the first year. To exercise the rest, you had to stay three more years—but by then, you would have been given three more sets of options, each on the same terms. This meant that every Intel employee wishing to leave had to walk away from a significant block of shares in the company.

MacKay, whose badge showed that he was Intel employee number 50, liked what Sanders told him. Biting the bullet, he told his immediate boss that he was leaving. The next day, Andy Grove appeared at his desk, insisted on taking him to a local bar in his rusty old Sunbeam Alpine, and sat him down at a table with a bottle of Scotch between them.

"How can you do this?" Grove demanded.

MacKay had his response ready.

"I want to work somewhere where manufacturing is taken seriously," he said. "You guys just don't think it's terribly important. Tell me, Andy: If you had the choice of two seminars, one on solid-state physics and one on inventory management, which would you choose? I know the answer already."

But Grove was not to be put off. He kept MacKay talking and drinking until three in the morning—and by the time MacKay staggered up from the table, he had agreed to go back to AMD and tell Jerry Sanders that he was staying at Intel.

From that day onwards, MacKay's job suddenly began to get more interesting. He was given responsibility for the chip assembly operation that was carried out for Intel under contract across the Mexican border in the town of Tijuana. Several times a week, MacKay would drive down Highway 101 past San Diego, cross the border into Mexico, and check on progress.

Strictly speaking, because he was a British citizen, MacKay did not have the privilege of free border crossing that an American would have. But after badgering the Mexican consul in San Diego, he obtained a six-month visa that effectively allowed him unlimited crossings. A bigger issue was how to get the finished silicon wafers with memory circuits laid out on them across to Mexico in good time for packaging. In theory, MacKay was supposed to clear them through customs, something that could only be done through a broker every Tuesday. In practice, he carried them in a leather carpet bag on the floor of his car, immediately behind the driver's seat. Because a two-inch wafer could carry as many as two hundred circuits, depending on the chip's die size, he could carry thousands of chips at a time. After a while, MacKay began to mark the bag every time he carried a shipment, in the same way that wartime fighter pilots used to mark the fuselage of their aircraft after shooting down an enemy plane. It was not always a clear run. On one occasion, MacKay was turned back at the border because his hair was too long. Undaunted, he turned the car back to the United States, changed places with his colleague in the passenger seat a mile up the road, tucked his ponytail under his baseball cap, opened his newspaper to the sports page, and lay back sleepily as he was driven into Mexico through a different customs lane.

With Intel's head office almost a day's drive to the north, communications were of paramount importance. Telephone service through the local Mexican phone company was out of the question, not merely because the line quality was so poor but also because of the delay. So MacKay struck a private deal with a telephone engineer working at the local phone company in San Diego and arranged for a five-mile cable to be run across the border so the assembly plant could be connected directly into the American phone system.

Another creative engineer at Intel was John Reed, who bumped into Andy Grove at a party while still working in his first job out of graduate school. Grove asked him what he thought of Intel's product line. Pouring himself a drink, the young Reed replied breezily that the idea of using silicon gate technology in a memory chip was "kinda neat," but added that he thought the rest of the company's circuits "lacked creativity." It was an off-the-cuff, ill-considered response—but a week later Reed received a call from Les Vadasz, inviting him to come and talk to people at Intel about whether he might like to put a little more creativity into their product line.

After joining the company, Reed soon discovered that Intel had been a great deal more creative than he realized. Ted Hoff, the young Stanford researcher who had asked Bob Noyce point-blank whether the world needed another semiconductor company, had drawn up a concept for an entirely new memory cell that needed only three transistors compared with the conventional four, and fewer interconnections. The concept had only one drawback; it would not produce stable storage when the computer was switched off. To maintain the information in the cell, the circuit had to be "refreshed" every thousandth of a second. This added a substantial overhead to the memory system as a whole—but it offered the promise of packing cells together three to four times as densely as any existing product. If Intel could build it, this "dynamic random-access memory," or DRAM, would store 1,024 bits, four times as much information as the highest-capacity semiconductor memory device currently available in the world.

Karp and Vadasz had been assigned to turn Hoff's one-cell circuit diagram into a working part. They had already produced one chip design—a part called the 1102, which was commissioned by Honeywell, the customer that had prompted Intel to design its original bipolar chip. It was their second version, the 1103 chip, that Reed was soon told to work on. Partly because of the complexity of the chip's design, the first prototype wafers that came off the line did not contain a single working circuit. Reed spent a number of months on the project, fine-tuning the design and the manufacturing process before finally coming up with something that he believed would be manufacturable.

When Reed arrived in the fab area late one night to see the first prototypes of his new design roll off the line, Gordon Moore was waiting for him.

"Reed, you screwed up," he joked. "Only seventy-five working die per wafer."

Achieving a yield of nearly 50 percent was thrilling news. Noyce and Moore were confident that with further improvements to the design and the process, the manufacturing cost of the 1103 chip could soon fall to a point where Intel could sell it for $10.24—a penny a bit. Computer makers would complain that this new dynamic semiconductor memory was more complex to work with than old-fashioned core memories. But it was smaller, much faster, and used much less power. And if its price per bit was lower than that of core memory, DRAM would conquer the world.

A delegation was hastily sent to Massachusetts to persuade Honeywell to abandon the 1102 project and to put its backing behind the 1103. Three people went: John Reed, a salesman named Bob O'Hara, and Bob Noyce himself. When the presentations began, the Honeywell engineers were highly dubious. They had been cooperating with Intel for many months on the 1102, and the part was designed precisely to meet the requirements of Honeywell computers. Why should they throw away this work and switch to a product that Intel would soon be offering to all comers?

Essentially, Intel had two answers. The engineering answer was that the 1103 design, for all its additional complications, was easier to manufacture. This meant not only that it was more reliable now but also that it offered better technical improvements in the future. The marketing answer was based on cost. Because of the manufacturability advantage, the 1103 was already considerably cheaper to build than the 1102—and the gap would only widen. But the Honeywell engineers remained unconvinced.

It was only when Noyce, the father of the integrated circuit, began to speak that they sat up in their seats. Talking without notes or preparation, Noyce repeated some of the points that his colleagues had already made. What he said was in itself not new. But Noyce's presence, his aura of authority, his seductively deep voice, won the day. Honeywell signed up for the 1103, and the three men returned triumphant to Mountain View knowing that Intel could now focus all its efforts on developing a single memory product.

The launch of the new chip in October 1970 proved to be a turning point in the history of the computer industry. As we'll see, it was by no means a perfect product. But by undercutting the price of core memories, the 1103 established semiconductor memory as the technology of choice for computer makers from 1970 onwards—and set the industry on a familiar path of falling costs, rising performance, and diminishing size. As the price of semiconductor memory fell over the coming decades, it would become cost-effective to build memory into lots of other devices too. Demand for memory products would become a multibillion-dollar market—a market that Intel could legitimately claim to have created singlehandedly.

Noyce's success at Honeywell was typical of his talents and proof that he was admirably qualified to be Intel's first CEO. He combined formidable technical expertise with a will to win and a sense of fun. In the passenger seat of his Mercury Cougar on the way to San Francisco Airport, Reed discovered that his boss was a terrifying driver—weaving back and forth at high speed between lanes on Highway 101 in a playful attempt to show that he could get to the airport before any other car on the road. When Noyce came back from a skiing weekend with a broken leg freshly set in plaster, he would challenge the first comer to a wheelchair race down the corridor, laughing uproariously as he spun the wheels of his chair faster and faster, clattering against the wall as the chair veered out of control.

The other role models inside the company were Andy Grove and Les Vadasz. Both of them were as determined to win as Noyce was. But they took life, and work, far more seriously. Grove told his old Fairchild colleagues that he believed their old company had been run far too much like a holiday camp. Vadasz, meanwhile, wanted tidy desks, proper filing systems, accurate lab notes, regular performance reviews.

The attempt to impose these qualities on the company's engineering staff soon began to lead to frictions. In March 1971, three months after the 1103 was introduced in commercial quantities, Vadasz wrote a performance review for John Reed that said as much about his own personality as about the engineer whose performance he was rating.

"One of the clichés one uses in reviewing," Vadasz began, "is to say that so and so is a 'capable engineer.' There is not much point, however, in a review to say only that. In fact, the more capable an engineer, the more need there is to explore not only accomplishments but to try to analyze problems, failures, and all that is negative about the engineer's job performance."

He then offered a paragraph of measured praise, and then six further paragraphs demolishing Reed's working practices point by point. He complained that the "problems the [1103] suffers from could fill a book." Reed had "disengage[d] himself" from day-to-day problems. He showed a "complete lack of initiative in taking (or identifying the need for) action." It was "inexcusable" that he did not keep himself familiar with vital technical data. Reed was "disorganized" and left "devices and data scattered about." He always wanted "to move on too fast to new projects."

"I want to emphasize," Vadasz concluded, "that I respect John's engineering capability very much. John can solve any circuit problem we will have. . . . My objections above all were all related to John's working habits. Habits can be changed. I hope that John will be able to use this criticism in a constructive manner."

Vadasz was wrong. The review made Reed incandescent with rage. He instantly wrote a furious memo for his own personnel file, headed

To Whom It May Concern, complaining about it. Reed opened his reply by pleading guilty to the charge of needing corrective feedback from above to keep him working on matters that were important. Then he went on the attack.

"Here is a typewritten, signed off, filed-in-my-records report," he wrote, "citing specific examples of bad things I have done in my eight-and-one-half-month tenure here, each one of which should have been directly criticized on the day they occurred! . . . The practice of saving up all these 'constructive' criticisms in one package, to be delivered below the belt (in the form of a *copy* of an already filed report!), after the fact, is an indefensible management policy."

So angered and disillusioned was Reed by the incident that he immediately cut back the eighty hours a week he had been spending at the plant and started devoting more time to his family and singing in a local choral group. Within another year, he had left Intel forever. When Andy Grove, hearing of his departure plans, asked him what could be done to make him stay, Reed looked at him uncomprehendingly.

"This company is like a woman," he told Grove bitterly. "You're madly in love with her, but then you find she's been cheating on you. After that, you just can't give your hundred percent anymore."

"We'd be happy with ninety-five," replied Grove.

But it was no good. Reed was determined to leave the company, and the only way for Intel to make the best of a bad job was to circulate the Vadasz review and the Reed response around the company as a lesson in how the business of reviewing performance should be approached. Intel would later institute a series of regular lunches at which engineers and technical staff would have a chance to make their grievances known to the company's top management. They became known as the "John Reed Memorial Lunches."

It was understandable that tempers inside Intel should run high. The conventional rule of thumb in the industry was "one man, one chip, one year." Individuals took personal possession of design projects in a way that would be impossible today, where teams of one hundred or more people can work on a single chip. A circuit designer would spend months drawing up his design. He* would work long

---

*There weren't any women engineers at Intel in 1971, or at most other electronics companies either.

hours working with a "layout girl," a designer whose job was to cut the image of the circuits into a giant sheet of a red plasticlike substance called "rubylith." He would check the design again and again over a period of weeks, following lines of different colors around the circuit with a finger to make sure that everything connected up properly. Finally, after months of perfecting the process, the first prototypes would be fabricated, with the designer waiting tensely outside the wafer sort area, where the devices would be tested and then sliced into individual chips, as if outside a delivery room. There were two possible outcomes: the horror of a stillbirth, or the elation of a working device. But it was an intensely personal experience. And nothing would make an engineer more angry than the hint that credit for an idea or a piece of work was going in the wrong direction.

One day in August 1970, Joel Karp opened the latest edition of *Electronics* magazine on his desk. To his astonishment, he found an article in the magazine about the 1102 chip written by Ted Hoff. True, Hoff had devised the dynamic memory cell that the chip was based on. But Karp felt the 1102 was *his* chip. Incensed, he rushed into Gordon Moore's office and threw the magazine on Moore's desk, open at the beginning of the offending article.

"I promise you," said Moore with tears in his eyes. "I promise you that as long as I am in this company, nothing like this will ever happen again."

But the jealousies inside the MOS group were nothing compared to the rivalry between the MOS group and the group of engineers working on bipolar circuits. As the 1103 began to make headway in the market, the company shifted resources away from bipolar technologies toward MOS. The bipolar engineers began to find it harder to book time on the testing equipment. Their prototypes would always take longer to emerge. Their projects would receive less attention from Noyce and Moore.

Commercially, this was probably the right decision. Even the most die-hard enthusiasts for bipolar, such as H. T. Chua, whose faith in the technology had brought in the $10,000 from Honeywell, would admit later that MOS was the more promising process. At the time, however, the team took the downgrading of the bipolar operation as a personal slight. How could they take it otherwise, when they had devoted so many late nights, so much effort, so much emotion, to making their bipolar projects work?

Vadasz, as head of the MOS engineering team, did not help matters. He had a knack of saying hurtful things to the bipolar people, not just in meetings but in corridors, in the company cafeteria, in the parking lot, that could spoil an entire day for them. Some of his greatest venom was reserved for Dick Bohn, the bipolar team leader. Bohn was under considerable stress to make bipolar perform. At the same time, he was left in no doubt that the company considered his beloved bipolar process no more than a transitional technology that would soon be phased out until it was used only for expensive niche products working at especially high speed. In the end, the pressure became too much. Bohn began to drink heavily, and his work started to suffer. He was later eased out of the company, into a downward spiral of alcoholism and mental illness from which he did not recover for some time.

The fate of Dick Bohn was a terrible reminder to everyone at Intel of the high human cost of the conditions they worked under. Even Andy Grove, who was largely responsible for setting those conditions, felt a pang of conscience. A few years later, at a company retreat in the resort town of Pajaro Dunes, Grove would confide to a colleague that his contribution to the departure from Intel of Dick Bohn was the one thing in his life that he regretted most.

7

Yellow Snow

It was becoming clear that Intel wasn't a start-up anymore. The company's sales had grown from a token $566,000 in 1969—largely earned from bipolar circuits built for Honeywell—to a more serious $4.2 million in 1970. Although a downturn hit the electronics market in late 1970, forcing the company to lay off workers, the introduction of the 1103 in October made it inevitable that the company would expand. Its workforce, which had passed the one hundred mark at the beginning of the year, was approaching the point where Noyce, Moore, and Grove could no longer expect to know every employee by name.

Intel was also on the move. Anticipating that it would be impossible to meet demand for 1103 from the old Union Carbide plant in Mountain View, the company had bought twenty-six acres of orchards farther south in Santa Clara, where property prices were lower. By spring 1971, the plum trees, apricots, and almonds that covered the site were uprooted to make way for a large new fabrication plant—and the company was ready to move its manufacturing operations into Santa Clara I, as the new plant was to be called.

Other companies nearby were expanding too. As the Bay Area was becoming a magnet for the electronics industry, new factories were rolling back the orchards that had covered the Santa Clara valley until the 1960s. As trees gave way to office buildings and fields to highways, a local reporter coined a new name for the area: Silicon Valley. The rise of Silicon Valley has been simultaneous with the rise of Intel.

Before the company could move to its new site, however, there was a small matter to deal with: its address. When Intel had bought the property, the street bordering the site was known as Coffin Road, apparently named after one of the property developers who had owned it during recent years. This didn't sound too auspicious for a company that saw its own survival as by no means to be taken for granted. To make matters worse, the street was badly lit and foggy: It had already been the site of a number of car accidents. So Ann Bowers, newly hired as the company's human resources manager, went to see the city fathers of Santa Clara to see if it would be possible to change the street name. She was told that the matter would have to go before committee. After a little internal discussion with her colleagues, many of whom favored names like Intel Way, Semiconductor Street, and Memory Boulevard, she wrote a letter formally requesting the name change.

Three weeks later, shortly before the great move was to take place, Bob Noyce marched into her office at 7:30 one morning and dropped a sheet of paper on her desk.

"What is the meaning of this?" he demanded.

On the paper before her, Bowers saw an announcement from the Santa Clara officials that the street outside Intel's new headquarters would henceforth be known as Bowers Avenue.

Stammering, she told Noyce that it could only be a coincidence—that she had sent in the street-name request just as she had been told to. Some weeks later, a local official explained to her that the city had chosen Bowers Avenue because that was the name of the continuation of the street on the other side of the expressway. But there seemed no reason to spoil a good story—so most of the company's employees believed, for years afterwards, that Ann Bowers had so much influence in Santa Clara that she had managed to have the company's permanent address named after her.

One of the more delicate tasks facing Ann Bowers was to find a secretary for Andy Grove. By March 1971, Intel's director of operations had got through a number of secretaries but still failed to find one that met his expectations. It got to the point where Bowers would have to warn candidates for the position in advance that he was a difficult man to work with.

The first person who survived undaunted the process of interviewing with Grove was a young Englishwoman named Sue McFarland. Brought over to California by an American husband, McFarland was working as a secretary in a financial software company. But her marriage had begun to crumble, and she had seriously considered going back to England to pick up her old life in the Worcestershire countryside. While she was thinking about it, though, McFarland had been told by a friend that Intel was a company that was going places—and she had sent in a letter of application.

Waiting in the lobby, Sue McFarland was met by a man with short, frizzy brown hair and very thick glasses, striding in from a corridor at high speed. He was wearing polyester trousers, a white short-sleeved shirt with an array of colored pens in the pocket, and a broad, rather loud tie.

"I am Andy Grove," he announced. "Please come through to my office."

The office was austere, and lit by a single small window. There was barely room for the two of them; perhaps that was why Ann Bowers hadn't followed them in. Covering the walls were dozens of charts, each filled in meticulously by hand using colored ink, with incomprehensible acronyms on the axes. *Switch on your professional smile, Sue. Look confident. Choose an opening line.*

"What do the graphs represent?" she asked pleasantly.

"Why do you want to know?" Grove snapped back. Or rather: *Vy-do-you-vant-to-know?* His English was still strongly accented with Hungarian.

"I'm curious," she continued, refusing to be thrown off her guard. "I know that you are in charge of operations, so I'm sure you must have industrial processes to keep an eye on. I'm interested to know what kind of things you are tracking."

Grove explained, as if he expected her not to know already, that Intel Corporation was in the business of making semiconductors. "Semiconductors are materials that neither prevent the passage of electrical currents nor allow them to conduct as easily as through a copper wire, for instance," he continued.

Sue McFarland sat back in her chair, trying to concentrate on the mini-lecture that her interviewer had begun. "This gives them certain behavioral characteristics that make them very useful in designing electrical circuits. But it also means they are sensitive to small changes in the manufacturing environment. Our business depends on being able to produce semiconductor devices in large volumes at high quality. Small changes in the production processes we use and the materials present when we build them can have dramatic effects on the percentage of the production run that is usable when we have finished. Higher yields mean that we have more products to sell from each production run, which means that our costs are lower. This in turn means that our profits are higher."

"I see," she replied.

"But we are here to talk first about you. Tell me a little about your experience."

It was when Sue McFarland explained that she was a qualified shorthand writer that Grove interrupted her.

"Shorthand?" he asked. "Not speedwriting? The difference is important, and speedwriting does not please me."

"Yes, I can write shorthand."

"Would you mind, then, if I were to check your skills by dictating a memo to you, having you take it down in shorthand, and asking you to type it?"

It was clear that the question was not merely rhetorical. The candidate took a notebook and a pencil from her bag, replaced the bag at the side of her chair, and waited.

Oblivious to the difficulty caused by his Hungarian accent, Grove began to dictate a quick-fire memo to members of his staff, dealing with a number of problems that had come up with a specific manufacturing process. Sue McFarland had little trouble keeping up, but she felt herself translating the words of the memo into the dots and squiggles of shorthand like an automaton, understanding nothing of what she was writing. *Why are you doing this?* she thought. *Why are you wasting your time and his?* It was almost an interruption when Grove said, "That's it."

He got up from behind the desk, led her outside into the corridor, and showed her an electric typewriter on a small table. She wheeled the chair out from below, sat down, and rolled a fresh sheet of white paper into the machine. Taking a deep breath, she looked at her notes and prepared to begin. Then something made her glance over her shoulder.

Grove was still there, watching her—and he clearly had no intention of going away.

As she typed, the words on the page blurred in and out of focus. People clattered past on the linoleum of the narrow corridor. All the time, Grove stood behind her, watching her as the memo appeared line by line. Ninety percent of it was right. *Considering the circumstances,* she said to herself, *you're not doing badly at all.*

By the time the memo was finished, Sue McFarland had regained her self-possession. She pulled the paper smoothly out of the typewriter and swung around in her chair as she handed it to her interviewer.

She gave him her coolest look. "Feel free to fill in the blanks," she said.

It was too much to expect that he would merely glance at the paper. Back in the office, Grove sat down at his desk and studied the memo intently for three, maybe even four minutes.

"Yes," he said. "This is not entirely correct, but you have made a good attempt. I will be happy to offer you the job."

Sue McFarland felt the quiet thump of the heart that comes with a sudden piece of exciting news. She felt herself able to relax for the first time in the morning. But it was not in the nature of a well-trained Englishwoman to jump up and perform a victory dance. Instead, she simply smiled.

"Thank you," she said quietly.

"Ann Bowers will make the necessary arrangements for your salary and your entry pass to get into the building. When can you start?"

"I'll have to think a little about that, Dr. Grove."

"Call me Andy. We use first names in this company."

A week into the job, Sue McFarland received a shock as she hung up her coat. Her new boss called her into his office and sat her down in front of him.

"You've been late three times," he said.

Sue McFarland looked at her watch. It was shortly after 8:10. The company's official starting time was eight o'clock, as it was at her last job, where she had always come in some time between 8:15 and 8:30, and nobody had complained.

"Work at Intel starts at eight o'clock," said Grove. "I expect everyone in the company to be here at that time, ready to do business."

McFarland gulped.

"How can I expect the rest of the staff to do this if my own secretary comes in late?"

She left the room shaking.

OK, she said to herself after she had pulled herself together. *Do we want to work under this pressure, or do we want to go and look for something else?*

Sue McFarland was nothing if not a fighter. This might be her first introduction to Grove's Hungarian work ethic, but she resolved there and then to treat it as a character-building experience.

Over the succeeding weeks, Grove began to reveal further insights into his character. The office, dark and small as it may have been, was scrupulously tidy. The filing system that Grove had managed himself until then, but now wanted McFarland to take over for him, was a model of simplicity: All paperwork, except certain regular production reports, was filed immediately under the name of the sender. Incoming mail and memoranda were to be sorted by her and put into three piles: one for "action required," one for "important information," and one for "background information." McFarland was to screen Grove's calls as well as she could, always asking people who wanted to speak to him exactly what they wanted, and taking very detailed messages in a standard form. His day consisted of a number of meetings punctuated by periods when he would work alone in his office with the door shut, and shorter periods when he would call her into his office to take dictation. Every week or so, they would sit down for fifteen minutes to discuss priorities for the period coming up. All meetings in Grove's office were to start on time, and the door would be closed five minutes after the starting time. No interruptions were to take place, unless Noyce or Moore insisted on talking to him.

Once her propensity to wake up too late had been dealt with, McFarland soon began to turn into a model secretary. Grove particularly admired her soft English accent and her precise manners and dress. But as an immigrant who had learned English as a second language, he prided himself on his command of grammar and syntax—and watched like a hawk for any mistakes in her typing. One day he handed her back a memo she had typed, with a word circled in thick red ink.

"What's wrong with this?" she asked him.

"It says *exemplified*," said Grove. "The verb comes from the noun *example*. You should have spelled it *examplified*."

Sue McFarland gave the smile of a native speaker who knew that for every rule in the English language, there was at least one exception.

"I don't think so," she replied. "Here, let me look it up."

She handed the office dictionary across to Grove, her eye twinkling with good humor at the opportunity to demonstrate that the boss was not always right.

He threw the dictionary at her.

If there was one point that Grove was keen to impress on Sue McFarland, it was that she worked for Intel, not for him. "I just happen to be your supervisor at the moment," he'd say. Nothing made him more angry than to hear that an executive had asked his secretary to take his suit to the dry cleaners, or to buy a birthday present for his wife. But there was one occasion when this principle collided inconveniently with the iron rule of promptness. Grove rushed into the office one day, fresh back from a meeting outside the building, and threw McFarland his car keys.

"Please park my car," he said. "I'm running late for my next meeting."

She took special pleasure in finding a space at the very far end of the parking lot, making sure that he would have the longest possible walk back to his car at the end of the day.

A few times, Grove sent her down to the company cafeteria to bring him some food, and spent the lunch hour dictating memos to her. The food he asked for was always the same dish: cottage cheese and fruit. He prided himself on maintaining his weight at the same level it had been when he was in college. After a few days of this, McFarland had had enough.

"Keep this up," she said, "and I'll leave the office in order to take the hour that I'm entitled to. And you'll have to get your own lunch."

But the two got on better and better. Sue McFarland realized that Andy Grove, for all his ferocious demand for precision, had awakened a tendency in her own character in the same direction. Always polite and proper, she liked things to be done correctly too. He began to refer to her as HMOS—Her Majesty, the Operations Secretary. He began to display a sense of humor, too. Three months into her new job, she stubbed her toe against a desk and swore. Grove appealed to the heavens. "Thank God!" he said. "She's human." Little did he realize that his secretary's Mistress Mouse manner was more a function of her initial terror of him than of her own personality.

Gradually, he began to trust her with greater responsibility. Not content with the three category piles for incoming mail, Grove asked her to go through his correspondence, highlighting key phrases with a yellow pen so that he would be able to scan the pages more quickly.

Once in a while, there was a pinprick to remind her what a tough man he was to work for. On Christmas Eve, 1970, Grove left the Santa Clara office just after lunch to go across to Mountain View for a meeting. Sue McFarland continued to work, finishing most of the jobs in front of her by half past three. There was no sign of Grove. Shortly after four, a colleague strolled into her office and asked her what her plans were for the holiday. *Heck*, she thought. *It may be Thursday, but it's Christmas Eve.* Ten minutes later, she was in her car on the way home.

The following Monday, she arrived back at work promptly at five to eight. Grove was already in the office, stony-faced and waiting for her. "Christmas Day is a holiday," he said, "but Christmas Eve is a workday. I came back to find you absent. In future, I'll expect you and everyone else in the company to stay at work until our normal closing time."

The following year, Grove made a preemptive strike to avoid misunderstandings. He sent around a memo to all Intel employees, reminding them not to cut their last afternoon before the holiday. This became an annual institution in the company, known as the "Scrooge memo," and it irritated people mightily. When she returned from the holiday, Sue McFarland would often find an in-box bulging with copies of the memo, which their recipients had sent back to Grove annotated with nasty comments.

May you eat yellow snow, said one of them.

The same year, Andy Grove presented Sue McFarland with her first bad performance review.

"As my job grows," he wrote in his most professorly tone, "Sue could be of increasing use to me by relieving me of many activities, from arranging dinners and bookbinding to efficient and prompt pursuit of office details, any of which may seem trivial but which if not done and well done distract me from what should more properly occupy my attention. Sue has the ability to handle all this and more, but evidently lacks the interest or the ambition to do so. I find this a pity; her capabilities will not be utilized more fully and as a result her usefulness to me and therefore to Intel will remain limited. For this reason, her compensation will also have to remain at its present level."

When he presented this review to her, neatly typed on a piece of company stationery, Sue McFarland burst into tears. Shocked and crestfallen, Grove did not know what to do. He walked stiffly across the room, took a Kleenex out of a box, and handed it to her. She dried her eyes, stood up, put on her coat, and walked out without a word. Terrified that his wonderful secretary would resign, Grove's first reaction was to call Ann Bowers to ask her advice on this delicate matter of human resources. Bowers's assistant explained that she was away from work, having a minor operation, but Grove would not be put off. A few minutes later, he had tracked her down by phone to her hospital bed. He asked Bowers what he should do.

"You should have thought of that before you wrote the review," she replied tartly.

The following morning, Sue McFarland returned to work to find a funny get-well card on her desk. Grove might have hoped that this sign of contrition would close the matter. But he underestimated her. By the end of the day, a memo in reply to the performance review was on Grove's desk, drafted without a hint of the emotional turmoil McFarland had displayed the previous day. In it, she explained that the growth of the company was making it harder and harder for her to keep up with her existing responsibilities, let alone take on new ones. The progress report for March 1971 was forty-two pages long, she pointed out; by October 1972, it weighed in at ninety-seven pages. All the new professional employees required her to write technical reports, she explained, all of which she had dealt with in a timely fashion. During the period, Intel had set up new assembly plants in three Far Eastern locations. Once again, this had increased her workload; once again, she reminded him, all her assignments had been completed in a timely fashion. She ended the memo by putting in a request for an assistant to be hired who could take much of the typing burden off her shoulders.

Grove granted the request.

"One could not allow oneself to be intimidated by Andy," she remarked afterwards, "or one would be squished. He would tend to treat people as doormats if they behaved like doormats."

"Not only myself, but everyone else who reported to him, we were constantly forced to make a decision. Do we want to continue to do this? Are we going to subject ourselves to this criticism? Are we going to keep pushing ourselves to do more and more? For a variety of reasons, the answer was 'yes.'"

One of those reasons was straightforward. Sue McFarland didn't just like Andy Grove. She admired him hugely. Grove was a brilliant problem solver, a fanatical master of detail, and a man with an absolute determination to master the difficult technical projects Intel had embarked on. He drove everyone else hard, but he drove himself harder still. "I learned more from him than from anyone else I ever worked with before or since," she said.

8

The Microprocessor

The news of Intel's breakthrough in MOS memory technology with the 1101 and 1103 chip caused some jealousy inside competing electronics companies, but there was one place where it provoked outright despair. Inside Fairchild Semiconductor's research department, a young Italian engineer named Federico Faggin was on loan from a European joint-venture company in which Fairchild had a stake. He had spent his time at Fairchild Semiconductor working on silicon gate—the technology that proved to be the key to Intel's 1101 memory chip—and had watched, with growing frustration, Fairchild's failure to do anything with the knowledge that had been created inside the lab. Noyce and Moore had hired dozens of people from Fairchild, down to the lab technician in the department who had been working most closely on the silicon gate process; now their new company seemed destined to commercialize it independently. But Faggin himself couldn't follow the stars of the Fairchild research effort across to Intel. He had decided to stay in America, and his change of status from temporary exchange visitor to permanent resident meant that he couldn't change jobs while his application was being processed.

It was another year before Faggin was ready to make his move. He called Les Vadasz at Intel, and told him that he would be interested in joining the young company. He made only one stipulation; he wanted to work on chip designs, not production processes. Vadasz invited him over to Mountain View for a chat but refused to say anything in detail about the work that Faggin might do if he came to Intel. So Faggin was taking a leap in the dark when he accepted an offer from Vadasz and Grove, gave notice to Fairchild, and reported for work at Intel two weeks later to the day.

Boredom was evidently not going to be a problem in the new job. Vadasz explained on Faggin's first day that Intel had entered into a contract to design a set of chips for a Japanese firm called the Nippon Calculating Machine Corporation. Faggin was to be the project leader, and his first job would be to meet a client representative who was flying in from Tokyo the very next day to check on how the project was progressing.

An afternoon of reading the files and talking to his new colleagues gave Faggin the background he needed. The product Intel was working on was a desktop calculating machine sold under the brand name of Busicom, and the approach had come from Japan at a time when Intel was desperate for work of any kind. At first, the client's technical people had asked Intel to tender for a project to design and manufacture a set of eight logic chips customized specially for their calculator and preprogrammed to carry out the basic arithmetical functions it would need to offer. But with three different memory circuit projects already in progress, Intel simply did not have the resources to carry out eight new logic chip designs. It was Ted Hoff, the brilliant Stanford engineer who had come up with the idea for the DRAM cell, who proposed an alternative solution. Why not build a miniaturized general-purpose computer, he suggested, which could then be programmed to do the arithmetic for the client's desktop calculator?

The key difference between a general-purpose computer such as the PDP-8 and the customized logic circuits required by the Busicom specification was that the PDP had a subroutine capability: It could stop in the middle of a series of program steps, go off and carry out another job, and then return where it had left off. Hoff saw that if he could only add a subroutine capacity to the Busicom design, he could then take all the high-level functions that the calculator required and turn them into a set of subroutines. The basic computer could then be stripped down to the point where it could perform only the simplest tasks, and everything else—even something as apparently basic as adding a pair of integers together—could be reduced to combinations of these simple tasks.

This was an insight of dazzling brilliance. Discussing it afterwards, however, Hoff managed to make it seem almost obvious. "I'd been using a Digital PDP-8 computer to run full-scale FORTRAN programs," he recalled, "yet the PDP-8's central processing unit was a great deal simpler than the Busicom machine. It got all its complexity from memory. The subtle bits were in the program, not the hard-wired logic."

After a few days of thinking about it, Hoff sketched out a plan that involved a four-chip set: a central processing unit (CPU), a memory chip for working data, a read-only memory chip (ROM) where the program written specially for the Busicom functions could be stored, and a fourth device to deal with input and output, or I/O. Such a plan would be considerably less complex to design than a set of specialized logic chips—and it might well prove cheaper.

The Japanese company had been initially skeptical, particularly since its engineers had already done months of preliminary work on the logic design in the specification. But gradually, the Japanese managers came to accept the merits of the idea. Hoff's general-purpose design would allow the company to offer a range of more complex calculators in the future without having to build an entirely new set of logic chips. In a market that was becoming increasingly competitive, anything that allowed it to sell a better calculator at a lower price than its competitors was to be welcomed. And if Hoff was confident that he could deliver its four-chip set, with a tiny general-purpose computer running the arithmetical programs, then who were the engineers in Japan to doubt him? The company had handed over an advance of $100,000, and it was expecting to see some evidence that the chips for its new product were well on their way to production.

There was just one problem. After coming up with this brilliant idea, Hoff was told to concentrate his efforts on other projects. The project made some progress when another engineer named Stan Mazor, who had joined Intel from Fairchild, added a few instructions to the architecture and wrote some sample programs to prove the feasibility of the calculator design. But by April 1970, when Faggin arrived at Intel, the chip was still very far from complete. The set of instructions that the CPU would handle had been agreed on and confirmed by the Japanese engineers as correct. Hoff had drawn up an overall design for the chip, indicating broadly how many transistors it would require and which jobs would be carried out where. But when Faggin asked to see the detailed design, he got a shock. There wasn't one—but a Busicom engineer was about to arrive in California for a progress check.

Masatoshi Shima, the Busicom engineer, was all smiles when Faggin and another designer met him at the airport. His tune changed when he saw the materials that Faggin had been ordered to show him. Shima, a talented engineer in his own right, realized immediately that it was no advance on what he had seen on his last visit.

"You bad!" he shouted. "You promised! You said design done! No design! This is just idea! This is nothing! I came here to check, but there is nothing to check!"

Faggin had been briefed not to let on that he had just arrived, but he realized that hiding the truth would merely make his position more untenable. He confessed to Shima what had happened and agreed to start work immediately. Carrying out the first piece of processor work of his career, he was now faced with an almost impossible schedule.

Working with Mazor, a fellow circuit designer, Faggin managed to turn the concepts into working prototypes of four chips at extraordinary speed. So rigorous was he as a circuit designer that the manufacturing prototypes of the first three devices of the four—the ROM, the RAM, and the input-output chip—worked perfectly when they came off the line. The fourth, the processor itself, proved a little more problematic. The first prototype was absolutely dead, and it took Faggin some time to work out what had happened: The circuit was supposed to be built on the chip in a series of layers, and one of the layers had been accidentally missed out of the manufacturing process. The second prototype worked, and needed only minor adjustments. Three months after Faggin's arrival from Fairchild and Shima's arrival from Japan, defying the "one man, one chip, one year" rule, Faggin and Mazor had produced four working chips.

By then, however, the calculator market in Japan had become a great deal more competitive. Shima's bosses back in Tokyo decided that they could not build the Busicom machine profitably if they were to pay Intel the price for its chips that had originally been agreed. They came back to Intel, demanding a price cut.

Had Intel responded differently to this demand, it could never have become the company it is today. But Bob Noyce, fed with good advice from Hoff and Faggin, knew exactly what he wanted. He was willing to refund $60,000 to the client—but in return, he demanded a change in the license terms. Instead of giving the client exclusive rights over the chip design, he said, Intel wanted the right to sell the design to other customers. The response from Tokyo was a qualified yes. As long as Intel would agree not to sell it to competing calculator companies, the general-purpose processor that had been designed for the Busicom machine was Intel's to keep.

Faggin's extraordinary achievement in delivering the chips so swiftly had not been without cost. With his wife and new baby back in Italy, Faggin had worked twelve, fourteen, sometimes even sixteen hours a day for weeks on end. Yet Andy Grove was in the process of a campaign to turn Intel into a more serious, more professional outfit—and Les Vadasz, following Grove's lead, relentlessly complained to Faggin when he arrived late for work. The complaints irritated Faggin mightily. Everyone in the lab, he said, knew that some nights he would still be at his workbench until dawn, going home only to snatch a few hours' rest before returning to the plant. But Vadasz would not be moved. The result was that relations between Faggin and Vadasz began to deteriorate—and the talented young circuit designer began to find his work in the Intel research department increasingly miserable.

But there were compensations. Although he still missed his home town of Vicenza, Faggin was confident that he no longer wanted to return to Italy. He was becoming accustomed to the brilliant blue skies of northern California and the beauty of the fruit orchards to the south that were still beyond the reach of the electronics industry. He was coming to terms with the strange food and drinks consumed by the Americans—Jell-O, cold milk, and weak coffee by the pint—and with their strange midwestern objection to the civilized custom of drinking a glass of wine with one's lunch. He was also beginning to appreciate the contrast between the orderliness of the engineers he was working with and the relaxed, timeless chaos still prevalent in Italy. And he devised a simple rule of thumb for life in America as a European. The ratio of everything was the same as the ratio of an inch to a centimeter. Cars, houses, refrigerators, shopping carts—everything in the States was two and one-half times the size of its equivalent in Europe. On balance, Faggin decided, he might as well stay in California. The future looked interesting.

"A New Era In Integrated Electronics." This was the headline that Intel used to announce the launch of its 4004 microprocessor in an ad in *Electronic News* in November 1971. Gordon Moore went further. He described the microprocessor as "one of the most revolutionary products in the history of mankind."

That wasn't how it looked at the time.

People in the computer business viewed the 4004 as a fascinating novelty. They knew that it matched the power of the ENIAC, the world's first vacuum-tube computer project, which was completed in 1946 at the University of Pennsylvania under contract to the U.S. government. Built to calculate ballistics and detonation tables for American weaponry, ENIAC occupied an entire room, used eighteen thousand vacuum tubes, and consumed 20 kilowatts of power— enough to heat several family houses. The 4004, by contrast, was small enough to rattle around in a matchbox, and cost under $100.

But a 1946 computer wasn't a practical comparison. In the quarter century that had passed since then, the ENIAC had long been superseded by more modern machines using integrated circuits. By 1971, the 4004 offered an extraordinary combination of price and performance, but in absolute terms it wasn't a serious contender for work inside "real" computers. With the ability to process only four bits of information at a time, it was many times slower and many times punier than the 1971 state-of-the-art in mainframe central processing units. One executive from the computer industry, entirely missing the point of the revolution that was about to take place, joked to Bob Noyce that he wouldn't want to lose his whole computer through a crack in the floor. Even Stan Mazor, one of the members of the microprocessor design team, was famous for telling his friends that they should never trust a computer they could lift. Only if you could foresee that the 4004 would be followed by improved versions that would double its performance every eighteen months for the next quarter-century was it clear that microprocessors would eventually displace the great monoliths of the mainframe era, and bring computing power to every office desktop.

Intel's marketing people looked at the new chip and made pessimistic noises. Even if the part's performance would increase as quickly as the performance of Intel's memory devices had done—and that was a big if—there was a worry about how big the market for microprocessors would be. After all, only twenty thousand mainframe computers had been sold in the entire world in 1971. Assume optimistically that Intel could gain a 10 percent market share, and you were left with sales of only two thousand units a year. This was about a week's production— and nowhere near enough to justify a serious R&D budget.

So if it wasn't going to put the mainframe computer out of business, what was this new gadget for? Its creators inside Intel's research lab were full of ideas. If the chip could go into a calculator like the Busicom machine, said the 4004's creators, then it could also add intelligence to a whole range of electrical business machines—cash registers, coin-change machines, traffic lights, weighing machines, blood analyzers, cocktail dispensers, microwave ovens, cars, whatever. Until now, building intelligence into such machines had been prohibitively expensive because it required designing a special dedicated piece of computer hardware for each application. The 4004 would change all that. Since it was a miniature general-purpose computer, it could be used by industrial designers to do any number of different jobs. The customization would be in the software—in the program that controlled the chip.

The target customers for this use of the 4004 were engineers in America's biggest industrial companies. But most of these engineers knew nothing about computer programming. Instead, it was smaller, hungrier companies without a strong, entrenched market position that saw the potential of the tiny chip first. This gave rise to a problem in Intel's sales department. The customer list for the company's memory products made up a *Who's Who* of the computer industry: big, reliable, blue-chip firms that could be counted on not only to pay this month's outstanding bill, but also to send in orders month after month to the far blue yonder. The early adopters of the 4004 were much more obscure. Someone inside Intel's marketing department described the 4004 customer list as "not so much *Who's Who* as *Who's That?*"

In August 1972, Intel released a second microprocessor. Like the 4004, it had started out as a custom design project—this time for a company called Computer Terminals Corporation, which wanted to build a new display terminal. In accordance with the specification that CTC had given to Intel, the new processor handled data in chunks of eight bits at a time rather than four. It was known as the 1201 during its development. When the time came for launch, however, Ed Gelbach discovered that most Intel customers were utterly mystified by the company's obscure system of numbering parts by function, capacity, and start date. They thought the 4004 had earned its name because it was the company's first 4-bit microprocessor. It seemed only natural to call Intel's first 8-bit machine the 8008.

The release of the 8008 helped awaken glimmers of interest in the idea of using Intel microprocessors inside business computers as well as to add intelligence to industrial products. But the 8008 was little easier to program than the 4004. Until a set of compilers were developed, you had to write assembly-language instructions for the chip, telling it step by step to input this chunk of data, store it in that register, add it to the contents of the other register, output the result, and so on. Once you had your program ready in assembler, you then had to turn it into machine code—a set of two-digit hexadecimal numbers that could be fed to the processor one by one from the memory chip where the program was to be stored.

If it sounds complex and unfriendly, that's because it was. Only two categories of people were likely to go to the trouble: engineers who could see a real commercial advantage from incorporating the chip into a product, and teenage hackers who thought the idea of messing about with their own computers was cool.

Two of the earliest hackers in this category were a pair of kids, aged seventeen and nineteen, from a private high school in northern Seattle. Bill Gates and Paul Allen clubbed together to raise the $360 they needed to buy an 8008 chip from a local electronics store. But not even the founders of what would later be Microsoft could make the 8008 support the BASIC programming language. Instead, they made an abortive attempt to use the chip to build a machine for a local traffic consulting company that would analyze ticker-tape counts of cars on suburban streets.

What made engineers in American industry take the microprocessor seriously was Intel's first development system. Sold in a big blue box and known as the Intellec 4, the system was a tool that made it much easier and faster for outside engineers to develop and test programs for the new microprocessors.

Development systems proved a neat way of hooking customers into Intel's product line. When a customer spent $5,000 on an Intellec 4, the chances were that it would spend another $50,000 on microprocessors over the next year or so. Then for every microprocessor, another half-dozen or more other peripheral chips including memory, ROM, and input-output devices would be needed. This was the kind of business Ed Gelbach liked.

Even to those who didn't believe the new device was the biggest thing that had ever happened to the electronics industry, the microprocessor began to look as though it had some promise. Perhaps it would never be a big money-spinner on its own account—but hell, if it helped to sell more memory, then that was just fine too.

9

Public Company

Fifteen years after Intel's founding, Andy Grove published a book called *High-Output Management* in which he set out many of the lessons he had learned from his experiences with the company.

The book began with a chapter called "The Basics of Production: Delivering a Breakfast." Grove set his readers a simple problem that he'd come across while working as a bus boy shortly after his arrival in America. "Your task," he wrote, "is to serve a breakfast consisting of a three-minute soft-boiled egg, buttered toast, and coffee. Your job is to prepare and deliver the three items simultaneously, each of them fresh and hot." Within a few pages, Grove plunged into the complexities of production management, using the breakfast "factory" as an example. Continuous egg-boiling machines, toast-making delays, problems with rotten ingredients and rude staff—these and many other issues were dealt with as the proprietor of "Andy's Better Breakfasts" learned how to deliver an acceptable hot meal at an attractive price.

"Bear in mind," the Intel veteran wrote, "that in this and in other such situations there is a right answer, the one that can give you the best delivery time and product quality at the lowest possible cost. To find that right answer, you must develop a clear understanding of the trade-offs between the various factors—manpower, capacity and inventory—and you must reduce the understanding to a quantifiable set of relationships."

Not too many people in the restaurant trade could tell you with confidence the link between the number of waiters they employ, the number of pieces of bread their toasters can handle every minute, and the number of eggs in the cold store at the end of the day. But in the infinitely more complex business of chip manufacturing, where there are dozens of different steps to making a product, scores of people with different skill levels involved, and new production processes and machinery being introduced all the time, the job of "reducing the understanding to a quantifiable set of relationships" is almost nightmarishly difficult.

Grove's determination to succeed at this piece of analysis made Intel's first years of production extremely stressful. Theoretician that he was, Grove had no truck with the touchy-feely approaches to manufacturing that he believed were common elsewhere in the industry. Instead, he wanted to be able to express Intel's production lines as a set of equations like those he'd published in his book *Physics and Technology of Semiconductor Devices*. To do this, he needed facts: statistics in huge quantities, regularly delivered.

But this was 1971, not 1991. There was no company intranet, no spreadsheet software—not even any desktop computers. The statistics that Grove demanded had to be collected and tabulated largely by hand—by people who were having problems enough just getting through the day, producing any output at all from the rudimentary designs and processes in Intel's fabs. Most Intel engineers were lucky if they got home before midnight in time to see their families. No wonder there were stresses.

The 1101, Intel's first silicon gate MOS product, had been hard enough. "We embarked on this new technology . . . because of its perceived superior characteristics, although nobody was using this type of technology at the time," said Les Vadasz afterwards. "And the damn thing didn't work! Week after week, we just pushed wafers through the line with zero yield! We were seriously beginning to doubt the correctness of our technology direction. But perseverance did pay off."

The problems Intel had with the 1103 were of a different order of magnitude. Grove, who admitted to suffering from weeks of sleepless nights while trying to get the part into mass production, looked back on it as "almost as much fun as your final exams at college."

"I can remember twice a day going out on the line and physically counting 1103s as the introduction date drew closer," recalled another engineer. "We almost knew each good unit by name."

Others came almost to hate the endless measurements and tiny changes they had to make to both the design of the chip itself and the process used to build it, in an attempt to find a "sweet spot" that would deliver reasonable yields. So heartily did they come to hate the troublesome 1103 that they referred to the job of getting it into mass production as "turd polishing."

The hourly paid people who worked on the production lines, mostly young women, could be offered the incentive of cash— delivered in crisp dollar bills at the end of every week, because Grove believed in the animal trainer's principle of making the reward immediately and visibly linked to the good performance that had earned it. They could be told to watch Betty or Jane, who seemed to be producing a higher percentage of usable parts, and imitate exactly what she did. They could be forbidden to wear makeup in the fab area, and they could be forced to tie up their hair behind a cap, and wear gloves, booties, a "bunny suit," and safety glasses. They could be ordered to pick up wafers with a vacuum wand instead of with tweezers to make sure that no physical contact took place that could break off microscopic chunks of material that would contaminate the processes further down the line.

But professional engineers were less unthinking than hourly paid line workers in their acceptance of orders from above. They would do what they were told if they could see a good reason for it, but not otherwise. As John Reed's reaction to a hostile performance review had shown, criticism that was too harsh could easily be counterproductive. So in 1971, Grove was caught between a rock and a hard place. On the one hand, he was answerable to Noyce and Moore as operations manager for getting prototypes into production at reasonable quality, cost, and speed; on the other, there was a limit to how hard he could drive the engineers beneath him to meet his goals.

When the pressure built up, it would be in meetings between manufacturing and marketing that the safety valve would blow. Bob Graham, who had less time to go fishing now that he had products to sell, was banging the table regularly, complaining that his customers in the computer business weren't getting the parts they had been promised and demanding to know why Grove had not met this production forecast or that yield projection. More frustratingly still, he would also complain when Grove delivered parts that he had not asked for. Graham had adopted the sales slogan of "Intel Delivers" for use outside the company. He was damned if he was going to let Grove get away with failing to deliver to him.

On one occasion, Graham was put in a particularly embarrassing position. Intel's Japanese distributor had a number of customers waiting for matching sets of memory chips and the drivers needed to make them work. What Grove actually shipped to Japan were a number of incomplete sets. When an incomplete consignment arrived at Yokohama, the distributor sent Graham an angry telex: HAVE RE-CEIVED MUSKETS STOP AWAIT BULLETS AND POWDER STOP.

After a series of furious confrontations, in which Graham taxed Grove with sending parts that he couldn't sell and failing to send parts that he had promised to sell, a compromise was brokered by Moore. In the company's internal financials, Grove's organization would receive credit only for boxed stock that was delivered in accordance with the production forecast. Any parts Grove produced that Graham had not been forewarned about would come "free."

What made the disputes particularly bitter was that Graham and Grove were of exactly equal status. They were founder-employees, though not founder-stockholders. Both of them had been given stock options along with every other Intel hire, but Noyce and Moore never even offered to sell them a chunk of shares at the outset. The pair also received promotion at the same time: When they were at a conference together in Tokyo, a congratulatory telex arrived from Noyce informing them that their job titles had been raised to vice-president.

From where Graham sat, it was clear that Grove knew how to take orders from Bob Noyce and how to ask advice from Gordon Moore; and he knew how to keep the people who reported to him in line. But Grove seemed unable to work cooperatively with a manager who was one of his peers. Graham resented what he saw as Grove's constant attempts to expand his own empire by ordering Graham's sales and marketing people around—and sometimes by trying to force Graham himself to take his advice.

"I'm not that kind of a person," Graham recalled afterwards. "You can't tell me what to do. You can tell me what you'd like me to do. You can tell me what *you're* going to do. But you can't tell me what to do unless I agree to it. . . . [Yet] Andy's tendency was to tell you what the ads ought to be like and what ought to be in them, when they ought to run, how much they ought to cost, and who the reps ought to be. He was delving into areas where he had no expertise."

To make matters worse, Grove had a strong tongue. For Noyce and Moore, both brought up in God-fearing households where cursing was very much frowned upon, it was little more than a tease when Grove would get up from the meeting table and announce his intention to "go for a piss." But Graham's resentment burned red-hot when Grove would tell him day after day that he was a "stupid son-ofabitch" or a "bastard" or a "dumb shit."

Grove also knew how to make the best of a disability. In his early years at Intel, as we've seen, the hearing problem he suffered from required him to wear an ungainly hearing aid that wrapped around his ears and over his crown like a pair of headphones. Just at the point where he was being told something he did not want to hear, the device would seem to fail—and Grove would interrupt loudly, bellowing "Huh? Huh?" He was also able to use the device as a weapon of battle. When a speaker at a meeting was running over his allotted time or straying from the point, Grove would take the hearing aid off his head, and with an eloquent gesture that said more than any complaint or expression of boredom, thump it down on the table to indicate that he would listen no further.

The last straw for Graham was a dispute over something apparently trivial: the data sheets on its products that Intel sent to engineers, providing technical specifications and performance information. When the 1103 chip was ready to ship, Graham discovered that the bipolar driver circuits that went with the 1103 wouldn't work with the chip over the full temperature range that the memory chip itself could tolerate. He immediately took up the problem with Grove.

"I could not get Andy to understand that the operating range over which the memory would work, the drivers needed to work too."

Soon it became clear that modifying the drivers to make them more tolerant of extremes of temperature would be technically unmanageable: it would raise the cost and make the devices clunkier. Graham then decided to aim for the next best thing. He told Grove that if the drivers and the memory chip would not work together across the memory chip's full temperature range, then the data sheets would simply have to be frank about the narrower temperature range in which they worked.

Grove disagreed. Few customers would care about the issue, he said, since their computers were already adequately air-conditioned and they would be unlikely to test the performance of the Intel parts below freezing or close to boiling point. Even if they did, the problems with temperature range would never be visible to the outside world. Tested on their own, the drivers worked across the full range; it was only when running together with the 1103 that their range narrowed.

Graham insisted that the honest thing to do was to make the problem clear on the data sheets. He wanted to eliminate even the tiniest risk that Intel might have to compensate a customer who discovered that its engineers had been misinformed. But Grove would not be moved.

Day by day, the dispute escalated, until finally it reached the point where the two men were no longer on speaking terms. Noyce was called in to adjudicate. Late one morning, he ordered Graham to publish the data sheets as Grove had specified.

"Bob, we can't do this," Graham replied.

"Do it anyway," snarled the Intel founder.

Thirty minutes later, Graham was sitting at a restaurant table facing his wife, Nan. He had gotten into the habit of calling her and inviting her out to lunch when the internal battles got too much for him, so she knew that this morning there must have been a bad one.

Graham looked into his drink.

"Nan," he said. "I'm not working at Intel anymore."

His wife's eyes filled with tears as she recalled the pressure they had been under over recent months, and realized that it would now all be behind them.

"Thank God!" she said.

On his way from the confrontation with Noyce to his lunch date with his wife, Graham had cleared his desk. He wasn't fired; he had simply been presented with an ultimatum: either leave or publish the data sheet the way Grove wanted. At that moment, he'd recalled that it was precisely in order to get away from issues of politics and style that he had left Fairchild. If Intel, for all its fine words, was going to revert to the characteristics of his old employer that had so dismayed him, then he wanted no further part in the venture.

For Noyce and Moore, the decision was tough but straightforward. It had increasingly become clear that Intel was too small a company for both Graham and Grove. They would therefore have to choose which one to lose. Whatever the rights and wrongs of the specific dispute that had precipitated the decision, Grove was clearly more vital to Intel's success than Graham. The marketing vice-president was talented, experienced, focused, well connected, and energetic. But the operations vice-president was more than that. He was a figure of towering intellect, an obsessive chaser of details, a fearless fighter who would allow no personal friendships or loyalties to get in the way of what he believed to be best for the company. He also possessed will power, self-discipline, and determination in quantities that were given only to one person in a million.

If Noyce and Moore wanted their young company to fulfill all their ambitions, they could not rely on their own combination of inspiration and scientific insight. It was inevitable that tough decisions were ahead. Research projects would have to be axed. Talented engineers would have to be fired. Requests for pay rises would have to be refused. Troops would have to be marshaled to drive imitators and competitors from the market. Noyce and Moore could not do these things on their own; in many cases, they shrank from the force that was needed. They needed a really tough manager. And neither of them had ever come across anyone tougher than Andy Grove.

There was just one aspect of the Graham affair that was surprising. Bob Graham and Gordon Moore had been great friends. Not only had they fished together; Graham and his wife would often go over to have dinner with Gordon and Betty, and Graham considered Moore his mentor inside the company. But after Graham's encounter with Noyce, Gordon Moore was nowhere to be found. Graham was of course too proud to ask him to intervene. Staying out of the dispute altogether, Moore had nothing to do with negotiating the departing vice-president's severance terms. From the moment of Graham's fateful conversation with Bob Noyce, he neither saw Gordon Moore nor spoke to him for the next five years.

The departure of Bob Graham marked a turning point in the structure of Intel's leadership. Although Bob Noyce and Gordon Moore were still CEO and executive vice-president, while Grove was merely one of three other vice-presidents, it was clear that the power of daily decision making was passing—less than three years after the company's start—into Grove's hands. It would be another fifteen years before Grove received the title of chief executive, but from 1971 onwards, he was to be the dominant influence over the company and its culture.

Shortly after Graham left Intel, the company began preparations for an initial public offering. There were just enough weeks left before the IPO for the company to hire in a talented new marketing vice-president whose name could appear in place of Graham's on the prospectus.

A headhunter hired to carry out a search came up with a number of names, of whom the most promising was Ed Gelbach, an intolerant but charismatic figure who ran the national sales operation for Texas Instruments and was suffering homesickness for the beaches of California. Asked by the search agent whether he would consider a move from TI to another firm, Gelbach replied that he had no interest in joining any other company—unless it was Intel.

Gelbach seemed a perfect match, but Noyce and Moore were determined to avoid a repeat of the Graham episode. Before hiring him, they handed the candidate over to Grove, making it clear that since Grove would have to get along with the new vice-president of sales and marketing, he might as well have a veto over his appointment. The outcome of the meeting was that Grove agreed for a job offer to be made, and Gelbach accepted.

By midsummer 1971, Ed Gelbach was back in California with his feet under the desk. Every bit the expert negotiator, Gelbach exacted a price from Intel that was fully commensurate with his talents— including options to buy twenty thousand shares, almost 1 percent of the company, at $5 apiece. Since it was clear that Grove did not believe that sales or marketing really mattered, he also took care that he would have the powers and the budgets to carry out his responsibilities.

When the IPO took place in October 1971, there were a few surprises in the prospectus. Gelbach's name appeared in the management section above Grove's. Many of the backers who had put up the money that funded Intel's creation were revealed as members of the Traitorous Eight, the crew that had left Shockley's operation en masse to set up Fairchild in 1957. The company's two biggest shareholders were still Noyce and Moore, with a combined holding of over 37 percent, worth nearly $20 million at the offering price of $23.50. Although the prospectus showed that both men were paying themselves less than $30,000 a year, neither of the two founders was proposing to sell a single share from their holdings. Both men clearly believed that Intel still had far to go.

10

Second Source

It was a symptom of the technological know-how Bob Noyce and Gordon Moore had assembled at Intel that the company was able to break one of the cardinal rules of the electronics industry. That rule was: You shouldn't try to develop a new circuit design and a new manufacturing process at the same time.

Jerry Sanders and his colleagues at AMD, based ten minutes' drive away from Intel in the town of Sunnyvale, had no such luxury. While Grove and Moore could claim formidable knowledge of both the physics and chemistry of silicon wafers, the team Sanders had assembled had no more insight into these matters than the average group of engineers and salesmen in the electronics industry. For AMD, the technological risks of trying to innovate on all fronts at once would have been too great.

There was also a financial issue. When you brought out an entirely new product, the customers you were trying to sell it to were all manufacturers of one kind or another—usually computer companies. They wouldn't design it into one of *their* products until they had seen a working sample—but even if they liked it, you would then have to wait until the computer they'd designed it into was finished and ready for manufacturing. Only then, two years or more after your engineers had started designing, would the customer want to buy the part in significant commercial quantities. This meant it took almost two development cycles instead of one before money invested in a new part started paying back.

Intel had raised a million dollars more than AMD and had started up nine months earlier. The industry was consolidating, price pressures were increasing, and experts were beginning to say that it was now too late to start a broad-based semiconductor manufacturing company. So the financial climate was simply too risky for Sanders to consider developing radical new products at the outset.

In the business plan for AMD, he had dealt with the problem diplomatically. The company's long-term ambition, the plan explained, was of course to develop a range of absolutely new products all its own. Such an ambition was as uncontroversial as motherhood; proprietary products brought in higher margins and were a sign of intellectual machismo. But in the short term, AMD's route into the business would be to operate as a "second source."

Second sourcing was effectively the invention of one man: Robert S. McNamara, President Kennedy's secretary of defense. When he arrived at the Defense Department from the Ford Motor Company, McNamara realized that one of the biggest sources of wasted public money in defense contracting was the fact that many parts came from only one supplier—which made it impossible for Uncle Sam to tell whether he was getting good value for money or not. McNamara decided to try to make it a rule that every part should come from at least two sources. Not only did this provide a useful reality check against fraudulent pricing; it also injected an element of competition into the market. When two companies were fighting for the government's business, they had an incentive to look for ways to make their manufacturing more efficient and thus their prices lower.

As the 1960s wore on, McNamara's ideas were taken up enthusiastically in the computer industry. The mainframe companies that were trying to compete against IBM realized that every single-sourced component they bought was a hostage to fortune. If its supply dried up—whether because of an earthquake under the factory, a fluffed introduction by its maker of a new process, or simply a supplier accepting a higher offer for the parts from another customer—then a computer worth tens or even hundreds of thousands of dollars could be left sitting in a warehouse, useless because of the absence of a single small component worth only a couple of bucks. To avoid this nightmare computer companies preferred to buy parts where there were at least two makers in business. For an electronics company with its own technology, a second source was a necessary evil: It took the cream off margins, but it was the only way to get customers to buy the part.

There were two ways to become a second source. The formal way was to sign a licensing agreement with the company that invented the product, paying an up-front fee and a royalty. In return, you got a set of the masks containing the master layouts of the circuits. Sometimes, if you were lucky, some engineering visits to help you get the line working properly so that the process would deliver reasonable yields.

The informal way to do it was to buy a few sample parts from a distributor as soon as the part came out, rush them back to the lab, pop the top, and take blowups of the circuits inside. You then assigned a team of people to perform traces on the part, carrying out a kind of electrical audit to try to deduce from the signals going in and out what was happening inside. This was slower and more difficult than official second sourcing, but cheaper. And although it was frowned on, the law of trademarks and patents, secrets, and copyrights was murky enough to make it possible without actually breaking the law.

Second sourcing, then, was the strategy that Sanders proposed to use to bootstrap himself into the semiconductor business. For this purpose, the key technical member of his team was Sven Simonsen, the Danish-born semiconductor specialist who had been one of AMD's eight founders. Simonsen had worked as a circuit designer at Fairchild, where he had conceived ten different logic devices, all in medium-scale integration, and had then as head of department presided over the development of fifteen more. By 1970, the devices were no longer state-of-the-art; they contained far fewer components than the four-thousand-transistor monsters that Intel was working on. But they were good, solid sellers, and Simonsen knew the product range so well that he did not need to take so much as a scrap of paper from Fairchild with him when he left to join AMD.

The great advantage of trying to redesign a chip that you had already designed once before was that it gave you a chance to correct all the mistakes you had made the first time round, without having the manufacturing guys on your back screaming about the production that would be lost every time you stopped the line to make a change. But it was risky to improve things too much. The object of the exercise was to produce a part that was "pin compatible" with the market leader—meaning that it could be slotted into the circuit board using the same number and placing of metal connectors, or "pins," as the other company's part. If the redesigned circuit used only half as much power and ran three times as fast, the computer company that was buying it would have to make design changes before it could start using your part. Far better just to aim for a 15 percent speed improvement and make it easier for the customer to switch.

There was just one problem. If the competition found out that its part was being second-sourced without authorization, it could always fall back on an old-fashioned strongarm tactic to squeeze out the interloper. "OK," it could say to its biggest customer. "You've received a bid from the guys down the street on three of our parts that undercuts us by 20 percent. But you're still buying six other parts from us where there's no second source. You're gonna have to choose: Do you want those six parts or not? Because there's no way we'll sell them to you if you're buying the other three from the competition." Alternatively, it could simply refuse to sell the different parts individually.

This form of defense was called "packaging out," and it raised the stakes dramatically for a company that was thinking of becoming a second source. Copying just a handful of products from the range wasn't enough. To get into the chip business seriously, you might need to clone ten different parts or more in order to protect your customers against the risk of retaliation.

It was a measure of the energy of the AMD engineers that even with the upheaval of changing jobs, moving into the company's site in Sunnyvale, and scratching their heads to think back over a number of past projects, they still managed to bring no fewer than sixteen finished circuits to market within nine months of starting work.

At first, AMD's parts were hard to sell. Purchasing managers loved to cut their costs, but they knew that switching a contract to an untried new company that failed to deliver might cost them their jobs. So it would take more than just a few nickels off the price before they would commit. It would also take credibility and good old-fashioned salesmanship. After several years of sitting in Fairchild's LA office telling a fleet of salesmen what to do, Ed Turney suddenly found himself pounding the pavements for AMD, visiting clients. Because credibility was crucial, he would often take Simonsen or another engineer with him. In particularly difficult cases, even the master salesman himself—Jerry Sanders—would occasionally be drafted in to help.

Just when pessimism was beginning to set in, the fledgling company received an unexpected bonus. The new management at Fairchild Semiconductor sent a memo around to its salesmen, attacking AMD and demolishing its product line point by point. When a friendly client sent a copy around to Turney, he immediately realized its value: The memo *proved* that Fairchild took the threat from AMD seriously. Since credibility was the company's greatest problem, this was a positive rather than a negative thing. Turney promptly ran off a few hundred copies of the memo and circulated them to all the purchasing managers who were still hemming and hawing about whether they were going to buy from AMD.

Once the customers began to look at AMD's product line more closely, they saw another attraction. Traditionally, the electronics market had been split into two: There were the standard components for the computer industry, which would work in a temperature range between zero and 75 degrees Celsius; and there were the parts sold to the military, which were guaranteed to work anywhere in a much wider range from −55 to +125. The two sets of components often ran off exactly the same production line; the only difference was that the parts that still worked during the extreme temperature tests would get sold to the military for three or four times the normal price so they could be frozen or boiled up in the sky or under the sea.

Sanders saw an opportunity in this. Because AMD was making design changes to the parts it was second-sourcing, and was fabricating them on a new production line with clean equipment, the yields were often higher than in the Fairchild plant where the original part was still being made. As a result, AMD found that an unexpectedly high proportion of its parts met the more rigorous military specification. Most civilian customers had no practical need for "Mil Spec" parts, since they weren't building fighter planes or missiles. But the military standard of quality sounded good, and helped the parts to sell.

Shortly after AMD's first advertisements appeared in the trade press, Simonsen took a call from an executive at Westinghouse Electric, the company he had worked for before joining Fairchild.

"Sven, you've been advertising a four-bit adder," said the voice. "Do you really make the part, or is it just a marketing ploy?"

The question was a reasonable one; plenty of companies in the industry saw nothing wrong with advertising parts that weren't yet in production. But Simonsen protested that AMD was innocent. Not only was the company making the part, a small logic chip that could add together whole numbers between 0 and 15, but AMD could even provide a thousand units the next day if his former colleague wanted them, he boasted.

"Not quite," he was told. The Westinghouse man explained that he was in charge of a project to develop a radar for the U.S. Air Force. The Air Force's standard practice was to "fly before buy"; it would happily issue development contracts, but to get a real production order, a company would have to demonstrate an aircraft that actually flew—or in this case a radar device that worked. Westinghouse's problem was that it was ninety days away from a crucial test of its new radar system, and it had just been told by Texas Instruments, the most powerful company in the chip industry, that a 4-bit adder crucial to the entire system was running late. There was no second source. To stay in with a chance of winning the contract, Westinghouse had decided to redesign the radar system around the equivalent Fairchild part. Having been bitten once already, it wanted a second source in case Fairchild in turn failed to deliver.

Simonsen realized that AMD had just been offered a great opportunity.

"Don't do that," he replied. "You don't need to redesign your system. Give us the specifications [for the TI part], and we'll build you an adder that works with your existing system design. The component price will be high, but it will cost you less than the redesign."

The Westinghouse manager was skeptical. Surely, he said, it would take too long for AMD to develop a second-source TI part from scratch. After all, there were only three months to go before the radar system test.

"We'll do it in six weeks," said Simonsen.

Six weeks later, to the day, Simonsen delivered the first production sample to Westinghouse. It was a smart move. AMD was not only guaranteed far higher margins than it would have received as a second source to an existing Fairchild part. More importantly, the Westinghouse guy was now convinced that everyone at AMD walked on water. The goodwill the company had earned would be worth many hundreds of thousands of dollars in future contracts.

The ideal kind of second source, people used to say in their cups at the Wagon Wheel, was a company that was just good enough to make customers *believe* it could build the part, but not quite good enough actually to build it. That was the kind of second source that Intel was lucky enough to find.

The product that proved the point was the 1103, the world's first 1K DRAM. Intel had advertised it in the trade rags under the screaming headline: CORES LOSE PRICE WAR TO NEW CHIP. The ads went on to invite potential customers to call Intel collect in Mountain View, tell its sales department what they were currently paying per bit for core memory, and hear from Intel how they could switch to smaller, faster semiconductor technology without spending a penny more.

So powerfully did this pitch grab the industry that Intel was soon inundated with calls from computer companies, none of whom wanted to be caught out by being last to switch to semiconductor memory. Five minutes into the conversation, however, would always come the dread question: Who was Intel's second source?

Andy Grove was temperamentally opposed to the principle of second sourcing. As anyone who had seen the charts on his wall could tell, he saw it as one of the greatest failures of the electronics industry that its members never seemed to be able to deliver on their commitments. The solution to the problem, he believed, was not to sacrifice revenues by allowing a know-nothing competitor to rip off your designs. Instead, he maintained, Intel should get its manufacturing working reliably enough that customers did not need to ask for a second source.

There was also a concrete issue at stake. The industry's graveyard was littered with the bones of companies that had come up with a couple of good ideas but then failed to mass-produce them at the right time and the right price. The great risk of signing a second-source deal was that if the chosen partner was one of the industry's leading names, Intel might hand over to a well-funded and well-organized competitor the very secrets that could be used to drive it out of business.

But Grove was before his time. Early in 1970, Intel had received a request for second-source rights from a Canadian telecommunications company called Microsystems International Limited. After extensive discussions, Intel's board of directors overrode Grove's objections and authorized Noyce and Moore to go ahead and negotiate a deal.

The MIL deal was fortuitously timed. It began to produce a stream of fees and royalties—starting with an up-front check for nearly $1 million—that kept the company afloat while Intel was suffering from the recession at the end of 1970. But the pain came in the winter, when Intel was forced to send teams of engineers out to Ottawa, braving the worst snow and ice that a Canadian winter could throw at them, to hand over to MIL the mask sets for the 1103 and to help get its fab lines running properly. The job proved unexpectedly difficult, but Intel was contractually obliged to do it, and the Canadian company had astutely inserted a provision in the agreement that meant that Intel would receive bonuses if it helped MIL to achieve certain yield levels by a specified date. The painful process of managing this, and the wasted time of repeated engineering visits, left Grove with a bad taste in the mouth. It was "not as emotionally satisfying as getting a product to manufacturing," he recalled, "but the degree of work was really quite the same." But he worked loyally to implement the decision that he had opposed, and did his best to make it a success.

Three months later, as MIL began to offer its own version of the 1103 in competition with Intel, it looked as though Grove had been right. Every time the subject came up for discussion, his face gave away his thoughts. *You should have listened to me. Was it really worth the front money? Look, we're losing money left and right here.*

But then MIL got too clever. In an attempt to get more chips out of each wafer on the fab line, the company made a change to its production system without consulting Intel: It tried to shrink the chip, and to increase the wafer diameter from two inches to three. The change was a disaster: yields dropped immediately to zero. To make matters worse, the Canadian company built up many months of useless inventory before the problem was properly detected, let alone solved. The result was a stream of former MIL customers, suddenly strapped for memory circuits, coming back to Intel begging for orders of ten thousand units for delivery as soon as possible. Intel profited handsomely, and MIL's failure helped to reinforce the company's reputation as an organization that could deliver on its commitments. By the end of 1971, Intel was able to boast that 14 out of the world's 18 leading mainframe computer manufacturers were customers for the 1103 memory chip. Even Andy Grove was forced to admit that this first experience of second sourcing had proven a success.

AMD's public relations were handled by Elliot Sopkin, a journalist who had come to California from Atlanta to work on a local paper in Oxnard, a beach town just north of LA. Sopkin had lived next door to Ed Turney, and had been impressed by the salesman's raffish lifestyle. Every morning, as Sopkin went out to work, he would see Turney stroll out onto the sand in a swimsuit, carrying a telephone with an enormously long extension cable. He would then sit down in a deck chair, telephone machine at one elbow and adding machine at the other, and start making loud sales calls to clients. When Sopkin returned from work at midnight, Turney would be back on the beach, full of drunken talk about the topless bar he had just visited in Santa Monica and the $100,000 sale he had just made to the purchasing manager he took there. It certainly seemed more fun than journalism. When Sanders appeared in Oxnard and offered Sopkin a position at AMD, he accepted without hesitation.

Six months into the job, Sopkin presented Sanders with a cartoon from the *New Yorker* depicting King Arthur sitting on a throne at a large table surrounded by knights. "The round table symbolizes our equality," said the caption. "The high-backed chair and the funny crown symbolize that some of us are more equal than others."

The cartoon captured Sanders's style perfectly; his colleagues soon began to refer to him as "the king." While Intel was nonhierarchical and resolutely insistent on the primacy of "knowledge power" above "position power," Sanders kept aloof. Even before the financing was in place, he made it clear to his seven colleagues that he would prefer to deal with investors himself—and followed this up by excluding the other founders from the company's board of directors. Once the company was formed, he awarded himself the titles of president, chairman, and chief executive officer. Nobody complained: They all had plenty to do themselves, and Sanders evidently had the capacity to lead.

He certainly looked the part. Sanders drove a Mercedes-Benz, and wore dazzling clothes that were evidently made to measure. Some of his colleagues thought he was the height of style; "always six months ahead of *GQ*," said one. Others thought Sanders's clothes simply revealed that he was a poor boy who had made good. But everyone agreed on one thing: Sanders's mane of hair, which would earn him the nickname of "the Silver Fox" when it turned prematurely gray, was always impeccably coiffed.

Sanders was not one to shirk work. When an important Friday afternoon meeting dragged on to 9:00 P.M., his fellow founders would groan, "Come on, Jerry, let's go and have a drink down at the Wheel."

"Okay," the king would snap, "I'll pick up again at eight tomorrow morning."

"Jesus, Jerry. Tomorrow's Saturday!"

"Sorry. Make it nine."

The king was not always an easy person to work with. Tom Skornia, AMD's general counsel, often heard his colleagues refer to the AMD chairman as "Monster Man." AMD's management meetings were also less participatory affairs than Intel's. While Bob Noyce and Gordon Moore would sit back at executive staff meetings, letting others fight out the big issues, Sanders's style was to treat his staff meetings as if he were briefing a squadron in the Air Force. AMD's key people would be summoned every Tuesday morning at nine to hear a succession of predictions, announcements, questions, instructions. Sanders used the meetings to keep track of how different departments were progressing with different projects. But he gave his colleagues little opportunity to raise issues of their own at the meetings. These he preferred to deal with, one on one, in his own office.

But it was in the board meetings that Sanders's instinctive political skill was most evident. Skornia, who served as company secretary as well as general counsel, began to notice how well the AMD chairman handled his fellow directors. To make sure that his proposals would be smoothly and speedily adopted in the board meetings, he would prime key board members in advance of a difficult decision. Only once in the first year, when he made an ill-judged proposal for AMD to take over a smaller electronics firm, was Sanders forced by his fellow directors to retreat.

In 1971, however, Sanders began to shake out his organization. One day, he summoned Sopkin into his office and began asking him questions.

"Elliot, do we have security guards on duty during the day?"

"Sure, Jerry. You know I look after that."

"You know what, it wouldn't hurt if we had a guard on duty right up here this morning."

"Where would he be?"

"I think he'll be walking between your office and mine, a bit closer to yours."

"When?"

"About ten."

At 10:00 A.M. precisely, Sanders called Frank Botte, one of his seven fellow founders, into his office, and closed the door behind him. He told Botte that he was performing below par and fired him on the spot.

Five minutes later, a strangled sound emerged from the office. Blazing with anger, Botte had grabbed Sanders by the throat and was squeezing as hard as he could. It required all the strength of the security guard whose presence Sanders had carefully prearranged to separate the two men.

Later in 1971, a similar fate befell Jack Gifford, the leader of the original group of four who had come to Sanders with the idea of building analog circuits. This time, the sin that the victim was allegedly guilty of was treason, pure and simple. Sanders believed, rightly or wrongly, that Gifford had tried to organize a palace coup against him and to take the chairmanship of AMD into his own hands. With a few well-placed phone calls, Sanders made sure that AMD's directors realized how important it was to remove this potentially divisive influence—and with the board's approval, it was not long before Gifford, too, left the company.

Thanks to the success of the engineers' second-sourcing efforts and Sanders's indefatigable sales campaign, AMD was able to go public less than a year after Intel. Its prospectus, issued at the end of September 1972, showed the company as making money—just. But there were a few surprises. Because Sanders had fired him without claiming cause, but then tried to force him to sell his AMD stock back to the company at ten cents a share, Botte had sued—and the case, worth over $1 million, was still pending.

More interesting was what had happened to the company's share capital. Unable to make its start-up funding last all the way to the IPO, AMD had gone back to its investors in a second round for another $650,000—ostensibly to follow Intel's lead and diversify from AMD's basic bipolar technology into a new line of MOS semiconductors. The prospectus for the IPO also revealed that the balance of power between the founders had also changed. Originally, seven of the eight founders had each received 76,500 shares, and Sanders 102,000 in recognition of his senior status. But in June 1972, the company had granted him options over an additional 48,000 shares.

Four of Sanders's five remaining founding partners were astounded when they got news of this. The original equity splits had been carefully negotiated; how had Sanders managed to arrange an extra slab of shares for himself? The fifth founder, John Carey, was probably less surprised: The prospectus showed that he had been promoted to vice-president in 1972 and had been given over twenty-four thousand shares in recognition of his enhanced value. Carey and Sanders soon found themselves facing furious demands by the other four to rescind the arrangement. But Sanders brazened it out. Without apologizing or explaining, he made it clear that the arrangement had been made, and that was that.

In the eyes of his partners, the issue of those stock options marked the beginning of what they believed would later prove to be a trend in Sanders's stewardship of AMD: a grabbing for himself of a share of the company's success that was considerably greater than what comparable managers elsewhere were being awarded.

At first sight, there seemed little need for this. At the time AMD went public, Sanders was already paying himself $34,000 a year in salary—considerably more than both Noyce and Grove at the larger, older, and more profitable Intel. But Sanders had always lived just a little beyond his means. Back in his Fairchild days, he had a house on a good street in Los Altos Hills, one of the smartest places in the Valley. Once at AMD, he moved farther north to the even more prestigious community of Atherton—and after the IPO, he would move to an imposing house on a seven-acre estate so large that it required a full-time gardener and a housekeeper to run it.

In January 1973, when the wage controls imposed by Richard Nixon's government were removed, Sanders set to work crafting a new contract covering his employment at AMD. The new terms included tight restrictions on the circumstances under which the board would be allowed to fire him, and salary and fringe benefits lavish enough to create a stir when they were published in a trade magazine the following year. Getting his new contract past the board was one of Sanders's toughest showdowns yet, but once again he succeeded by brazening through. The AMD chairman's favorite phrase was "A man's reach should exceed his grasp." Never had a life been lived so literally through that maxim.

11

Turning Failure to Profit

Intel's 1103 chip was the world's first commercially successful semi-conductor memory device. But engineers in the computer industry designed it into their products because its high performance and small size forced them to—not because they wanted to. The first version of the 1103 that Intel produced was—as Gordon Moore admitted a decade later—"the most difficult to use semiconductor ever created by man."

It wasn't simply that the device required a host of peripheral circuits to make it work. It also needed three different power supplies, and it had a capricious timing cycle that any system using it had to accommodate. Once the feeling of triumph and excitement at simply being able to manufacture the chip at all had subsided, Intel's top management realized that the company faced a crisis. Unless the flaws of the 1103 were quickly corrected, they might prevent the chip from making the transition from technological curiosity to commercial triumph.

Intel came up with two responses to the problem. One was to start, immediately, a program of looking again at the chip design to see how it could be simplified and improved. But it would take time to prepare the new masks, prove a new process, and move from samples to full-scale manufacturing, so the redesign could not be expected to bear fruit for nearly two years. Intel's second response to the problem was more short-term and small-scale. Ted Hoff and Stan Mazor, two of the company's engineers, took a few weeks off other projects to build some demonstration systems. They hoped the systems would help convince customers that designing the 1103 into a computer system was less difficult than it looked. But Intel's customers didn't behave as expected. Instead of nodding their heads wisely and putting in their orders for the 1103s, the engineers at computer companies who saw the demo systems began to ask to buy them in mass-production quantities, so they could leave to Intel the job of designing the entire subsystem that accommodated hundreds of individual chips.

While Intel was pondering whether to manufacture these integrated memory systems, a telegram arrived at Bob Noyce's house. It was from Bill Jordan and Bill Regitz, two senior staff at Honeywell, the computer company that had collaborated on the original MOS development project that led to the creation of the 1103. Jordan and Regitz had hit a rough patch at work; their boss had suddenly told them that his travel budget would not allow them to go to the International Solid State Circuits Conference in Philadelphia, which every semiconductor engineer worth his salt had to attend. So the two men had simply taken a week's vacation from work and bought themselves tickets to the conference from their own pockets. After the sessions, they had drowned their sorrows in a few beers and had come to the conclusion that they would both be better off working for Intel than Honeywell.

Their telegram to Noyce said nothing about Honeywell's internal politics; it asked simply whether he would be interested in seeing a business plan to set up a division at Intel to build "memory systems"—integrated units that companies could plug into their mainframe computers to increase their memory capacity. The answer, of course, was yes. Although they did not know it, their telegram landed on Bob Noyce's desk just when he had come to the conclusion that Intel needed to do more than offer only loose components. At his suggestion, Jordan and Regitz mailed over a business plan outlining in five handwritten pages how the new division might make money. Noyce and Moore then flew over to Boston to see the two men. Within a month, they had moved their families to the West Coast, ready to set Intel up in the memory systems business.

On their first day at work, Regitz and Jordan were told that Intel's plans had changed. The yield problems with the 1103 were so severe that the company could not afford to spare both men for the memory systems effort. One of them, Regitz, would be assigned to "turd polishing"—the project to redesign the 1103. Jordan would have to work on his own to set up the new Memory Systems Operation. (Almost from day one, the new division was referred to as "MSO." Intel was big on abbreviations.)

Poaching one engineer from a disgruntled Ted Hoff and more from Honeywell, Jordan soon put together the beginnings of a memory systems operation and of a product range—essentially large boxes full of circuit boards to which thousands or even tens of thousands of 1103s were mounted, together with the appropriate driver circuits. Selling 1103s in this way brought Intel two great advantages. One was simply the strength of numbers: With a single sales call, a single invoice, and a single goods shipment, Intel could bring in tens of thousands of dollars. This was a source of great excitement for a company that had never had a product that sold for more than a couple of hundred dollars. It meant that the work of Intel's sales operation could be better leveraged.

The other advantage was that Intel could now make use of parts that did not meet the specifications laid down in the company's data sheets. When it was selling only individual components, parts that ran a little too slowly or consumed too much power were useless. Yet these parts could account for a quarter, a half, or even more of the output of the fab line. Now that Intel could build these substandard parts into memory systems, the only thing that mattered was to make sure that the system as a whole performed adequately. Half the parts inside might not meet the specification of the components sold individually—but customers would not even know, let alone care. On the contrary; for the extra convenience of having all those substandard 1103s built into a complete memory system, they were ready to pay a premium.

An added attraction to the memory systems business was the marketing strategy of IBM, the granddaddy of the mainframe business. To make its computers look more price-competitive against those of the "seven dwarfs," IBM accepted modest margins on the basic computer, but then made its real money on the add-ins that customers came back for in a year or two when they needed to upgrade their systems. This was a high-tech example of making money from the blades instead of the razors. But it also opened up an opportunity for Intel. Since IBM built all its own memory devices and wouldn't even consider buying 1103s from Intel, why not design some memory systems especially for IBM machines and sell them straight to IBM's customers? The margins would be astounding, and the division would gain an entry into a previously closed market that accounted for nearly 70 percent of the world's memory sales.

Venturing on to IBM's turf required a little more expertise and care than the average new product introduction. Jordan not only had to make sure that quality was acceptable; he didn't want any of his division's customers to get fired, if something went wrong, for failing to buy IBM. Jordan also had to try to copy some of the excellent customer service that was part of the IBM package. For example, the division had to devise a leasing program that would allow companies to rent the memory systems for a fixed period of months and then send them back to Intel. These things were not difficult in themselves, but they, like Jordan himself, were all new to a relatively small company like Intel.

It was only when the memory systems operation was up and running smoothly that stresses began to emerge. The issue was how the new division's accounting should be done. Should the chips that it obtained from the components' business and then built into systems be charged at their full arm's-length price, just as if the memory operation had bought parts in the market? Or should they be valued at cost, since the parts that were now going into Jordan's memory systems had simply been thrown away before his arrival?

Both approaches had problems. Booking the incoming units at the full price hardly reflected their opportunity cost to Intel, since the company had never tried to find any takers in the market for components that failed to meet specifications. Equally, it seemed too generous simply to give the chips to the new division; this might give rise to such accounting distortions that the company would be tempted to pour money into the memory systems operation because the figures made it look more profitable than it really was.

Clearly the sensible answer was to choose some number between the two. But since each division manager was supposed to be responsible for the profit and loss of his own operations, the question was more than merely academic. Every extra penny that Bill Jordan was forced to pay for his chips would increase the profits of the components business and cut his own division's profits; every penny that he managed to negotiate away in price breaks would make the components business look worse but him look better. The outcome could make or break careers.

The question would remain unresolved for nearly seven years, and both Gordon Moore and Bob Noyce would resist pressure to arbitrate between the two sides. But as the years ran on, a couple of trends would become evident. First, memory systems might be a fine business, but even on a favorable set of numbers it could not claim the 55 percent gross margins that were imposed elsewhere in the company as the test of viability of a new project. Second, the growth rate of the division was not as great as the growth rate of Intel's other semiconductor-based businesses. Mainframes were a giant market in the early 1970s, but the arrival of low-cost memory and low-cost processing would change the face of the entire computer industry—and offer better opportunities for profit elsewhere.

Sometimes, understanding why a device fails is as important as finding a way to make it work. One of Intel's cleverest engineers was a tall, thin physicist named Dov Frohman who had devoted most of his working life, including a Ph.D. and a spell inside Fairchild's research lab, to the study of an obscure metal–nitride oxide semiconductor technology. When Intel decided to bet on silicon gate, Frohman was reassigned to troubleshoot the process. Looking at the broken devices, he began to wonder whether part of the reason the silicon gate devices had failed might be that some of the gates in the circuit had become disconnected, or "floating."

Some weeks later, Frohman wheeled a demonstration trolley into Gordon Moore's office. In the course of ten short minutes, he demonstrated a way of turning the phenomenon that caused Intel chips to fail into something that could form the basis for a new product. "We put together a 16-bit array with primitive transistor packages sticking out of the sixteen sockets," Frohman recalled. "There were red bulbs to indicate the bits. This was all new to us, and we were thrashing around. We showed Gordon that by pushing the button you could program the device, and we demonstrated that it would hold a charge." Frohman had discovered something truly astounding: a semiconductor that behaved like read-only memory (ROM) but could be programmed with incredible ease.

This discovery had the potential to change the lives of engineers who needed to store information permanently on a chip. The standard way to do this was to "burn" the data onto a standard ROM by drawing out the circuit on sheets of rubylith, turning the design into a set of glass masks, and then waiting for the circuits to be etched on to silicon wafers on the fab line. Usually, the process took weeks, if not months. Now engineers would have a shortcut: they could "write" the data into this new kind of ROM in a few minutes—and the prototyping cycle for a new computer product would be cut from months to hours.

Moore did not need to see Frohman's demonstration twice before committing the company to turning it into a commercial product. Soon after the development program began, however, Frohman came back with some even better news. It wasn't just writing data to his new kind of ROM that was easy. The chip could be easily erased too, using ultraviolet light. So if the circuit designers found that they had made a mistake, or decided to make some improvements to their design, all they needed to do was to take the ROM chip off the circuit board it was installed on, open up its top, and shine a UV beam on it. The chip would then be like new, ready to receive a fresh set of data. Intel decided to call it an erasable, programmable read-only memory (EPROM).

Before the EPROM was ready for sale, the company had to find a way of manufacturing it at reasonable cost. The design's first manifestation, a chip with a capacity of two kilobytes, was from this point of view a disaster—it was half as big again as the biggest chip Intel had ever made. Simple arithmetic meant that you'd get fewer devices, or "dice," off each silicon wafer if the chips were bigger, so the average cost of each one would be higher. But there was a further penalty for trying to build bigger devices. One of the key sources of failure came from random flaws in the silicon wafer itself. Other things being equal, a bigger die size would mean that a higher percentage of the devices that came off the fab line would be flawed. The outlandish size of the first EPROM also presented a more prosaic problem. The chip was so big that its design didn't fit on the layout tables. The circuits had to be assembled from four smaller layouts stuck together—which created alignment problems.

The first working EPROM emerged in September 1970, and by the following February Moore felt confident enough in the project's process to give Frohman the go-ahead to make a presentation on the new technology at the International Solid State Circuits Conference in Philadelphia. To demonstrate the power of the circuit's ability to handle swift erasing and programming, Frohman projected a film in front of the conference delegates.

"The movie showed a pattern of bits being erased—bit by bit, this sea of dots would disappear until only an Intel logo remained," recalled Moore. "With continued UV, the last bits gradually faded until one single, persistent bit was left. Finally, it too disappeared, and the audience burst into applause." The discovery of a new way to program a ROM was as astounding to the wider community of the electronics industry as it had been to Moore himself.

One of the engineers in the audience most impressed by the demonstration was a researcher called Joe Friedrich, who was working as a circuit design manager in Philadelphia. Friedrich had been friendly for some years with both Gordon Moore and Andy Grove, because he had been one of Fairchild's star memory researchers before being poached away by Philco Ford Electronics shortly before the foundation of Intel. But Friedrich had kept up with the Intel crew; in 1969, he had set up a technical seminar at his new employer's offices to coincide with the timing of the Philadelphia conference. Moore had agreed to deliver a presentation under the title "An Industry Built on Sand." The attendance had been an all-time record, and the two men had chatted amicably at length as Friedrich drove Moore back to the airport.

Now, two years later, Friedrich was back at the solid-state circuits conference looking for a job. One Friday in February 1971, Ford had announced to the workforce that it was to close down its electronics subsidiary. The following Monday *Electronics News* had reported the closure, and on Tuesday Friedrich had taken a call from Andy Grove asking if he would be interested in coming to Intel. Friedrich agreed to meet Les Vadasz when he came to Philadelphia a couple of weeks later with the rest of the Intel delegation. Sitting down with Vadasz over coffee, Friedrich asked what he could expect to work on if he moved to the new memory company. "Watch out for Dov Frohman's presentation," Vadasz had said. "That'll explain everything."

Once he'd seen the film, Friedrich needed little persuasion. Two months later, shortly after his thirty-third birthday, he moved his wife and four children to California and started working at Intel. Only after his arrival did Friedrich discover the bad news. The EPROM was in production, under the part number 1702, but manufacturing yields were appalling. On average, only one good circuit was emerging from every two wafers—and for each working part, more than a hundred nonfunctional devices had to be thrown away. This was hardly Frohman's fault. In an attempt to avoid the internal politics that had kept so many good ideas locked in the lab at

Fairchild, Intel had laid down almost as an article of faith that the people who developed a technology should also be responsible for bringing it into commercial production. But Frohman was a physicist, after all, not a circuit designer—and yield improvement and process changes were not his specialty.

Friedrich set to the task at hand with a precision that was all Andy Grove could have wanted. Before he started, he had to design his own test programs and testing boxes. Then he reworked the circuit itself to try to reduce its power consumption, changing it from a parallel design to serial and incorporating a sense amplifier. His next objective became to "characterize" the behavior of the device. "If you couldn't understand it theoretically," he said afterwards, "you had to understand it empirically." What this meant in practice was that Friedrich had to play with each good circuit, watching what happened when he applied different currents and different voltages to it. For weeks on end, he tried combination after combination, carefully noting down the measurements of its electrical behavior.

Friedrich's approach was in startling contrast to that of John Reed, the engineer who fell out with Les Vadasz over his work on the 1103. Reed had once written in his lab notebook the words "The device behaves funny," provoking Vadasz to demand scornfully in his performance review, "What the hell does that mean?" Friedrich would never need to be ticked off in his appraisal for such sloppiness. It wasn't in his character simply to say that what a circuit did was "funny." He needed to know exactly how funny, in what respect, and for how long.

Sitting down with his new circuit design and his careful behavior measurements, Friedrich recalled that the EPROM normally worked in two modes. When reading back data stored on it, the chip required two different power supplies, running at +5 and −12 volts. To program the device by writing data on to it, however, Friedrich was supposed to use a higher negative voltage. The trouble was that for the writing operation to work, this had to be done very precisely. A couple of volts too little, and the data would not be recorded on the chip; a couple of volts too much, and the oxide would break down and zap the device permanently. With Intel's current manufacturing technology, it was hard to make the write voltage consistent over the potential millions of die that could come off the line. Since customers would not know the unique voltage appropriate to each part, they would be in danger of destroying half the devices the first time they tried to use them.

But Friedrich's data showed something startling. If he ran a very high negative voltage across the device—a process he called "walking out"—the result was that the device suddenly became much easier to work with afterwards. Instead of using a voltage that came dangerously close to destroying the chip before successfully writing data to it, he could now use a much lower voltage. The resulting margin for error was so wide that even with the unpredictabilities of 1971 vintage manufacturing, a far higher proportion of the chips would be usable when they emerged from the fab. Sure enough, the first set of wafers showed an increase in yield from half a chip a wafer to an astounding sixty per wafer.

It was only later, when the theory of the device was better understood, that Friedrich was able to learn why "walking out" the virgin device had such an effect on its future behavior. But for the moment, knowing that it did was enough. Intel was able to put out a modified version of the EPROM, called the 1702a, which came off the lines at such consistently high yields that its manufacturing cost was a fraction of its predecessor's. Once the process became stable, the EPROM actually became so cheap to produce that it cost less than its own packaging. (Because the EPROM's ceramic box required a special window in the top to admit the ultraviolet light needed for reprogramming, each box cost well over $10.) As a result of Friedrich's efforts, the device could be built for a total cost well under $30—and sold for over $100.

Moore, Noyce, and Grove realized as soon as the part was in production that they had a winner on their hands. But two factors made EPROM technology spectacularly more successful than they ever dreamed. One was an unexpected link with the microprocessor that Intel brought to market almost at the same time. Every time a customer designed a new product that incorporated the intelligence of a microprocessor—such as the Busicom calculator that provided the impetus for the original design project—the customer would need read-only memory to store the program that drove the processor. When you were working on a prototype, it made sense to buy EPROM rather than standard read-only memory, because mistakes could be ironed out or changes made immediately instead of taking weeks to implement. Intel had expected that once the prototyping was complete, customers would switch back to the lower-cost basic ROM when ordering in production quantities. But to the delight of the company's sales department, that wasn't how customers behaved. Once they got used to the instant gratification of being able to burn data into an EPROM in a matter of minutes, they didn't ever want to go back. Engineers inside the companies that Intel was selling to could justify sticking with the more expensive part by saying that this let them bring new products to market immediately and make instant upgrades to existing products. Of course this cost more than using standard ROM. But the new chips were often going into high-tech products that end-users were willing to pay more for anyway—so the extra cost could be passed straight on.

It wasn't only high demand that made the EPROM a hit; a second factor appeared as an added bonus. Friedrich's trick of "walking out" every new circuit was the perfect kind of trade secret: Not even the most accomplished second-source engineer would be able to detect what he had done to improve the performance of the part. So when competitors all over the Valley started trying to produce knockoffs of the 1702a, they were unable to deliver yields that made it economical to produce the device. As a result, Intel maintained a complete monopoly over EPROMs for nearly two years. The phenomenon that Dov Frohman had discovered by accident while trying to work out why something else failed became a cash cow that contributed tens of millions of dollars to Intel's revenues. In 1971, Intel's sales were $9 million; in 1973, thanks in great part to Frohman's device and Friedrich's work in making it manufacturable, the figure had risen to $66 million.

Flush with the success of the EPROM, it seemed that Intel could do no wrong. So it was no wonder that when an opportunity to diversify into consumer products came along, the company's board of directors enthusiastically backed a proposal from Noyce and Moore to expand into a new line of business. The product was the digital watch—and the idea was that Intel would be able to combine the new liquid crystal displays that were just coming on to the market with its proven expertise in making and assembling chips. With such an apparently neat fit, Intel bought a start-up digital-watch company called Microma in July 1972. The plan was to do to the consumer watch business what Intel had just done to the computer memory business: jump in at a time of great technological change and emerge a few years later with a high market share that would have been impossible to attain at a time of greater stability. As a measure of Intel's confidence that it could pull off this achievement, the company's

1973 annual report predicted that within seven years, digital watches would account for one-third of the watch industry's entire annual sales of 300 million units. For this to happen, two changes would need to take place. The selling price of LCD-based watches would have to fall from over $100 to around $30. And the leading digital-watch technology would have to move over from standard light-emitting-diode (LED) displays to liquid crystal displays that showed the time continuously without a button having to be pressed.

Soon after the Microma acquisition, which Intel financed by issuing nearly seventy thousand new shares, Les Vadasz called Joe Friedrich into his office and offered him a new job as a reward for his work on the EPROM. Friedrich was to be sent over to Microma, where he would head up the group of engineers designing the chips at the core of the new generation of digital watches. The job would be based in Cupertino, where Microma ran a separate operation. So although Friedrich would be able to keep in touch with his old Intel pals, he would continue to work in a small, friendly environment while the parent company became bigger and more impersonal.

The offer seemed impossible to refuse. By the end of 1972, Friedrich was happily ensconced at Microma, full of optimism and excitement about the future.

12

A New Standard

Federico Faggin was a relentless champion of the microprocessor. Soon after the launch of the 8008, he was back in Les Vadasz's office, demanding the resources to convert the chip into a form that could be built using a new process called NMOS. Based on negative charges rather than the positive charges of the early MOS process, NMOS raised the possibility of making the device run twice as fast without any design changes. Les Vadasz was not keen. Microprocessors might help to sell other products, but they were still a tiny sideline to Intel's core business of selling memory chips. The company needed to make sure that the new microprocessors did not gobble up more than their fair share of research spending. With heavy existing commitments on the memory side, Vadasz refused to sanction work on a new generation of processors so soon. But Faggin would not be put off. In meeting after meeting he persisted until finally, nine months later, Vadasz went to Grove for permission to convert the 8008 to NMOS.

Once they had approval to do the preliminary work on the conversion, Faggin and his colleagues realized that they would need to make some changes to the circuits—and so they would need to produce a new set of masks that were used to etch the circuits into the silicon wafer. Since they were going to this trouble of new masks, it was decided, they might as well make a few improvements to the processor design itself. Almost by accident, therefore, a development program began on an entirely new processor—a processor that would double the number of transistors in the 8008 and would also take advantage of a new generation of chip packaging. The standard way to connect a packaged chip to a circuit board was by means of sixteen metal pins, each of which could carry one incoming or outgoing signal. The new packaging used forty pins—making it possible to get information into the chip and back out again faster. Taking all these changes together, the objective was to make the new processor ten times as fast as its predecessor.

Ted Hoff and Stan Mazor worked on the instruction set. Responsible for the circuit design were Faggin and Masatoshi Shima, who by now had moved over to Intel from the Japanese makers of the Busicom machine. The maximum number of operation codes, or basic instructions, that the chip could accommodate was limited to the 256 different possible 8-bit "words." Mazor was determined to use all 256; Shima, when he was going through the list, lost patience when there were still ten op codes to work into the design. "No more," he begged—and the result was that the new chip, known as the 8080, left the remaining op codes unused. This decision would prove to be of great significance later.

Putting the 8080 into manufacturing was not a significant problem. Whereas the memory devices had often required a new process, with a host of technical problems all of its own, the 8080 was built using technology that was already in place and working smoothly in mass production. The big issue was whether there were any major flaws in the design of the chip itself. There weren't. By April 1974, the first 8080 processors were being shipped out to Intel customers. The production cost of each chip would be anywhere between $5 and $50, depending on how many good chips came off each wafer. But there was nothing already in the market that was remotely comparable, deciding a price for the 8080 could hardly be a scientific process. Ed Gelbach decided to pitch it at $360, making a wry joke at the expense of IBM's best-selling 360 mainframe. Then all they had to do was to sit back and wait.

By the time of the introduction of the 8080, Intel had commercialized three technical innovations of great historical significance—the first DRAM, the first EPROM, and the first microprocessor. It had also increased its annual sales to $134 million and its workforce to 3,100 people. It had built a third fabrication plant, or "fab," in

Livermore, California, augmenting its existing two fabs at Santa Clara and Mountain View. To reduce labor costs, it had moved the job of final assembly of chips into their packaging to two overseas sites, one in Malaysia and the other in the Philippines.

By 1974, when the 8080 was formally released, Intel had become the world's fifth largest maker of integrated circuits. Arthur Rock, the venture capitalist who had rounded up investors to fund the company's start-up, had stepped aside as chairman of the board in favor of Bob Noyce. Gordon Moore had become president and CEO. Andy Grove, who had been promoted over Ed Gelbach's head to executive vice-president, was now publicly acknowledged as the third member of the founding troika. While Moore made the big decisions over technological direction and strategy, and Noyce traveled around the country as a sort of corporate supersalesman and ambassador, it was Grove who was now formally as well as informally responsible for the company's internal operations.

The most obvious mark that Andy Grove had made on Intel was a procedure known as "constructive confrontation." As enshrined in the company's statement of values and taught in its internal training sessions, constructive confrontation meant that Intel people should try to get problems out into the open so that they could be discussed and solved in a practical way, without arousing personal animosities. That was the theory. In practice, "constructive confrontation" owed a direct debt to its creator: It captured exactly how Grove himself liked to operate. He could be abrupt, aggressive, and interrogatory. He relished a fight. And he seemed to take a positive delight in shouting at people. One senior manager happened to be in his office when Grove took a call from a subordinate who was asking for authority to spend money on something. Grove refused him immediately, haranguing the hapless maker of the request at high volume and with great anger. Then he hung up the phone and turned calmly back to the colleague in his office to resume the discussion that had been interrupted. "That got his attention, I think," he said.

Grove's style inevitably put off some of the company's fainter hearts. Joel Karp, who left Intel after pressure at work had helped to precipitate a divorce, was once asked by Les Vadasz to stand in for him at one of Grove's staff meetings. The experience shocked him. "It was really an eye-opener for me. At one point, Grove was yelling and screaming at this guy. I thought: 'How can people be treating adults like children?' " The experience left Karp with a strong feeling that he didn't ever want to have anything to do with management. "I thought we all got yelled at enough by our parents when we were kids. Now we're grown up, we shouldn't have to be in environments like this."

But it wasn't only Grove who set the tone. The style that Ed Gelbach had learned at Texas Instruments before he came to California was probably no less robust. Others whom Gelbach brought into the marketing department with him from TI, notably Jack Carsten, were also famous for tough and often cutting talk. But it was Grove who established the day-to-day objectives for his managers and who put in place the disciplines under which they were to achieve them.

Grove used two methods to control his managers. One was budgets: He insisted on a rigorous, regular budgeting process in which general managers and department heads were required to make detailed predictions of costs and revenues, and were required to update the predictions regularly with an explanation of why changes were necessary. The other method of control, suggested to the company in its early years by a management consultant, was that every employee of the company from Grove downwards was required to define a set of medium-term objectives, and to come up with a list of "key results" by which success or failure in achieving the objectives would be measured.

Grove's control was cemented by a structure of regular, standardized meetings. Others might dismiss meetings as intellectual and emotional overhead that got in the way of running the business rather than contributing to it. Grove was undaunted. In his book *High Output Management*, he would later offer a succinct account of why he thought meetings were so important. A manager's work, he said,

is to supply information and know-how, and to impart a sense of the preferred method of handling things to the groups under his control and influence. A manager also makes and helps to make decisions. Both kinds of basic managerial tasks can only occur during face-to-face encounters, and therefore only during meetings. . . . [A] meeting is nothing less than the *medium* through which managerial work is performed.

There were many kinds of meetings in Grove's lexicon. One was the "one-on-one"—a discussion every week or two between every employee and the supervisor he or she reported to, in which small and big problems could be brought up. One-on-ones were used to define objectives and key results, and then to check on progress. They were also the place where written performance reviews were delivered. At first, Grove's practice was to read out the review he had written at the meeting and hand a copy of it to the employee on the way out. Later he changed his system, and began sending out the written review a day or two in advance so that the employee had a chance to absorb the information properly and respond to it during the one-on-one.

Grove also encouraged Intel's human resources department to institute a standardized system of "ranking and rating." Rating meant that most Intel people were put in one of four performance categories: "superior," "exceeds expectations," "meets expectations," or "does not meet expectations." These soon became so ingrained in the company consciousness that Intel people in casual conversation would describe an underperformer as simply a "does not meet." Ranking meant that every employee was also told how the company believed he or she matched up against others doing similar jobs. Pay raises—and, more important, awards of stock options—were based on this system. As Intel's stock soared to a high of $88 a share in the final quarter of 1975, the stock options that were granted to all professional employees emerged as the most important incentive element in every pay packet.

Another kind of meeting was the MOMAR, or "monthly management review." Here a group of peers from different parts of the company would attend to hear a presentation by one division of its current strengths and weaknesses, problems, and opportunities. The purpose of MOMARs was to make sure that even in the busiest working schedule, Intel managers were forced to raise their noses from the grindstone of their current concerns and look at the wider picture of the company's business as a whole. Grove hoped the system would also provide a constant source of free consultancy, as talented managers from one department came up with good ideas for how to solve problems in another. He thought it even more important for people to make presentations as a matter of self-discipline. Only if you were able to set out the issues facing your part of the business in a way that others could understand could you claim to understand them yourself.

At the opening of every MOMAR, Grove was always to be found taking notes. He made a point of keeping the presentations that every department made, and bringing them with him next time the same department was under the spotlight. Sitting at the back, he would then lob a series of difficult questions, pressing the hapless manager giving the presentation to explain why his team had failed to live up to the lofty ambitions announced last time around.

A more relaxed kind of meeting was the management retreat, in which Intel's executive staff and a few other senior people would decamp for a few days from Santa Clara to some attractive resort where they would brainstorm about big issues facing the company's future. Here the objective was to inject new thinking and new approaches. Often, outsiders would be brought in to lecture on the importance of learning how to listen, or the latest fashionable management theory.

Grove's favorite kind of meeting was one that didn't look like a meeting at all. Acutely conscious as he was of the value of his own time, he hated to invite someone to his office for a discussion that needed only a couple of minutes, but then be forced by politeness into a half-hour chat about the world. Instead of allowing this to happen, he would make a point of going to see the other person in their office, so that he could have the two-minute word and then get on his way.

To make these encounters easier, Grove set up a regular system of inspections of all Intel plant and facilities that people began to refer to as "Mr. Clean." He, and later on other senior managers, would walk around the building, checking on everything from the janitor's cubbyhole to the cleanliness of the boardroom, and ordering whatever he found out of order to be set right. Because Andy Grove was one of those people who believed that a tidy desk indicated a tidy mind, the Mr. Clean inspections trickled down to a system of enforced neatness for the entire company. You wouldn't get an immediate pay cut if there were too many papers in your in-box or a pile of books on the floor. But you'd get asked pointed questions—about whether you had just come back from a business trip that accounted for the backlog of unanswered mail, or whether you were waiting for a new bookcase to arrive—which made it clear that the company viewed untidiness as incompatible with doing your job properly.

Plenty of people found the inspections petty and irritating. On one occasion, Grove walked into an office and drew the attention of one of his managers to a hole in the wall that he had noticed on his last Mr. Clean inspection, three days earlier.

"I thought I told you to get that fixed," he said.

"Andy, I've got bigger problems to worry about than that," replied the manager.

"There are no bigger problems," came the cold reply. "There are just problems."

But it was the Late List that was the most controversial of the management techniques Grove introduced to Intel. The idea arose in 1971 because of Grove's irritation at not being able to find engineers at their desks early in the morning. According to an Intel engineer quoted in a company publication over a decade later, Grove was sitting in a corner conference room with a sweeping view of the parking lot, waiting for a meeting to start, when he lost his temper.

"We'd periodically look up from our discussions and glance at the parking lot, watching people straggle in long after 8:00," Thomson recalled. "Finally Andy pounded on the table and said he couldn't take it anymore, that this was a manufacturing organization, and that we should all start at eight o'clock."

A few days later, the security officers who staffed the employee entrances at Intel's three facilities were told to ask all employees who arrived after 8:00 A.M. to sign their names. There were no immediate plans for retaliation against latecomers, but Grove wanted Intel's staff to know that he—which meant the company—both cared and noticed when they arrived. The idea was strongly opposed by most of Intel's management and also by the human resources department. But it was a measure of Grove's influence over the organization that the Late List was put into practice and stayed in place for the rest of the 1970s and most of the 1980s.

Of course, it could not be foolproof. Employees who were moving from an early meeting in one building to a later meeting in another were often irritated to be forced to sign in—though they were consoled by the spectacle of seeing Gordon Moore undergo the same humiliation even though he was Intel's chief executive. But people who made a habit of working late found it galling to be singled out as disloyal employees, particularly when they compared themselves to others who left the office promptly at 5:00 P.M. So the sign-in sheets, which were circulated to senior management, would often contain angry messages: I WAS HERE UNTIL MIDNIGHT LAST NIGHT, DAMMIT! Sometimes a close inspection of the signatures on the sheet would reveal that a number of the late arrivals had identified themselves as Andy Grove or Mickey Mouse. Some employees would simply evade the list altogether, taking what they saw as the system's absurdity to its logical conclusion by sitting in their cars in the parking lot until after 9:00 A.M., when the company assumed that the only arrivals at its facilities would be customers, and the security guards therefore had instructions to stop asking for signatures. One Intel manager, interviewed for this book ten years after he left the company, identified himself as one of a group of people who found a way around the sign-in procedure. But he refused—out of concern that former colleagues still with the company might be subject to retaliation—to say how he'd done it.

Federico Faggin was one of the earliest to rebel against the attempt to impose a standard starting time to the day. By 1974, he had become the manager of a team of eighty or so engineers and technicians—but he felt just as unhappy having to impose the rigor of the Late List on the people who reported to him.

To Faggin, the Late List was a symbol of the regimentation that was becoming part of life at Intel as it grew. Faggin saw it as a symptom of a bigger issue; with a staff of professionals to cover manufacturing, marketing, and finance, the company could no longer offer him the same exciting chance to learn new skills as it had when he first arrived. Nor, paradoxically, could it offer appropriate rewards. Faggin had received the standard engineer's allocation of one thousand share options when he arrived—and every year he got another tranche, subject to the rule that new options could only be exercised gradually over a four-year period. With Intel's stock price rising promisingly, he could expect the stock to be worth several years' salary before too long. But Moore and Noyce, who had started the company, were each sitting on nearly a half-million shares whose value fluctuated between $20 and $50 each. To achieve financial security on that scale, Faggin would have to start up his own company.

It was probably the dispute over the patent that prompted his decision.

As we've seen, Faggin was the scientist who had invented the silicon gate process that was the basis of Intel's memory-chip business. The work had been done while he was at Fairchild working under the supervision of Les Vadasz, and Intel had been able to turn it into a moneyspinner because Fairchild had failed to put it to commercial use. Faggin had never received formal recognition inside Intel for the work he had done; in any case, lots of work by lots of people had been needed to turn his laboratory demonstration into a robust manufacturing process that worked reliably at high volumes.

Yet Faggin always felt a quiet satisfaction for having come up with the key innovation that made Intel's memory chip business possible.

One day when he was working on the 8080, a chance remark from Dov Frohman, the inventor of the EPROM, sent him scurrying off to the patent office. Frohman had indicated to him that Faggin's idea of a "buried contact"—a diffused resistor whose connections were made with polysilicon to silicon contacts—had been patented, that the inventor credited with it was Les Vadasz, his former boss at Fairchild, and the company to whom rights in the invention had been assigned was Intel Corporation.

This discovery made Faggin burn red hot with fury—for he recalled that the key idea that led to the invention, of using a "buried contact," was one that Vadasz had not wanted him to try out when he was working in the Fairchild lab. "I tried anyway," Faggin recalled later. "I made it work. When he found out at Intel that he needed it, what could he do? Someone must have said to him: *Hey, we can patent this.*"

Faggin stormed into Vadasz's office and demanded to know how and why he had patented his idea. Vadasz, for once, was at a loss for words.

"Let's go see Grove," he said.

Grove did all the talking.

"Well," he began, "these things happen. The idea must have stuck in his mind and he didn't know where it came from."

"Come on," retorted Faggin. "He knew exactly where it came from."

It was Faggin's belief that Grove had knowingly encouraged Vadasz to patent the invention to protect Intel's commercial interest, in the full knowledge that it had not been Vadasz's idea. Faggin made clear his accusation.

Both men tried to pacify him. Faggin was even offered a copy of the first page of the patent to hang on his wall. He refused in a blaze of anger—not least because it would have been an odd thing to explain to visitors, a patent hanging above his desk that didn't even bear his own name. But in the end, Faggin swallowed his feelings. "Was I to sue them?" he asked afterwards. Obviously not. That wasn't the kind of thing that engineers did in 1974.

Faggin was not the only engineer in the Intel design department with itchy feet. Another member of his team, Ralph Ungermann, was chafing under the Andy Grove disciplinary system.

Ungermann had come to Intel in 1971 from Western Digital, a start-up that was trying to build logic chips for customers on a one-off customized basis. A graduate in communications from Berkeley and in computer architecture from the University of California at Irvine, Ungermann had seen firsthand the effect that the micro-processor could have on the custom logic business. Instead of buying his company's custom circuits, customers had begun to migrate toward Intel's 4004, which they could customize themselves at far lower cost.

On the principle that he might as well be a beneficiary of the change he could see occurring, Ungermann moved up to Silicon Val-ley from his home in southern California, and began attempting to get a job in the microprocessor design department at Intel. Only once he was inside did Ungermann come to the conclusion that Intel's management didn't at all understand the true potential of the micro-processor. He was also astonished to discover that Intel had only a couple of people working on microprocessor circuit designs, when he knew that Motorola, the country's fourth biggest maker of integrated circuits, had been so impressed by the 4004 that it had set up a team of forty people working on microprocessors and the chips that went with them.

To his great chagrin, instead of working on microprocessors, Ungermann was assigned by Les Vadasz to a relatively minor custom project—a job to build a chip that could recognize coins, which was being carried out for Mars, Inc. At first, the idea of devoting all his hours to a system for selling candy bars in vending machines seemed depressing; but Ungermann soon began to appreciate that although he was not working on the general-application microprocessors that he believed had the greatest business potential, there was still a great deal to learn from the discipline of designing custom chips for par-ticularly subtle tasks.

Another initial disappointment turned into a bonus. Instead of reporting to Vadasz, as he believed he would, Ungermann found himself reporting to Federico Faggin. It took him only a short time to realize that Faggin was a thinker of rare talent and a wonderful engi-neering manager. "He knew where the industry was going. He knew what could be done on the technology. He pushed you hard to be on the edge of greatness," Ungermann recalled.

Ungermann was always a mysterious figure to the loyal foot sol-diers at Intel: He seemed to have part-time activities running alongside his day job. This was a legacy from his old days at Western Digital. Some years earlier, he had noticed that no simulation tools were available that allowed chip designers to try out their designs cost-effectively before putting them into production. Working with his wife, a computer programmer, Ungermann designed a piece of software that did logic simulations. He distributed his service through one of the companies offering "timeshare" on mainframe computers to small businesses, and found to his great delight that his package was a hundred times faster than the nearest competing product. The business began to produce nice royalty flows—so much so, in fact, that Ungermann bought himself a brand-new Porsche in 1973 with the proceeds.

By 1974, Ungermann had come to the conclusion that he didn't have a long-term future at Intel. Not only was he outside the clique of Ph.D. physicists, visible at company parties around Noyce, Moore, and Grove, who he believed were the real inner circle that ran the company. He was also nettled by the Late List, which he felt was humiliating and counterproductive. But the last straw for Ralph Ungermann was another of Intel's innovations, the cubicle.

When the company moved its headquarters from Mountain View to Santa Clara, its rate of growth was so fast that the offices were in a constant state of reorganization. Walls would be built to form new working spaces, and then torn down again a few weeks later to accommodate a group of new hires. Finally, Intel's management realized that all this building work was not only causing noise and inconvenience but also costing money—so, taking a rational engineering solution to the problem, it decided to abolish offices altogether. In their place, every employee up to Noyce would have a cubicle—a small working area with a desk, chair, bookshelf, and telephone, surrounded by a shoulder-high padded divider. The hope was that this would break down barriers to internal communication. Ungermann hated it—he was the kind of person who needed peace and quiet to get his work done, and having a door to close really mattered to him. He wanted out.

It was a piece of bad luck that finally prompted Ungermann to act on his own inclination. In July 1974, he exercised a group of options for several thousand Intel shares. Under the rules of the option scheme in force at the time, employees who exercised their options were not allowed to sell the shares they received immediately; they had to hold the shares for at least one business day before disposing of them, because the transfer process could not take place immediately.

To exercise his options, Ungermann had borrowed $100,000 on a day when the current price of Intel stock in the market was somewhere between $60 and $70, and the options allowed him to buy the shares at $20, locking in a profit of 5,000 lots of $40. When he got around to selling, however, news of an impending downturn in the electronics industry had driven the company's stock down to $16. Instead of making $200,000 in profits, he was now $20,000 out of pocket. Not only would he have to sell the Porsche to pay back the money he had borrowed; it would also take several years of scrimping and saving before he was back to where he had been a few short weeks before. To make matters worse, the electronics downturn also had an immediate effect on Ungermann's sideline business, since many companies using his logic software package halted design projects in order to pull in their belts until business improved.

So there it was: a disputed patent and an unlucky bet on the stock market. Ungermann grumbled to Faggin, and Faggin grumbled to Ungermann. And just as Noyce and Moore had resolved to start Intel after getting frustrated with their position at Fairchild, so also the two younger men decided to leave Intel and set up in business on their own.

When Faggin handed in his notice, the company's first response was to make it clear that great things might be on offer if he were prepared to stay. Faggin replied that he was not interested. He was willing to work out three months of notice if the company wanted him to, but his decision to leave was irrevocable.

Shortly before he left, Faggin received a summons to Grove's office. Grove had recently instituted a system of "exit interviews." Some employees saw these as an alarming reminder of life in the Communist bloc, where the right to leave the country was so sharply curtailed that dissidents needed an "exit visa" before they were allowed to board the aircraft to the West. In fact, these interviews had no such sinister intent; they were simply a reflection of Grove's belief that something useful could always be learned from a talented employee who had decided to leave. Departure was the ultimate criticism of how Intel ran its business. It made sense to try to find out how to change things so that the company would not lose others through the same mistake.

With Faggin, however, there was little to say. Grove knew every detail of Faggin's conflicts with Vadasz, his dissatisfaction with Grove's approach to discipline, his hurt at what he believed to be the appropriation of his invention. All Faggin would say was that he was going to work with Ungermann and planned to do something with microprocessors. He had been so busy over the past few months, Faggin said, that he hadn't even had a chance to decide exactly what he would do.

Grove's response was chilling. Now that it was clear that nothing could keep Faggin inside Intel, he sent the brilliant engineer on his way with a dismissal that amounted almost to a parting curse.

"What will you do if you leave Intel?" he asked. "You will leave no heritage for your children. Your name will be forgotten. You will fail. You will fail in everything you do."

Shaken by the almost medieval brutality of these words, Faggin made for the door. Grove had tried to destroy his self-confidence, to plant a seed of self-doubt in the mind of a potential competitor. But the departing engineer was not so easily cowed. "I will succeed," said Faggin to himself. "I will not be forgotten."

PART TWO

DOMINATION

"Are we doing this as an exercise to improve our position in the market place, and achieve the recognition we deserve? Or are we doing this to fucking kill Motorola? . . . We have to kill Motorola, that's the name of the game. We have to crush the fucking bastards. We're gonna roll over Motorola and make sure they don't come back again."

—Jim Lally, former Intel executive,
    describing the thinking behind Operation Crush

13

Borovoy Wins a Patent Battle

There weren't many people who turned down a job offer at Intel in its earliest years. One of the few who did was Roger Borovoy, a friend of Bob Noyce's who was one of the smartest company lawyers at Fairchild. When Noyce invited him to join the new company, Borovoy made it clear that he didn't see himself working for a start-up. He jokingly told Noyce that Intel wouldn't need a lawyer of his horsepower for some time—and suggested that the two men should talk again in a few years when Intel was bigger. So another lawyer was hired to keep his seat warm. Three years after the IPO, Noyce renewed the offer—and this time, Borovoy accepted. He resigned his position at Fairchild and decided to take a few days of vacation at home before joining Intel.

That was when the call came in.

"Roger, it's Andy Grove."

"Hi, Andy." The lawyer delivered the expected pleasantries about looking forward to joining Intel, and waited for Grove to respond in kind.

But Grove, never a man for small talk, hadn't called to welcome him aboard. Instead, he pitched straight into the purpose of his call.

"I want you to fire Ted."

"What?"

There were two guys in Intel's legal department, and Noyce had agreed that both of them would report to Borovoy. The more senior

of the two, who held the title of "corporate counsel," was Ted Vian—
not a dazzling lawyer, maybe, but certainly a thoroughly competent
one. This was the man Grove was asking Borovoy to dismiss.

"I want you to fire Ted. You know the industry's just entered a
downturn? Well, I'm laying off engineers, and you don't hire another
lawyer when you're laying off engineers. If you want to come, you
gotta fire one of them: Ted or the other guy."

Let me get this right. I haven't even walked through the door yet, I
haven't even joined the company, and he wants me to fire the first
guy who's supposed to be reporting to me?

"Andy, I've never worked with Ted. I don't know him."

"I don't care which one, but over my dead body do we increase the
head count of lawyers while letting engineers go. Fire one of them."

Borovoy replied that he'd be happy to look at the issue once he had
his feet under the desk, but he certainly wouldn't do anything for at
least a couple of weeks. "I don't know the other lawyer from a hole in
the wall," he said. "And besides, I really think you'd do better to talk
to Ted yourself," he told Grove.

A few days later, Borovoy reported for his first day at work and
found Ted Vian now working alone as the sole member of Intel's legal department. Andy had talked to Ted, and Ted had fired the other
guy. Borovoy had extricated himself from a bruising situation with
some skill by standing up to Grove's bullying, but he learned a useful
lesson from the experience about the real balance of power inside
Intel.

"Andy was president of that company from the day it opened," he
recalled, looking back on the Vian incident. "There was never any
question in my mind. Andy was everybody's boss. He was the guy
who made things hum."

So although Borovoy was formally supposed to report directly to
Bob Noyce as the company's chairman, he recognized from the outset
that in practice, he would be reporting to Grove. "From the day of
that phone call, before I set foot in the door, I knew who was boss."

In the six years between the first job offer and the day that
Borovoy actually joined Intel, the legal landscape of the entire electronics industry had been transformed. Back in 1968, people and
ideas had flowed easily between one company and another, their passage oiled by conversations in bars such as the Wagon Wheel. By
1974, electronics companies had become a great deal more territorial

about both their employees and their intellectual property. Court cases were becoming commonplace; companies would use patents either to extract high royalties from competitors or to strike wide-ranging "cross-licensing" agreements in which two companies would agree to let each other use their patents without fees. Managers were finding themselves under pressure to sign contracts that prevented them from moving quickly to competitors.

Borovoy had experienced these changes firsthand. Shortly after Les Hogan arrived with his band of heroes to take over Bob Noyce's place, Fairchild had been hit by Motorola with a suit claiming breach of trade secrets—and Borovoy had spent much of the next five years fighting the case.

It was not long before the new general counsel at Intel faced his first real test: a lawsuit against the company from Western Electric, a division of AT&T. Over the past few years, Western Electric had been gradually pursuing all the big names in the semiconductor business, demanding royalties for what it alleged was their use of a very old patent, dating back to the 1950s, that covered a key stage in the oxide processing of transistors. Some companies had already paid up; when he was on the Fairchild payroll, Borovoy himself had signed an agreement to license the technology. But Intel and a number of smaller new companies had always maintained that there was no reason why they should pay for the technology—and they'd refused to do business with Western Electric.

Borovoy's first move was to ask around the Valley to find out how many other companies had received the same complaint. The answer was eight; Intel was the biggest. Because of his knowledge of this particular patent, Borovoy decided that he would litigate the case himself instead of hiring in outside counsel. Within a few weeks, he found himself elected lead counsel for the entire group of companies.

As part of the process of discovery, in which each side in a court case is allowed to read relevant documents held by the other side, Borovoy demanded the right to go over and inspect papers relating to the patent at Bell Labs, the famous research center in Murray Hill, New Jersey, where the original work on the transistor had been done. Looking through the center's patent records, he noted down the names of some of the people who were involved in different patents in the field of integrated circuits. Then he asked to see the lab notebooks of all the scientists involved.

The fact that the notebooks had been carefully kept in storage was no surprise; any company that took patents seriously had to preserve the raw data and daily notes on which patent applications were based. Otherwise it might risk losing a piece of evidence that could be crucial if an outside party tried to interfere. But Borovoy was still a bit surprised when a clerk led him into a room deep in the Bell Labs and sat him down at a grimy metal desk. On the desk, neatly piled, were over a thousand dusty notebooks. Ten feet above the desk was a single naked 40-watt bulb.

"Here you are," said the clerk. "You have to leave by 5:00 P.M. every day. There's a cafeteria around the corner."

As the echo of the slamming door died away, Borovoy gazed wearily at the pile. He wasn't quite sure what he was looking for. He knew that the patent covered the use of oxide masks for diffusion in chip manufacture. He knew it had been awarded to two men named Derick and Frosch, one an engineer and the other a lab technician. And he knew that the patents were a politically sensitive question at Bell Labs at the time. Faced with an antitrust probe by the Department of Justice, AT&T had signed a consent decree to get the trust-busters off its back—and had agreed among other things to offer free licenses to competitors on all the patents that the company earned before January 1, 1956. The patent that Western Electric was now using against Intel had been filed after that deadline, so it wasn't subject to the consent decree.

Reaching for the first notebook on top of the nearest pile, Borovoy felt a glimmer of excitement at the intellectual challenge of looking at all this raw material—closely followed by second thoughts: *Jeez, I'm going to be here for two weeks.* But he proved himself wrong. Two hours and a couple of dozen notebooks later, the lawyer pulled out a notebook belonging to a researcher named Fuller and compared it with the contents of the Derick and Frosch patent. *My God, there's the Derick and Frosch patent, and here's the same goddamn thing in the other guy's notebook, nine months before.*

The Fuller notebook was by no means conclusive, but it strongly suggested that AT&T had incorrectly dated its invention when it applied for the original patent. There was clearly a motive: If it could hold off from patenting the idea until after the justice department's deadline, then Ma Bell might be able to earn some royalties from it. But misattributing and misdating an invention weren't allowed under the patent law—and there was a good chance that AT&T's monkey business, if proven right, might invalidate the patent. There was only one way to find out: take depositions from Derick and Frosch. But before Borovoy put on his coat and reached for his briefcase, he picked out half a dozen other notebooks at random. Carrying the notebooks out of the room to the AT&T clerk nearby, he asked for permission to use the copying machine, and ran off a hundred copies from different notebooks so it would not be too obvious what he was interested in. He then replaced the notebooks in date order on the pile, made a couple of phone calls, and left.

It took less than a day of depositions to extract some useful information about the circumstances of the original invention from the two men named on the disputed patent. When he arrived the next morning to continue the depositions, Borovoy was handed a note. *Western Electric's licensing manager would like to talk to you*, it said.

Calling the manager back during the morning break from the depositions, Borovoy was surprised to find himself invited to lunch.

"But you know I'm out here in Murray Hill," said the Intel general counsel. "I can't come into Manhattan today—I've gotta be back here at 1:30 to resume the depositions."

"No problem."

The mountain was offering to come to Mohammed.

Over lunch, the licensing manager made it clear that he had been contacted by Western Electric's lawyers after the previous day's events. All of a sudden, the licensing rates he was asking for became very reasonable. Instead of demanding 1.5 percent of Intel's annual sales—an astoundingly high figure in those innocent days—he said: "How about we give you a five-year license, we'll try and be reasonable about it, and then agree to a royalty for use of the whole of our company's patent portfolio from this year onwards?"

They haggled briefly, and then settled on the spot for a lump sum of $50,000 to cover everything up to that date, with a tiny fraction of a percentage point as the royalty in future.

"Look," said Borovoy. "If this were just Intel, we'd fold up the depositions and I'd leave. But I'm lead counsel for all eight companies and the others haven't settled yet."

A few weeks later, the entire dispute was over. Thanks to Borovoy's detective work among the Bell Labs notebooks, Western Electric was forced to offer all eight companies a similar deal. The savings to Intel alone were worth a lifetime of the new general counsel's salary.

Roger Borovoy was not so lucky in the second battle he fought for Intel. This time the opponent was the Shell Oil Company, which had patented some technology related to the sense amplifiers that Intel used in its memory chips. The patents were well drafted, and Shell had picked Intel as its first target. Borovoy sat down with the attorneys from Shell and put together what he believed was a creative settlement. Intel would concede that its latest generation of chips infringed the patent, and would pay a $2 million onetime royalty to Shell for future use of the technology. But the two sides could not agree on what to do about the past. Borovoy believed that Intel's earlier generations of chips didn't infringe; Shell insisted that they did. To resolve the dispute cheaply, the two sides agreed that they would take depositions, write briefs, and ask a neutral patent lawyer to arbitrate. If there was infringement, Intel would pay Shell a half-million dollars. If not, no further money would change hands.

After the briefs had been exchanged, and just before an oral hearing was due to take place, the Shell attorney called Borovoy.

"Do we really want to have this hearing?" he asked. "We're willing to split the difference. For $250,000, you have a license."

Borovoy thought about it and went to see Grove.

"What do you think I ought to do?" he asked. "The reason I'm coming to see you is because I thought maybe the difference between a quarter-million and half a million could impact on a quarter's earnings."

"No," replied Grove. "They're the same order of magnitude. What do you think the chances are of winning?"

"Better than fifty-fifty, I'd say."

"Go for it."

Two days later, Borovoy turned down the Shell offer and announced Intel's intention to go ahead with the hearing. Unfortunately, he lost. Two days after the company sent off the check for $500,000, Grove was due to give Borovoy a performance review.

"Do you want the good news or the bad news?" Grove asked.

"Gimme the bad news. No, on second thoughts I know the bad news. It's Shell, right?"

"No."

Grove then picked up some other problem with Borovoy's work, which wasn't of great importance. "Now do you want to hear the good news? It's Shell."

"What do you mean? How can it be good news? We lost it."

"Roger, we were in litigation. You fashioned a clever settlement where you paid what you thought was reasonable. You found a scheme to resolve the difference. Better than that—when the other side offered to split the difference, you were willing to go for a full victory anyway."

Borovoy walked out of the room with a raise and a favorable written review in his hand. *Perhaps Andy Grove isn't so bad after all*, he thought to himself.

14

A Competitor
on the Horizon

Once they were both out of Intel, Federico Faggin and Ralph Ungermann were ready to sit down and talk about what products they might develop. Ungermann favored the idea of trying to build an electronic typewriter. Faggin wanted to take the concept of the original 4004 microprocessor that he had worked on with Hoff and develop it into a one-chip microcontroller that would hold all memory and input-output devices together with the processor on a single piece of silicon. *Electronics News* picked up a rumor of his idea, and the next week's edition of the trade magazine contained a prominent article reporting that Faggin and Ungermann were going into the processor business together.

A week later, the two men received an unexpected visitor at the offices they shared in the prosperous community of Los Altos, a few miles from Palo Alto. He identified himself as being from a subsidiary of Exxon, the world's most powerful oil company, that had been set up to invest in start-ups. Exxon Enterprises, as the company was called, had looked at Faggin and Ungermann and liked what it had seen. If they'd like to develop a new processor, the firm would be willing to back them.

A deal was swiftly signed between the two men and Exxon Enterprises giving the oil company a controlling 51 percent stake in return for $1.5 million. Ungermann had a good name for the new business: It was to be called Zilog, an acronym indicating that the company

was intended to be the "last word [z] in integrated [i] logic [log]."
Two months down the line, Faggin had second thoughts. He had
been keeping an eye on the fate of his old project, the Intel 8080
microprocessor, for some time. And judging by the enthusiastic response that the 8080 was getting—not just in the trade rags but in
anecdotal evidence from how companies all across the United States
were beginning to use it—Faggin realized that it would be a mistake
not to capitalize on the upswell that seemed to be beginning for the
general-purpose microprocessor. In December 1974, he persuaded
Ungermann to abandon the controller project and switch to developing an improved version of the 8080 chip.

In an attempt to mend bridges with Andy Grove and Les Vadasz,
Faggin went back to Intel with some ideas and offered to produce the
improved 8080 on contract to Intel. He was turned down. Ed Gelbach retorted that it would be "too tempting" to the rest of Intel's
employees if the betrayal of leaving the company were to be rewarded
so swiftly with a lucrative contract. But the visit did have one effect.
To Faggin's great surprise, he received a job application from Masatoshi Shima, the engineer who had commissioned the 4004 project,
and later joined Intel. Since Shima had done the detailed layout work
of the 8080, Faggin was enthusiastic about welcoming him aboard.

Intel's response to the Shima defection was swift. Roger Borovoy
called Ungermann and issued blood-curdling threats of the legal
remedies he would immediately seek if the two men poached just one
more Intel employee. In vain Ungermann protested that Shima had
approached them, not vice versa. Intel had drawn the line, and it
seemed risky to overstep it.

The development of Zilog's new chip proved to be quicker than either Faggin or Ungermann had dared hope. Working eighty hours a
week—and with nobody to complain what time he arrived in the
mornings—Faggin completed the chip architecture in less than nine
months. The detailed circuit design was handed over to his partner
and Shima, who displayed a brilliance that astounded both his colleagues. When Ungermann, for instance, wanted to add an extra instruction to the chip's instruction set, Shima shook his head. "It will
increase the die size by two mils [thousandths of an inch]," he said.
His two colleagues were stunned by Shima's instinctive ability to see
the consequence that a minor increase in the logical complexity of the
device would have on the silicon "real estate" it required.

Since Zilog was initially made up only of the three of them plus a handful of other layout artists and helpers, it was out of the question for them to fabricate the chip themselves. Instead, Faggin drew designs on "thousand-x" Mylar with a lead pencil; Shima oversaw the conversion of the designs into masks; and the completed set of masks was shipped off for manufacturing to Mostek, a spin-off from Texas Instruments that was now one of Intel's hottest competitors in the MOS memory market.

Two weeks after receiving the masks from Zilog, Mostek returned a set of sample chips. The chips didn't work fully, but the design flaws were not hard to detect and fix. By March 1976, Zilog had a working part that it was ready to unleash on the world.

When the Zilog Z80 came out, the response from the trade press was immediately positive. The new chip could run any program written for Intel's 8080 chip, and would fit interchangeably into the same place as the 8080 on a customer's circuit board. But it incorporated a number of refinements that made it twenty times easier to program. The new chip had a "serial I/O" technology that made it easier to address peripheral devices. It offered a facility called "direct memory access" that made an attempt to resolve the curious addressing system used in the 8080. And best of all, it took advantage of the op codes that had been left unused in the 8080 design to deliver some advanced functions that were well thought out and truly useful to computer designers.

With a price tag of only $200, the Zilog Z80 began to capture the imagination of individual hobbyists. People who had previously spent long nights in front of a ham radio were now, thanks to the glories of large-scale circuit integration, tinkering with electronics. The Z80 made it possible for the first time for them to contemplate the revolutionary possibility of building a computer of their own. Since there were fewer computers in the world in 1974 than airplanes in the world in 1997, telling your friends you were doing this had the same kind of ring then as announcing that you were assembling a Boeing 767 in your backyard would be today. But the job was a bit less daunting. In 1974, a crop of new magazines were spreading the word about the new large-scale integrated circuits and offering step-by-step instructions for putting them to use. New companies had sprung up, offering kits with intriguing names like Altair or Mistral that included everything you needed to build a computer. The part would later even be designed into Radio Shack's TRS-80, the machine that many claim as the first real "personal computer."

Having spent $400,000 developing its chip, Zilog could hardly afford to spend lavishly on an army of salesmen. Instead, it bought space in *Electronics News* and ran a series of provocative ads. THE BATTLE OF THE 80s, said the headline—indicating not only Zilog's claim to prominence in the coming decade but also the comparison Faggin wanted to be made between his own Z80 and Intel's 8080. The campaign worked like a dream; as Faggin and Ungermann traveled around the States and abroad in search of wholesalers, second sources, and big industrial customers, they often found the ad pinned to the walls inside the offices of potential customers. Rumor even had it that Bob Noyce had a copy of the ad strategically placed immediately above his desk.

This was not a surprise. From an engineer's point of view, Z80 was an unmistakably superior product to the 8080. Not only did it run considerably faster and cost only slightly more than half the price, it was also easier to program and easier to design into larger systems.

Zilog's efforts were soon rewarded with the most sincere form of flattery: imitation. Both Mostek and Sharp approached the company with a request to build second-source chips that were identical to the Z80. Since Faggin and Ungermann's business were such a new company, and since both men had learned from Intel that getting quick market acceptance was the key to success, they granted royalty-free licenses to both companies. Faggin realized that the two second sources would undoubtedly force Zilog to cut its prices. But he was convinced that Zilog's own manufacturing costs would fall even faster than prices—and so the result would be greatly increased sales and thus higher profits.

The most important priority, however, was not to rest on the laurels of the Z80's success. Faggin recalled with some bitterness how it had taken him three-quarters of a year after the launch of the 8008 just to get Les Vadasz's permission to start developing a new processor. Now that he was his own boss, he would not allow the same mistake to be made twice. So as soon as the Z80 was sent to manufacturing, before it had even hit the market, Faggin sat down with his partner.

"We need to start work on the next one," he said.

Some months later, Zilog began development on its next chip, to be called the Z8000, which would process data 16 bits at a time instead of 8, and would deliver another tenfold improvement in performance. And the company behind it would be a more serious outfit.

New employees had been hired, bringing the design team up to a strength of ten—and Faggin and Ungermann, encouraged by their masters at Exxon, were already looking at the possibility of designing DRAMs and EPROMs.

To Intel, Zilog was beginning to look like a daunting competitor.

15

Penang Burning

To continue pushing out the envelope of semiconductor technology, Intel needed an ever-growing supply of scientific talent—not just device physicists, computer architects, and circuit designers, but also materials scientists who could understand the behavior of the packaging of the company's products.

One of the more unusual people who joined the company was Paul Engel, a talented chemist fresh from his Ph.D. Engel was identified with a technique that Intel would find increasingly useful as it grew: a careful process of keeping up contacts between Intel's scientific staff and their former teachers and fellow students at the leading universities. By 1974, an invitation to come and talk to Intel was an honor to any student who was aware of what was going on in the electronics business.

With Engel, the call for interview came in by phone one Friday from Gene Meieran, one of the senior people working for Les Vadasz. As soon as he realized the opportunity that had been offered to him, Engel's mind began racing. *Work in the semiconductor business? In California? For Intel? Tell me what I need to pay! An arm? A leg? You got it.*

Engel agreed immediately to fly to California the following Monday morning.

"Go to the airport," said Meieran. "You'll find a ticket waiting for you. We'll meet you when you get here, and take you to your hotel."

Three weeks later, Engel was back in California permanently. He checked into the Vagabond Motel—considerably more economical than the place where Intel had put him up when he was still considering the job. He bought an old VW and started to look for somewhere to live. An apartment in Sunnyvale would come into the picture later on, but since Intel was Engel's home from eight in the morning until ten at night most days, the place he slept did not have much of an impression on his life. If you'd asked the young scientist what he thought of work six months later, he'd have overwhelmed you with enthusiasm. *Couldn't ask for a better job. I just love it. It's terrific.*

It was not long before Engel faced his first real challenge. Bill Jordan's memory systems division sent a message down to his engineering group, complaining that a number of 1103s, Intel's best-selling 1K DRAM chip, were failing on test. Before leaving the factory, a certain number of parts were picked out of every thousand and put through a battery of tough working conditions—ranging from the "burn-in," where the parts were left running while being baked in an oven, to another test in which they were operated in a chamber cooled to ten degrees below freezing using liquid nitrogen. It was this latter test that the chips were failing.

On opening the boxes, Engel and his colleagues saw immediately that corrosion had caused the chips to fail. The issue was where that corrosion had come from. After all, the packages in which the chips were installed were supposed to be hermetically sealed against the outside world. The obvious suspect was the airtightness of the box itself— especially since the problems had only begun recently, after Intel had switched to a new system of using cerdip packaging. (*Cerdip* is an abbreviation for "ceramic dual in-line package," and it refers to the black box with a set of metal prongs on each side that is most people's idea of what a computer chip looks like.)

When the assembly process was working properly, a newly manufactured chip, or die, would be sandwiched between two pieces of ceramic. Tiny wires would then be used to link the metal connectors on the edge of the die with connectors inside the ceramic box. The box would then be baked, with low-temperature glass acting as a glue between the top and the bottom. Result: an airtight sealed chamber, easy to connect to the outside world by plugging the two lines of pins, or "leads," into a circuit board.

To test the hypothesis that water was leaking in from the outside air, causing the corrosion inside the failed chips, one of the team's technicians set up an experiment to pump hot steam into the chamber in which the packages were sealed. That increased the error rate enormously, so the presence of water inside the packaging was clearly part of the problem. The trouble was that it wasn't the whole problem. When Engel arranged for a supply of a special desiccant material from a leading glass company and ran a test assembly process with a little desiccant inside every chip, some of them continued to fail. Evidently a second force was at work, too.

As a temporary solution to the problem, Intel reverted to the old, more expensive form of packaging. But the difference in price between the two kinds of package was nearly seventy cents per chip. On sales of a million units a month, that meant it was costing the company the equivalent of over $8 million a year to hang about while the problem remained unsolved. Engel and his colleagues suddenly began to feel pressure from the top of the company to find an answer quickly. Over the July 4th holiday weekend, the Santa Clara parking lot contained twenty cars—evidence that all the engineers on the team were inside, tearing their hair out, terrified that they (or at least their leader) would be fired if they didn't solve the problem.

Nearly a year after the problem had first been diagnosed a technician named Carl Ito came up with a clue that saved them. He reminded them of the "outgas" phenomenon—where alcohol could break down at high pressure when the glass melted, giving off water as a by-product that turned into miniature bubbles in the seal between the two pieces of ceramic. A quick test confirmed that Ito was right: Steam could be detected inside the furnace not only at 100°C, when water boiled, but also a second time when the temperature rose to 170°C. But how could the problem be eliminated?

Engel decided to try heating up the packages to 170°C *before* sealing them. The trouble was, he didn't have any special equipment for doing this. No matter; he'd invent some. Engel went off to the warehouse at the back of the fabrication area and dug out an old furnace. With a few adjustments, the furnace could be arranged to sit directly in front of the furnace in which the attached chips were normally sealed into their packages, with the belt from one furnace dropping the parts directly on the incoming belt to the next. With beating hearts, the engineers fired up the new "preheat" furnace and ran a set of die through the new process. This time, when the chips were cooled and put through their low-temperature test, they survived.

There was no corrosion to be seen inside. The problem was solved—and Intel could now save millions by switching back to the cheaper packaging.

Before the switch could take place, though, the new system of preheating the packages had to be up and running—not just in Santa Clara but also in Malaysia, 8,500 miles away. Intel had now moved the bulk of its assembly to a newly built site near Penang, the trading hub close to the country's northern tip. Late in spring 1975, Engel flew over to oversee the installation of a new preheat furnace that would allow the company to save that crucial seventy cents a million times a month. The trip would leave him with some extra time to look around the assembly plant and do a little sightseeing too.

On his return to Silicon Valley some weeks later, Engel submitted two trip reports. The first was part of Intel's standard practice: to get best value when it sent employees traveling around the world, the company asked them to write a detailed account of what they had done. The second report was something Engel had come up with on his own.

The young engineer had bad news for his bosses: He believed that a management group that had gone over to check on Penang in early 1974 had been given the runaround. The earlier visitors had praised a well-ordered plant; they'd reported smugly on how the operators were so disciplined that they would push their chairs neatly back in beneath the workbench when they got up to leave. By contrast, Engel found scenes of chaos. Engineers were holding completed silicon wafers in their bare hands. The plant managers didn't know what was going on in the plant; they were being snowed by the supervisors, who kept them from understanding what was happening with the workforce. More alarming still, there were problems with safety inside the plant. The equipment, by and large, was American-made, and designed to run at 110 volts; but the local power supply was 220, so the company had installed step-down transformers to convert. There was evidently a chronic shortage of spare parts, so where fuses had blown on the transformers or on other equipment, the plant electricians had *replaced them with normal electrical wire*. This was a cardinal sin, as even a trainee electrician could immediately tell. The whole purpose of the fuse was to blow if there was a sudden jolt of current, and act as a safety device to protect the expensive and sensitive equipment. By replacing the fuse with standard electrical wire, the plant electricians were almost guaranteeing that equipment would be damaged in the event of a problem with the power supply.

Loyal employee that he was, Engel submitted this second report, complete with a photograph of a smiling engineer holding a wafer in his bare hands to prove his point about the sloppy management in force. He explained in the report that the problems were more likely to be due to poor communication between Penang and California than to the electricians' incompetence. Engel sent one copy of his report to Gene Meieran, his boss, and another to Keith Thomson, the production chief who was Meieran's boss.

A few days later, when Engel had plunged into a new project, Meieran strode into his cubicle.

"Where's your copy of the memo?" he snapped.

"What memo?"

"The Penang trip report. The second one."

"I sent a copy to you, and another copy to Thomson," replied Engel, puzzled.

"I want the original."

"Why?"

"Just give it to me."

Intel's management had good reason for wishing to suppress the memo. On May 1, 1975, hours after Engel had submitted his report, a fire had broken out in the Penang plant, burning the entire facility to the ground and destroying all the equipment inside and much of the inventory.

The incident was troublesome enough because Penang accounted for more than half Intel's entire worldwide assembly capacity. To make matters worse, the plant had been in the middle of a particularly important production run of new parts, one hundred of which were due to be shipped off to Burroughs Corporation. Burroughs was about to bring out a new computer, and wanted to "qualify" the new parts before committing itself to buying tens of thousands of the new chips from Intel. Unable to deliver those hundred chips, Intel was now doomed to lose the Burroughs contract.

But the company was determined to get back to work as soon as possible. Rebuilding the Penang plant—and finding alternative capacity for chip assembly—became the company's number one priority in the second half of 1975. The plant manager proved an outstanding leader: By the end of the second week following the fire, his staff had assembled 100,000 devices in the old company cafeteria and shipped them out to California. For the medium term, however, another solution needed to be found. To their surprise, Noyce and Moore found that Intel's most bitter opponents in California—Mostek, for instance, which competed with Intel for DRAM business—suddenly displayed a kind of national solidarity after the incident in Penang. The local managers of competing companies in Penang offered Intel the chance to use their capacity temporarily at night, during the graveyard shift, while the rush job to rebuild the assembly plant went ahead. By the end of 1975, business in the plant was almost back to normal. Intel celebrated by throwing a giant party and giving out little plastic promotional plaques and ashtrays to employees who had worked extra hard to help get Penang back to normal.

Meanwhile, there was an insurance claim to make—not only for the loss of the plant and equipment but also for business interruption and the loss of contracts that resulted. Here Intel had been astonishingly lucky. Its business-interruption insurance had expired at the end of April 1975, and someone had forgotten to renew it. Only because of the zeal of Intel's insurance agent, the former New York Giants quarterback Y. A. Tittle, was the company able to make a claim. The faithful agent, assuming that Intel's credit would be good, had gone ahead and renewed the insurance without waiting for payment.

With millions of dollars at stake, the insurance companies soon appointed loss adjusters to make sure that they were not being required to make an excessive payout. Late in 1976 or early in 1977, the insurers asked to send an investigator to interview Paul Engel. Meieran briefed Engel before he went into the meeting, warning him just to answer the questions and not to volunteer anything. Asked to hazard a guess as to what might have caused the fire, Engel made no reference to the dangerously faulty wiring that he had noticed during his visit. Instead, he reminded the investigator that there were communist insurgents in Penang. One theory among the locals, he said, was that communists had actually launched a rocket at the Intel plant during the night.

That was not Engel's only brush with Intel's insurers. In November 1975, six months after the fire, he had been sent out to supervise the installation of two new custom-built furnaces that Intel had ordered from BTU, a manufacturer in Massachusetts. Knowing that its insurance company would pick up the tab, Intel paid over $15,000 to charter a 747 cargo jet so the bulky pieces of equipment could be drop-shipped directly from Boston to Penang. The first furnace arrived safely. The second, for some reason, was delivered to Hong Kong instead, where it was off-loaded from the aircraft in the middle of a monsoon and damaged by rain.

Late in December, the local plant manager called Engel aside.

"I need some help," he said.

He led the young engineer over to a building, burned down in the fire, that was now almost rebuilt.

"I've got one furnace in that factory," he said, pointing over to the makeshift shed where assembly was being carried out on a temporary basis until the new building could be occupied, "but if I shut it down and move it here, we'll lose a few days of production."

The manager went on to explain that if he tried to move the furnace, it would take three days after shutting it down before it was cool enough to move. But the second furnace that had been damaged in Hong Kong was sitting in a nearby warehouse.

"I want you to take a look," he asked. "Tell me if you think you can rebuild it."

Engel took a few men down and opened the box. The core of the furnace was a thirty-foot stainless steel tube, eighteen inches or so in diameter. It was divided into twelve horizontal zones, each with its own heating element and controller, surrounded by a layer of insulation. Beneath the sodden insulating materials, the electrical wiring was badly corroded.

"It's wiped out," reported Engel. "I'm not able to rebuild all this."

"Don't worry," said the plant manager. "We've got guys here who can fix the electrical stuff. What you need to do is find some replacement insulation."

The next day, Engel and a colleague boarded a plane for Singapore, where they started a frantic search for industrial furnace insulation ten thousand miles from home. They failed, but Engel did come across a company that was making a different kind of insulation that looked as though it might just fit the bill. Back at the hotel, he realized that he didn't have a choice. He ordered the insulation and took it back with him to Penang as excess baggage.

Three days later, Engel saw the sun rise over Penang as he and the local electricians finished the long sleepless job of reassembling the furnace with its improved insulation. They were ready to carry out a dry run. To everyone's delight, the repaired furnace not only worked the first time; also, the dials showed that when the furnace reached the required temperature, the controllers were delivering less power than intended. The replacement insulation was actually better than the original—and it would allow Intel to return to the rebuilt building without losing the crucial three days of production.

A month later, the plant manager grabbed Engel again.

"We have a small problem," he said. "We have an insurance guy here. You know that furnace you rebuilt?"

"Yeah?"

"We're trying to collect on it. We told this insurance guy that it wasn't salvageable, and he wants to see it."

Engel pointed impotently into the plant. "It's in there. We're running production on it," he said.

"Why don't you just tell him we're qualifying it?"

So Engel was forced to give a long, technically incomprehensible explanation to the insurance man, explaining that the operators had just started it up and were feeding a few qualification units through so that the reliability of the real production furnace on the other side of the plant could be checked. The insurance investigator looked skeptical at first, particularly since it was clear that there were thousands of units running through the furnace every hour. But Engel did a good sales job on him.

"Any qualms?" Engel asked rhetorically, looking back on the incident. "I was a committed soldier of Intel, and I was trying to help Intel. I figured I'd let Intel make the moral decisions. Am I going to burn in hell for it? Is the world a worse place for it? The answers to those questions are 'I don't know' and 'no.' Intel at the time was a very insecure company. People talk about it today, but we always thought that we were going to be put out of business the very next month. We didn't trample on anyone. We were just doing our best to stay ahead of the pack."

16

Gopen Beats the Union

Looking back on the hectic days of working at Intel during the mid-1970s, one employee picked an image that could only make sense after the popularization of the VCR.

"It was like life on fast-forward," he said.

Intel was engaged in a perpetual struggle to make its products not only more powerful but also smaller, faster, and cheaper. Dramatic improvements on these fronts were the best way to grab the attention of customers, and also the best way to keep ahead of the competition. But it wasn't only the company's chip-design engineers who were under this constant pressure to improve: Their work often resulted in a new product that was bigger and more complicated than its predecessor. The toughest battles were often fought elsewhere—in the fabs where the semiconductors were actually built.

In the early 1970s, with new people making new products using new processes in new plants, there were so many variables that yields in the industry were often very low. Even when a product was in full-volume manufacturing, it was common to get only five or ten good chips out of the hundred or more on each wafer—a ratio that would be simply laughable in most manufacturing industries. In the semiconductor business, which added so much value to its raw materials, a ratio like that could still make manufacturing profitable. A single working chip could fetch tens or even hundreds of dollars, while the raw materials it contained had been bought for only a few cents.

The axiom of the business was that the way to greater profitability lay in process improvements. If you could raise the number of good chips per wafer from five to ten, then your costs per chip went down by half and you could cut your prices sharply and still make more money. Equally, you could achieve the same effect by using bigger wafers, which had space for twice as many chips, thus potentially doubling your output every time you processed a set of wafers. Or you could use a tighter "design rule"—leave the circuit design the same but shrink it down further, like making the type smaller to get more words on a page—and magically get more chips for the same quantity of raw materials and processing.

The trouble was that any of these improvements would require changes to working practices inside the fabs. An increase in yield didn't happen by magic; in the absence of a major process change, it was the result of long months of examining carefully how the fabrication process worked and looking at ways to do it more cleanly and efficiently. To take the silicon wafer size up from two inches in diameter to three inches, as Intel did in 1973, you had to find a reliable source of perfectly regular crystalline silicon, precisely sawn into wafers of the right thickness—and then you had to change over much of your processing machinery to deal with the bigger wafer and find out the best way to lay out the circuits on the bigger wafer. Shrinking the design rule didn't just require using new lithographic techniques; it often necessitated a change of chemicals for the etching process, or a rearrangement of processing steps.

So Intel's fabs, like those of other semiconductor companies, were stressful and constantly changing places to work. Every few weeks there would be a new procedure to watch for, every few months a new piece of equipment to learn how to operate, every few years a change so major that the whole manufacturing process had to be almost relearned from scratch. And yet the people who worked in the fabs were not all engineers who had joined up in the hope of making hundreds of thousands of dollars in profits from stock options. Most of them were hourly paid people, often young women starting on little more than the minimum wage, whose principal skills were dexterity, attention to detail, reliability, and resistance to boredom.

Working in a wafer fab could make the most regimented job on a car assembly line look free-and-easy by comparison. You couldn't smoke, eat, drink, or wear cosmetics. You had to wear a protective suit, complete with white booties over your feet and a "snood" over your hair. And—at least in the days when many jobs were done by hand—you were liable to be criticized for picking something up in the wrong hand or attaching a wire one thirty-second of an inch too far to the left.

After Intel had built two fabs, one in the old Union Carbide plant in Mountain View and the other in a purpose-built site in Santa Clara, the company began to look further afield for its manufacturing sites. Skilled labor in the Valley was getting expensive, and there was the perennial problem of staff turnover. Nothing was more frustrating than spending months helping an operator to learn how to work a sensitive and unpredictable piece of machinery, only to see the same operator take a job down the street at National or Fairchild for a dollar more per hour. So it became a company objective to limit its workforce in the Valley to only around six thousand and take on new people by building plants elsewhere. Livermore, an hour's drive to the east, was the first of these. Oregon and Arizona, an hour's flight to the north and southeast, would follow later in the 1970s. By the 1980s, Intel abandoned the rule that no fab could be too far to get there and back from Santa Clara in a day, and built fabs in Israel and Ireland. Each time it built a new fab outside the Valley, the company could feed off a fresh labor pool, with few competitors to lure its best people away.

As the number of fabs grew, maintaining consistency among them began to be a problem. An essential starting point was to take some of the most productive people in one plant and send them over to the new one to teach the new hires how to do their jobs. This was harder to do than it sounds, because the consequence would always be a productivity hit in the first plant, with a resulting complaint from the angry fab manager that his best people had been taken away. But even with this "seeding" process complete, there could still be sharp differences between plant productivity.

With Andy Grove's scientific conviction that there must always be a best—that is, lowest-cost—way of running a fab, pressure grew to standardize completely. Grove called the campaign "McIntel," and told his staff that he wanted to see the same consistency between wafers fabricated in different Intel sites as he could see between hamburgers bought at different branches of McDonald's. Just in case the point wasn't clear, he had a large replica of a chip—silicon, not potato—made with a combination of Intel's logo and the golden arches of McDonald's stamped on the side. He posed behind it for *Intel Leads*, the company's internal newspaper.

Grove set up a series of groups of engineers from different plants and gave them the job of deciding which raw materials, which equipment, and which methods should be used throughout the company. One group, the Die Production Technical Review Board, was known familiarly as "Dipterb." He also encouraged the writing of a fat procedural manual that covered everything from how the floors should be swept to how plant managers should format their memos and file their expense claims.

In this sea of change, one stable rock was taken for granted: Intel was a nonunion company. It did not need to negotiate with an outside body when deciding how much to pay in wages, whom to promote, what rules to set. In the prospectus that took Intel public in 1971, the company's management had declared, "None of Intel's employees is represented by a labor union. Intel has experienced no work stoppages due to labor disputes and considers its relations with its employees to be excellent." And in the four years since, nothing had changed.

Then Howard Gopen, manager of Fab 3 in Livermore, saw one of the leaflets. Not yet thirty years old, Gopen was in charge of over five hundred people and several hundred million dollars' worth of plant, equipment, inventories, and work in progress.

He had been sent to Livermore when it opened in 1973 to work as the fab's first engineering manager. The job was a reward for a highly successful couple of years as process controller at Mountain View, where he had presided over an increase in yield from ten to thirty chips per wafer. He was a graduate of the City College of New York—the institution where Andy Grove received his first degree—but his origins were in Brooklyn rather than Hungary.

Gopen had participated fully in the rivalry between the fabs. He took a certain pride in the fact that Livermore, its interior painted persimmon instead of the company's standard shade of blue, could claim significantly higher yields than Mountain View. Now that he had overall responsibility for the whole plant, things were moving ahead still faster.

"We were running ten thousand wafer starts a week," he recalled. "This was a lotta product, a whole variety of processes and [devices]. Logic chips, SRAMs, EPROMs, everything except DRAMs because those were made in Oregon." Since Oregon was still relatively new and Fabs 1 and 2 were older and smaller, Livermore probably contributed more than half the company's entire output.

Its success was visible to even the most junior hire. Three shifts—the day, the swing, and the graveyard—were running every day of the week. All you had to do was go into the wafer sort area, look at the number of good die that were coming off each wafer, and go look them up in the trade mags to see how much they sold for, and you could see: This factory wasn't just making money. It was printing it.

And yet not much of the proceeds seemed to have trickled down to the workers. The standard Intel pay structure started people off at slightly above the minimum wage—never all the way down to the minimum, for that wouldn't give the right impression—and then gave them a series of promotions depending on productivity, seniority, and service. Because the plant was so new, the average wage at Livermore was considerably lower than at Mountain View. Yet there weren't many managers around to explain why this made sense, because the senior staffing had been done in a pretty spartan style too. Such engineers as there were had no time to stroll around and chat with operators.

"The mistake we made at the time was that we had very few supervisors," recalled Gopen. "The reason was because we gave people a title called assistant supervisor. This was the way we thought we could reward well-performing operators. We had a structure that had the operator working for assistant supervisors, who were working for supervisors." The ratio of operators to supervisors was like that of students to teachers in a school—something around thirty to one. As a result, much of the direct supervision was left to the assistants, who had had little training in dealing with the people who reported to them. So two explosive factors were coming together at the plant: a lack of humane, professional line management, and a growing feeling among the workforce that joining a union would bring them the rewards they deserved for their hard work.

Gopen got his first inkling of the problem only when he saw a flyer, handed out by one of the fab operators, calling on the workers in the fab to demand a vote on union representation.

"I remember the day when it happened. I had a tremendously sick feeling. Boy, something had gone astray."

In the quiet of his office, he picked up the phone and dialed a number in Santa Clara.

"Will, it's Howard."

Will Kauffman had been Gopen's fab manager back in his days at Mountain View. Now he was in charge of all fab areas across the company, plus all assembly and test. Kauffman was known as a "pressure sponge"—a calm, thoughtful man who could keep his head when under pressure from people above and below.

Quickly, he asked Gopen for more details. The young fab manager explained that there weren't any union reps on the site yet; it seemed simply that some of the employees had contacted the union and asked for help in organizing the facility. The management of the plant hadn't been forewarned, and some members of staff were already handing out leaflets to their colleagues, putting forward arguments why they needed to be represented.

The union was the United Auto Workers, one of the most powerful in the country. The UAW had broken managements at Ford, Chrysler, and General Motors. The prospect of having to communicate with the Livermore workforce through a local UAW organizer was one that filled Gopen with dread. He had not learned anything about labor unions in college, and at Intel, not only was there no training on how to deal with them, they were never even discussed.

Kauffman asked Gopen to obtain one of the leaflets and send it down to Santa Clara. He convened a meeting with Jim Olsen, Intel's VP of personnel, and Gordon Moore, the company president. For good measure, he also invited a senior labor lawyer from a prominent local firm that Intel used regularly on employee issues. Together with Gopen patched in from Livermore at the end of a telephone line, the group began to plot Intel's strategy.

Two principles were axiomatic. First, Intel must make sure at all costs that no union won representation rights at Livermore or anywhere else: to allow one to do so would be to invite a string of problems with personnel and management issues. Second, Intel must not allow its employees at Livermore to discover how much it cared about the issue. The response must be low-key, and coordinated through Gopen. No indication should be given that legal firepower was involved or that the company president was sitting in on the crisis meetings.

From those principles emerged a practical solution. The problem would be tackled with a series of communications. Intel would tell its Livermore staff that they had a legal right to a ballot over union representation, but it would bombard them with arguments—financial, practical, technical, intellectual, emotional—why voting for a union would be bad not only for the company but also for *them*.

By the time the Livermore workers who wanted a union had got signatures from 30 percent of the workforce asking for a ballot on representation, the Intel campaign was ready to roll. For every flyer

the UAW handed out, Intel had two more—apparently generated from inside the plant's management, but of course carefully prepared by the outside lawyers and vetted by the crisis committee in Santa Clara.

Then the bomb scares began.

Gopen was sitting at his desk in Livermore when the security guard rang up from reception.

"I've just had a call," he said. "There's a bomb in the plant."

A bomb? Intel's procedural manual was hundreds of pages long but it told you nothing about what to do when someone was about to blow up the entire plant. Down the corridor in the fab area, dozens of sensitive processes were taking place, many at high temperature, many using extremely dangerous chemicals, almost all of them precisely timed. You couldn't just tell everyone to drop their tools and walk out: Doing that might destroy weeks of work in progress, worth hundreds of thousands of dollars.

Gopen called Olsen in Santa Clara. They agreed to send out an order over the intercom to evacuate the building in as orderly a way as possible, while sending someone into the fab area to make sure that as many fabrication processes as possible that were actually in progress were completed safely before the shutdown. Gopen's next job was to go out to the parking lot to address the hundred-odd employees who had been evacuated. The staff made a strange group. Many of them, shivering in the brisk wind, were still dressed in bunny suits and snoods because they hadn't had time to change back into their day clothes before leaving the fab area.

Next, Gopen had to grab the plant security staff and arrange for them to make a thorough search of the entire site—with volunteers from the clean room on hand to make sure that nobody contaminated the fab areas by inadvertently breaching the rules on protective clothing and cleanliness inside.

Three hours later, the evacuated staff were back indoors and the plant was back to normal. No bomb had been found, and Gopen suspected that the hoax was perpetrated by someone who was taking the pro-union campaign to a new level. But something was missing. *Gopen hadn't called the police.* His instructions from Santa Clara were to handle the problem using only his own internal resources. Bringing in the cops, he was told, wouldn't substantially reduce the chance of another bomb scare—but it would certainly waste a lot of time to have a couple of beat officers escorted around the plant

asking dumb questions about processes and procedures they knew nothing about. There was also the question of publicity. The last thing Intel wanted was to see a headline in the local paper the next day saying BOMB HOAX HITS CHIP PLANT. Everyone knew that the first consequence of any such publicity was to encourage every crank in town to phone up and say he'd planted a bomb. So the scare was kept secret.

But it wasn't the only one. Over the coming weeks, Gopen was forced to shut down the fab five more times. Every time it happened the plant took a productivity hit; but it helped that the Livermore facility had suffered a few power failures in the past. The damage to work in progress always seemed to be minimal. Meanwhile, the company had put some proper procedures in place for what to do when there was a scare. Point one was to try to get the caller to provide a code word. This meant that if a scare ever did actually get followed by an explosion, then the company would be able to distinguish the real bomber in future from hoaxers. Point two was to step up the plant security all the time, so that there could be no risk from unattended packages anywhere on the site. People weren't such a problem, because entry to the site was already strictly controlled; if a bomb were ever to be planted, it would almost certainly have to be an inside job. Point three was to assess how serious the scare sounded. If the caller simply said there was a bomb in the plant, *forget it*. Only when the caller specified a time that it would go off and gave some location information showing at least a basic understanding of the plant layout would Gopen evacuate the staff. This approach was of course very different from the immediate evacuation that the police would probably have ordered after every call. But Intel had a business to run. Losing a few hours' output every week really mattered. After all, the mantra inside Intel ran, this is a small company in an industry of giants. *We might go under any moment*.

During the campaign running up to the ballot on unionization, Gopen decided to hold a number of meetings with the operators— arranged by supervisors, but without the supervisors themselves present. The idea was to impress on the staff that, quite separately from any issue of labor representation, Intel wanted to hear about their concerns, wanted to deal with any problems or complaints they had. To a young woman straight out of a community college, sitting down with Howard Gopen, the plant manager himself, was something of an honor.

Gopen learned two useful things during those meetings. One was that the support for bringing in the UAW was concentrated among the people who worked the swing shift and the graveyard—not surprisingly, since they were the people who saw Intel's senior management least frequently and were most at the mercy of capricious behavior by an untrained assistant supervisor. The other was that there was a real groundswell of discontent about one of Intel's personnel policies.

In accordance with Andy Grove's principles, the plant paid and promoted people on the basis of their performance reviews. For a worker in the fab area, those reviews were decided by three things: the standard of work the operator did (particularly the yield figures that could be traced back to that individual's own work); the output the operator did, measured by average number of wafer operations per hour or whatever; and attendance. Turning up late, everyone knew, was a disciplinary issue. You couldn't just walk in and out of the fab area when you felt like it—you had to go into your working area with the rest of your team when your shift began. What irked the staff most was that they were allowed to take time off without any penalty, if they gave the plant twenty-four hours' notice—but if they were sick one morning and couldn't come, there would be an immediate effect on their compensation. A low attendance figure affected your performance review for the month, your bonus, *and* your pay increase.

From the company's point of view, this seemed to make perfect sense. Unscheduled absences forced the plant management to scramble to find people to fill in for the missing body, and if an appropriately trained replacement couldn't be found then there would be an immediate loss of product. But to the operators, who didn't have any experience of what it was like on the other side, the system seemed manifestly unfair. Why should you be allowed to take a few days off just for fun, when you got penalized for being sick after the first eight hours? "I can't predict when I'm going to be sick. It'll count against me."

It was a delicate balancing act to find ways of resolving the employees' complaints without making it look too much as though the company was backing down under pressure from the union ballot. To help distract attention, Andy Grove himself went down to Livermore. The visit was billed as just a regular site visit from the company's senior VP—but it was carefully timed to allow Grove to talk to the people on all three shifts. He'd arrive early in the morning and address the graveyard operators as they came off. Then a second meeting with the day shift. Then a day's work at the fab, talking over strategy with

Gopen and other people there, and filling in the free time with a couple of hours of phone calls from a spare desk. And then, at the end of the day, another talk with the swing shift people who had just arrived. As the voting drew to a close on the day of the ballot, Gopen waited anxiously with his colleagues to hear the result. Over 50 percent, and Intel would be dealing for the first time in its history with the United Auto Workers. Below 50 percent and life would return to normal.

The result was a walkover: Only one in five members of the work force voted for representation. Part of the victory was due to a conviction among the fab operators that Intel was, after all, a good employer who would treat them well and reward them fairly for their work. Part of it was due to a genuine attempt by Gopen and his colleagues to make their management of the facility more open and to listen more carefully to what the individuals under their charge had to say. But part of the victory was also the result of a successful, military-style campaign, convincing the staff of the carrots they would receive if they stayed unrepresented and the sticks they'd get beaten with if they didn't. For instance, the leaflets had pointed out in a dry, factual way that if workers went on strike and picketed outside the plant, they needed to realize that the company had the right to fire them and bring in replacements to take over their jobs.

That representation ballot at Livermore was probably the closest Intel ever came to dealing with a labor union. The effort that the company put into defeating the prorepresentation movement was an indication of how much the company wanted to avoid unionization. But the outcome of the ballot was also proof of something else. When there was a contest between Intel and the UAW to see who best could manage a campaign for the hearts and minds of employees, who could offer the right mixture of hope and fear, who could deliver the most cogent arguments in the most persuasive leaflets, there was no contest: Intel won hands down. In the end, the ballot result was proof that Intel knew its own workers better than the outside organizers of the labor union did.

17

The Stopgap

When Andy Grove was trying to hire someone into the company, he usually made great predictions about Intel's future. It helped that he believed every word he said. But sometimes, his hard sell went too far.

A case in point was Bill Lattin, one of the leading experts on semiconductor fabrication processes at Motorola. Grove contacted Lattin in 1971 and delivered an uncompromising pitch intended to make him join Intel.

"Grove had a very abrasive style," Lattin recalled. "It didn't work well with me. . . . The recruiting style was: Motorola doesn't have a chance—we're going to kick their butts."

Lattin's response was to refuse, politely, and go back to his job at Motorola determined to work with renewed vigor to prove his interviewer wrong. When Intel developed the 1102 memory chip for Honeywell, Lattin obtained a copy of the specification from Honeywell and led a small team that built a copy of the chip. Motorola also produced a second-sourced 1103, by which time the team was confident enough to design a new memory chip of its own. But every year, Grove would pass through Phoenix and ask Lattin again to come and interview for a job at Intel.

"So Andy was still telling me I was with the losers? That inspired me to go to work with the losers and work harder."

It took a little more time for Lattin to win a moral victory against

Grove. When Intel's first 8-bit microprocessor came out, Lattin started a program inside Motorola to develop a more powerful 8-bit processor. Soon after the appearance of Intel's 8080, Motorola was in the market with the new chip, which it called the 6800. The Motorola offering was a shock to Intel: It was neater than the Intel chip in a number of ways, most importantly that it required only one 5-volt power supply instead of the three different power supplies that the 8080 demanded.

What was it that made Grove so determined to hire his engineer? Partly it was that he had taught Lattin, and knew how good he was. When Grove was lecturing a course on semiconductor physics at Berkeley—a part-time assignment he had taken on while still at Fairchild—Lattin had been one of his most promising students. It had been a source of irritation to Grove that Lattin audited the course instead of taking it for credit, and the teacher had given his student a hard time as a result.

But maybe there was more to it than that. Lattin's background was quite different from Grove's, the refugee from Hungary who worked his way through City College before going on to Berkeley. Lattin had done badly in high school and volunteered for the U.S. Navy. But his history revealed the same pattern: an unpromising start, with an advance to academic distinction through raw talent. His first real education came at the Navy's own electronic technician school, which he quit to go to Bible school in Portland, Oregon, after undergoing a religious conversion. Lattin then joined a local company as an electronic technician and started studying at night. After two years at Ventura Junior College in southern California, he switched to Berkeley and decided to stay on for a master's. By 1975, when he was manager of Motorola's entire MOS division and responsible for all memory and microprocessors, he was working in his spare time on a Ph.D.—and Grove was still trying to persuade him to come to Intel.

Internal politics finally made Lattin give in. After the electronics recession in the second half of 1974, Motorola asked him to move his department from Phoenix to Austin, Texas. Before going, Lattin extracted a commitment from his boss at Motorola that the engineers who showed their loyalty by moving would be secure if they went. The move took place in the summer of 1975. Four weeks later, the man who had made the commitment lost his own job, and his successor demanded layoffs. Lattin told the new boss he'd rather leave than break his promise to the engineers. Within weeks, he had moved to Intel, bringing half a dozen of Motorola's brightest in his wake.

Lattin's first job was to lead a team of chip designers working on an extremely advanced architecture, to be called the 8800. Since this would reduce the number of people reporting to him from three hundred at Motorola to just five, he was not at first impressed. But then he began to look at the processor that the team had begun to design. In typical Intel style, it wasn't trying to make an incremental improvement on the 8080; instead, the company's ambition was to make a revolutionary jump ahead of current microprocessor technology. The new chip was going to have fault tolerance and self-checking hardware. It would handle true multitasking and variable-length instructions. Most radical of all, it would recognize different data types and would exhibit the "object-oriented" approach that was only to become fashionable in the computer business more than a decade later. It was also going to be the biggest chip Intel had ever built: 300 mils (thousandths of an inch) on each side, compared with the 166×125 that was the die size of the 8080. This alone was a technological leap of amazing daring; since errors tended to be scattered randomly across the silicon wafer, Intel had to do a cluster study just to find out what chance there was of finding a defect-free part of the wafer big enough to hold the chip.

Lattin was so astounded by what he saw in the project plans that he went to see Gordon Moore, the company's resident stargazer as well as its chief executive.

"Gordon, you want me to be program manager on this thing," he began. "But this computer is so sophisticated that I'm not going to be able to tell you whether it's a good architecture. . . . This is not like 6800s. This is all the mainframe concepts kinda rolled into a microprocessor."

Moore was undaunted. For all the success of the 8080 to date, Intel wasn't making any serious inroads into the computer business itself. The architects of mainframes were still laughing at Intel's microprocessors as too puny and short on features to be taken seriously as the basis of a computer architecture. This new design, Moore believed, would be the one that would catapult Intel into the computer business. He sent Lattin away inspired, reassured, and convinced that the company's top management was behind the project 100 percent.

But it was to Grove, not to Moore, that Lattin had to report from month to month as the 8800 project progressed. Once he had agreed to take on the new processor, he became responsible for whatever obstacles the team encountered. There were many such obstacles—and with Grove's system of management by objectives and key results, with regular one-on-ones to probe the details of exactly what was going on, there was nowhere to hide.

"Every review, the schedule slipped," Lattin recalled. "Andy wanted hard schedules, hard facts, and we were in research. I got my butt cleaned every review we had—brutally. I'm kind of from the Motorola culture, where it's a lot less confrontational."

Lattin was caught between Grove's demands for progress and the reluctance of the researchers working for him to make decisions. Justin Rattner, the brilliant architect who was supposed to be responsible for finalizing the new chip's specification, was particularly difficult in this respect. He was never quite done; in the end, Lattin would find himself in the office late at night pulling the specification pages off the printer one by one in an attempt to meet his deadlines and avoid the humiliation of another dressing down.

After one particularly painful session, Lattin was reduced to making a personal appeal to Grove.

"Andy," he said, "if you're going to criticize me, you've got to spend some time coaching me."

Wiser heads at Intel could have reassured Lattin that this intense pressure was just one of the problems of making great technological jumps. The company would crank up the heat month by month, but it wouldn't kill the 8800 project. And whatever people said, there was enough money, enough patience, and enough technical know-how to give the research the time it needed.

While Intel remained as committed as ever to Lattin's project, it had hired a new hotshot marketing ace to take the company's microprocessor effort by the scruff of the neck and turn it into a serious business for Intel. His name was Bill Davidow, and his arrival signaled the company's realization that microprocessors could no longer be dismissed as a market made up just of hobbyists and calculator manufacturers. Until then, funding of microprocessor projects had always been attacked by the memory guys as a waste of resources. "Let's quit dicking around," they'd say. "Computer memory is where the big money is. This microprocessor stuff may be good publicity, but it isn't bringing in any profits. We should get out of the business now, and concentrate on what we're good at."

Davidow's contribution to the debate on the 8800 was simple but effective. He agreed that work on the radical new processor should go ahead, but he raised a tough question: Did Intel need something to fight off the competition with in the meantime? All the company had was the 8085 chip, an 8080 with a few catch-up modifications that followed Zilog's lead in putting the unused op-codes to work. But Zilog was known to be developing a new 16-bit chip known as the Z8000—and Bill Lattin brought with him the knowledge that Motorola had already begun a 16-bit development project that would be called the 68000.

Davidow pondered for a while how best to obtain an impartial assessment of the new project and its problems. He picked a young software engineer named Steve Morse, who had been on the payroll for less than a year and therefore owed no great allegiance to either its supporters or its detractors, and asked him to write an assessment of the new processor design. Brilliant and intense, Morse shared with Grove the distinction of having spent some years teaching at Berkeley. He could be expected to apply some academic rigor to the task. To help him, Morse brought in as an assistant a junior Intel engineer who happened to be one of his former students.

Morse's report, when it arrived in April 1976, confined itself to an assessment of the architectural flaws in the design of the new chip. Over fifty-seven pages long, it identified fifteen errors and omissions from the specification; nine points that needed clarification if the spec was to make sense; four problems that, if uncorrected, would slow down the processor's effective operating speed to a crawl; and thirty-seven software-related issues of varying degrees of importance that Morse suggested needed attention. Nowhere did the report say that the processor was fatally misconceived and should be abandoned. But line by line, point by point, it destroyed the new chip's credibility.

Too much was riding on the project already for Intel to kill the work solely on the advice of a pair of young scientists. But Davidow and his colleagues had to face facts. Morse had uncovered enough problems to reveal that this processor would not be ready for some years to come. Unless Intel acted quickly, it would have no response to the two new superchips promised by Zilog and Motorola. And everyone knew what happened to technology companies that allowed others to improve on their good ideas without fighting back.

"Terry, you've got ten weeks to design a processor."

Bill Davidow looked at the faces around the table to gauge their reactions. The other participants in the meeting were all men, all in their late twenties or early thirties, and all wearing open-neck shirts.

All had fought their corner vociferously, shouting and swearing at their fellow engineers and rapping the table to get their points across. As the windowless room had filled with cigarette smoke over the past two hours, one idea after another had been suggested, only to be dismissed as "crazy" or "idiotic" by someone who thought differently. But gradually, a consensus had begun to form.

Now the time had come to enforce a decision. At forty-one, Davidow was the oldest man in the room. His job as general manager of the division gave him authority, or "position power," as the guys liked to call it; but it was his depth of experience—notably at the helm of General Electric's R&D labs and later Hewlett-Packard's minicomputer business—that gave him "knowledge power." When he spoke, the others knew that they were listening to the accumulated wisdom of twenty years in the computer industry.

Terry Opdendyk, the man Davidow was addressing, was almost a self-parody of an Intel manager: very young, very talented, very brash. After graduate school, he had learned the ropes of software design at Hewlett-Packard; now, at twenty-eight, he was running a department that most companies would have made him wait another ten years for. To him, the "constructive confrontation" favored by Intel was natural. His Dutch ancestry had given him a streak of obstinacy and a taste for a fight. Although he could never say that Intel was a pleasant place, he would later describe it as "the most exciting, stimulating, demanding, exhilarating, fatiguing place I've ever worked." But not even Opdendyk could get his engineering team to deliver a new processor architecture in ten weeks.

Sure, he understood the reason for imposing such a deadline. Once the big architectural decisions about the processor had been made, there was still much to do. First came the basic circuit design, then checking, then months of prototyping and fine-tuning, then sampling on silicon, and then tweaking the production process in order to manufacture it at reasonable cost. At any stage, a single missed connection to any of the hundreds of thousands of transistors in the design could send the team back to the drawing board. When all the stages were timetabled, the conclusion was inescapable: if the project was to be completed within Davidow's one-year deadline, the basic architecture could only be given ten weeks.

Young though he was, Opdendyk knew that if he accepted the demand being pressed on him by the rest of the meeting, he would be up against the conventional wisdom in the industry: one man, one chip, one year. The ten-week deadline was barely realistic. Yet if he committed himself to delivering the architecture in ten weeks, there would be no going back. At other companies, he might have been able to find excuses: He could say afterwards that the commitment had been conditional on this or that, which had not materialized. At Intel, Andy Grove could be relied on to scribble down what had been said on his agenda sheet, and to pull out the sheet triumphantly months later, quote the undertaking verbatim, and demand to know what had gone wrong. Self-preservation told Opdendyk that he must refuse.

Yet for once, his Dutch grandparents failed him. Knowing that the ten-week deadline was impracticable, he still couldn't argue his colleagues into giving him more time. They knew that once the architecture was finished, they would have just as tough a time in meeting their own deadlines; and they knew that giving their colleague more time meant giving themselves less. When the meeting broke up, he had agreed to a ten-week delivery. As he walked down the corridor, Opdendyk could console himself with one thought: At least there was no difficulty in finding a specialist to design the chip architecture. Steve Morse had already shown himself to be a gifted engineer in an earlier project. As author of that damning report, he had been the chief critic of the 8800. Justice required that he should be made the architect of the stopgap. Others would have to take part to make sure that the architecture was suitable for the circuit designers and the manufacturing people. But the bulk of the work during the ten weeks would be carried out by Morse himself. This would be the first time that a software specialist rather than a component man from the hardware side had been entrusted with a processor architecture but that might well prove an advantage rather than a drawback. Opdendyk knew that Intel's early processors had been designed by people who knew little about programming computers. With his own background at HP, he had spotted some features that would make the 8080 troublesome and difficult to use, and had successfully incorporated some changes that made it a little more friendly. Offering the prototype 8080 to a programmer accustomed to the ease of use of an IBM machine, he believed, was like offering a military-specification field telephone to an old lady who wanted to call her grandchildren across town.

Morse needed no prompting to see things from a programmer's point of view. But the young software engineer also had a quality that was of great significance in chip architecture: his academic discipline. This was evident not only in the rigorous approach he took to his work but also in everything else he did. When Morse decided to trace his family's immigrant origins, for instance, he'd spent painstaking hours in the registry at Ellis Island looking for possible misspellings of his family name and cross-checking the boats on which his grandparents and their cousins had arrived from central Europe. His research done, Morse had photocopied the documents and gummed them neatly into a series of albums together with his photos, every edge perfectly aligned and every caption carefully phrased. The same fastidious attention to detail was evident in every chip he worked on.

And so it was that in May 1976, Steve Morse set to work on the architecture of Intel's new stopgap processor. Every morning at eight sharp, he would meet Opdendyk to deliver a progress report. For the rest of the day, and often late into the night, he would work at his design with pencil and paper, occasionally making use of the adding machines that were still rare in the office. Discussions with the people who would take the processor to the next stage were essential; for this, Morse would trot between Intel's two Santa Clara buildings, or into the annex that had been built on the other side of the Central Expressway. Meanwhile, Opdendyk's job was to field the political flak.

In essence, the design challenge that faced Morse was a simple one. If the new 16-bit chip was to offer a significant speed advantage over the 8-bit 8080, it had to be different in a number of important respects. But Intel also wanted to encourage repeat business from its customers, and one way to do so was to allow them to upgrade a system designed for the less powerful processor so that it would also work with the newer one. Ideally, therefore, the new stopgap processor should run every program ever written for the 8080.

Morse soon came to the conclusion that it would be impossible to meet both of these objectives. The 8080 chip had offered programmers a range of 111 possible instructions; his design required 133. But the new chip's instruction set was not just the old set plus twenty-two new instructions. It left out a few of the old ones. When Intel's marketing people got wind of this, they were terrified. Wouldn't this seemingly small change, they asked, mean that programs written for the 8080 chip would fail to run properly on the new model? Not so, replied Morse. All that was needed was a little translation scheme that mapped each of the dropped instructions from the 8080 onto one or more instructions on the new processor that would have the identical effect. So with a little extra work, customers would after all be able to benefit from the time they had spent learning the intricacies of the 8080, and reuse software written for the older chip. In its ads and its data sheets, Intel would still be able to utter the magic word "compatible."

The need to make the new processor compatible with the old threw up a second, more serious problem: what to do about memory capacity. When the 8080 was in design, Intel had only recently launched its 1103 chip, and memory had still been an expensive, scarce commodity. Since then, Intel had improved its manufacturing as well as its designs, and was able to build chips at much higher yield. More important, competitors had come into the market, forcing prices to fall sharply. By 1976, the price of memory was less than a tenth of what it had been four years earlier. So customers were beginning to dream up products that required not only a faster processor but also much more memory. How could Morse give his new design a big increase in storage capacity without destroying the work he had done to preserve compatibility with the current model and without taking so long to implement his ideas that Terry Opdendyk would overshoot his deadline?

Morse's starting point had to be the 8080 design. To keep track of what was where, the processor assigned an "address" to each place where a number was stored, like a numbered label on a pigeonhole. The addresses were 16-bit binary numbers, implying a total capacity of 65,536 addresses. This had been an acceptable ceiling when designers had to be careful with their use of memory. But buyers now wanted to use more memory—and would start bumping up against the 64K limit.

The obvious answer was to make the addresses longer. By adding four more binary digits, Morse could increase the potential memory capacity sixteenfold at a stroke, to something over one million possible addresses—a megabyte of memory. But then the question arose: How could the new addressing system work with software designed for the old system? Here Morse had a flash of brilliance. He decided to group the addresses together, sixteen at a time, into "segments." If you were running 8080 software, the old address would still work: Since there would be up to 65,536 different segments, an old-style short address would simply point to the first slot in each segment. If you were writing software for the new machine, you would use the longer address, with the 4 extra bits added at the end to give you access to the other fifteen addresses in each segment.

This approach did have a drawback. The new processor dealt with numbers 16 bits at a time; yet the "segmented addressing" system required 20 bits. This meant that to work with the 20-bit addresses, the processor had to do some funny additions using a "segment register," shifting the 16-bit addresses four digits to the left and back again so they could make sense in a 20-bit addressing scheme.

What Morse produced—and what the circuit designers and fab people would within the year turn into a finished chip, manufactured and ready for sale to Intel's customers—was something that purists would view as a kludge: an inelegant, botched design. But it fulfilled brilliantly the task that it set out to do. It took users of the old, slow 8-bit 8080 into the age of much faster 16-bit processing. It allowed them to build systems with a megabyte of memory. And, most important of all, it allowed them to continue to use all the software they had written for the old processor—with only very minor modifications. To convey these two key selling points of backward compatibility but higher performance, the new stopgap chip was given the part number 8086. It was introduced in June 1978.

The contrast between the delays that plagued the 8800 and the speedy development of the 8086 can be reduced to two key points. First, the 8800 suffered from what people in IBM called "second system syndrome." The designers of a new computer system, the folklore ran, always had to drop some of their best ideas along the route—and could never resist the fatal, counterproductive temptation to try to incorporate all of them the next time around. This had happened in abundance with the advance architecture under Bill Lattin's reluctant management. Second, the unreasonable deadline and the compatibility compromises had proven a blessing in disguise for Morse. By constraining his room for maneuver—like a classroom teacher giving the students an essay topic instead of letting them write about whatever they want—his supervisors had forced him to exercise his creativity in a more focused way.

At the time of the launch of the 8086, it was impossible to tell how the chip would fare against the yet unannounced competing products from Motorola and Zilog. But the result of the rushed development program was that Intel was still in the microprocessor game. The big battle was yet to come.

18

Marriages and Divorces

Ann Bowers, Intel's head of human resources, had always been slightly in awe of Bob Noyce since that day when he came into her office to confront her about the naming of the street outside Intel's Santa Clara facility as Bowers Avenue. Intimidated by his legendary status as one of the fathers of the semiconductor industry—not to mention his chairmanship of the company—she took to calling him "Dr. Noyce."

"Would you please stop calling me that?" he'd complain. "It makes me feel a hundred years old."

Noyce was well into his forties, ten years older than Bowers, and apparently happily married with children. He was as keen as ever on tennis, scuba-diving, and sailing—and his sense of humor and presence all made him a man of immense personal magnetism to both men and women. Bowers was not immune to his charms.

"We didn't see much of each other," she said afterwards. "I was very careful that it stayed that way."

Every so often, Noyce would stand by her cubicle and start one of those casual conversations that from anyone other than the company chairman would have sounded like a come-on. *I want to talk to you about the way you got to be the way you are*, he'd say. *Because I've got a daughter, and I'd like her to be like you.*

"There was always some chemistry, but Bob was married. . . . Then one Friday afternoon he appeared in my office and said: 'I'm going to take some people up to the Nut Tree for dinner. Would you like to go?' He frequently asked other friends I knew, and for God knows what reason, I said yes."

Ann Bowers canceled her plans for the evening and went to join the party at dinner. Somehow, there'd been a car shuffle, so Bob had to take her back in his car—and the two of them were together for the first time without anyone else around.

"By the way, I presume you know that I'm getting a divorce," he said. Bowers was so shocked that she almost jumped out of the car.

"I thought: *This is going to be very dangerous, very messy,*" Bowers recalled. Noyce explained that he had told Gordon Moore and Andy Grove about the breakup of his marriage, assuming that they would pass the word around the company. But neither of them did; office gossip wasn't exactly high on their list of priorities. Ann Bowers, the woman who had told herself the very first time she met Bob Noyce five years earlier that he was the man she wanted to marry, was the last to know that he was now available.

What Noyce had done wasn't unusual. The rigors of work in the semiconductor industry were often too great for marriages to hold together. In his 1983 profile of Noyce for *Esquire*, Tom Wolfe wrote:

In the Silicon Valley a young engineer would go to work at eight in the morning, work right through lunch, leave the plant at six-thirty or seven, drive home, play with the baby for half an hour, have dinner with his wife, get in bed with her, give her a quick toss, then get up and leave her there in the dark and work at his desk for two or three hours on "a couple things I had to bring home with me." Or else he would leave the plant and decide, well, maybe he would drop in at the Wagon Wheel for a drink before he went home. . . . So then he wouldn't get home until nine, and the baby was asleep, and dinner was cold, and the wife was frosted off, and he would stand there and cup his hands as if making an imaginary snowball and try to explain to her . . . while his mind trailed off to other matters, LSIs, VLSIs, alpha flux, de-rezzing, forward biases, parasitic signals, and that tera-sexy little cookie from Signetics he had met at the Wagon Wheel, who understood such things.

But there was something odd about this happening to Bob Noyce. He was, after all, both the son and grandson of ministers of the church. He was a guy whom everyone looked up to. He was the leading advocate of the view that Intel should try to be a more ethical company than its competitors.

Who knows what went wrong during his twenty-one years of marriage with Betty Noyce? While Bob had accumulated his fame, his job title as company chairman, his hundreds of millions of dollars, his Los Altos house—Betty was not content to be just the spouse of everybody's best friend. She put her foot down early on and made it clear that she was not willing to be just a dutiful company hostess. When someone introduced her at a party as "Bob Noyce's wife," it was with a little glint of steel as well as a smile that she replied, "No, actually I'm Betty Noyce."

Her insistence on carving out for herself a life independent of the company and Bob's achievements earned Betty Noyce the reputation of being a "feminist." In those days, that was the only word you could use for a woman of intelligence and spirit, strength and independence, who wanted some life outside her husband's shadow.

The divorce, when it took place, followed a monumental row at the house in Maine where the family spent their summers. Betty took the house in Maine; Bob took the house in Los Altos, and they divided the Intel stock between them. Betty Noyce immediately became such a large shareholder that even the rumor that she was planning to sell her shares in the company was enough to send Intel's stock price spiraling down.

Meanwhile, a few miles up Highway 101 in Sunnyvale, Jerry Sanders was having partnership problems of his own. Not with his wife: That would come later. This time, Sanders's parting was with Ed Turney, the fast-talking salesman who had been Sanders's best man at his wedding in Las Vegas.

AMD had survived the 1974 chip recession, but only just. The company's stock bottomed out at $1.50, one-tenth of the price set at the IPO two years earlier—and its losses during the recession wiped out all the profits it had earned to date. Looking back on the problems of 1974 during a public speech the following year, Sanders would joke that just about everything that could go wrong had gone wrong. "If I'd owned a dog," he said, "it would have died."

Turney had a reputation for betting big on the stock market—and also on the silver market. In December 1974, under pressure to meet margin calls, he put his long-standing friendship with Sanders to the test. Turney went into the AMD chairman's office and asked for a personal loan of $50,000.

Jerry Sanders had a high income to dispose of. With the approval of the board of directors, he had awarded himself a princely salary in the depths of the trough—and when he discovered that Wilf Corrigan, who had recently taken over the helm of Fairchild, used a Rolls-Royce Silver Cloud as his company car, Sanders had felt obliged to trump him by buying the British carmaker's new Corniche model. Yet whether Jerry Sanders could afford to lend even his closest friend such a sum of money from his own pocket was debatable. Despite his handsome terms at AMD, Sanders still lived beyond his income. Not only were there the two houses, one in Malibu and one in Atherton; there were also racks of lavish clothes, a taste for fine restaurants and French champagne, and the annual shopping trip that he took with his wife, Linda, to Paris, always stopping in New York on their way back to California. Jerry wasn't the kind of guy to leave $50,000 in the bank when there were so many great ways to spend it. But the company was a different matter. Despite its temporary financial difficulties, AMD was clearly in a position to make a modest loan to a valued officer in need—if that was what the company's chairman believed was in the company's interests.

Asked about the incident afterwards, Turney would say little about that fateful meeting: "Some personal things . . . evolved out of that [which] I won't get into between Sanders and myself relative to stock positions." But some of the other AMD founders soon heard an account of the meeting between the two men. They were told that Turney had asked for a loan. Sanders had complained about what he saw as slipping performance in Turney's work. Turney had then walked out of the room without the $50,000 check he had asked for. Whether he jumped or was pushed, Jerry Sanders's best man left AMD on December 4, 1974—and was forced by the need to support himself to sell his 76,500 shares in the company. Turney's timing was terrible; at the point when he sold, AMD stock was close to its all-time low. Had he been able to hold on for another couple of years, Turney would have been able to retire with nearly $3 million in the bank.

With Turney now out of the way and business beginning to recover within a year, Jerry Sanders now had bigger things to worry about—the most important of which was a potential lawsuit from Intel, where Roger Borovoy had begun to take the initiative himself. He had threatened to launch a complaint against AMD, claiming that Sanders had infringed Intel patents by second-sourcing the company's highly profitable EPROM. Thanks to Joe Friedrich's tricks, discovering how to get the EPROM to yield had been an unusually troublesome business, and it had taken AMD nearly twice as long as expected before it had a working part that was yielding reasonable quantities in production. So it was a particular disappointment for Sanders to be faced with a legal challenge when the profits had just begun to flow after so much hard work.

The AMD chairman was forced to recognize that a turning point had been reached. In the past, AMD had been so light-footed that it had delivered its second-source parts with impressive speed. On one occasion, with a 4K static RAM chip, Sanders had actually beaten Noyce and Moore to it. His ad campaign for the part ran under the headline: WE WERE GOING TO SECOND SOURCE INTEL, BUT WE COULDN'T WAIT. No matter that the AMD part was expensive to make and cumbersome to use. Although it had been swiftly superseded by better designed parts from both Intel and TI, AMD had still managed to make an excellent return on the chip because it got designed into military systems. This guaranteed AMD a steady flow of repeat orders at prices far higher than those in the commercial market.

But it was getting increasingly hard to keep up. AMD's ambition to build a range of its own proprietary chips was beginning to look impossible to achieve. Profits from the EPROM and DRAM had allowed Intel to grow to three times AMD's size—and the creation of the microprocessor had changed the rules of the game by introducing new complexities and raising the costs of research. There must now be serious doubt as to whether AMD could keep up if it tried to develop a range of parts of its own. Sanders was forced to recognize that second sourcing was his destiny. But second sourcing was no longer as easy as it had once been. The industry was concentrating, and its players were increasingly using patents, trade secrets, and copyrights as bargaining counters to strengthen their lead.

Gordon Moore, who had given the go-ahead for Borovoy to start pursuing AMD, was second only to Andy Grove in his disapproval of the behavior of second-source companies who stole ideas from the real innovators and sought to make money from them. One Intel engineer, discussing with Moore the components that would have to be brought in from outside to build a development system, had unwisely suggested that Intel save money by buying a second-sourced Fairchild part from AMD. Abandoning his usually mild demeanor, Moore had declared angrily that he would never even consider the idea. But Jerry Sanders knew that he had a fan in Bob Noyce, so it was to Noyce that he went in an attempt to resolve the EPROM dispute. A meeting was soon set up at Intel's Santa Clara headquarters.

The participants must have made a striking contrast. On one side of the table in the conference room was rumpled, charismatic Bob Noyce, lighting one True Blue from the stub of the previous one. Next to him sat a testy and visibly hostile Andy Grove, still in his gold-chain and muttonchops whiskers phase, with four or five other Intel microprocessor people all in open-neck shirts and ready to let rip a bit of constructive confrontation at the first opportunity. On the other side, were a handful of members of the ADM crew, trained by their chairman to speak only when spoken to, and Sanders himself. From the toes of his polished shoes to his pressed Italian suit, from his crisp white shirt to his even crisper silvering hair, Sanders looked as though he still had ambitions to be in the movies. It was only when you listened to his presentation and heard him delivering his spiel about patents and partnerships, intellectual property and litigation, with a full command of the jargon of the chip business, that you remembered this was electronics, not entertainment.

"Jerry is very self-assured," said one of his partners many years later. "When he speaks extemporaneously, he's at his best. From prepared notes, he doesn't come across so well. He has a method, a unique way of stating a premise and building a faultless logical argument that you can't confute. The trick is, the premise is incorrect most of the time. So you have to listen real carefully to what he says."

After he had said his piece, Sanders sat back to hear what Noyce and his colleagues had to say. It soon became clear that the news was better than it had first appeared. Intel was not out to drive AMD out of business. After an hour's talk, not exactly friendly but not hostile either, Sanders drew the meeting to a close and led his followers back to camp.

Two months later, Sanders strode into his office at AMD's headquarters and called his executive staff meeting to order.

"Tomorrow," he said, "I'm going to sign a license agreement with Intel for the 8085."

A couple of the members of his executive staff smiled. They had spent the last six weeks waist deep in negotiations, with Sanders staying away from the meetings but determined to keep control of every detail. The rest of the company's officers had been kept in the dark about the negotiations that followed the set-piece meeting on Intel turf—and when they heard the news, the meeting broke into spontaneous applause. They had never believed it possible that Sanders would persuade Intel formally to give him the rights to one of its processors. Yet he seemed to have succeeded in doing just that. How?

Intel had wanted three things from AMD. It wanted money for what it believed to be the use of Intel's intellectual property in AMD's knockoff EPROMs. It wanted the right to second-source AMD products when it chose—notably a neat little gadget called a "floating-point unit," which was designed to slot in next to an 8080 microprocessor and carry out complex math calculations at blistering speed. And it wanted to strengthen its own position in the microprocessor market. With Zilog's Z80 out there hammering sales of the 8080, Intel needed to increase the credibility of its own 8085 while the 8086 design worked its way to manufacturing. Having AMD as a credible alternative source of supply was a good start.

Appreciating what Intel wanted, Sanders had been able to extract some surprisingly valuable concessions. He'd won full second-source rights over the 8085, including the right to use the name, to advertise full compatibility with the Intel product, and to repackage Intel's technical manuals with an AMD cover. The second-source rights meant that AMD would not have to go to the trouble of painstakingly photographing, studying, and testing the Intel part. Instead, it would simply receive a set of Intel's masks, which it could then use in its own fab to start pumping out 8085s. But Sanders had instructed his negotiators to make it clear that rights to the 8085 alone would not be enough to start AMD off on the track of paying royalties to Intel: The larger company would have to offer something more.

Intel had then placed one more card on the table. The offer came from Roger Borovoy, Intel's general counsel.

"Roger was telling us that certain future circuits were likely to be microprogrammed, and he would give us the right to copy this microprogram," Sven Simonsen recalled. "As we came out of the meeting, [our lawyer] asked me: 'How significant is this? Is it significant or a throwaway?' I told him that it could very well be significant."

Simonsen, who was by then in charge of all AMD's new product development, explained the principle of microprogramming to his lawyer. The instruction set of a chip like the 8085 included over a hundred different instructions. Some were basic, and could be carried out by the processor in a single step during just one cycle of its internal clock. Others required many steps before they were complete. Chip architects were beginning to notice that you could use shortcuts to carry out these more complex instructions. Instead of designing dedicated logic for each instruction, you could write a miniature program that would break down the complex instructions into a series of simple instructions, and store it on the chip. The result was to save space on the chip—and also improve performance. The set of these programs was known collectively as the chip's "microcode"—and it was the microcode, Simonsen explained to the lawyer, that Intel was now offering AMD.

Now that the offer was sweet enough, Sanders was ready to sign. He wrapped up the details in accordance with the timetable he had given AMD's executive staff—and set to work publicizing the deal as an alliance of peers. AMD took out double-page spreads in the trade press showing two extended white-shirted arms, hands clasped in a friendly shake, with the cuff link on one arm carrying its own logo, and the cuff link on the other carrying Intel's.

The acquisition of second-source rights over the 8085 was a big deal for AMD, but the following year Sanders trumped it with a bigger deal still.

By 1976, even the most conservative and slowest-moving of electronics companies had noticed that the large-scale integrated circuits were changing the face not just of the computer industry, but also of industries that made many different kinds of consumer and industrial goods. Large, cash-rich companies in America and Europe began to look at semiconductors and wonder whether they needed to be part of this exciting, fast-growing business. Exxon, with its investment in Zilog, was a perceptive early mover. But soon others began to move in. Siemens AG, a German industrial combine whose origins stretched back to the beginnings of electricity in the last century, made an unsuccessful attempt to buy Intel. Sprague Electric acquired 20 percent of Mostek, the upstart that had jumped neatly into the DRAM market shortly after Intel invented it. And a consortium made up of Bosch and Borg Warner bought 20 percent of American Microsystems in early 1977.

Jerry Sanders looked with envy at the companies that had banked fat checks from these new investors. AMD had survived the 1974–75 recession, but only with difficulty. The company's history, he liked to say, consisted of springing through a succession of doors that slammed shut immediately behind it. What AMD needed, he believed, was a cash infusion large enough to make it "bulletproof" and better able to weather the ups and down of the cycle. The quest for the financial equivalent of a flak jacket was Sanders's top strategic priority.

He therefore let it be known, discreetly, that although AMD wasn't for sale, it was "for lease"—meaning that he was willing to sell a minority stake in the company to a partner who could make him a suitably handsome offer. The most enthusiastic taker was Siemens, which had been rebuffed after making an approach to Intel. Since Intel wasn't interested in being acquired, moving to its second source—to the company that touted itself as Intel's strategic partner—seemed a logical step. Negotiations began between Siemens and AMD over the size of the slice and the price.

At first sight, AMD must have seemed a slightly raffish outfit by comparison with other firms in Silicon Valley. Cruising around in the convertible Rolls that the company leased for him, pictured at the front of every AMD annual report in the latest and most eccentric style of suit, Jerry Sanders looked like a big talker who treated the company as his private possession. But closer inspection showed that he ran a tight ship. Lavish though the Rolls-Royce was, it was the only luxury car that the company paid for. Sanders's office boasted an antique desk, but despite the growing popularity of the term "mahogany row" to describe companies' executive quarters, every other officer of AMD had to make do with plain metal. The economics went all the way to the bottom; Sanders had made a firm rule that employees were forbidden to make personal calls from the office, and he had installed pay phones within easy reach of everyone's desk to reinforce the point.

Sanders also impressed the visiting president of Siemens by taking him out to a thoroughly inexpensive restaurant in Sunnyvale. The Siemens man, unaware that Sunnyvale wasn't exactly the world capital of haute cuisine in 1977, mistook the choice of venue as a welcome sign of parsimony. When the talks moved to Munich, Sanders took the opposite tack: To convince the people he was negotiating with that he was a man of substance, he installed himself and his wife in the best suite at the Four Seasons Hotel while the rest of the AMD delegation were sent somewhere more modest around the corner. When a senior Siemens manager appeared at the hotel with his wife to take Jerry and Linda Sanders out to dinner, the American couple made a point of strolling down the hotel's main staircase together, wearing matching ankle-length fur coats.

The culmination of the negotiations came in December 1977, when a group of senior people from each company, with their investment bankers, met in New York. Sanders happened to be in Hong Kong with Linda at the time. According to the recollection of Tom Skornia, still the company's general counsel, a banker from Donaldson, Lufkin & Jenrette dialed Sanders's hotel number in order to patch him into a conference call. It was dusk in New York; members of the team were looking out the window at the New York skyline when the AMD chairman picked up the phone on the other side of the world.

"Sanders."

"Jerry? Joe here, with your representatives to the Siemens negotiations in New York. How are you doing?"

"Just sitting here watching the sun come up."

"We have a few open issues here on which we need your guidance, not least of which is the stock price. They're stuck at $42 and we at $48, with both of us claiming lack of authority to settle the other's number."

"Well, you're certainly right about your side."

As the team members in New York laughed, Sanders made it clear that he expected to settle the deal directly with Friedrich Bauer, the head of Siemens' components group.

"Just remember," he told the New York team before hanging up, "We don't need the money."

Seeing his wife stir in bed as he dropped the phone back in its cradle, Sanders spoke. "As we get down to the short strokes on this one, Linda, just make sure I remember that we *must* have the money."

They settled soon afterwards for $45. Sanders had done a marvelous sales job. Not only was the price nearly 75 percent higher than the market price of AMD's stock; the timing of the deal was also perfect. Siemens bought into AMD at the end of a series of nearly three years of rising quarters, when the company was flush with the success of its second-source arrangement with Intel, and when it had a 4K DRAM chip in the market and a 16K under development.

Within a few weeks of signature of the memorandum of intent, however, matters began to look less rosy. The company announced its first down quarter, and later revealed that its 16K DRAM chip was seriously behind schedule. The top management at Siemens, however, were undaunted. One of them reminded Skornia that since the company had been in business for 130 years and through two world wars, it had suffered a few down quarters itself.

When the deal went final early in 1978, AMD's officers were astounded to discover an element in the package that they had not known existed. They knew that Siemens and AMD had agreed to set up a sixty–forty joint venture called Advanced Micro Computers to explore the potential for putting microprocessors to work on the desks of engineers, and they knew that Sanders was to be the CEO of the new subsidiary. To their surprise, however, they discovered that Sanders had made a deal with Siemens whereby the German company would buy a huge slab of shares at the $26 market price and award him options over those shares in compensation for his work, for exercise at $28.

The reaction inside AMD to this news was fury—especially since this was the second time that Sanders had enriched himself with stock while an important transaction on the company's behalf took place. Sven Simonsen, who became friendly with his opposite numbers at Siemens, asked the Germans later what they thought of the deal.

"I was told by them that the one point that took the longest time and the longest debate and the biggest hand-wringing was exactly that detail. They were very worried about what it would mean to them and their image if there came a major class-action suit of potential shareholders of AMD. How would Siemens look if they were paying off the AMD president to get a deal? They were very worried about it. They debated it extensively at the highest level in Siemens, [but] ended up concluding, 'Let's go for it.' "

Jerry Sanders's delight over the 8085 deal with Intel lasted little over a year. In early 1978, Intel started shipping samples of the stopgap 16-bit processor that Steve Morse had architected in ten weeks. The 8086 was not the world's first 16-bit processor; that honor belonged to National Semiconductor, which had introduced an underpowered 16-bit product based on obsolete process technology as early as 1974. Nor was the 8086 central to Intel's strategic plan to capture control of the microprocessor market. But it was out there, and neither Zilog nor Motorola had a 16-bit machine ready for market.

Sanders waited, with increasing worry, for Intel's invitation to come and discuss a second-source agreement for the 8086. As the weeks wore on, it became clear that the invitation would never come. AMD was faced with an unpalatable decision. Should it second-source the 8086 without permission, a job that would be fraught with practical difficulties and legal risks? Should it develop its own microprocessor architecture, pitting its own meager technical resources against those of both Intel and other companies several times its size? Or should it make a clean break with Intel and sign up as someone else's second source?

After looking around and talking to Simonsen and some other senior AMD people, Sanders came to the conclusion that the third option was the least unpalatable of the three. He examined the work that Motorola was doing and discovered that its chip looked technically superior to Intel's, but would be at least a year behind. Zilog, however, expected to have its Z8000 on the market within six months of Intel. With Faggin's formidable technical mind, and with the Z80's proven success, the new chip seemed to have a good chance of prevailing in the market. Better still, Zilog was a small and very new company; it would probably be easier to do business with than either Intel or Motorola. The conclusion seemed clear: AMD should become a second source to Zilog and put all its weight behind the Z8000.

19

Organization and Alpha Particles

On August 10, 1978, Andy Grove circulated a memo around Intel's directors, executive staff, department managers, and supervisors. Its title was "GET ORGANIZED (AGAIN)—Chapter 2," and its purpose was to deliver a progress report on a campaign Grove had started the previous quarter.

"For starters," he wrote, "the Executive Staff decided in reviewing progress against the specific milestones that we set for ourselves that our overall performance in this area rates a 'not done.' Basically, we have not achieved any of the detailed key results that we set in April. Because of that, and because of the continuing immense importance of this issue to both our short and long term success as a company, we have again decided to adopt 'Getting Organized' as our top corporate objective for the third quarter, with an updated set of specific key results."

Grove went on to explain that the news was not all bad: Awareness of the problem had grown, even if this had not yet manifested itself in measurable results. As examples, he pointed out that several key departments had hired lots of new people. The recruiting process was being handled more professionally; 180 new graduates had just been hired. And in the second quarter of 1978, Intel had hit its shipment targets in all areas and in balance—resulting in an all-time sales record, 17 percent up on the previous quarter.

The memo was a perfect illustration of how Intel worked under

Andy Grove. Its very existence—several hundred copies, efficiently distributed through the company's internal mail system—said something. Intel ran its Xerox machines night and day; Grove believed that writing things down, particularly plans, objectives, progress reports, and the like, was much more important than whether anybody actually read what was written. But the use of objectives and key results was evidence in microcosm of how Intel worked. After it had been suggested to the company by a management consultant, Grove had adopted this system throughout the company, starting with a set of objectives for the entire company at the very top, and trickling down through divisions and department to work groups and "individual contributors," as the company politely called people who didn't manage anyone else. In each case, the objectives and key results would be set, and progress would be measured periodically and reported upwards. The system was formally known as Intel Management by Objectives. Colloquially, people would refer to their list of objectives and key results as their "imbos"—as in "Yeah, I got 70 percent of my imbos done this quarter."

Also on display in the memo was Grove's obsession with measurement. Gene Flath, the first manager of Fab 1, had come up with the image of the manufacturing process as a "black box" and had pointed out the usefulness of being able to cut a window into it to see what was going on. Grove had adopted this metaphor enthusiastically, and was keen to cut as many windows as possible, with the window in each case consisting of a set of statistics showing how well the job was being done. He believed that this discipline should apply to the company's administrative activities as well as its manufacturing. In *High-Output Management*, he actually included a table showing each administrative function and the indicator that should be used to measure its output. For accounts payable, for example, the company should count the number of vouchers processed; for janitors, the number of square feet cleaned; for customer service, the number of sales orders entered.

The other startling thing about the memo was its relentless focus on the negative. Most companies would be quite pleased to be growing so fast, to have just completed the best quarter ever, and to have hit all targets. For Grove, this was not enough. His attention was focused on a few more quarters and years down the line, and he noticed the risks that would arise if the company failed to keep control of its operations. So his memo homed in on the fact that the glass was half empty, and pushed his colleagues hard to fill it higher.

Grove's focus on organization was probably the feature that distinguished Intel most from its competitors. While other companies might look at recruiting as a soft, emotional job that involved finding good people and inspiring them, Grove saw it as just another manufacturing process—with the applicants on campus as the input, and the output as NCGs ("new college graduates"—another one of the many abbreviations Intel used) who accept job offers to work at Intel. Grove also included in *High-Output Management* a "linearity indicator"—a chart showing how the company could try to predict, as the academic year progressed, whether it would hit its hiring target by year-end.

The process started with a concerted effort by everyone at Intel to contact old friends and professors at college, asking for suggestions on who were the brightest, best students. Then the company's recruiting people would go out to campuses and carry out the prescreening. Being invited to Santa Clara for an interview was the "limiting step" in the process, according to Grove: like putting an egg in to boil in the breakfast factory described in his book, it was an expensive business to pay for someone's air ticket, so the objective was to screen the invitations very carefully so as to get the highest possible ratio of hires to on-site interviews. Once at Intel, candidates would be intensively checked out by a half-dozen people and sometimes more. The interviewing process was taken so seriously that at times an order would come down to block out one or two whole days each week so that no meetings could be scheduled that would interrupt the hiring process. One potential hire, a computer scientist from Northwestern University named John Wharton, had his interview interrupted by a secretary walking in with a message that Bob Noyce was holding on the phone for his interviewer. To his astonishment, the interviewer replied that he couldn't talk to the chairman of the board. "I have a candidate," he explained simply. At Intel, that was an excuse for missing almost anything.

Sometimes, Intel went to even greater lengths to hire the people it wanted. On one occasion, the company's head of human resources, Roger Nordby, told Andy Grove that a new college graduate he had been hoping to bring in had received offers from a dozen other companies and wasn't likely to take up Intel's offer.

"Tell you what I'll do," said Grove. "If this guy's such a star, you write him a letter from me saying why he ought to come, and I'll sign it."

Three days later, the letter had been signed and mailed out—and the young graduate, astounded to receive a letter from the same guy who had just been on the cover of a business magazine, called to say that if the company was that keen for him to join, then Intel was the place he wanted to work.

Another effect of Grove's repeated demands to get organized could be seen in the company's efforts to market microprocessors. The issue was that microprocessors were fundamentally different from the rest of the components that the semiconductor industry was used to marketing. While other parts needed little more than a specification and a short explanation of how to install them, microprocessors were tools of much greater general use. This meant the company had to do more than just provide technical support to engineers who were having problems using them. First, it had to send out reams of manuals, data sheets, applications notes—a volume of information that grew to such a point that by the end of the decade, Intel's internal publishing house was turning over $2 million a year, even though customers were charged no more than the cost of producing the materials. Second, Intel had to go out and show people what they could do with the microprocessor—at seminars, at trade shows, and in customers' own sites.

There would usually be two people assigned to each client: an FSE and an FAE. The FSE was a "field sales engineer"—a salesman who had the appropriate background in electrical engineering to talk intelligently about parts and what they did. The FAE, was a "field applications engineer" who would divide his or her time between the clients of two different sales engineers and discuss with them what they were trying to do and how they could achieve it. Sometimes, this support could be extraordinarily imaginative: One engineer, Nick Nichols, spent an entire weekend in discussion with clients at a company called Magnavox, who wanted to use an Intel processor to design games. When he returned to base, he started working on a design, patented it, and helped Intel build a special game chip that brought in several million dollars' worth of sales.

But Intel's engineering expertise was not handed out to clients indiscriminately. The order came down from somewhere near the top of the microprocessor division—Davidow, perhaps, or maybe someone like Jim Lally or Jack Carsten—that the company didn't want its field staff spending valuable hours helping with a problem if the customer was not going to place a big order. If the technical assistance wasn't going to generate orders of ten thousand pieces in the first year, forget it: "Send the bastard some stuff on paper."

Gordon Moore had a plaque hung prominently in his office: "This is a profit-making organization," it said. "That's the way we intended it . . . and that's the way it is." To make sure the message percolated through the company's ranks, entire departments would be drafted in every Friday afternoon to hear a lecture on marginal cost calculation, or how to qualify a sales prospect. Even if your job gave you no contact with the outside world, you'd still learn that there was no point wasting your time with someone who didn't have the authority to make a buying decision. The recommended technique, the speaker would explain, was to ask, point-blank, whether the guy you were talking to could sign the purchase order himself. If not, you'd ask him to bring in the person who would.

When a potential client was evidently of great strategic importance, signing them up could become an MB for the entire company. A case in point was the Ford Motor Company's decision to put microprocessors into its automotive engines. There were dozens of potential microprocessor applications in automobiles, but one in particular was compelling: The chip could be connected to a monitor in the engine's exhaust to detect the oxygen content. Less than half of one percent oxygen in the exhaust meant that the fuel was probably not being completely burned—which would result in poisonous emissions of carbon monoxide and bad consumption numbers. More than that meant that the input mixture was not rich enough—harming the car's performance. The chip could decide every fraction of a second to open and close the carburetor to adjust the fuel flow.

The business argument for "electronic fuel injection," as this approach was called, was self-evident to Intel long before the car companies took it seriously. But by the time Intel discovered Ford was interested, the carmaker was on the point of signing up with Mostek to buy a single-chip implementation of a Fairchild processor. Once the news reached Intel, the wheels went immediately into action. Noyce got on the phone to someone very senior at Ford and extracted a promise to postpone the final decision for a month to give Intel a chance to come up with an alternative. Meanwhile, the word went down to the applications engineers that they had twenty-five days to come up with a redesign of Ford's system using an Intel product.

The job was given to John Wharton, the computer scientist whose interviewer had refused the call from Bob Noyce. The product he was to adapt for Ford was Intel's 8048—a "microcontroller" descended from the old 4004, which included memory and input-output functions on the same piece of silicon as the central processing unit. Working night and day for nearly a month, interrupting his progress for frequent checks with Ford's technical people to make sure he was answering the right questions, Wharton produced a solution to the problem that could be taken over to the client and demonstrated.

When the chip was tested on site, Wharton was shocked to see what the Ford engineers did to his baby. They started by simulating the harsh environment of a working engine, with its constant vibrations and high levels of electrical "noise"; then they brought in a spark generator, using the distributor coil that created the sparks in the spark plugs, and decided to simulate what would happen if the cable came loose, flopping around inside the engine compartment, scattering two-inch lightning bolts every few hundredths of a second directly on to the metal case housing the computer. The result was that the program's counter became corrupted, and the electronic fuel injection process came to an abrupt halt. Undaunted, Wharton went away and redesigned the hardware so that a constant check would be carried out to make sure that the process was working properly. If not, his program would automatically reset and start again.

Considering that Ford's management had started out by insisting that the decision was already made, it had been an expensive gamble for Intel. But a few weeks later, flush with pride, Wharton found himself sitting down to dinner with a group of senior Intel executives at the Hyatt Hotel in Dearborn, Michigan, celebrating their first microcontroller sale to the Ford Motor Company. Nobody said it, but the conclusion was clear. It was all a matter of Getting Organized.

Even in this increasingly disciplined atmosphere, there was still space for a few mavericks among Intel's new hires. One such was Tim May, a student of relativity and astrophysics from the University of California at Santa Barbara.

Immediately after graduating, May was recruited to join the company's technology development department, reporting to a Stanford University professor named Craig Barrett who had taken a sabbatical to spend a year at Intel. Barrett discovered that May exhibited a strange mixture of discipline and chaos. On the one hand, his lab notebooks were always fastidiously neat and precise. On the other, he was quite unable to obey Andy Grove's orders to arrive by 8:00 A.M. and he was too indiscreet simply to sign in quietly and allow the matter to be forgotten.

Once, he scrawled "THIS IS BULLSHIT!" across the top of the Late List—which resulted in a call from Grove a few days later, demanding angrily in the Hungarian accent that was still evident: "What is zis bullsheet?" Unabashed, May retorted that it was bullshit to force latecomers to sign in without making any provision for explanations. May proved a talented solver of engineering problems who worked so hard that he never found out what kind of fruit grew in the orchards outside the Santa Clara buildings. But despite his devotion to the job, May couldn't resist teasing his bosses by making it clear from time to time that he felt the chip business was a step down from studying black holes.

One day in late 1976, a senior Intel engineer stuck his head around May's cubicle, asking for help with a problem that had recently come up with Intel's new charge-coupled devices, which it was making for a number of clients including Singer, DEC, and Reticon. The new 16K CCD had just come out, and Intel's test people had come across a series of random, single-bit errors in the device. The discovery was frightening because a number of thinkers in the semiconductor business were beginning to wonder whether the process of miniaturization down toward atomic scale was about to come up against physical limits.

"You know, Tim," said the engineer who had looked into May's cubicle, "I was at a meeting today, and Gordon said he remembered a 1960s paper by a guy at RCA." May's colleague went on to explain that the paper had posted a daring question: At what stage in the scaling downwards of devices would cosmic rays become a problem? "I think it's a pretty strange idea, but Gordon thinks we should take a look at it. Since you're a physics guy, could you do it?"

May dug out the paper from the modest technical library the company kept. He looked at it and discovered that there was an entire body of literature on what could happen to semiconductor devices if they were close to the explosion of a hydrogen bomb, or if they were in orbit around Jupiter. He soon came to the conclusion that Moore's question had been far-fetched. At sea level on earth, cosmic rays were unlikely to be an issue.

But his interest had been aroused—and grew to the point of

becoming an obsession. Some weeks later, Western Electric sent back to Intel an entire shipment of 4K memory chips that had been intended for use in the first electronic telephone switchboards, complaining that they were showing signs of random single-bit errors. At the same time, Intel began to hear rumors that competing chipmakers were experiencing the same problem. The company's testers reported that the problem didn't come up with chips in white packages with gold metal lids, but only with those encased in black ceramic. A task force was set up, which May was not invited to join, to investigate possible causes. But it made no headway.

One night in February 1977, May was sitting in the hot spa attached to his apartment complex in Sunnyvale when he suddenly had a brainwave. In his geophysics classes at Santa Barbara, he had been taught about a new method scientists had discovered for dating pottery. When a pot was fired, the heat from the kiln would cause the uranium and thorium present in the clay to shoot out subatomic particles into the flecks of mica that were also present—and the disrupted structure of the mica would from that moment on emit almost imperceptible radiation, gouging tiny holes in the pot over the years. By measuring the holes, a scientist armed with knowledge about the half-life of radioactive materials could estimate how long it was since the pot had been fired.

May knew that the ceramic packaging used in the semiconductor industry was very slightly radioactive. Suppose, he asked himself, this radioactivity was linked to the random-bit errors. The decaying radioactive elements emitted three sets of particles that might be responsible, known as alpha, beta, and gamma. The alpha particles were slow-moving, almost like heavy bowling balls, but they could be easily stopped by a sheet of paper. To block the smaller betas, you needed a centimeter of aluminum, and to protect against gammas required a meter of concrete. Half an hour's research in a textbook, followed by a few calculations on his programmable Hewlett-Packard calculator, and May had the answer. Chips of 1976 vintage were sufficiently miniaturized that fewer than one million electrons were needed to store the electric charge that represented the difference between 1 and 0. Yet a single alpha particle could affect the equivalent of 1.5 million.

The next day, May strolled into the lab and picked up two bins of 4K chips, a selection of working chips encased in white and gold, and a set of chips packaged in black ceramic that had failed. He carried them over to the assembly group and put them in a machine called a tracer flow whose job was to detect packaging leaks by pumping krypton gas around the chips. On this occasion, May was not interested in using the krypton to look for leaks; his purpose was just to use the machine's radiation detector. He lowered the clean group of chips into the lead-lined well, hit the button marked "integrate," and carefully wrote down the radiation level. Then he replaced the white packages with a set of black ones and pressed again.

"The needle practically pegged—right across," he recalled. "It was Eureka time—the errors were correlating with the radioactivity level."

Further experiments confirmed the hypothesis that it was radioactivity, not leaking, that was the issue with the packaging. When May did a comparison, checking four circuit cards full of white-packaged chips for errors against four circuit cards with black-packaged chips, it was the blacks that failed. When he put the black lids on the white boxes, the chips failed. When he put the black lids on, but covered them with a layer of masking tape—thicker than the sheet of paper that could block an alpha particle—the problems disappeared and the chips worked again. To make the point more convincingly, May asked a friend to crack open a smoke detector. It was illegal to release the tiny quantity of the radioactive element americium 241 that was inside, but the result was striking: In the presence of the radioactive element, even good chips went haywire. Finally, a lump of uranium ore was commandeered from an Intel scientist who was a keen rock collector. The lump, which was about 30 percent pure, was radioactive enough to produce a chart: number of alpha particles running along one access, error rate along the other. Over ten orders of magnitude, the chart showed a straight line. So the conclusion was that the semiconductor business had not, after all, come up against a natural brick wall against further miniaturization. It was just that the radioactive elements in the ceramic lids were throwing zingers into chips that would once in a while cause a failure.

Resolving the problem took two steps. One was to change the way the devices worked so that more charge was built up in each cell, thus reducing the chips' susceptibility to alpha radiation. The other was to change the ceramic used in the packaging.

Since May's analysis of the problem and its solution were clearly a source of competitive advantage, Intel did not want to give the rest of the chip industry any help in solving the problem. So it contacted its leading packaging supplier, the Japanese firm Kyocera, and told it under the terms of a strict nondisclosure agreement what May had discovered. Kyocera changed the formulation of the ceramics it supplied to Intel so that they would be nonradioactive from then on. Craig Barrett was sent with a group of sales people to Western Electric's offices in Denver to explain why the chips Intel had supplied for its phone switches had proved unreliable. He came back grinning. "We just blew them away," he said. IBM and one or two other key customers were also told, again under terms of nondisclosure.

The matter remained a company secret for another year, when Western Electric's research people came to Intel a year later, threatening to announce the discovery to the world if Intel was unwilling to. Intel's engineers concluded that it was time to take the credit by making a presentation at an academic conference on reliability physics. But the marketing department was furious. One senior manager, who like Ed Gelbach had come from Texas Instruments, was incensed at the idea that Intel should give up its advantage to his former employer so easily.

"No fucking way," he said. "We're not going to suck hind tit to TI on this one. I don't want some two-bit engineer like this May character doing this."

In the end, the marketing department lost. May made his presentation, and won the award for best paper at the conference. Intel no longer had the secret of the alpha particles to itself, but it had achieved a valuable one-year lead over the rest of the industry.

20

The Microma Mistake

In 1979, Intel was not used to direct competition.

During its first decade, the company had prospered by using its strength in research and development to invent entirely new categories of products, and using its ability to master complex processes to win the race to manufacture those products in commercial volumes. Intel could claim to be the pioneer behind the first memory chip, the first DRAM, the first EPROM, and the first microprocessor—the four most important innovations of the decade. But the company had little experience of the disciplines that occupy most companies: slugging it out with the competition on cost, quality, service, and delivery time. The result of this inexperience was that when circumstances took Intel's technological lead away, the company began to stumble.

The first signs of this problem came in the DRAM market that Intel had itself invented. Intel's IK DRAM, the 1103, had the market to itself for nearly two years and brought in the cash flow that allowed the company to invest in the microprocessor. In the 4K generation of memory chips—capacity grew fourfold in each generation—Intel built a good product but was beaten to market by Mostek, the start-up company that spun out of Texas Instruments. By the 16K generation, Intel had definitely lost market leadership: The design that became the industry standard belonged to another company, and Intel was both late and a relatively high-cost producer. It was a measure of the unprecedented growth rate of the market that with these handicaps, the company's memory operations still managed to turn in sparkling figures quarter after quarter.

Then problems began to emerge with Intel's range of development systems—"blue boxes" like the Intellec-4 and Intellec-8 that could be used by engineers to design software and systems for microprocessors. Development systems were an essential tool in encouraging customers to pick Intel processors instead of competing models, and it was a rule of thumb that the sale of one development system would bring in a steady stream of component sales after it. But the manufacturing quality of the blue boxes was patchy. At one point, return figures showed that 80 percent of the boxes were either DOA (dead on arrival) or sent back as defective within ninety days. Jim Lally, a former HP computer marketing executive who had been the first marketing manager for the development systems business, was hastily brought in from another division to fix the problem.

Lally found a shocking lack of communication between the engineers who had designed the product and the manufacturing people who were supposed to build it. Both blamed the other for the reliability problems—and because the division as a whole was under pressure from above to meet its production targets, the result was that lots of badly assembled units were being allowed to leave the factory. Lally's first attempt to solve the problem was to order the manufacturing manager to give every machine a weeklong "burn-in" test—which revealed that only 60 percent of the finished units coming off the line were working properly, compared with the 95 percent that should have been an absolute minimum. Matters started to improve, but too slowly; yields were rising only a few percentage points a month.

"So I said OK, that's it," recalled Lally. "Nothing ships. Nothing ships out of this fucking place until we understand what all the problems are on those machines."

The managers reporting to him were at first horrified: How did he think the company would react, they asked him, when the division missed its target for the quarter? But the stoppage had a salutary effect. It demonstrated that at least in this corner of the business, Intel's management was serious about trying to solve the problem—and it helped Lally to restore manufacturing quality to a reasonable level.

Another issue arose with the Microma watch business. Intel's acquisition of the Microma company in 1972 had been based on the belief that digital watches, as prices fell and volumes grew, would become an important new outlet for Intel's chips—and would also provide a neat route from the industrial to the consumer market. Both predictions came true, but not quite as Noyce and Moore had hoped. They had expected digital-watch prices to fall to $30 by 1980. In fact, discounters were selling digital watches with LCD displays for $19.95 or even $9.95 as early as 1977. This turned the manufacturing of watch chips into a commodity business with razor-thin margins. Worse, the demands of consumer marketing proved too much for Intel. Microma's first TV ad cost an astounding $600,000, and Intel's management plainly lacked the skills needed to produce a succession of fashionable designs season after season.

Even with the watches being assembled at Intel's Penang facilities by workers earning less than $1 an hour, the business was not making money. In late 1977, Intel's board were forced to admit that they had made a mistake. They decided to sell the watch business, taking a charge of $2 million in the third quarter of the financial year to cover its losses. Luckily, the company was able to reduce the charge by $700,000 a few months later. Dick Boucher, the Intel general manager put in to help Intel make a graceful exit from Microma, managed to sell Microma's designs, equipment, and name for more money than expected.

The episode was still an expensive mistake, but in a year when the company's sales were $283 million and its income $32 million, not a disastrous one. For years afterwards, Moore used to wear a Microma watch—and when people asked him about it, he would explain that it was the most expensive timepiece he had ever owned.

But all these problems were flea bites compared with a more fundamental malaise inside Intel—the company's attitude to its customers. It was understandable that Intel should have more of an internal focus than most of its competitors in the industry. After all, it had risen to prominence by ignoring the conventional wisdom and developing products that people did not even know they would want—not by painstakingly researching the market and asking customers for their opinions. Years later, Akio Morita of Sony would joke that if his company had carried out market research before proceeding with the Walkman, the product would never have seen the light of day. Intel's EPROM and its microprocessor were earlier examples of the same phenomenon.

For a while, this deficiency was obscured by the extraordinary talents of Bob Noyce. Using to the full his reputation as inventor of the integrated circuit and father of Silicon Valley, Noyce would fly around the country on Intel's behalf in his private jet, dropping in on important customers at just the moment when they were about to make an important decision or when Intel had screwed up and needed to retain their loyalty. He was the dream company chairman.

"Bob could stand up in front of a roomful of securities analysts and tell them that we were facing a number of major problems in our business, and the stock would go up five points," said one Intel manager.

Casey Powell, the sales manager for Intel's East Coast region, noticed the Noyce halo when the Intel chairman dropped in to participate in a sales call.

"Noyce would arrive in town, and you'd hand him the company's annual report and a one-page blurb of problems, questions, solutions, answers," he recalled. "Having skimmed it, Noyce would walk in, and people would think he'd been following their company and had been a shareholder for twenty years."

That air of easy familiarity was only the beginning. Revered by every engineer who knew anything about the industry, Noyce could start chatting in his low-key way about Intel's current products and those it had under development; by the time he left, he had gone through the entire product range pointing out its advantages over the competition. The point was, it didn't *feel* as though that was what he was doing. Noyce's great knack was that he sounded far too authoritative, too technical, too learned, to be just a salesman.

But Bob Noyce had hardly been involved in running Intel from day to day since 1970. With his cars and planes, his venture capital investments, his speaking engagements, his invitations to meet politicians and grandees in Washington, with his divorce from Betty Noyce and remarriage to Ann Bowers, he had gradually withdrawn from Intel as the decade progressed. Finally, in the company's 1979 annual report, he disappeared altogether from the executive photo on the first spread. Instead the picture accompanying the management report showed just Gordon Moore and Andy Grove. Noyce had become Intel's vice-chairman, while Moore had been bumped up to chairman and CEO, and Grove had become president and chief operating officer. Given that the company's senior founder had formally withdrawn from its top slot, it might have seemed strange to investors that the change was not even mentioned in the management report. Employ-ees knew better: They knew that Andy had been running the show for years anyway.

Andy Grove's style in dealing with customers was very different from Noyce's. Since he expected the senior management of other companies to be as busy and as rigorous with their time as he was, he would always get straight down to business when he paid a sales call. This meant that he wanted to be armed with the answer to every pos-sible question he might be asked—so much so that he once forced Powell to wake Bill Davidow in California at 5:00 A.M. one day in or-der to provide a statistic that Grove thought he might need before going into a 9:00 A.M. sales call on the East Coast. And instead of strolling down the shag pile of mahogany row, glad-handing the vice-presidents one by one as he made his way slowly to the presidential suite, Grove would march straight into every meeting, firing intellec-tually on all cylinders.

The contrast was most marked when Grove arrived at a high-level lunch that Powell had organized for the chief engineer, the company that had booked the largest ever order for 8080 microprocessors. The client was to eat with a half-dozen of Intel's most senior people in Lorenzo's restaurant, and the objective of the occasion was to mas-sage his ego, to convince him how much Intel valued and respected and admired him. Contrary to his normal practice, Grove failed to turn up on time. Then suddenly, sometime after the party had begun their meal, they heard a familiar voice. Looking around to the chair that had previously been empty, they found Grove sitting in it, talk-ing at the speed of a machine gun.

"How do you do? I'm Andy Grove! What is the purpose of your visit here today?"

Powell was keen for Grove to cool down. "The guy wasn't about to commit to anything. He was going to make a choice and then play a political game of deciding." Yet Grove was utterly oblivious to the human subtleties of the situation. On hearing that the client was about to make a decision between an Intel product and a competi-tor's, Grove launched into a point-by-point comparison of features, and wound up by asking the client to commit to an order there and then. The approach was unsuccessful: They came away empty-handed.

On another occasion, Grove paid a courtesy call at Wang Labora-tories in order to promote the one-megabit bubble memory device that Intel had just produced. Invited into the office of Dr. An Wang, who had founded the company in 1952 after leaving Harvard's computer lab, Grove placed a sample of the device on Wang's desk and leaned forward.

"I'd like to ask you a question, Dr. Wang, since you were the inventor of core memory. What do you see as the applications for the magnetic bubble memory device?"

Wang glared at him disparagingly and starting flipping through his mail.

"*Doctor* Grove," he replied. "If you had to ask me that question, you never should have built the product."

To the mortification of his visitors, the distinguished inventor gave Grove very little time, and interrupted their meeting several times to take incoming phone calls. In the trip report that Grove filed afterwards, he wrote: "I feared at one point that I was to be consumed by his cavernous yawn."

With Andy Grove at the helm, it was not surprising that Intel's sales efforts should be deficient in diplomacy. Grove abhorred the fast cars, Dom Pérignon, and expense-account entertaining that epitomized the Jerry Sanders way of doing business. He would never admit to believing in the old saying that if you invented a better mousetrap, the world would beat a path to your door. But his instinct told him that the job of an Intel field sales engineer was to visit a customer, take the better mousetrap out of his briefcase, put it on the table, tell the customer what the unit price was for orders of ten thousand, and then ask how many he wanted. And if the customer wasn't interested, you didn't waste time arguing; you just packed up your bag and moved on to the next call.

Intel's sales department was nonetheless well staffed and run. Sales came under the responsibility of Ed Gelbach, the former TI executive who had replaced Bob Graham back in 1971. Gelbach had an almost regal presence; you knew he was someone important simply from the way he walked into the room. The people who reported to him came to learn from experience that when he arrived somewhere by air, Gelbach would step out of the terminal, assuming that someone else would pick his bag off the carousel, and climb straight into the largest limo waiting on the curbside. So revered was he that the staff who worked for him imitated his clothes and his mannerisms. People used to say that if Ed came back from the men's room one morning with the front of his shirt protruding from his fly by mistake, everyone else in the department would take it as a signal of a change in fashion and would follow suit that afternoon. And while he was less senior than Grove, Gelbach had more autonomy than anyone else in the company.

What Gelbach concentrated on was the more strategic process of trying to define new products and new market segments, and making decisions about distribution channels. He did a superb job of assembling the set of support products, from in-circuit emulators to testers and development systems, that made it possible for Intel's customers to design microprocessors into their new products. But the 1970s were a time of production constraint, when Intel was only rarely able to manufacture enough chips to satisfy customer demands. Inevitably, this meant that Intel's 180 direct salespeople did not need to spend much time sweet-talking their customers. A whole range of skills counted more highly: technical expertise; ability to squeeze product out of the factory for a favored customer when it was "on allocation"; and all the standard Intel virtues of hard work, good technical support, good record keeping, promptness, and market knowledge. Intel salesmen did their job well, but the competition at AMD, a company that had a much less sparkling product range, looked down on the Intel sales operation from a great height.

21

Crush!

In 1978, the members of the Intel sales force found themselves facing an unfamiliar situation. Customers were saying that Motorola's 68000 microprocessor, released nearly a year after Intel's stopgap 8086 part, was actually technically superior. Similar gripes had been heard on the comparison between the 8080 and the 6800 a few years earlier, but this was far more extreme. Customers now were saying that the Motorola part was better designed, faster, cheaper, *and* easier to use. What possible reason could they have for buying the 8086?

At first, the rumblings from the field were ignored at Santa Clara. The sales force obviously wasn't doing its job properly, people said. If only those lazy sales engineers would pull their fingers out, customers would come to realize that they had already invested heavily in 8080 technology, and that choosing Motorola's part over the 8086 would devalue their investment. It was simply a matter of waiting until the industry realized what was good for it. Like the memory chip and the EPROM, said the guys in Santa Clara, Intel's new microprocessor would eventually receive the recognition it deserved.

Then came clues that were harder to close your eyes to. Jim Lally, out in the field giving a briefing to the sales force about new systems development products, asked some Intel salespeople casually what they thought of the 8086.

"They started laughing," he recalled. "Wow! If that isn't a wake-up call when your own FAEs start laughing, what is?"

The demoralization in the sales force was understandable. After being treated to years of the Andy Grove school of salesmanship, with the take-it-or-leave-it offer being followed by a swift departure if the client quibbled over the price, customers reacted to the inferiority of the 8086 with relish rather than sympathy. You'd been buying from this guy all these years not because you liked him but because the products were so good you couldn't allow your resentment of his arrogance to get in the way of good business. Now there was a better product elsewhere, and you had a perfect opportunity to stick it to him.

But it was not until the message arrived at Intel's head office in writing that it was taken seriously. Casey Powell, still in charge of the East Coast region, had been receiving complaints for a while about the difficulties of selling the 8086 from Don Buchout, a field applications engineer whose advice he valued. Finally, Powell lost patience with telling Buchout not to worry and ordered him to set down his concerns in writing to Bill Davidow, the division's general manager.

Buchout's message, eight pages long, was constructively confrontational in the best Intel style. It started out by telling Davidow that he could sit there and make whatever excuses he wanted, but that it was undeniable that Intel's 8086 was losing out to the competing Motorola part in the market. *These guys are beating us,* was the conclusion. *What are we going to do about it?* And just in case Buchout's finer points were lost on Davidow, Powell used a meeting with him a couple of days later to reiterate how seriously he took the problem.

Davidow got the message and relayed it to Intel's executive staff the following Tuesday. Although it was only a temporary stand-in for the 8800—which Bill Lattin continued to promise was coming soon—the 8086 was a strategic product for Intel. On it depended not only all the bigger development systems and test equipment but also millions of dollars' worth of memory and EPROMs. The news from Buchout indicated that the company had a full-scale crisis on its hands.

"The discussion of [the message] at the executive staff meeting . . . couldn't have been more unpleasant," Davidow wrote later. "By the end of it, I had either volunteered or been asked by Grove to run a marketing task force charged with solving the 8086 problem."

Task forces were a favorable Intel device. The person in charge was designated the "czar"; dealing with the issue the task force had been set up to address would become his number one objective.

Davidow assembled what he believed to be a group of the company's best sales and marketing talent and kept them in continuous session for three days. They emerged with a plan, which the executive staff endorsed two working days later. Within the week, over 100 Intel people were summoned to the Hyatt House in San Jose for a kickoff meeting where Andy Grove would present the new program the task force had developed. As they walked through the doors, the participants were each handed a brown button bearing the word CRUSH in orange letters. There were two reasons for naming the campaign Operation Crush. One was that the Denver Broncos defensive team was known as "Orange Crush" that year. The other was articulated by Jim Lally in his usual forthright style.

"Are we doing this as an exercise to improve our position in the marketplace, and achieve the recognition that we deserve?" he asked. "Or are we doing this to fucking *kill* Motorola? Because the other guys are so stupid that they won't make any difference at all. The Z8000 is nothing because Zilog doesn't know what it's doing. The 16016 is even more of a joke because National doesn't know what it's doing. There's only one company competing with us, and that's Motorola. The 68000 *is* the competition. . . . We have to kill Motorola, that's the name of the game. We have to *crush* the fucking bastards. We're gonna roll over Motorola and make sure they don't come back again."

The difficulty was that Intel's part was clearly inferior to Motorola's. Even inside the Intel departments that suffered most from the "not-invented-here" syndrome, people realized this. So the task force concluded that what Intel needed to do was to divert attention from the deficiencies of its device and come up with a wider definition of "product" on which Intel could use to vanquish Motorola. Davidow argued that Intel had five advantages:

A fine image as a technology leader: Customers were concerned if they left Intel they would lose out on future developments.

A more complete product family and a plan to enhance it: Motorola was weak in this area. If we could make customers aware of that fact, it would be a great advantage to us.

A well-focused and superbly trained technical sales force: The Motorola sales force was a group of generalists. They lacked technical support in the field as well. Many were afraid of the microprocessor. We knew that if we could just get the customer to ask Intel before making a design decision, we usually could beat the competition.

Better performance at the system level: If the customer evaluated total capability—a system with the 8086, math coprocessors and peripheral circuits—we came out ahead. We also had a well-thought-out interconnection scheme. Here, too, Motorola was weak.

Ultimately, perhaps the most important advantage Intel had was that *Motorola's customers were experiencing great difficulty making that chip work in their products.* Intel had great customer service and support. We could assure a customer's success with our device. By comparison, choosing the Motorola path clearly presented a risk to the customer.

To make Intel's claim to superiority at the system level plausible, a rush program began to get fifty articles published in the trade press, and to develop a set of system-level benchmarks showing that Intel's package as a whole outperformed Motorola's. The company also began a new ad campaign, coordinated by Regis McKenna, the veteran Silicon Valley publicity consultant, using the line "There is only one high-performance VLSI computer solution—Intel delivers it."

But the most revolutionary step taken by the task force was to abandon a rule that had guided Intel from its very inception: never to announce products until they were in manufacturing and on distributors' shelves. "Intel delivers" was an important idea to keep in customers' minds; that was why it had been adapted by McKenna for the new slogan. But it was now more important to tell them what Intel expected to be delivering in future. Over the next three months, Davidow therefore commissioned a hundred-page Futures Catalog—a set of specifications and preliminary data sheets for parts, starting with a coprocessor chip that would allow the 8086 to crunch numbers more than five times faster than a 68000. Many of the parts in the catalogs had not yet been designed, let alone manufactured. But that didn't matter. The idea was to show customers what they could expect over the coming five years if they stuck with Intel.

Motorola fell for it. Instead of dismissing the products that Intel had preannounced as "vaporware" or "paper tigers," the company rushed out its own far less impressive futures catalog. And instead of redirecting customers' attention to the microprocessors themselves, where it had a strong lead over Intel, it allowed itself to be drawn into a marketing battle over wider systems performance, which it was doomed to lose.

So the objective became to displace Motorola as market leader. Following Intel's system of management by objectives, this objective was expressed in terms of a set of "key results" against which success or failure could be measured. The key result here was the long-term market share of the 8086 against the 68000. The best way to determine this would be to count "design wins"—to count the number of new products that were designed around Intel's part rather than Motorola's. How many would be a reasonable number to aim for? A few hundred, perhaps? A thousand? No, said Lally. We should expect each salesperson to bring in one design win per month. With nearly 170 people in the field, that meant the target for Operation Crush would be two thousand design wins by December 1980.

In 1979, Bill Handel wasn't a star salesman. He worked at a little-known computer company in Silicon Valley, where he had had an undistinguished record of performance. But Intel was so desperate for new people that he was given only one day of training before starting work at its Santa Clara sales office.

That one day, packed with explanations of the differences between EPROM and ROM, microprocessors and microcontrollers, development systems and in-circuit emulators, came close to making him quit. Armed only with his happy-go-lucky temperament and his degree in sales engineering from Purdue University, Handel felt immediately out of his depth.

Things began to look up when he realized that he'd be working from a sales office on Lakeside Drive, not at the company headquarters. The office was full of regular guys, not propeller-heads.

"Selling chips was a front," Handel joked. "Everyone was doing real-estate deals. The regional manager had set up a venture to buy and develop commercial buildings and apartments in Atlanta, Georgia. He was general partner, and we were all limited partners."

When the time came for some real work, Handel was assigned a sales territory in Sacramento and another in San Francisco's East Bay, plus as much of the unassigned territory in northern California as he chose to grab. He soon realized how a salesman met his targets. The secret was "sandbagging"—a term borrowed from stock-car racing, where drivers would throw a little sand in the trunk to make their cars run slower in the qualifying rounds and thus get a place further forward in the line for the real race. At Intel, sandbagging meant being highly pessimistic about the amount of business you expected to do. That way, you'd be given an easily attainable target— and if you did just half-reasonably, you could expect to collect a pat on the back and a big bonus at the end of the year.

When the Crush campaign began, Handel had little experience on his side. But he did have an engaging, boyish smile and a kind of shambling amateurism that worked like a dream disarming customers who were instinctively suspicious of fast-talking salesmen. Beneath this exterior, his immediate ambitions were straightforward: to make an income of at least $40,000 a year—and to win the Crush contest. The prize, appropriately enough, was eighty-six Intel shares: It would be given to the field sales engineer and field applications engineer who turned in the largest number of design wins. All the engineers who met their targets would go directly to paradise at the end of 1980: They'd win a weeklong sales conference in Tahiti.

Handel and his FAE scoured northern California. They started with the big, serious accounts, and progressed downwards to the cranks and start-ups. No venture was too small or too insignificant for Bill Handel to pay a visit, to deliver his little spiel about the 8086 and its wonders, and to walk out with an order just big enough to qualify, and a letter confirming that the 8086 chip had been designed into a new product.

By the fall of 1980, Handel looked as though he was doing well— but another salesman in the Santa Clara office, Wayne Garten, had over sixty design wins and looked as though he was going to win the prize.

"Jeez, Wayne," Handel would say. "You got it, man." And right up to Christmas, Wayne thought he had won the prize.

Then Handel pulled his trick. On the last working day of the year, he opened the top drawer of his desk and drew out a sheaf of thirty or forty letters from customers, each of them confirming a design win. Some of them were products that sounded implausibly eccentric; Handel's favorite was a professor at the University of California at Davis who had designed an electronic brassière that would use an 8086 chip to monitor the wearer's breast temperature and let her know when the most fertile period of her cycle was approaching. But the letters were all in place, and Handel's total was approaching one hundred different design wins.

"All's fair," he told his disappointed colleague, "in love, war, and sales."

Handel knew, long before the trip to Tahiti, that he had won the contest.

So had Intel. Never mind whether the electronic bra ever made it to the mass market. The bigger issue was that Operation Crush had created so much momentum in the business market that by the end of 1980, the 8086 had clearly vanquished the rest of the market.

Operation Crush was aimed squarely at Motorola, Intel's leading adversary. It succeeded in squeezing Motorola's share of the microprocessor market down to 15 percent. But the first two victims of the operation were Federico Faggin and Ralph Ungermann, the two engineers who had left to form Zilog.

Faggin and Ungermann had fallen prey to the most common problem of small companies: They'd become too ambitious too fast. Their decision to diversify from microprocessors into memories, enthusiastically supported by the company's ill-informed paymasters at Exxon, diverted resources from the task of bringing the Z8000 to market. The extra people they hired to work on the Z8000 slowed down the development process instead of making it quicker. While it had taken them only nine months to bring the Z80 to market, the Z8000 took three full years. Like its predecessor, the Z8000 was a neat design, but it arrived too late. Intel had already shipped the 8086.

To make matters worse, Faggin and Ungermann received an unpleasant surprise late into the project. Like the people they had left behind at Intel, both men understood the concerns of customers who had invested time and money in building systems around their previous product. They set out with the objective of protecting those investments by making the new chip able to run software written for the old one. But the architect they hired to design the Z8000 had different ideas. He never told either of Zilog's founders so, but he was determined not to design what he viewed disparagingly as a "wart on a wart on a wart"—a botched upgrade to the Z80, which was itself a botched upgrade to the Intel 8080, which was itself a botched upgrade to the 8008. The result was that the Z8000 that emerged from three years of development was compatible with nothing. Zilog had the industry's narrowest product range, only a dozen salespeople, and no futures catalog of its own. All these factors together tested the loyalty of Zilog's customers base to destruction. Faced with the uncertainties of adopting a chip architecture whose future even a couple of years out was hard to predict, Z80 users turned their backs on the Z8000 and headed straight into the Intel camp.

Zilog's struggling sales effort looked like a disaster for AMD. It proved that Jerry Sanders's instinctive wish to hitch himself to the Intel star had been right to begin with. Once he had thrown in his lot with Ungermann and Faggin, Sanders had worked tirelessly to establish the Zilog part, or rather the AMZ8000 as his version was called, in the market. He had flown around the country and the rest of the world singing its praises; he had even tried to persuade his new shareholders and partners at Siemens that they should abandon their second-source agreement with Intel in order to take up the Zilog processor. (This approach was probably a little disingenuous, since Sanders would never have abandoned Intel if he had been offered the second-source terms that Siemens received.) But in autumn 1980, Sanders returned disconsolately to California from a trip to the Munich Oktoberfest, convinced that any further effort would be wasted. He walked into the office of Tom Skornia, who had abandoned his law practice and was now on the AMD payroll as company secretary and vice-president.

"Tom," he said miserably, "I'm making the wrong part."

22

Whetstone's Design Win

In 1965, three years before Intel was even founded, Gordon Moore wrote an article for *Electronics* magazine predicting that the power and complexity of the integrated circuit would double every year.

The number turned out not to be quite right. Moore's later experience at Intel demonstrated that it would be about once every eighteen months, rather than once a year, that the power of the integrated circuit would double. Throughout the 1970s, the trend had continued so smoothly that you could draw a log chart showing years along the x-axis and capacity running up the y-axis, and if you marked a point for every new product, the points could be joined up in an almost perfect straight line. This was true for just about any measure of capacity—number of transistors on a chip, clock cycle speed, whatever.

It was Moore's appreciation of the consequences of this phenomenon—which later became known as "Moore's law"—that guided Intel's strategy throughout the 1970s. If the price of semiconductor memory was going to fall by half every eighteen months, then you could predict in advance approximately when semiconductors would displace magnetic cores. If microprocessors doubled in power every eighteen months, then you could predict in advance when it would make economic sense to put a microprocessor inside a weighing machine, a digital watch, or a car.

But Moore had one curious blind spot: He was unable to see the application of his own law to the computer industry. While he appreciated that rising capacity would cut the cost of the mainframe computers that most big companies relied on, Moore did not recognize that the microprocessors Intel was developing might radically change the whole basis of the business by making computers, in a phrase he used in the 1965 article, "more generally available throughout all of society."

Lesser minds at Intel, by contrast, did see exactly what was coming. Rich Melmon, a young marketing planner who had written a paper about Intel when he was in business school in 1973, kept nagging his colleagues about the idea of a mass-market computer—so much so that Bill Davidow, his boss, told him he'd only have lunch with him "on condition that you don't bring up the subject of personal computers." In 1975, four of the company's best technical people— Ted Hoff, Justin Rattner, Stan Mazor, and Terry Opdendyk—started brainstorming about what they called a "desktop computer" intended as a tool for engineers. After working on the idea for a number of weekends, they produced a plan to equip an 8080 processor with a keyboard and a monitor and sell it in the home market. Gordon Moore was not interested.

"What's it good for?" he asked. The only concrete example the four engineers could offer was that "a housewife could keep her recipes on it."

"I personally didn't see anything useful in it," recalled Moore, "so we never gave it another thought."

In a sense, Moore had a point. To make a computer useful to the average person, it was not enough to have just a powerful, cheap combination of memory and central processing unit. You had to have devices that would make it easy for a consumer to use, starting with a keyboard, a good-quality screen, and a printer. And you needed dozens of programs—hundreds, maybe—that would allow the machine to do useful things, whether it was typing a letter, maintaining an address book, or keeping a set of accounts. Where would those programs come from? Certainly not from inside Intel; the company's resources were fully stretched as it was trying to cope with the proliferating industrial uses of the microprocessor. Nor were there many small companies outside that would wish to write these programs. Computer software was a highly specialized industrial market, and companies that wrote useful programs sold them for thousands of dollars each. Would they really want to write software for Intel's microprocessors, which were still considered ungainly and hard to use by comparison with "serious" computers?

By 1977, however, with another halving of the cost of processing power, people outside Intel were beginning to see the potential of personal computing. MITS came out with its Altair computer kit, using Intel's 8080 chip as a base. Radio Shack produced the TRS-80 computer. But by far the most important personal computing innovation of the 1970s was the work of Steve Wozniak and Steve Jobs, working in their garage with a couple of high-school kids as helpers. Their Apple II computer, portable in the sense that you could lift it, was the first computer that someone without a degree in engineering could seriously contemplate buying. The two young enthusiasts were introduced to A. C. "Mike" Markkula, an Intel employee who had been fired from the marketing department at Andy Grove's behest in 1976. Markkula had invested every penny he had in Intel stock when the company went public in 1971, and this, together with the options that came as part of his job, had made him so much money that he could afford to retire at the age of thirty-three. Instead, Markkula put $91,000 of his fortune into Apple, helped the two Steves arrange venture financing, and guided the company to a successful IPO in December 1980—the very month that Operation Crush ended.

By then, a program called Visicalc had been written for the Apple II. It was the world's first commercial spreadsheet, allowing accountants and bookkeepers to automate the brute calculations that had taken up much of their time until then. Visicalc was the first real answer to Gordon Moore's question, "What's it good for?" But Intel still didn't get it. Personal computers remained low on the list of the target markets into which the company was trying to sell its processors.

One of the good things that came to Intel from Operation Crush was a design win at IBM. Intel's relationship with the world's biggest computer company had long been an uneasy one. In keeping with its tradition of building all its components internally, IBM had refused to buy Intel's pioneering memory chips, and had been furious when Intel responded by moving into the memory systems business and selling add-on boxes for IBM mainframes that undercut the price of its own add-ons by as much as 50 percent. Andy Grove thought Intel was wasting its time trying to sell to a company that was so obviously irrational in preferring its own inferior technology. The salesman appointed by Intel's East Coast sales manager to work on the IBM account made regular sales calls for a year without receiving a single order, and Grove tried to have him fired. But he was prevailed on to wait, and eventually IBM came around. The company soon gave Intel its single biggest order of its first ten years: a request for memory chips worth $30 million. The chips were a special 32K design just for IBM: one 16K chip mounted on top of another, in a configuration that Gordon Moore referred to affectionately as "love bugs." But IBM was still suspicious of its smaller and much faster-moving competitor.

Late in 1979, just before Operation Crush had begun, Intel had released a strange, stripped-down version of the 8086 called the 8088. In an attempt to appeal to the segment of the 8-bit market that wanted to move up to 16-bit processing but found the 8086's price unpalatable, the 8088 was a low-cost hybrid. Its internal guts were the 16-bit engine of the 8086, but it used an 8-bit "bus" to communicate with peripheral devices and with memory. As well as making the device cheaper, this modification allowed the chip to be inserted into old 8-bit systems with only minimal modifications. It was a classic example of Intel's practical approach to the market. The 8088 might be hated by purists, but it did a useful job for users in the real world who didn't have the resources to convert their 8-bit products to a full 16-bit architecture immediately.

Earl Whetstone, a field sales engineer in Florida, was as keen to win the Crush sales prize as anyone else. Big Blue had never bought a processor from Intel before, but what the hell—it might be worth a try. He made a call on IBM's development facility in Boca Raton, Florida, and found an unexpectedly receptive audience.

Whetstone didn't realize it, but he had stumbled into one of IBM's internal political minefields. IBM had already taken the decision to build a desktop business computing device, to be known as the IBM Personal Computer. The project was being run out of Austin, Texas, and it was to be based on a Motorola processor. But Motorola was running late with its processor, and the IBM project was in jeopardy. Don Estridge, a senior IBM executive who was in charge of developing new distribution channels for the IBM PC, had made a deal with Sears, Roebuck & Co. that the new IBM machine would be distributed through Sears stores—and he knew that if IBM was unable to deliver the product as promised, the Sears deal could go down the drain.

With only partial approval from above, Estridge had set up a project to build a second version of the PC, referred to inside the company as Project Chess. To prevent jealous rivals in Texas from sabotaging it, he emphasized that the project was only intended as a test of the Sears distribution channel. Just as Intel had built the 8086 as a botched stopgap until the "real" project came good, so also Estridge was building a pared-down PC to keep the seat warm for Texas. Since he was in Florida, and supervising a team of engineers working out of trailers outside the DisplayWriter word processor and printer division, Estridge ordered his engineers to take the circuit boards out of the DisplayWriter and put them into a box so they could be used as a computer prototype. The DisplayWriter's processor, however, wasn't the 8086. It was the slower, crippled version of the 8086—the 8088.

Such was the secrecy of the project that IBM decided not to let even Intel know what was going on. Whetstone and his applications engineer were therefore asked to help build something without knowing what it was.

"When we went to provide technical support," he recalled, "they'd have our technical people on one side of a black curtain and theirs on the other side, with their prototype product. We'd ask questions; they'd tell us what was happening and we'd have to try to solve the problem literally in the dark. If we were lucky, they'd let us reach a hand through the curtain and grope around a bit to try to figure out what the problem was."

The guys at Intel realized that something was up when IBM demanded a second source for the 8088. You only asked for second sources when the component was strategic to your product line, when you couldn't afford for the source of supply to fail. Gradually, as 1980 turned into 1981, it dawned on Intel that the processor it was selling IBM wasn't going to go into a printer or a dedicated machine for word processing. It was the world's biggest computer company's first step into personal computing.

One of the design decisions made by IBM that caused most puzzlement at Intel was the company's choice of operating system for its new PC product. Intel knew a bit about operating systems because of the work it had been forced to do in making its microprocessors usable. The company had developed an OS of its own, called ISIS, which made it easier for users to write programs in high-level languages or run applications written by third parties.

Intel had turned down a number of opportunities to move into the computer business. In 1976, a consultant named Gary Kildall, who had written some software for Intel processors, offered the company rights to a new operating system for microprocessors that he'd written, called CP/M. He wasn't hoping to get rich from his creation; the terms that Kildall proposed were simply that Intel should give him a development system in return for CP/M. His point man at Intel, Brian Halla, looked at the package, talked to some colleagues, and came back to Kildall with the news that Intel wasn't interested; it was convinced that ISIS, its own operating system, was a better piece of software. But Halla offered to give Kildall the development system he'd asked for anyway, because the company was on good terms with him.

Five years later, Kildall's CP/M had attracted enough of a following among the hobbyists and hackers who built their own computers that IBM approached his company, Digital Research, with a view to negotiating a deal that would make CP/M the standard OS in the new PC. What happened next has become the subject of controversy and legend in Silicon Valley: Kildall was out of his Monterey office when the IBM team came to call, and the representatives that he left behind felt unable to agree to the tightly drafted confidentiality document that the guys from Big Blue insisted they sign before any discussion could take place. The result was that IBM left Digital Research empty-handed and went instead to Bill Gates at Microsoft. Gates didn't actually have an operating system to sell to IBM, but he promised to provide one anyway, which he later picked up for a song from a small company called Seattle Computer Products.

The Seattle Computer package, whimsically known as Q DOS, standing for "quick and dirty operating system," looked superficially similar to Kildall's CP/M, but was actually not compatible with it. Shortly before the launch of the IBM PC, Gates brought a copy of the program down to Intel, hoping that the chip manufacturer would give him a boost by endorsing it in some way as the standard operating system for its microprocessors. The Intel engineers were not impressed.

"My boss, Chuck McMinn, walks into my office one day and dumps a manual on my desk," recalled John Wharton. "He says a company up north is trying to convince Intel to license or endorse his operating system." Two days later, Wharton had studied MS-DOS, the product that would later become the best-selling piece of software in history, and had come to some harsh conclusions. "My advice was an unqualified no. These people are flakes. They're not original, they don't really understand what they're doing, their ambitions are very low, and it's not really clear that they have succeeded even at that." Wharton's negative impressions were compounded by the disarray he witnessed when he went up to spend a day in Seattle meeting the Microsoft developers. From then on, Bill Gates found that people at Intel stopped returning his calls.

In the company's defense, it must be said that Intel had its hands full working out what to do to satisfy IBM's demands for a second source for the 8088 processor. In the end, Intel bowed to the inevitable. It would give the second-source rights to AMD, its old sparring partner.

The first that Sanders heard of the matter was when IBM approached him with a request for a high-level briefing on AMD's future technology plans for microprocessors. A delegation of vice-presidents was sent to an IBM facility in upstate New York to give presentations on AMD's sales, marketing, MOS semiconductors, bipolar chips, and new product development. Shortly afterwards, a call came in from Intel asking if AMD would like to talk about future co-operation. Within a couple of meetings, it became clear what was on offer: Once again, Intel wanted AMD as a second source.

This time, Sanders and his colleagues hesitated before deciding whether to proceed. Of course Intel was the ideal company to second source—particularly since Operation Crush, whose existence was still an Intel secret but whose results were visible for all to see, had catapulted the company to unquestioned dominance of the micro-processor market. But Andy Grove had screwed AMD around once before, Sanders felt. AMD was going to look stupid enough switching back from Zilog to Intel after only a couple of years. If Intel reneged on the deal two more years down the line, Sanders would be the laughingstock of the Valley.

So Sanders sent his negotiators to Intel with a clear idea of what he wanted and how he proposed to get it. On balance, he decided that AMD would be willing to return to the Intel camp—but only as part of a long-term partnership that would guarantee AMD rights to a wider range of Intel products for a long time to come. In other circumstances, this might have been an unrealistic expectation. But news of the imminent launch of the IBM PC had leaked out, and it didn't take a rocket scientist to connect the two approaches to

AMD from IBM and Intel and to work out what was going on. Intel was asking AMD to be a second source for one reason and one reason only: IBM had held a gun to Andy Grove's head and told him that signing up Sanders was what he had to do to get the 8088 inside the PC.

AMD started out by refusing point-blank to pay any more royalties or license fees to Intel on the grounds that it simply couldn't afford to. After all, it was less than half Intel's size. Instead, the two sides came to an agreement whereby AMD would initially second-source Intel's parts for cash, but after 1985 a system of exchange would come into effect allowing AMD to offer its own products to Intel for second sourcing. The idea was that if the two second-sourcing programs were in balance, no money would need to change hands. Since chips could vary enormously in size and difficulty of design, a "complexity factor" system was agreed to allocate points to each chip. The balance of points would decide who owed what to whom. This agreement would last for ten years, with either side having the right to cancel at a year's notice after year five. The deal was signed in February 1982, just six months after the IBM PC hit the market.

These two events had a profound effect on both Intel and AMD over the succeeding decade. The inclusion of Intel's chip architecture in the IBM PC was to increase the market for its microprocessors a thousandfold, give the company real power over the market for the first time, and cast it forward into a new and utterly different stage of its history. The second-source deal was to give AMD a generous share of this bonanza, but ultimately lead to a court case between the two companies that would bring AMD perilously close to collapse.

And the other players? Motorola might be crushed, but it was not yet destroyed. Its 68000 processor architecture would live on in the Apple Mac and, in a different incarnation, in a highly profitable range of microcontrollers.

Zilog, by contrast, was already done for. The company was tottering managerially, because the arrival of a new executive nominated by Exxon had created ill-feeling between Faggin and Ungermann. But the news that IBM had designed an Intel chip into its new PC hit Federico Faggin "like a blow in the stomach." He knew the game was up. Before Operation Crush ended, he had found a discreet way to leave the company. He persuaded Exxon to promote him to the exalted title of Group Vice-President for Computer Systems, a job whose only responsibility was to move to New York and wait six months before moving on to something else. Ungermann left later to start a new networking company. Zilog limped on regardless, and is still in existence today. Faggin and Ungermann, cashing out with $4 million apiece, had made a well-timed exit.

That left just one chip not yet accounted for: Intel's 8800, the earth-shattering new 16-bit processor whose delay had led to the creation of the 8086, 8088, and IBM PC. Bill Lattin handed on the project to a successor, and the 8800 finally made it to market in February 1981. By then, the chip had been renamed the iAPX432—iAPX standing for Intel Advanced Processor Architecture. Its launch took place just at the time when the victory of the 8086 as the dominant microprocessor standard was complete, and was the biggest anticlimax in Intel's history. Entirely by accident, the company had found the microprocessor that the market wanted. The chip Intel had intended to make the industry standard was underpowered, late, and a shrunken disappointment compared to the grandiose ideas that had gone into it.

PART THREE

EXCLUSION

"Don't let your employees do to you what you did to your former boss."

> —The Golden Rule of protecting
> trade secrets, as defined by
> Intel general counsel Roger Borovoy

23

Seeq and Destroy

Shortly before Christmas 1980, a head appeared around the side of Gordie Campbell's cubicle in Santa Clara.

"Come in."

Five people walked into his cubicle. Five sheepish Intel employees looked at him, and then one began to speak.

"We've decided to leave Intel."

"I kinda guessed that," said Campbell.

"The trouble is that none of us will work for each other."

"Oh?"

"But we will work for you."

Gordie Campbell was one of Intel's more flamboyant marketing men. He'd joined the company in 1975 to work as manager of the company's major accounts, when Intel first realized that it needed to give special attention to the top twenty or so buyers of its semiconductors. After three years in that job, jetting around the country with Intel's top management in tow, Campbell had then been invited by Andy Grove to solve a problem in the nonvolatile memory business.

The problem started from the fact that Intel's EPROMs were too popular. Originally intended just as a prototyping tool, EPROMs had taken off as a mass-market device because companies realized that the ability to program a ROM chip electronically cut their development times sharply and allowed them to get products to market more swiftly. Intel's competitors had been slow to develop their own—with the consequence that even if the company charged truly wicked margins, which it did, people still queued up to buy. "We had guys showing up with suitcases of cash offering to buy parts," Campbell recalled. "They'd call to say that their chairman of the board would be thrown out unless we agreed to sell them parts."

With such overwhelming demand, the division's sales and marketing people had been unable to say no to their customers. The result was that the business had a backlog so large that on current production volumes, it would take five years to clear. It wasn't unusual in the semiconductor industry for customers to have to wait a few months for a popular part—maybe nine months in the middle of a real boom with capacity constraints. But five years? That was crazy. It made the company look foolish to its customers, it caused a great deal of unnecessary work in processing orders that never got fulfilled, and it made people angry when the company failed to deliver on its promises. Only 10 percent of orders were going out on the date that the company had committed to.

With some knocking together of heads, Campbell took a year to remove the backlog and to bring some semblance of order to the marketing process, to the point where "performance to first commit"—the measure of how many orders Intel processed as promised—was up to 87 percent. But Intel then decided to move part of the operation from Santa Clara to Albuquerque, New Mexico. Campbell, who had just divorced his wife and needed to stay nearby to see his children, immediately arranged a transfer within the company to a different job in California. But the division's move to New Mexico prompted others to reconsider their position, and the five people who had just walked into his office had done just that. Rather than stay at Intel and leave California, they preferred to stay in California and leave Intel.

Campbell chewed the matter over during the holiday, and then told his five colleagues early in the New Year that he accepted their invitation. Later in January, after some preliminary work had been done on their business plan, he led the group into the office of Ed Gelbach, who ran the whole of Intel's sales and marketing.

"Ed, we need to see you," said Campbell.

"Why all of you?"

"We thought this would be the best way to do it. We're resigning."

Gelbach, cool as ever, listened to their account of their plans to leave Intel and start up their own business manufacturing EPROMs under the name of Seeq Technology. He then got up from his chair and walked them straight out of the building. As they handed in their security badges, the six men might have been tempted to believe that leaving Intel had proven less traumatic than they expected.

A week later, Campbell and his new colleagues knew better. While they were away talking to the venture capitalists who had agreed to fund their new business, Intel served writs on them all—at their home addresses, which had the effect of intimidating the men's families.

To increase the intimidation factor, Intel also hired a blue-chip law firm from New York to fly over to California to take depositions from the Seeq founders. Cravath, Swaine & Moore was the partnership that IBM had used to fight the U.S. federal government through a decade of antitrust litigation. Tom Barr, one of the company's biggest stars, spent an entire week interrogating Campbell over his role in the affair.

"I'm sitting on one side with my one attorney," recalled Campbell as he pictured the occasion. "On the other, Tom is sitting there with *seven* other attorneys, four on one side and three on the other. I tell you, Intel had three or four law firms on this deal. I don't know what they paid Barr to do this."

The move succeeded in convincing Campbell that Intel was ready to spend big money to stop Seeq in its tracks. But Barr himself could not get Campbell to admit any wrongdoing. They talked the company's foundation over eighteen ways from eighteen different angles, but Campbell's answers were always the same.

It was not just the Seeq founders' decision to leave en masse that had provoked the lawsuit. Intel was terrified that the renegades might break its highly lucrative monopoly over 5-volt 16K EPROMS, which nobody else knew how to manufacture. The company was also incensed by some indiscreet observations that one of the founders of Seeq made to a local newspaper. The last straw was the discovery that Seeq had arranged for its telephone number to end in the digits 2764. Intel's 16K part was known as the 2716; the 64K version was under development, and Seeq's choice of phone number, anticipating the Intel product it aimed to compete with, seemed like a deliberate taunt.

But there was a bigger issue beneath the litigation. Intel was now clearly the dominant company in its industry, and Moore and Grove were determined that it should not become a 1980s equivalent of Fairchild. Fairchild had spun like a firework out of control, scattering valuable technology and talented people over the whole of Silicon Valley while itself falling into decline and unprofitability. Intel had already suffered defections since Faggin and Ungermann left to start Zilog—notably one group that left to start Daisy Systems, and another that founded Xicor, whose name was reputed to be an abbreviation for "ex-Intel Corporation." The company now had to decide what its strategy should be toward those who split off to set up on their own.

Inside Intel, the issue was hotly contested. Roger Borovoy, Intel's general counsel, took the relaxed, and slightly cynical, view that the departure of talented people who set up in competition with you was a long tradition in the Valley—and that you could minimize the losses by judicious legal maneuvering, but hardly prevent them altogether. Borovoy had written a short foreword to another lawyer's book on the protection of trade secrets, in which he suggested that the Golden Rule of the whole process was, *Don't let your employees do to you what you did to your former boss!*

Andy Grove was much less sanguine. He refused to accept that there were any relevant parallels between the current break-offs from Intel and Intel's own break-off from Fairchild thirteen years earlier (or come to that, Fairchild's break-off from Shockley eleven years before that). He did not believe that any of the parting managers was a 1980s Noyce. And frankly, he thought Borovoy was a wimp. In order to get the kind of action he wanted from his general counsel, Grove put the system of Intel Management by Objectives to work. He ordered Borovoy to initiate two new lawsuits per quarter. This case against Seeq was one of the consequences.

Yet even to Grove, it must have seemed a little odd to be suing Seeq. Campbell had raised funding for the new company from Kleiner, Perkins, Caufield & Byers, the Silicon Valley's leading venture capital firm. One of Kleiner's bigger investors was Gordon Moore: Like many other successful entrepreneurs in high-tech industries, his own experience of the spectacular rewards to be gained from start-ups had encouraged him to invest in other people's. To make matters worse, the partner at Kleiner, Perkins who had put together the Seeq deal was a keen young computer scientist by the name of John Doerr—the very same John Doerr who had spent a highly successful five years as a rising young marketing ace at Intel. The Seeq deal was his first transaction since leaving Intel; wisely,

Doerr had chosen to pick people from a company he knew and starting out in an industry that he knew.

Under the standard rules of litigation, Intel had the right to force the Seeq team to disgorge documents that might be relevant to the case, even if those documents harmed the start-up's own defense. But Borovoy found to his surprise that the Seeq files demonstrated little evidence of nefarious intent. Far from walking out the door with a cookbook full of Intel secrets, they had done the very thing that Moore and Noyce themselves claimed to have done to Fairchild— they had left to commercialize a research program that their existing employer had not yet brought to fruition, let alone put to commercial use. Asked afterward whether he thought the Seeq team had ever intended to steal Intel's secrets, Borovoy answered simply:

"No, I really don't. . . . They did not take a technology, they took an idea that Intel was not pursuing. That's a very good way to express it. But it was still Intel's idea. Intel owned it, and Seeq had no right to take it. That's what Intel did when it started from Fairchild."

But Intel's objective in the court case was not merely to seek after truth. Andy Grove wanted to stop the bastards—and with this in mind, any reasonable legal technique would do. "Once you're suing," said Borovoy, "you might as well put in everything that has any scintilla of credibility." So Intel took a daring step. It amended its action to complain of conspiracy to damage Intel instead of simply theft of trade secrets—and it brought Kleiner, Perkins into the battle by suing the venture capital firm too.

Suing the VCs was actually Art Rock's idea. The venture capitalist who had raised Intel's original funding was still a big shareholder, and still sitting on the company's board and attending the occasional executive staff meeting. It seemed to him that the lawsuit against Kleiner, Perkins might help *pour encourager les autres* as the French revolutionaries said in 1789 when guillotining aristocrats. But this tactic proved a disaster. Had Intel confined its attentions to Seeq, the lawsuit might have persuaded the venture capitalists that backing the fledgling EPROM company was too much trouble—and led them to stay out of any future rounds of financing. By threatening Kleiner, Perkins itself, however, Intel made the lawsuit a matter of principle and a matter of survival. The firm's partners knew that if they knuckled under, it could become much harder to raise money for start-ups in future. The suit also put Kleiner, Perkins in a position where it needed to clear its name. The implied allegation that it had conspired to steal secrets from a prominent Silicon Valley company was itself damaging to the venture capital firm's reputation. Within days, the partners hired one of the best law firms in town and made it clear that they would fight Intel to the end: millions in defense, as the old saying went, and not a cent for tribute.

Then the Seeq founders made a mistake that played right into Borovoy's hands. They made the tactical blunder of announcing a plan to license some basic EPROM technology—which looked much more likely to have come from Intel—to Zilog.

"We took the documents we had, and we crafted a detailed brief showing where our technology was being used," recalled Borovoy. "We didn't have a very strong case—I'd be the first to admit that, and they knew that—but there was stuff that was close. It would have been an up-and-down case at trial, but since they were greedy and wanted to give it away, we filed a motion for preliminary injunction. . . . We convinced the judge to grant it."

Denied the cash flow from royalties, Seeq was therefore forced to continue with the more difficult project of developing its own 64K EPROM technology alone and getting it to market. Gradually, the pressure of the court case began to tell. Almost a year after Seeq's founding, Campbell realized that the cumulative cost to date of fighting off Intel had grown to $1 million—nearly a quarter of the entire start-up capital that Seeq had raised. And there was a management issue too: Although Campbell and one other founder had taken on the job of managing the defense themselves, leaving the remaining four to focus on developing new technologies and building the business, the case was still depleting managerial resources needed elsewhere.

Faced with the preliminary injunction against technology transfer to Zilog, Borovoy guessed that Seeq's founders would now see that it made sense to settle. So he consulted the EPROM team at Intel and drafted a settlement that Campbell might bite on. Its principle was simple: Intel would allow Seeq to manufacture chips using the technology that the court had forbidden it to transfer to Zilog—"if you can make that work, God bless you," Borovoy put it—but Seeq would have to agree not to go back to the old technology that Intel had been using. The expectation inside Intel was that the newer EPROM process that Seeq was working on would be difficult, slow, and expensive to implement, and that Intel would keep its profits higher for longer by forcing Seeq to go with that instead of with Intel's more reliable and better understood process.

Bill Davidow was deputed to make the call.

"Gee, Gordie," he said when Campbell picked up the phone. "What do you think about this? Your emotions run pretty high when you go through a year of wasted time and money. Why don't we get together and have lunch and discuss this?"

"Y'know," he said at the lunch, "through the discovery of documents, we've determined that you guys have a different process than we have. Would you be willing not to use our process?"

Campbell consulted his colleagues and concluded that since the Seeq team were convinced their process would be better anyhow, they might as well agree. Davidow then replied that the two sides seemed to have grounds for a settlement.

So that was the end of Intel's lawsuit against Seeq and Kleiner, Perkins. Grove was happy, because Borovoy's tactics had cost Seeq a hell of a lot of time and money and had prevented the start-up firm from directly implementing anything that Intel was already using. Campbell was happy, because Seeq was now free to go ahead and try to make its new process profitable.

Campbell still felt a lingering resentment, however, at the way that the Seeq renegades were painted inside the company. With an eye to discouraging repeats of the incident, Intel had done a highly successful job at portraying them to its employees as cheats and thieves.

"Guys I thought were my friends wouldn't even talk to me," recalled Campbell. "They said *How could you have done this?* I said: *Done what?* They said: *Taking our technology out and starting a company with it like that.* Yes, it was a fairly subtle but a fairly effective campaign. Gelbach wouldn't speak to me for three or four years."

On the core issue—whether Intel had played fair in launching the lawsuit in such an aggressive manner—Campbell was less sure. At the time, he was hot with resentment and moral disapproval of Intel's tactics. Five years later, however, he changed his mind. By then, he had left Seeq and started a new company called Chips & Technologies—and Chips was suffering defections from engineers who left to start on their own. Campbell responded in a way Intel had taught him: He sued. It was a neat proof of Borovoy's Golden Rule.

Ultimately, the case had only one casualty, which neither Campbell nor Borovoy was aware of. It destroyed one innocent career.

John Doerr, the venture capitalist at Kleiner, Perkins who had helped to start Seeq, was married to a talented engineer who had joined Intel before he had, and was still there. As the Seeq battle became more embittered, Ann Doerr began to feel uncomfortable at Intel, being cast so clearly as a member of the opposition.

"John's firm had invested in Seeq," she recalled, "and Roger Borovoy used to kid me in the lunch room about the lawsuit, and I just felt I could not work freely if . . ." She stopped.

"It just became uncomfortable to have my husband aligned with the enemy," she said. "So I left."

24

Checkmate Powell

The fact that Intel's iAPX432 was brought to market at all, given its lateness and its technical deficiencies, was an indicator of how tenacious Intel could be in persevering with a project long after it was proven mistaken. But the chip's launch was also something else: a personal triumph, of a sort, for Casey Powell.

Powell, the East Coast sales manager who had encouraged the sending of the message that prompted Operation Crush, had spent most of 1980 in the trenches helping to run the campaign against Motorola. His appointment as general manager of the iAPX432 project was a sign of how divided opinion inside Intel was on the project. The supporters of the new megachip believed that if anyone could bring it into the light of day, he could. Its opponents, on the other hand, believed that if the project really deserved to be killed, Powell would not hesitate to administer the blow.

It was a painful few months. Development work proceeded at Intel's site in Oregon, and the chip already had one general manager, Jean Claude Cornet, with whom Powell was supposed to cooperate. Cornet, an engineer's engineer, did not think he needed any help, and it was some time before Powell had observed enough of the operation from the sidelines to take control.

After serving as midwife to the iAPX432, Powell was then given two jobs by the company. One was to combine the chip operations and microprocessor operations into a single organization; the other, to be carried out concurrently, was to run a renewed marketing campaign against Motorola. The problem was that Operation Crush had achieved everything that could be asked of it except for its original objective: Intel had not, in Jim Lally's words, "fucking *killed* Motorola." Indeed, the competition was still very much alive.

Motorola's 68000 chip was less of a success than Intel's 8086 and 8088. The launch of the IBM PC, with half a million machines sold in its first two years, had greatly increased the gap. Inside 80 percent of those machines was an Intel chip; the remaining 20 percent were made by other firms under license, notably AMD. But Motorola's semiconductor division in Phoenix had not lain idle in the meanwhile. It built a stripped-down version of its 68000 chip to match Intel's 8088. And it increased its position in consumer electronics and telecommunications spectacularly as the decade wore on.

Hence the call inside Intel, a year after the end of Operation Crush, to go back and finish the job. The executive staff decided to repeat the exercise—buttons, rallies, design win targets, vacations for the salesmen if they delivered, all the standard stuff—under the title of Checkmate. Casey Powell was designated the czar of the operation.

The campaign began against a dismal background for the company generally. Following the second oil shock, the world economy was in sharp recession. Competition had whittled away the margins on Intel's memory business. And in an attempt to avoid mass firings, Grove had instituted a program called the "125% solution." This campaign, with alarming echoes of *Animal Farm*, George Orwell's satire of Russian communism, was based on the belief that the company would pull through better if everyone worked harder. Accordingly, all Intel's staff except those who were paid hourly were asked to put in an extra two hours every day—even though many of them were already working weeks of sixty hours or more.

Even with these measures in place, it was hard to convince people that Intel's survival depended on zapping Motorola—no matter how persistently Andy Grove might repeat the assertion. Operation Crush was the kind of thing that happened to a company only once in its lifetime. The freshness of thinking, the sense of urgency, the suddenly shared common purpose—all of these were features of Crush that had jolted people out of their standard ways of doing things at Intel. Being jolted a second time with Operation Checkmate just didn't feel so spontaneous and exciting.

Nevertheless, the company put on a spectacular engineering spurt in 1981. By the month of March 1982, it was ready to launch four new chips—an embedded 16-bit processor called the 80186, a special coprocessor for local-area computer networks called the 82586, a coder-decoder chip for telecommunications called the 2914, and a new generation of the 8086 called the 80286. This last device was arguably the most important of the four. It answered the concerns of hundreds of thousands of people who had bought an IBM PC and only later discovered that their new computer was painfully slow when trying to carry out any kind of serious work. The 286 became the basis for a new, higher-powered IBM PC, known as the PC AT, with the "AT" standing for "advanced technology."

With all these marketing balls to keep in the air, Casey Powell also had to devote half his time to the narrower job in chip and microprocessor operations. But Grove thought Checkmate should be working better. He knew that Motorola was working on a world-beating new chip, to be known as the 68020, which would be 32-bit, would contain 200,000 transistors, and would be able to execute eight million instructions a second. And he felt that Intel had only a short time in which to solidify its lead.

Then Powell suffered a political setback. Bill Davidow, the microprocessor marketing guru who was his principal mentor, went off on sabbatical. Powell then found himself reporting, against his will, to Jack Carsten, a senior marketing executive brought in by Gelbach from Texas Instruments, who had become a senior vice-president of the company and general manager of the components group. Powell feared that Carsten hated his guts. The relationship wasn't helped when Powell had on one occasion refused to take orders from Carsten, bluntly telling him that it was to Davidow that he reported.

As 1982 wore on, Powell came under growing political pressure. Dave House, the general manager of the microcomputer group, warned him that Carsten was sowing doubts about his commitment in Grove's mind. Losing Grove's confidence, of course, spelled the end of your career at Intel.

It was House who told Powell one day the real definition of fear. "You're standing over your desk, you're going through your in-basket, and you find a Grovegram [also known as an Andygram] dated two weeks ago that your secretary forgot to put there until that morning, and which has an AR ["action required"] on it. And while you're reading it, *the phone rings.* You know it's Andy. You just know it is."

Matters came to a head at a meeting of the Intel executive staff when Powell, four months into the new job, was called in at Carsten's instigation to give a progress report on Checkmate. As he walked into the meeting, he had a terrible foreboding. He had been warned beforehand that Grove was likely to lay into him—and looking around, he could see the company's entire executive top brass assembled, staring at him with cold, unsympathetic faces. Powell had no choice in the matter. With a perceptible tremor in his voice, he launched into his presentation on the problems facing the Checkmate program four months in.

Carsten interrupted.

"Well, aren't you the problem?" he demanded.

Before Powell could complete a defense of his management of the project, Grove asked a question. Before Powell could complete his answer, Grove snapped out a follow-up. Powell paused. Then Grove began to shout and hammer the table with his fist. His voice rising to an angry roar that reverberated around the room, Intel's president took Powell's presentation apart piece by piece. Red with anger as he warmed to his theme, Grove accused the Checkmate chief of incompetence, inexperience, everything.

"I put you into this job," he said, "and I'll take you out of it if you don't perform."

As his outburst continued, other members of the executive staff fell silent. Inured as they were to aggressive combat in the name of constructive confrontation, they could only look on, stunned. Powell just stood to attention, frozen in his place. Finally, Ed Gelbach stood up and threw his pencil down on the table.

"If you're going to do this to the guy, take him out and don't do it in front of everybody."

Another member of the executive staff got up from his place.

"I'm leaving," he said. "I'll come back when this is over."

Grove had by then come to his senses.

"All right!" he said. "Continue!"

Voice shaking, Powell wound up his presentation with a set of recommendations for fixing the problems of the campaign. "OK," he said. "Does that satisfy you that this will solve the problem?"

"We'll just have to see," replied Grove. "OK, fine, thank you."

But Powell was not yet done. "Now let's talk about my problem," he said.

"What do you mean, *my problem?*" demanded Grove.

"Well, evidently I'm a does not meet as general manager of microprocessor operations," he said, referring to the Intel rating system of "meets requirements," "does not meet requirements," and "superior." "Right, Dave?"

Dave House shrugged.

"I'm a does not meet at running Checkmate."

Carsten shrugged.

"Let me tell you something else. I'm a does not meet as a father and a husband. I am *not* a does not meet performer. What are you going to do about *my* problem?"

Grove, now calmer: "What do *you* think the solution is?"

Powell threw a look of death at Jack Carsten. "If you leave it up to me," he said, staring into the eyes of the man he believed to be his tormentor, "I can solve the problem just like *that.*" He snapped his fingers, and the sound echoed around the room.

Seeing that a fight was about to break out, someone said "Stop the meeting, Grove." And for the first time in living memory, Intel's executive staff broke up for an unscheduled recess.

As Powell walked toward the door, he saw Grove standing there, Carsten at his elbow. "I'm sorry," said Grove.

"I didn't know whether to cry, to hit him, I felt so violated," recalled Powell. "Until that point, if you cut me, I bled blue [the company's color]. I was a total Intel person."

Powell turned to Grove. "How can you tell me you're sorry when I knew last week that you were going to do this?"

"I don't know what to say . . . ," began Grove.

But Powell had already turned on his heel and walked out of the room. He continued straight past the reception desk, out into the parking lot, and into his car. Then he drove back to his hotel, ignoring the furiously blinking message lamp on his telephone, and took his six-year-old daughter out to the Great America theme park just off Highway 101.

After a few rides, he had cooled down enough to pick up his messages. The first was to call Dave House—with special instructions to tell House's secretary to put the call through immediately, no matter what.

"What would you do if you were me?" House asked him.

"You leave me alone for a while," replied Powell. "Because emotionally, I've [already] quit. . . . But I can tell you something I know already. Carsten's the guy who precipitated this. I will not bend down to him even on one knee. The plan I have in place is going to work. I'll finish Checkmate. I'll make it work. Then I'll either find another job in Oregon with Intel, find another job in Oregon outside Intel, or start another company."

Six months later, Powell received an Andygram—a little message of congratulation, written in red ink in the president's soft, oddly feminine continental letters, initialed at the bottom with his trademark curving AG.

"On that fateful day, I doubted you," it began. "You were right and I was wrong. You've now proven that everything you said was true."

Powell took that as his exit visa. "I could leave knowing that he had acknowledged I was right. That gave me permission. I wasn't running away from anything. I wasn't leaving a failure."

A few days later, he went into Dave House's office and resigned. But Casey Powell had learned the lessons of Gordie Campbell and the foundation of Seeq. He had telephoned the attorney who had defended Campbell against Intel's lawsuit, explained who he was, and explained that his intention was to quit the company.

"It was like sitting down *knowing* that you're going to be audited, saying 'I want to fill out my tax return and I don't want to do anything illegal,' " Powell recalled.

The lawyer gave him all the details. Don't use any company property in getting your new business together, not even a pencil. Don't do anything on company time. Don't write a business plan before you leave. If you've got the balls to do it, take people with you—but meet them off the premises. And when you do take people, take them all at the same time, because otherwise if you go back for a second bite then they'll consider it so threatening that they sue.

Following these instructions to the letter, Powell gave up his job at Intel. He took seventeen people with him from Intel's Oregon operations, and they all handed in their notice on the same day. When Intel asked him what he planned to do, Powell replied with sweet simplicity that he refused to give any details. He would not preclude doing something that competed with Intel but he had no plans at the present time to do so.

Andy Grove was incensed. He wanted to sue—on the basis that Casey Powell *must* have used inside information to know who the seventeen people were and that they were any good.

"Andy, that's an also-ran. You've gotta have something better," replied Roger Borovoy, the company's general counsel. "You can't make that the centerpiece, or you'll be laughed out of court." But Borovoy could not dissuade the Intel president from sending lawyers around inside the company, interviewing anyone who seemed to have come in contact with Powell or his seventeen colleagues during the past six months. Of course, Intel's lawyers had no right to take depositions from the renegades themselves, since no suit had been filed against them.

Borovoy counseled Grove against going too far. "A lot of people at Intel liked those people," he said. "It made people inside edgy if you were too aggressive."

Many months later, one further Intel employee applied for a job at Powell's new company. By then it had defined its business as building powerful computers, and its name as Sequent. Powell had wanted to use the name Sequel, to mark the symbolic change he had made in his life by leaving Intel, but he was advised that the trademark office wouldn't accept the name because Hawker-Siddeley already owned the name for a gas turbine product. As soon as this eighteenth Intel employee gave in his notice, Powell received a call from Ed Gelbach asking to come and meet him at Sequent.

Gelbach walked into his former colleague's office and dropped two draft complaints on Powell's desk. One was for the actual expenses and costs that Intel claimed it had suffered from his defection, amounting—curiously, given Powell's involvement with the iAPX432—to precisely $432,000. The other demanded punitive damages, and ran to a total of many millions of dollars. Both named Powell in person, rather than his company, as the defendant.

"Hey," said Gelbach. "These guys want to sue. I keep telling them no. I've come to make a deal."

"I'm not going to make any written deal with you," Powell replied. "But I'll tell you now that I'm not going to hire anyone else. If you want to sue me, go ahead. Make me a martyr. Go ahead."

It was only Andy Grove who couldn't make a clean break. When Sequent's first products came out, they used processors made by National Semiconductor—and the chipmaker, anxious for any ammunition to use against the market leader, ran pictures of Sequent products prominently in its own ads in the trade press. On one occasion, Grove found a National ad featuring Powell that had by chance been printed opposite an ad for Intel. He mailed it to Powell, with a handwritten note on it, signed with a smiley face inside his trademark capital A: "CP—I always knew your heart was in the right place." The message seemed to be clear: *You don't leave Intel. We win. You don't win.*

Later on, Powell relented, and decided that Sequent would do better to base its machines on Intel architectures. He contacted Grove to arrange a meeting.

"The past is behind us," he began. "I never did anything wrong. I'd like to do business with you."

"Fine," said Grove.

Some years later, Powell bumped into Grove again on the podium at an industry event. "Powell," he said, a smile on his face and the Hungarian accent still audible in his voice, "the best thing you ever did was to come back to Intel."

25

Microcode

By 1982, Sven Simonsen and Jerry Sanders were the last two of AMD's eight founders still associated with the company. Larry Stenger had always told his friends that he would quit as soon as his shareholding was worth $1 million—and in 1976, he was as good as his word, saying a cheerful farewell to AMD. Jim Giles, an outstanding analog circuit designer, had never had ambitions to manage others the way Sanders did. Keeping to himself, he remained an "individual contributor" to the company, devoting his spare time to photography and the care of a sick child. The penultimate departure was John Carey. In 1978, as Sanders was putting the final touches to the Siemens deal, Carey suffered a minor collapse during a corporate outing to the opera in Munich. Covered in sweat, he showed clear symptoms of nausea and loss of balance. It was evident to his colleagues that his illness was related to stress—and perhaps also to the tensions in his relationship with Sanders. Within a year, he had left AMD to concentrate on his garden and his collection of vintage cars.

With the help of the generous salary and options he extracted from AMD's board of directors, Sanders had become increasingly flamboyant. He acquired a second Rolls-Royce, a third mansion, and a nubile former beauty queen to serve as his second wife. Linda Sanders, his first wife, had served a divorce writ on him as he walked up the steps of AMD's headquarters shortly after the couple returned from a monthlong vacation in France.

It had to be admitted that Sanders looked and acted every bit the successful CEO. For one of AMD's famously luxurious Christmas parties, costing an astounding $500,000, he hired Bruce Springsteen to sing—and later made his own grand entrance on a sleigh. He gave away a red Corvette as a prize to an AMD employee—milking the resulting publicity with the slogan, "America's hottest car for America's hottest company." He gave away $240,000 of the company's money— $1,000 a month for twenty years—in a lottery to a twenty-one-year-old woman from the Philippines who had recently joined AMD to work at $4 an hour on the graveyard shift. He chose to be photographed for a book on Silicon Valley pioneers in his dressing gown, lying lubriciously on an enormous four-poster bed in one of his houses.

Sanders was always ready with a snappy line. When a securities analyst asked him in 1981 why, if the company's fortunes were as bright as he was claiming, he had just sold thirty thousand AMD shares, Sanders replied: "I've been selling stock primarily to finance my rather lavish lifestyle." At a speech to the Semiconductor Industry Association's annual dinner during the pit of the oil-shock recession, Sanders held a sheet of paper above his head.

"For those of you who are relative newcomers to our industry, having joined our ranks over the last twelve months, I would like to show you something perhaps you have never seen. This is a purchase order. [Laughter] As we conclude calendar 1981, the U.S. semiconductor industry is meeting the challenge. We have matched the Japanese in yields. We have matched the Japanese in price. We have matched the Japanese in quality. And by year-end, it appears we will match the Japanese in lack of profitability!"

The next speaker on the podium was Bob Noyce, who was to offer a forecast for sales during the coming year.

"It's sort of like following Bob Hope with a reading of the obituaries," he said.

But Sanders was a difficult man to get on with if you tried to get behind his presidential mask—particularly if you had known him since the tough days of AMD's start-up. Not only did Sanders like to micromanage the company's most senior executives—in some cases going over their travel schedules to make sure they were flying the most economic routes and not spending too much time in hotels at the beginning and end of their trips. Sanders also continued to keep power over the company tightly in his own hands.

A case in point was the SEC's recommendation in 1980 that

membership of the boards of directors of public companies should be set by a nominating committee. The SEC's objective was clear; it wanted to make nonexecutive directors more independent of the full-time officers, by taking the power to hire and fire outside directors away from the full-time insiders. Since it was Sanders's good relations with members of the board, and his influence over the board's membership, that was at the heart of his ability to extract such generous compensation from AMD, it was not surprising that he did not like this idea. With the help of Tom Skornia, he concocted an ingenious circumvention of the new rule: Instead of appointing a subcommittee of the board to decide who should serve as directors, Sanders arranged for the board to sit as a "committee of the whole"—as a subcommittee of itself, made up of the entire board membership—with the effect that he complied with the SEC rule, but had the same control over the crucial issue of board appointments as he had over any other decisions of the board.

"We got away with this for twelve years until Calpers [the pension fund representing California state employees, which had a reputation for being a strong defender of shareholder rights] figured out what was going on," recalled Skornia.

After Carey's departure from AMD, Simonsen's professional respect for Sanders's managerial abilities remained undiminished. But he felt a sense of growing distance from Sanders—a distance that was exacerbated when Sanders named a new senior vice-president and asked Simonsen to report to him instead of directly to Sanders. So when an opportunity came up for Simonsen to join a venture capital partnership, he took it. By late 1982, the last of Jerry Sanders's original seven partners had left AMD.

An equally important change happened inside Intel during the same year. Roger Borovoy, the lawyer who had once said that Bob Noyce's new company was not yet large enough to require someone of his horsepower, had decided after more than eight years at the company's legal helm to move on. Like Simonsen at AMD, he too had been downgraded. Andy Grove, deciding that he only wanted to have three or four people reporting to him, had asked Borovoy instead to report to Larry Hootnick, who had been promoted from CFO to senior vice-president for finance and administration.

Borovoy had no difference of personality with Grove. He remained one of the greatest admirers of the man's irascible, driven, obsessively intellectual leadership of Intel. But Borovoy was simply "Inteled out," as he put it. His life had become too scheduled. He would go to three rigorously timed meetings in a row and return to his office to find a dozen phone messages requiring attention. In his new career—venture capitalism, like Simonsen—Borovoy would still come back to the office to find twelve messages. But his time felt more his own, and he had become an entrepreneur in the sense that his mission now was to go out and look for deals. After leaving Intel, he felt that a great weight had been lifted from his shoulders.

Talking to Andy Grove about who should succeed him, Borovoy had pressed the claims of Tom Dunlap, a young engineer who had started studying law in night school while on the company payroll. Dunlap had attracted Grove's attention early on in his legal career, when a senior executive of National Semiconductor had reported to Gordon Moore that he had been offered the chance to buy a stolen computer tape containing secret Intel chip mask designs. In order to apprehend the thieves, someone needed to pose as an executive of National Semiconductor and make the buy. Placing his loyalty to Intel above his own safety, Dunlap volunteered. He went to an apartment in San Jose, wired with a radio-microphone and badged up with a false ID card identifying him as a National employee, and agreed on a buying price with the thieves. When Dunlap gave a preagreed signal—"It's a deal!"—police waiting in an unmarked van outside burst in and made the arrests.

Andy Grove was deeply impressed by the lawyer's willingness to risk his life for the company. When Borovoy asked him to back Dunlap's candidacy above that of Ted Vian, the corporate counsel who had been waiting fifteen years for the top slot, Grove jumped at the idea.

"It's fine with me," Grove said. "I'll always remember what Tom did with that stolen stuff—I'll always admire Tom for having done that. But Art Rock's gonna have a cow because Dunlap's so junior."

"I'll handle Art Rock," Borovoy replied. Rock, the venture capitalist who had started Intel fourteen years earlier and served as the company's first chairman, was still a force to be reckoned with inside the company—even though he had abandoned the company's chairmanship a decade earlier.

Borovoy went to see Rock, and told him that Dunlap was one of the best lawyers he had ever seen. "I'm convinced he'll grow into the job."

The wizened financier looked unconvinced. "I'll go along with it," he growled, "but he'll be *corporate* counsel, Ted's old title. If he does good, then he'll be general counsel."

Borovoy was proven right, and Rock was as good as his word. Dunlap, appointed in 1983, did grow into the job—and within a year, his title had been upped from corporate to general counsel.

These two departures—Borovoy from Intel, Simonsen from AMD—were to prove more important than anyone realized. Both men had exerted some degree of restraining influence on their bosses. Once they had gone, relations between the two companies deteriorated rapidly.

The background to the issue was that the balance of power between Intel and AMD began to change almost as soon as the ink was dry on the ten-year technology-sharing agreement that they signed in 1982. Once the pressure from IBM to appoint a second source was off Intel, the deal with AMD began to look less attractive—and as Intel consolidated its lead over Motorola in the battle for dominance of the 8086 processor generation, the need for a second source diminished.

Meanwhile, Jerry Sanders was unable to resist crowing in public about how well he had done from the agreement. Before he had left AMD, Simonsen had writhed in agony as the AMD chairman told an invited group of securities analysts visiting from New York what a great deal it had been, and how foolish Intel had been to sign it. Simonsen had tried a number of times to warn Sanders not to shoot his mouth off. *Say we're successful, by all means. Tell them whatever you want about how good the company is. But you don't need to continually address this contract and rub Grove's nose in it.*"

Tom Skornia, AMD's general counsel, had detected the same problem even earlier. On the very day the deal was publicized in 1982, he had sat in the audience at the press conference and scrutinized Andy Grove's reaction while Sanders was repeating his mantra about how the agreement was an "alliance of peers."

"The look on Grove's face was priceless," he remembered. "Intel and Grove, in their own estimation, are without peers."

By 1984, Sanders was beginning to take serious risks. At an analysts' meeting at the Pierre Hotel in New York in September, one analyst asked the AMD chairman to explain how it could be possible that Intel had invented the "E-squared" PROM, a new type of EPROM, and yet that AMD seemed to have brought the product to market almost simultaneously and sold more units. In answer, Sanders proceeded to trash Intel's manufacturing process in Albuquerque. He explained, in detail, how this was a case in which Intel had failed to execute on a good piece of technology development—and added that the problem was not that unusual, either.

"I thought: *Why would he do this to a guy who came to America after throwing Molotov cocktails in front of Russian tanks in Budapest?*" recalled Skornia. "Andy Grove must have picked up the trade press, read about those remarks, and said 'That's it.' It's clear that [the relationship] went downhill from there. It was clearly a tremendously imprudent thing to do. But [Sanders] just had to crow about the fact that he had a bigger market share and Intel was the inventor."

In 1984, AMD and Intel renegotiated the terms of the 1982 agreement. Sanders wanted early second-source rights to Intel's two newest processors, the 80186 and the 80286; in return he agreed to pay extra royalties, this time not a percentage of AMD's factory-gate price but a flat rate per processor. This made a huge difference: It meant that as each processor generation matured and selling prices fell, the cost to AMD of second sourcing would rise from a modest percentage of the proceeds to a much higher revenue slice that would seriously curtail the smaller company's ability to undercut Intel. But Intel also agreed, subject to confirmation of final specifications, that it would accept two important new parts under development at AMD. If Intel chose to second-source the parts, then AMD would win points under the old 1982 formula based on complexity and form factor, and no royalties would be payable on the processors.

The amendments to the deal, like the original agreement they modified, were handled on both sides without much involvement of the lawyers. The fine points were fixed between Dave House and Tony Holbrook, AMD's COO. Holbrook became worried that Intel's engineers might choose to reject the two parts. A week after the amended agreement had been signed, he called House to express his concerns.

"Don't worry, Tony," House replied. "I'll make them take [them]."

The two parts were a hard-disk controller, known as HDC for short, and a graphics chip called a quad-pixel display manager, or QPDM.

Ten days later, House called Holbrook back.

"Remember the HDC and QPDM?" he asked. "We're not taking them."

House's call provoked a fierce reaction inside AMD. One faction said that Intel was simply hard to please. With a history of distinguished innovation, and with a large dose of NIH, or not-invented-here syndrome, Intel was always likely to look down its nose a little at other companies' parts. Intel could also claim, with some justice, that some of the parts AMD offered were too large to be manufactured cost-effectively. AMD's job, said the proponents of this point of view, was to work as hard as possible in meeting Intel's demands for improvements and changes.

The other faction insisted that Intel wasn't playing fair. It seemed clear, its members complained to Sanders, that the larger company was trying to stop the technology-transfer deal from working. It was deliberately putting up obstacles. It was imposing impossible conditions. Intel was determined, they argued, to reject the HDC and QPDM and to force AMD to pay through the nose for access to the 286.

Sanders decided to proceed on the assumption that Intel was acting in good faith. He told AMD's technical people to work harder at getting the two parts in the shape that Intel wanted, and to keep coming back with amendments, no matter how troublesome and difficult the Intel engineers might be.

Sanders was wrong. He would not discover the evidence for several years, but Intel had definitively decided, while the amendment was being negotiated, that it wanted the whole technology-sharing deal to collapse. A secret internal memo from one senior Intel official to another stated the company's strategy in two succinct bullet points:

- Assure AMD they are our primary source through regular management contact and formal meetings.
- Take no more AMD products under the current agreement.

Jerry Sanders had finally received his comeuppance for baiting Andy Grove. Intel had decided that its position in the market was strengthening so fast that in its very next chip generation—the 386—there would be no need for a second source at all. The computer and electronics industries would all say they wanted a second source, and Intel would encourage that belief while samples of the 386 were being designed into new products. When the chip was ready to go into mass production in the fabs, however, Intel would reveal to the world that no other company would be licensed to manufacture it. By then, it would be too late for customers to protest—and the momentum behind the chip would carry Intel through as the sole source. With no Jerry Sanders to cut into its margins, the company would be able to price the chip higher to begin with and to slow down the swift price erosion that came with second sourcing. The strategy would add hundreds of millions of extra dollars to Intel's bottom line.

But to make the strategy work, Intel needed AMD's cooperation in the 286 generation—and to win that, Intel needed to make AMD believe that it was going to be given the 386. Otherwise, there was a danger that Sanders might try to harm Intel by switching his support to another company's 286-class architecture.

In 1985, another internal Intel memo defined this objective succinctly: "Keep AMD in the Intel camp." It continued: "Key point— we are in no hurry. We don't need a 386 second source, especially since everyone assumes AMD will be one." Another memo, a year later: "Maintain a second-source, business as usual posture in the market place. . . . Our strategy is to keep talking. . . . We do not want them [AMD] to go to Hitachi or NEC, and should not stimulate them to do so."

After having already made two switches, Sanders was in no mood to change camps again to a competing processor architecture. But in 1986, he lost patience and decided to invoke the arbitration clause of the 1982 agreement. The clause laid down an informal procedure for settling disputes under the agreement before a private arbitrator.

Rich Lovgren, AMD's general counsel, called an outside lawyer called Terry MacMahon to ask him to handle the case.

"It'll be a twelve-week trial, Max," said Lovgren. "Can you commit to that?"

"Yes," replied MacMahon.

Lovgren was wrong. The arbitration would last three years—with hearings over 313 days, 61 witnesses, 2,093 exhibits and 42,000 pages of transcript—and the dispute between the two companies would soon widen into a number of related cases in open court. The longest and most bitter litigation in semiconductor history had begun.

26

Gold

The ad in the paper didn't name the company, but the job sounded like fun—and Rob Miller, just graduated from the California State University at Sacramento, known familiarly to its alumni as Sack State, needed a job. He had majored in criminal justice, and the position advertised was for an investigator at one of Silicon Valley's leading technology companies. The mystery of not knowing who the employer was added to the excitement. Instead of being invited to the offices of a potential employer, Miller was told to meet a recruiter at the Radisson Hotel in Santa Clara for an interview.

By 1983, Intel was a billion-dollar business with twenty-one thousand people on its payroll—and like any other company of its size, it needed an internal security department. There would always be work for a small team of people that could gather information swiftly and discreetly: petty thefts, harassment cases, workers' compensation claims, and industrial accidents. But the nature of its product made Intel a little special. When you were pumping out, a million times a month, little chips of silicon the size of a fingernail that were worth hundreds of dollars apiece—considerably more than their weight in gold, incidentally—the wages of sin were high, and the precautions you needed to take against sin had to be in proportion. The job opening, Miller learned, was part of an expansion of the company's internal security operation.

Rob Miller's first duties were an indication of how thorough a management machine Intel had become. Arriving at the company's Santa Clara headquarters and reporting to a former probation officer named Marvin Zietzke, he was shown how to use a microfiche reader and set to work on a pile of application forms. Each one gave someone's personal details; Miller's job was to check that none of the people on the list had criminal records in Santa Clara County. The pile of forms to be processed was not limited to résumés from new college graduates who had applied for jobs at Intel. Anyone who walked through the doors and spent time unaccompanied had to be checked: a temporary worker, a contractor working on the installation of equipment or the repairing of an air conditioner, even someone whose job was to replenish the peanut machines, *anyone*. This made sense: If you wanted to insinuate an industrial spy into a rival company, it was much easier to get them hired as an office cleaner than as a circuit designer—so even the shortest stays and the most menial jobs still required the basic check.

Soon Miller's job began to broaden. The rookie investigator found himself doing surveillance on company employees who Intel's security chiefs believed might be selling secrets to competitors. With a sensitive job appointment, sometimes a résumé needed to be checked in the finest detail; Miller would be sent out to go and chat with former coworkers or landlords to find out what was going on.

But the exciting stuff, which really needed initiative, was in the sting operations. Knowing there was a thriving black market in stolen semiconductors, Intel did not wait to suffer loss before trying to find the fences who helped stolen parts find their way back into the system. Instead, it would set up operations to find buyers for stolen parts and smoke them out. The procedure was complex, and required time and care. Acting incognito, without revealing their association with Intel, members of the security department would establish a company in the Bay Area. Using the trading name of the dummy company, they would then place ads in the local papers and trade press offering Intel parts at prices so low that anyone could see they must be stolen.

As soon as a taker appeared, one of Intel's security staff would be detailed to meet the intended buyer, make it clear that the units on offer were stolen, and wait to hear a reaction. If there was the slightest sign of a bite, Intel could call in the police to arrest the buyer immediately. The team would then wind up the company it had created and start the operation afresh under a different name in a different town.

A year after he started Miller stumbled on his biggest case. A call came into the company from someone who wouldn't give his name, but explained that he knew of an Intel employee, aged twenty-nine with a wife and two kids, who worked as a technician but seemed to have a great deal more money than his occupation would suggest. The anonymous caller went on to make a specific allegation: "He's stealing gold from you." He identified the employee by name, adding that the employee had just bought a new house in the California town of Modesto in addition to his existing property in Los Gatos, close to Intel's Santa Clara headquarters. With a salary of only $30,000, suggested the informant, the guy clearly had found some lucrative second source of income.

Miller discovered from research inside Intel's personnel records that the employee worked shifts like a firefighter, twelve or fourteen hours at a time with long rest breaks in between working days. His job was to service peripheral machinery in the fabs—and among his jobs was a twice-monthly cleaning of the inside of a centrifuge machine. One of the materials deposited on the inside of the centrifuge when the factory was running was pure gold—a material that was used in chips in only tiny quantities, but quantities that built up considerably when you were shipping millions of parts a month. Intel had budgeted a half-million dollars a month for its gold needs. But in a startling illustration of the fact that the company was now too big for Andy Grove's rigor to reach into every last corner of its operations, there was no mechanism in place to check that all the gold the company bought was either being shipped out of the door inside semiconductor packaging or was being recycled.

Rather than simply haul the technician in for questioning, Miller was ordered to investigate further. A closed-circuit TV system was rigged up near one of the centrifuges from which the technician was believed to be taking the gold, and the security team spent several hours glued to a screen nearby, trying to capture evidence of theft on videotape. But the technician seemed to have a knack of always turning his back so that the position of his hands was shielded by his body from the camera. In the end, Miller and his colleagues had to resort to direct surveillance. Four or five of them would lie in wait in various hiding places inside a giant machine room full of tanks and machinery and catwalks with metal steps. For hours on end, in the middle of the night, they would remain hidden in their places, waiting to nail the technician as he carried the gold he had retrieved from the centrifuge to the safe where he was supposed to store it for later weighing and recycling.

"We were never seen," recalled Miller. "We watched him come out. He would go . . . through this boiler area to the room where he changed. We suspected somewhere along the way that he was dumping the gold.",But after nearly twenty attempts, the security men were still unable to *prove* that the technician was making off with the gold. If he was stealing it, he had certainly found a smart way to do so.

Only when Miller started to do some lateral thinking did the investigation begin to progress. Assuming that the guy was stealing the gold, what would he do with it? Sell it, of course. Since the sale of pure gold in the United States was an obvious route for money laundering by tax evaders or criminals, it was subject to regulation and reporting. Miller discovered that any dealer who bought gold in bars was obliged to keep records of who had sold it to him and to issue receipts. A check of the local pawnbrokers, however, drew a blank. Since all the local pawnbrokers knew that semiconductor makers used gold, they would hardly be able to buy a hand-molded gold bar without provenance and maintain with a straight face that they'd never guessed it had been stolen from a fab. But that left unanswered the question of what Intel's thieving technician was doing with the gold that he was taking.

Miller was told to find out the hard way—and as preparation for the operation, he was sent to watch the technician's street for a few days. The next Wednesday, he stayed awake watching TV until nearly three in the morning, and then drove a small van down to Los Gatos. Drawing up outside the technician's house, he hoisted into the back of his van the three garbage cans left out on the street for the regular Thursday morning collection. He then drove a few blocks down the street and around a corner, stopped the van, and emptied the contents of the garbage cans into heavy-duty plastic sacks. Then he drove back to the house, deposited the empty cans back on the street as quietly as possible with their lids in place, and went home with the booty. Opening the plastic sacks one by one, he spread the messy contents of the technician's garbage on his own kitchen table, donned a pair of rubber gloves, and began to sort through it. His objective was clear: to find anything that would give any clue as to where the suspected gold thief was disposing of his ill-gotten gains.

It was a messy job, and produced no results. But Miller's orders were to persevere until he had solved the problem. The following week, he rolled up at the house in the early hours of Wednesday morning once again, picked up the garbage, and did the switch around the corner into bags. Again nothing. Soon it became a routine: Once or twice, Miller even brought his girlfriend with him. But as the weeks and months went by, and the countless sacks had been painstakingly sorted through on the Miller kitchen table, there was still not a single indication as to what the technician was doing with the gold. Miller began to wonder whether the phone call had been a hoax. Maybe the guy was innocent after all.

Nearly a year later, Miller hit pay dirt. Scrabbling among the empty cans of pet food and soiled diapers, he found a letter from a pawnshop in the gambling resort of Reno, Nevada. Within days, the shop had been checked out, the local police had been contacted, and the storekeeper had been challenged to produce his gold purchase records. He was already known to the cops for having a reputation as an under-the-table gold dealer, so it required little persuasion to convince him that he could save his own skin by helping to turn in the gold thief. Some weeks later, with the cooperation of the crooked pawnbroker, Intel was able to document the technician's next sale— an eight-inch-long ingot of solid gold weighing several pounds and worth $20,000.

The arrest did not take long. Intel alerted the local cops in Modesto, where the technician kept his second home, and Miller agreed to wait outside the house while they arrived and went in. After the arrest had been made, he was called in and searched the house together with the police. In the garage, they found a high-temperature vessel for molding the ingots and some gold that was still waiting to be melted down.

Oddly, Intel decided not to prosecute. Was it because the pawnbroker had not kept enough records to pin down the total value of all the sales to date, while the technician insisted that he had only done it once before? Was it because Intel thought that it would cost less in the long run to write off the couple of hundred thousand dollars the technician had stolen than to disclose publicly that it had allowed such a brazen theft to take place in the middle of a supposedly secure fab area? Miller never found out the answer. But Leonard Balli, a former police officer who worked with him in the investigations department, told Miller afterwards that the company had allowed the technician to leave quietly. A few weeks later, with the help of a good reference from Intel, he got a job at AMD.

27

The Vancouver Complaint

Scott Gibson, one of the seventeen Intel employees whom Casey Powell took with him when he left, had his own personal experience of Andy Grove's temper. It happened at the first high-level meeting he attended inside the company. Gibson arrived a few minutes before the 9:00 starting time, and settled in a discreet seat to observe with excitement the entry one by one of some of the company's most senior and most famous figures. Five minutes after the hour, when the last participant arrived, there was a deafening crash.

Recovering from the shock, Gibson turned to the end of the table. Andy Grove was sitting there, holding a stave of wood the size of a baseball bat. At the end of the stave was a hand shape, encased in a protective glove of the kind used inside Intel's fabs, with the middle finger extended in an obscene gesture. Grove had just slammed the wood onto the surface of the meeting-room table—and was now shouting at the top of his lungs: "I DON'T EVER, *EVER* WANT TO BE IN A MEETING WITH THIS GROUP THAT DOESN'T START AND END WHEN IT'S SCHEDULED."

Later, Gibson discovered that the stick with the finger was a tool that accompanied Grove frequently. Years after the introduction of the Late List, Intel's president was as touchy about promptness as ever. On one occasion, company legend had it, Grove had even bawled out one of his most senior managers with the words: "You're wasting my time. All I have in this world is fucking time. Get *out*!"

Luckily for Gibson, he was spared the experience of being at the sharp end of Andy Grove's temper—or bat. His own departure from Intel was not precipitated by a single humiliating incident, as Casey Powell's had been. Instead, it was the result of a deep-seated belief that Intel had lost strategic direction, that it was failing to respond to a change in the market that Gibson believed would be momentous. That change was the growing competition in the memory market.

At the age of twenty-seven, Gibson had received the title of general manager and had been given control of his own profit-and-loss account. His background seemed almost ideal for success at Intel: a midwestern childhood, like so many of the naturalized Californians who made up the top ranks of the company; an engineering degree at the University of Illinois, followed by an MBA. Gibson had also run his own business in college. In partnership with a fellow student, he had started a venture to retail stereo equipment to students at three local university campuses.

The business that Gibson became responsible for was memory components operations. He was a member of the team that achieved Intel's first sale of memory chips to IBM. The IBM relationship was to bring Intel nearly $1 billion of revenue over the succeeding five years, and would later culminate in IBM's choice of an Intel processor for its first personal computer. At the time, however, the deal was controversial inside the company because Big Blue demanded, and received, a guarantee that Intel's selling price for the memory device would fall by 20 percent a year throughout the life of the contract. Intel hoped that its own costs would fall fast enough to make such price cuts possible while leaving the contract still profitable. But since there was no guarantee that they would, the deal exposed Intel to considerable risk.

Intel's basic memory business had run into problems as its interest in microprocessors grew. As we've seen, the company had created the silicon memory market single-handedly with the invention of the 1103 chip in 1971—and had followed up that product with a new 4K chip, four times the capacity, in mid-1972. But the new chip suffered from a number of problems which it was left to Intel's competitors to correct. Mostek, the Texas Instruments spin-off, had dominated the 4K generation of DRAMs; the same company had also beaten Intel to market with the first really reliable and usable 16K DRAM. The underlying issue was probably that the qualities required to make quantum-leap innovations in thinking and then follow them through to

market were very different from the qualities required to take an existing product, make a few refinements, and bring an improved version
to market quickly. Although Intel had fallen behind in this respect, its
memory operations still performed more than respectably. Revenues
from DRAMs had risen from $9 million in 1974 to $15 million in
1975, $23 million in 1976 and $38 million in 1977. It was in 1978—
the year of launch of the 8086 chip that created Intel's dominance of
the microprocessor market—that things began to go wrong. The company's DRAM sales grew a little, to $41 million. By 1979, Intel had
under 5 percent of the mass market for 16K devices. The new 5-volt
device it introduced that year—requiring just one power supply instead of the three separate voltages that were standard in the market
at the time—was not enough to compensate for a sharp fall in average
selling prices. The company's total memory sales that year shrank
back to $32 million.

Competition from Japan, rather than Silicon Valley, was the real
problem. A number of Japanese companies, including Hitachi, Fujitsu, Toshiba, and NEC, had seized on semiconductor memory as a
business that they needed to be in—and with the industrial weight of
an entire family of linked companies behind each one, they were
throwing money at the business as if there were no tomorrow. In the
early and middle 1970s, California engineers used to laugh at the
newcomers. They were the "Japs"—the guys who came to the trade
shows and conferences, smiling uncomprehendingly because their
English was so lousy, and snapping away at the slides with their little
cameras so that they could pore over them when they got home and
try to understand what they were about.

This prejudice was understandable; most American engineers had
formed their views of Japanese manufacturing quality in the 1950s,
when "Made in Japan" was synonymous with cheap and tacky. As a
result, the prevailing view in Silicon Valley at least until 1975 was
that you could license your technology to a Japanese company with
impunity, secure in the knowledge that the licensee would never be
able to do anything threatening with the intellectual property that it
had bought.

Another factor gave U.S. industry a false sense of security: the
cavalier view that Japanese chip companies took of intellectual property. More than a decade after U.S. companies began to take patents,
copyrights, and trade secrets more seriously, Japan's chip companies
were stuck in a 1960s time warp, believing that it was still OK to

knock off other people's designs. As late as 1982, NEC was selling an unlicensed copy of the 8086 chip that it had made by photographing the Intel chip's layout. An alert Intel engineer, Peter Stoll, discovered evidence of foul play when he noticed that a connection between two transistors on the NEC's chip layout had been blown at exactly the place where he had blown a connection on the 8086 in order to correct a logical error. In the same year, employees of both Hitachi and Mitsubishi were caught by the FBI in a sting operation trying to buy what they believed to be stolen papers containing secret information about IBM computers.

So it was tempting to·dismiss the Japanese chip industry as made up of a bunch of know-nothing copycats who could never do any serious harm. Intel was as prone to this view as any other company. Roger Borovoy, for instance, was asked by the *Palo Alto Times* for a reaction to the news that the Russian military had copied an Intel chip and were using it in their aerospace industry. Borovoy replied jokingly that he would be more concerned if it was the Japanese who were doing the copying, since they had more serious manufacturing capabilities—"but on the other hand, if the Japanese do it then the chips won't come back to us inside missiles."

Borovoy may have been right about the missiles, but he was certainly wrong in thinking that the Soviet Union was more of a threat to the United States than Japan. For the Japanese chip companies may have been copying chip designs and process technologies from their U.S. counterparts, but they were now making great strides in chip manufacturing itself. As latecomers the Japanese firms had to try to carve out some advantage that was uniquely their own—and this they proceeded to do with considerable skill.

While the people who worked in Silicon Valley's fabs tended to be flighty, moving from one company to another when an offer of an extra fifty cents an hour came along, Japanese fab operators were far more loyal to their employer. This, combined with a very high boredom threshold—acquired in the country's efficient but highly regimented and inflexible education system—meant that many Japanese operators could stay at the same place on the line for years on end, honing month by month the subtle technical skills that made the difference between silicon wafers that were spotted with flaws and those that were almost entirely clean. Another by-product of the Japanese education system was that fab operators tended to be more disciplined and almost militaristic in their habits. In a fab plant where a single particle of dust could cause an error on a chip, yields could be affected by such apparently trivial things as how strictly the operators obeyed the rules against cosmetics or long hair, and how many times the clean-room door was opened per shift. If Japanese fab workers were willing to be herded out all at once to take their bathroom breaks, rather than going one by one as they needed to, this could have a measurable effect on productivity.

Two other Japanese advantages were crucial. One was that Japanese semiconductor companies, in common with Japanese car companies, had much closer relationships with suppliers and equipment manufacturers than their American counterparts did. Equipment suppliers and chipmakers in Japan would work together on one of the dozens of stages in the fabrication process, making repeated small adjustments until everything worked as close to perfectly as possible. In America, by contrast, chip companies tended to make changes to their manufacturing equipment without even telling the original vendor. "We sometimes didn't even let the vendors into our fabs," recalled one senior Intel engineer.

The other advantage was intellectual: During the 1960s and early 1970s, Japanese companies were studying the work of American manufacturing experts such as W. Edwards Deming, who argued that the key to cutting costs in many manufacturing processes was to increase quality, since defects were always much more expensive to fix at a later stage than to prevent in the first place. It was not until the 1980s that this notion truly caught hold in U.S. industry. But the Japanese chipmakers were listening a decade earlier. They paid fastidious attention to their chip fabrication as a whole, devoting considerable effort to the search for any change—no matter how small or apparently insignificant—that could make the process work better or cost less. One example: Instead of embarking on the hugely expensive process of trying to keep the entire fabrication area free of dust particles, some Japanese chipmakers were focusing on the most dust-sensitive areas of the process, and using the highest-specification filtration and air-conditioning systems on just a few key pieces of machinery.

The result of all these factors together was that by the end of the 1970s, the best companies in the Japanese semiconductor business were considerably better at fabrication than the best companies in America. One source suggested that while peak yields on DRAMs in the United States were 50 percent, in Japan they were 80 percent. Since yield was directly related to cost, this meant that Japanese companies were able to make the same profits as their American competitors while selling chips at much lower prices.

The problem for Intel was that none of this was visible on factory tours. When senior Intel executives were taken around fabrication plants in Japan—something that happened once in a while at least, because it was a standard courtesy extended to a partner who was licensing technology—they would almost never be allowed to see the wafer sort area, where operators would check every die on the finished silicon wafer and mark with a dot those that were defective. "Die per wafer out"—the number of good chips that emerged from the process—was one of the most closely guarded secrets of every fab, because it gave away valuable information about costs and profitability. Apart from that, there were no magical indicators capable of conveying immediately to an Intel executive that things were simply being done better in Japan.

There was, however, one way in which Intel might have found out what its Japanese competitors were up to: by building an Intel plant on Japanese soil. This possibility was actually raised at the end of the 1970s—and Jack Carsten, as general manager of the components group, was an enthusiastic supporter of the idea. But in the end, the company decided against it, and the opportunity was missed.

"I had actually obtained leases on Japanese soil so that Intel could locate its first overseas fab area in Japan," Carsten recalled. "The plant would have provided some insulation from currency fluctuations, but the Israel plant [the alternative under consideration] had tremendous government subsidies and a good labor market. A Japanese plant would also have put us into the pipeline of Japanese equipment vendors, and linked us to the Zaibatsu [sic] network. We could have tapped the expertise of Japanese DRAM technology development, silicon makers, mask makers and the infrastructural support. This is what Texas Instruments did, because they had a commitment to local manufacturing. Eventually we chose Jerusalem, largely because of the subsidies."

No matter how tightly Intel tried to close its eyes, there was one irrefutable piece of evidence that something was afoot in Japan: the low prices that Japanese manufacturers were charging for DRAMs in America. The first effect of their entry was to drive down prices faster than before, with the result that Intel's line managers in the fabs began to decide, independent of the company's top management, to devote more of their production resources to high-margin microprocessors.

When you had the choice between filling a silicon wafer with microprocessors that would bring in several hundred dollars each, or filling it with DRAMs that would bring in only $10 or $20 each, you didn't need an MBA to see that reallocating wafer starts from memory to microprocessors would increase the company's profitability. But at the top of the company, Intel's official stance was no different from that of other companies in Silicon Valley. The reason the Japanese were quoting such low prices, went the mantra, was not that they were better at manufacturing. It was because they were buying their way into the market. And their quality was high simply because they shipped their best parts to America, leaving the junk for the domestic market.

The first Intel employee to see this view proven wrong was an engineer named Henry Gregor, who joined the company in 1980 from Tektronix. Gregor was initially disoriented when he arrived at Intel; he was assigned to a part of the company called the Microcontroller Instrumentation Operation. Recently moved out of Silicon Valley, the MIO group was referred to inside Intel as "Missing in Oregon"—and its members were certainly at one remove from the Intel mainstream. Gregor realized how far out of the mainstream when he was invited to join a meeting with some of the company's most senior people.

"The meeting started," he recalled. "I couldn't remember who was presenting it, and I didn't know too many of the characters in the room, though I knew Andy Grove and had seen him. . . . Suddenly, I noticed this guy at the back wearing a plaid shirt, who would appear to have a yelling fit every so often, after which he would sit down and get all red-faced. *Who's that?* I asked the guy next to me. *Oh,* he said, *that's Jack Carsten*"—as if the name was sufficient explanation for the behavior. Later, Gregor discovered that Carsten was not unique: Another character on the opposite side of the room would periodically go berserk and start shouting. Gregor's neighbor explained that this was Les Vadasz.

A few months later, Gregor was sent down to Hewlett-Packard's corporate center in Palo Alto with Intel's national sales manager. The meeting was almost as confrontational as the internal meeting Gregor had witnessed earlier—but for an entirely different reason. Hewlett-Packard was trying to implement a just-in-time manufacturing program, a revolutionary step in the States in 1980, where inventories would be kept to the very minimum and parts be delivered by suppliers on specified days shortly before they were needed. The management of HP was full of complaints about Intel's performance, and presented a detailed list of data where Intel had failed to meet commitments, missed delivery dates, and delivered parts of bad quality. The point was reinforced when Gregor later paid a visit with one of Grove's most trusted lieutenants to the Hewlett-Packard printer division in Vancouver. HP's vice-president of materials pointed to Gregor and turned to the Intel executive.

"You know, I see this guy here all the time," he said. "I know he's trying to design [Intel] stuff into our products. But I go out of my way to design stuff *out*, because I don't want service the way you do it and I don't want quality problems the way you do things."

Within a few months, the issue became public. At a conference of the Electronic Industries Association of Japan in Washington in March 1980, the general manager of HP's data systems division showed a slide comparing semiconductor quality from different manufacturers. During the previous year, he explained, HP had bought 16K DRAMs from three American and three Japanese firms. The results of this company's incoming quality checks were shocking. The parts that came from the very best American firm showed six times as many errors as those from the worst Japanese firm. Although HP was too discreet to name names, everyone present knew that the U.S. companies were Intel, TI, and Mostek and the Japanese were Fujitsu, Hitachi, and NEC.

Inside Intel there was surprisingly little interest in HP's findings. Only two people seemed to be seriously troubled by the company's complaints. One was Larry Hootnick, who had joined Intel as chief financial officer in 1974 after learning the ropes of corporate finance at Ford. Hootnick took great pride in telling people that he knew nothing at all about semiconductors—but he knew the numbers better than anyone else. Long before Grove began to take the issue seriously, he would complain repeatedly to the fab managers that their manufacturing costs were too high and their yields too low. The trouble was that Hootnick did not at that stage have any operational control over Intel's manufacturing; he could too easily be dismissed by the manufacturing guys as a nagging voice from outside—an armchair quarterback.

"When he had finance responsibility, I always saw him as an antagonist of the manufacturing world," recalled Will Kauffman, the soft-spoken vice-president who was responsible for all of Intel's silicon fabrication. "He was trying to get more productivity and lower costs from the manufacturing people. He was openly critical of what we were doing." But Kauffman himself took the complaints seriously. His interest in the issue aroused by Hewlett-Packard's complaints, Kauffman went out and bought some books on Japanese management and began to study them on his own time. But it was over a year before his reading delivered any concrete ideas for change inside Intel—and by then, relations between the finance and manufacturing people had broken down to such a point that it was too late for him to make common cause with Hootnick.

Meanwhile, a shocking new development had taken place in the industry. At the end of 1979, Fujitsu introduced the first mass-market 64K DRAM. This was an unexpected coup for a company that had for so long been dismissed as a copycat. Without access to the new designs and process technology at Intel or any other U.S. company, Fujitsu had beaten the Americans at their own game. The inexorable economics of the experience curve would now work in Fujitsu's favor, against Intel. Everyone knew that fabrication costs fell sharply as the cumulative number of units shipped grew; that was one of the factors behind the doubling of chip performance every eighteen months that had been encapsulated in Moore's law. The difference was that Intel would now play latecomer—and by the time Intel was ready with a 64K chip, which would not be for more than two years, Fujitsu's costs would have fallen so far that it would become impossible for Intel to compete profitably.

Recognizing the seriousness of the problem, Moore and Grove authorized Intel's researchers to accelerate their work on two powerful technologies that might turn the tables. One was a new production process called CMOS, or complementary metal oxide on silicon. This had the advantage of reducing the power consumption of the chip because it allowed the transistors in a cell to draw no current except when the cell state changed from on to off or 1 to zero. Makers of battery-powered portable computers would undoubtedly be willing to pay more for it.

The other killer technology that Intel hoped would help it to regain its lead of the memory market was called "chip-level redundancy." In the memory systems devices that Intel built for IBM computers, extra circuitry had been used to bypass the faulty cells of under-performing chips—allowing Intel to make use of parts that it would otherwise have had to throw away. The new idea was to incorporate this bypass principle onto the chip itself. It was explained by Ron

Whittier, manager of the memory products division, in a case study at Stanford University's Graduate School of Business:

"Essentially," Whittier explained, "you have a row-and-column addressing system on a memory chip. The periphery of the chip contains logic and refresh circuitry necessary to control and update the DRAM. In the 64K version, Intel added an extra column of memory elements, so that in the event of a process-induced defect, the auxiliary column could be activated. There was a physical switch, or 'fuse,' built into each column which could be addressed by the tester machinery. When a bad element was detected, current would be passed through the switch and would blow a 'fuse,' inactivating the defective column and kicking in the auxiliary column. In this fashion, a defective memory chip could be 'reprogrammed' before shipment, and overall yield could be improved."

It was a wonderfully clever idea—a way to circumvent the Japanese superiority in producing defect-free silicon wafers without having to achieve any underlying improvement in manufacturing quality. Chip-level redundancy was to high-yield processing as brain was to brawn: It allowed you to make a dramatic increase in the usable percentage of parts coming off the line without making any substantial changes to the operation of the line itself.

There was just one problem: It didn't work. Or to be more precise, Intel's engineers discovered after they put the redundant-design chip into production that the fuse-blowing process that was supposed to knock out the flawed column of memory cells was not permanent. Some time after the polysilicon fuse had blown, it would mysteriously "regrow"—with the effect that some time after the chip had been installed, the dud column would periodically be switched back on and the user would start to see data errors. It was not until early 1982, the third year after Fujitsu had introduced its part, that Intel was able to come out with a reliable 64K DRAM using a replacement design. The CMOS process would eventually be a big technical success, but that took time too: Intel was not able to ship its first CMOS 64K chips for yet another two years.

As general manager of memory components, Scott Gibson came to the conclusion in 1982 that Intel could not sustain its position as a participant in the broader DRAM market. He tried to convince his colleagues that the problem was long term rather than short, because Intel had picked up the habit as early as the 4K generation eight years earlier of making for the hills as soon as margins fell below a certain threshold. Gibson argued that Intel should now pursue a niche strategy in DRAMs just as it had in static RAMs and EPROMs. Let others slug it out in the commodity market for cheap memory. The company should focus on the new CMOS process, he recommended, and become known as the company that made memory devices for the new personal computers.

But just as Hootnick was outside the manufacturing mainstream and Kauffman was still in the process of being converted, Gibson was too junior in the organization for his proposal to withdraw partially from the DRAM market to be taken seriously. Two of the company's three most powerful individuals had their own reasons for violently opposing even a limited withdrawal. Ed Gelbach, at the top of the sales and marketing tree, knew that his salesmen liked to have a full product line. They liked to be able to offer one-stop shopping for customers, including memory, EPROMs, and processors—and customers who bought from Intel liked to know that the same product would still be available some years down the line. The decisions to phase out less profitable chips that Intel had taken from time to time had always made a few customers very angry. Also, a full product line allowed the stronger products to help sell the weaker ones. When a processor was in short supply and "on allocation," fair trading law did not allow you to *refuse* to sell it to a customer unless he bought a load of memory as well; but you could send a discreet signal that you welcomed simultaneous purchases of different products by offering discounts based on the total value of the sale rather than the quantity of each item. So Gelbach was dead against any withdrawal.

Gordon Moore, Intel's chairman and CEO, had a different set of reasons for wanting to stay in. DRAMs were the industry's "technology driver." Because every memory cell on the chip was the same, it was a relatively simple business to lay out the entire chip once you had the peripheral circuitry and the cell right. So Intel always used the DRAM, not the more complex chip designs, to try out new fabrication processes. The other advantage of DRAMs was that their very nature as a commodity meant that they were built in very large volumes. Only by processing large numbers of wafers through the same fab under the same process, believed Moore, could you make the improvements that allowed you to cut your costs.

Shortly before Gibson left to join Casey Powell, another Japanese bombshell dropped. Less than six months after Intel had introduced a 64K chip that ironed out the problems with its new redundancy technology, the first chips of the next generation—256K, four times the capacity of the 64K—came out. This time it was not just Fujitsu producing the chip. Hitachi, too, had developed a working 256K process.

As 1983 turned into 1984, it became clear that the industry was headed for a bloodbath. While many of the American companies had carried on investing through the last recession, building and then mothballing new factories if necessary, the Japanese had gone on the biggest spending binge in semiconductor history. By 1984, the total cumulative Japanese investment in plant and equipment for the chip industry was greater than the total cumulative U.S. investment. It became clear that when demand started to falter, massive overcapacity would result.

The Japanese response to overcapacity was different. They saw price-cutting as a fight to the death. Intel and to a lesser extent AMD were willing to sell a little below their cost in an attempt to keep factories running. But Hitachi sent a memo to its EPROM distributors, later published by the *Wall Street Journal*, outlining a very different strategy: "Quote 10% below their price; if they requote, go 10% again. Don't quit until you win."

When these were the new rules of the game, it was clear that the only ones left standing would be the companies with the deepest pockets. Here the Japanese firms had the clearest advantage—for their chip operations represented only a small part of their businesses. While semiconductors accounted for over four-fifths of AMD's sales, three-quarters of those of Intel and National Semiconductor and half those of Texas Instruments, they accounted for one-fifth of Fujitsu's sales and only one-ninth of Hitachi's. This allowed the Japanese companies to spread chip losses over a longer period across a wider range of other products.

Was it immoral to sell below cost? Arguably, no: It was something that the U.S. players had done for more than a decade. The introductory statement to Intel's own IPO document contained the following warning among the "high risk factors" that investors should consider before investing:

4. Because of severe competition and anticipated cost reductions, Intel and its competitors typically offer products for future delivery at prices below current production costs. If costs do not decline as anticipated, such sales may result in losses.

The difference was that while American managements, including Intel's, avoided selling below cost except as a last resort, the Japanese saw it as their best chance of getting into the market. DRAM prices fell nearly 70 percent in the space of a single year. It was the first time that Moore's law appeared to have underestimated the pace of technological change.

Before long, the turmoil in the DRAM market had became a matter of high politics and international diplomacy. Bob Noyce, now Intel's nonexecutive vice-chairman, helped get the point across to Intel's political friends in drawing rooms in Washington, DC. Not content with stealing technology from America, Noyce argued, the Japanese companies were now dumping their products below cost in the States. Their government was picking up half the tab for R&D. Their system of *keiretsu*, industrial groupings linked by cross-shareholdings, gave the Japanese companies a source of low-cost finance. Result: They were charging considerably lower prices in America than in their closed home market, in which U.S. suppliers had achieved only a 10 percent market share compared with over 50 percent elsewhere. Wasn't it time to do something?

Trade in semiconductors had become one of the most contentious issues between the United States and Japan. The office of the U.S. Trade Representative filed an antidumping complaint against Japanese DRAM manufacturers, and a wider complaint under section 301 of the U.S. trade law for unfair trade in semiconductors in general. Intel joined up with AMD and National to file its own complaint on EPROMs. In 1986, the governments of Japan and the United States signed a semiconductor agreement, which included a secret side letter in which the Japanese side said they "understood, welcomed and would make efforts to assist the US companies in reaching their goal of a 20% market share within five years." Later on, the side letter was made public, embarrassing both sides by revealing as empty rhetoric their stated view that the U.S. chipmakers' market share was not something that bureaucrats or politicians should try directly to influence. The letter provoked a further round of recriminations over whether the 20 percent market-share "goal" was or was not backed by a guarantee by the Japanese government.

For Intel, much of this was academic. After the dumping and unfairness were stripped out, after the short-term circumstances of market oversupply and technical problems with its own products had been overcome, the company still faced the fundamental issue: Should it—*could* it—continue to compete in the DRAM market?

The trouble was that almost nobody in the company, from Gordon Moore and Andy Grove downward, was able to approach the matter in an objective way. Intel's association with the DRAM was too long and too close. The company had created the memory-chip market, and the memory-chip market had created the company. To abandon memories in order to focus on the more profitable microprocessor business would be a betrayal of the company's roots. Yet what were the alternatives? To continue to offer a full lineup of chips, while hemorrhaging red ink? Or to retreat to a higher-margin niche within the memory market, if such a niche existed and could be defended?

It was the middle of 1985 before Andy Grove was finally ready to bite the bullet.

"Gordon Moore and I were discussing our quandary," he recalled. "Our mood was downbeat. I looked out the window at the Ferris wheel of the Great American amusement park revolving in the distance, then I turned back to Gordon and I asked, 'If we got kicked out and the board brought in a new CEO, what do you think he would do?' Gordon answered without hesitation, 'He would get us out of memories.' I stared at him, numb, then said, 'Why shouldn't you and I walk out the door, come back and do it ourselves?' "

In his 1996 book *Only the Paranoid Survive*, where the quotation above appears, Andy Grove argued that at times of technological change, any business can face dramatic changes in its environment— changes that he called "strategic inflection points." Make the right decision at the inflection point, Grove said, and your company can look forward to sunny years of future growth. Get it wrong, and you will slide inexorably into decline.

Yet there was no single point in mid-1985 when Intel had to make a snap decision about whether or not to continue as a major player in the DRAM market. The trends that provoked the 1985 crisis had been at work for at least five years, and possibly more. Had Intel taken steps to respond to them early, it might never have been forced to abandon one of its two core businesses.

Nor was it true that 1985 was the last point at which Intel could implement an exit from the memory chip business. In fact, it took a full further year before Intel had implemented the decision to pull out—and another full year before the company could return to profitability. First, Grove moved the general manager in charge of the operation to a new job, because it was clear that he was incapable of wielding the ax. Then he brought in a replacement with the specific instruction to get the company out of making memories. But the new general manager "went native": he wanted to continue the R&D program for the next-generation 1M (one megabit) chip, even though it was a forgone conclusion that the device would never be built. This was the clearest possible case of throwing good money after bad. It took several more months before all of Intel's employees, now down to 18,200 from a 1984 high of 25,400, recognized that the company was out of the memory-manufacturing business for good.

In the chapter on performance appraisals in his book *High-Output Management*, Andy Grove devoted a section to what he called "The Blast"—the kind of review where the boss has to tell the subordinate that he is doing the job badly and is likely to get fired unless things start to change fast. Grove accompanied his analysis with a diagram of a staircase in which a word appeared on each rising step. First came "ignore"; then came "deny"; then "blame others"; then "assume responsibility"; then "find solution."

Hewlett-Packard's presentation of its data on semiconductor manufacturing quality was a corporate-level "blast" at Intel and the other chipmaking firms in the Valley. Yet the response of Intel, as a company, was exactly as the book described the response of an underperforming individual. Ignore, deny, blame others, assume responsibility, find solution—it took Intel from 1980 to 1986 to make this progression.

28

A Scandal in Malaysia

At the end of 1985, as Andy Grove was grappling with the strategic dilemma of whether to take Intel out of the memory-chip business, the company's security department was facing a smaller but nevertheless highly irritating problem: what to do about the persistent losses that Intel was suffering from thefts at its Penang assembly plant.

The underlying problem was the disparity between the very low rates that the Malaysian women who worked in the plant were paid each hour and the very high value of the semiconductors they were handling. When a single chip in a package less than a half-inch long could be worth more than a month's income, and when hundreds of them passed through everyone's hands in the course of a day's work, it was not surprising that the temptation to steal was hard for some employees to resist. An inventive cottage industry developed whereby middlemen would board the morning buses that brought the assembly workers to the plant and give them instructions on what they were to steal that day. The women would then get the chips out of the plant by hiding them inside their bras.

Intel installed metal detectors at the plant exits, but that didn't solve the problem. The thefts merely became more daring. One group of robbers discovered that Intel was crushing defective chips to prevent them from being sold on the black market, and then sending them back to a recycling plant in Gilroy, half an hour's drive south of the company's California headquarters, so that the gold could be recovered from them. The crushed chips were transported across the Pacific in fifty-gallon oil drums. At midnight one night, the gang executed a daring switch. The chip fragments were whisked away to be sold in Singapore; in their place, sand was dug up from in front of the plant entrance and put into the drums. The result was that the theft was not detected until the oil drums made their way to the recyclers 8,500 miles away. On another occasion, thieves broke into a container of Intel parts that had been assembled in Penang and were bound for California. Leaving behind the low-value and commodity items, the robbers stole the highest-margin microprocessors and replaced the sealed boxes containing them with specially prepared replicas. Even the timing of the theft was carefully chosen: On the day when the chips were discovered missing at an inbound check in California, it proved impossible to reach anyone at the Penang plant because it was a public holiday in Malaysia.

In late 1985, Marvin Zietzke, the former probation officer who had hired Rob Miller into the Intel security department in California, ran a successful sting operation in Hong Kong, uncovering a Chinese gang specializing in semiconductor theft and sending one of its members to jail. But it was becoming clear that Intel's problems in managing security for the region were too big for Zietzke alone. Since it was clear that the company needed a full-time security person in Asia, an ad was placed in the *Asian Wall Street Journal*, and an investigator resident in Hong Kong with long experience of the U.S. private sector was hired. His name was Robert Westervelt, and his résumé included stints working for Howard Hughes, Levi-Strauss, Mattel, the U.S. Air Force, and the FBI.

From his very first day at Intel, Westervelt was a round peg in a square hole. At fifty-five, he was fourteen years older than Zietzke himself and considerably older than anyone at Intel except for a handful of the longest serving employees. That alone was not a problem. But a symptom of the difference in outlook was that Westervelt seemed to like not fitting in. While everyone else wore open-neck shirts, he reported for work in a suit. Steve Kopp, Intel's director of corporate security, told him that the company would prefer him to dress more casually.

"If you insist," replied Westervelt, "I'll just wear a sport coat from now on."

Two weeks after being hired, Westervelt completed his orientation and was sent out to Penang with Zietzke. Their first job on arrival was to review the success of Intel's latest antitheft operation in Malaysia. Westervelt, being new to the company, sat in on the meeting as Zietzke discussed the security operation with P. Y. Lai, the locally hired plant manager, and his local security chief.

As details of the operation unfolded, Westervelt could hardly believe his ears. He understood that Intel had set up an arrangement with an employee who had recently been fired for theft. The plant security manager would give the employee a package of Intel chips, and the former employee would act as a fence: He would contact potential buyers for the chips, explain that they had been stolen from the assembly plant, and then sell them. An Intel employee would then sign a sworn statement "confirming" that the goods had been stolen from the company. The buyer would be arrested by the local police, and the "seller" would be paid by the company for his help in getting the buyers behind bars. This operation, Westervelt understood, was being run with the full knowledge of Steve Kopp, Intel's director of corporate security, and Dick Boucher, the administrative vice-president of the company who was his supervisor. More than twenty arrests had already been made using the ex-employee as bait

Yet something had gone wrong with the operation. Because Intel chips were often in short supply, there were *two* unofficial markets for the company's products. As well as the black market, which was straightforwardly criminal, there was also a gray market in which customers who had overordered from Intel to make sure they received enough parts to meet their needs would then quietly sell whatever they didn't need. So legitimate buyers of chips might also get innocently entangled in the operation. Apparently, one of the buyers had been in just this category. When the local police arrived, he screamed that he had been framed—and receiving no satisfaction, he went down to Government House in Penang and made a complaint to the chief of police. To avoid a scandal, Intel paid the fence to leave for Thailand. The problem now being discussed in front of Westervelt was that an investigation by a new police chief was in progress, and the fence had returned to Malaysia. The question was how could he be prevented from spilling the beans to the local police.

Zietzke turned to Westervelt.

"What do you think of it, Bob?" he asked.

"The way you explained this in the meeting," replied Westervelt, "there's definitely been a crime committed. But not by the twenty-odd guys who bought the chips. The crime has been committed by you guys. You fabricated evidence, which is a felony in Malaysia and any other part of the world."

Zietzke turned to him.

"Well, Bob," he said. "If you want to make an omelet, you've got to break some eggs. That's the way the police operate in the U.S."

"I've been in police work a lot longer than you have, and I don't know of any police department that works in that way. I will not be part of it. What you're doing is wrong, and I won't be a part of it."

Two days later, Zietzke and Westervelt moved on to visit Intel's site in Singapore. Over the breakfast table in their hotel, Zietzke referred to the meeting that had broken up in disarray after Westervelt's intervention.

"Do you have enough money to retire on, Bob?" he asked.

"Why do you ask?"

"Because if you don't go along with us on this thing, you're going to be out on the street."

"Marvin," said Westervelt, "I think I'd better have a talk with your boss."

When Westervelt called Santa Clara, Steve Kopp seemed shocked. He disclaimed any knowledge of the sting operation, and listened carefully as Westervelt gave an account of the meeting, detailing why he believed the faked chip thefts were illegal. After twenty minutes of conversation, Kopp said that he would look into the matter.

For his part, Westervelt reiterated his determination to have nothing to do with a program that he considered to be illegal. "Some maids don't do windows," he said. "I don't do felonies."

When the introductory tour of Intel's Asian facilities was finished, Westervelt returned to his new base in Penang and Zietzke to California. Meanwhile, Kopp instructed Howard Hunter, the security manager reporting to him who was responsible for issues inside the United States, to fly out to Malaysia to investigate the operation. On his arrival in Penang, Hunter arranged to go and talk to the local police chief to find out what was going on—but refused to allow Westervelt to be present at the meeting.

With some independent information on the affair gathered by Hunter, Kopp was now in a position to act. He called Zietzke into his office in California and told him that since he seemed incapable of managing Westervelt, Zietzke had a choice: either to stay in his job while Westervelt was asked to carry out a full investigation of his past activities, or to move sideways into a different job. Zietzke replied that he would prefer to leave Intel. By June 1986, three months later, he had left the company and taken up a new job at National Semiconductor.

Meanwhile, unknown to Zietzke, Westervelt was firing off memos to Kopp, to the Penang site manager, to Kopp's boss, and even to Andy Grove, about what he had seen in Penang. Dismayed at the way in which Westervelt seemed to have run out of control, Kopp called him back to Santa Clara and sat him down in a closed conference room.

Kopp never told Westervelt that he was to be fired because he had blown the whistle on the Penang operation. He also did not offer any reasons why Westervelt was to be fired. Instead, he simply told the older man:

"You've won the battle, Bob, but you've lost the war."

Westervelt was sent to two further meetings, one with a company lawyer and another with a manager from human resources. On June 20, less than four months into his three-year contract with Intel, Westervelt was turned around and ordered back to Penang. He was given just over a month to pack up his household and his life, and move on to a new job.

Three weeks later, Westervelt telephoned an old friend. Mike Fehr, Westervelt's boss at Levi-Strauss for five years, to tell him he'd just stepped off a plane from Asia and was now back in San Francisco.

"It was out of the blue. He called me and asked if he could stay in my apartment," Fehr recalled.

When Westervelt arrived, he began telling Fehr an almost incredible story.

"The first thing he said was, Intel tried to have him killed. . . . He said that on leaving Malaysia he had been stopped by the Malaysian authorities and accused of narcotics trafficking. His story was that had he not known a guy who was head of Malaysian customs there, he would have been detained."

Westervelt had also brought documentary evidence with him backing up his claim that he had been asked to participate in an illegal operation to frame innocent buyers of Intel chips.

"When he arrived in my apartment, he had a very thick file of documents. I went over them with him, because I was a bit skeptical about such a program. Skeptical because it didn't seem to me that a company of the reputation and size of Intel would do such a thing. [There were] a lot of risks in doing this that went far beyond trying to stop people stealing your chips."

"He wasn't lying to me," continued Fehr. "After I saw the documents, I came to believe that he was in fact being persecuted by his own company. A series of documents had gone back and forth between him and his boss in the U.S. where Bob was refusing to do things and explaining why, and the documents from Intel were saying, 'We don't care what you think—do it anyway.' They never admitted that what he was being asked to do was an illegal exercise. But if you looked at the documents he sent in conjunction with the responses, it was clear to me that there was a disagreement between the two sides about whether he would do what he was being told, or would be fired."

Fehr was most astonished by Westervelt's claim that the company had tried to have him framed for drug trafficking. "I found it hard to believe. There was no evidence he could show me . . . [but] if you saw his demeanor, you could tell he was afraid for his life. Before, he was always very full of bravado. . . . [It was] too much of a coincidence that he would be leaving the country and detained when this had never happened before. There seemed to be a relationship. I believed him at the time, I definitely believed him. He was relating these incidents to me the same day [they happened], because of the dateline. It was very fresh in his mind. [There were] some pieces of evidence he talked about that tied together: One was that there was only one person who knew which flight he would be on, and that was the Intel guy that fired him. It looked very suspicious."

Westervelt's departure from Penang had taken place shortly after a Malaysian court sentenced two young Australians convicted of drug trafficking to death by hanging. When he was ready to leave the country, he told Fehr, Intel had ordered him to return his car to the plant because it would be needed by an engineer who had just arrived from the Philippines. It was promised that the engineer would drive him to the airport. Instead, the security chief's assistant drove him in a different car. Twenty minutes before his flight was due to leave, two plainclothes officers had approached him in the airport departure lounge and asked for his passport and hand baggage. They then took him into a detention room, where he saw another set of officers opening up his bags. Fearing that he was about to be framed, Westervelt immediately drew out of his pocket the business card of a senior police officer and demanded to call him. After Westervelt explained over the phone what had happened, the senior policeman then asked to speak to the officer who had arrested him. A few minutes later, he was put back on the aircraft, which had been held waiting at the gate.

Whether or not Westervelt's astounding story was correct, one thing was clear: His personality had undergone a sharp and apparently permanent change. After his return from Malaysia, Fehr found that his formerly happy-go-lucky friend was now introverted and obsessed with the fear that Intel was out to get him. Westervelt, who now lives in Nevada, carries a gun with him when he travels. He appears to be fearful that his life may once again be in danger.

Shortly after leaving Intel, Westervelt sued for wrongful dismissal. In his complaint, he accused the company plainly of firing him because he had been a whistle-blower. He said the company had given him "inconsequential assignments" and "unrealistic deadlines" in order to find an excuse to discharge him, and he accused the company of being involved in the "making of false charges against him to the Malaysian police authorities, resulting in his detainment at the local airport on July 31st, 1986." In support of his case, Westervelt produced a set of tape recordings that he had secretly made of allegedly incriminating conversations with Intel employees. Astoundingly, the lawsuit went unnoticed by the normally vigilant Silicon Valley press. It was settled in January 1989, under a confidential agreement in which Intel made an undisclosed payment to its former employee.

Bob Westervelt was not the only member of Intel's security department who fell out of favor with his bosses for refusing to break the law. Another was Terry Hudock, a former member of the Air Force Office of Special Investigations.

Hudock joined Intel on February 10, 1986. While Westervelt's job was to manage security at the company's Asian facilities, Hudock was assigned to investigations on the West Coast. At first, it was the standard stuff: minor sting operations directed against shady chip dealers, surprise audits on inventories at Intel plants, surveillance of employees who seemed to be behaving suspiciously. Often, the investigations would turn up nothing more than individual inadequacy or unhappiness. On one occasion, for instance, the security department tailed a lonely employee who had been taking unusually long lunch breaks, and discovered that he was visiting a topless bar during working hours—an offense for which he was promptly fired.

But it took only two months before Hudock was first asked to do something that disturbed his conscience. Howard Hunter, the head of Intel's domestic security, told Hudock that an Intel employee was being investigated under suspicion of drinking at work—and ordered the newly hired investigator to break into the employee's desk and his car to search for evidence of illicit alcohol consumption. Hudock, too surprised to refuse outright, asked Hunter whether this was proper. Did Sandy Price, the member of Intel's legal department who normally handled the issue raised by internal security, know what was going on?

"These are things we don't discuss with Sandy Price," came the reply.

Nonetheless, Hudock was able to resist the pressure to violate the employee's privacy. Instead, the employee was watched and followed by Intel security—and Hunter came to the conclusion that the drinking problem, if it existed, was not serious enough to justify any action by the company.

Meanwhile, a problem had been passed down to the investigators by Andy Grove. A former Intel engineer, apparently suffering from mental illness, had written a series of bizarre letters to Grove and other senior figures inside Intel. In the correspondence, the engineer had alleged that Grove was betting away the company's profits at the gambling tables in Las Vegas. He also declared himself in love with the daughter of Bill Hewlett, one of the founders of Hewlett-Packard. He demanded that he should be made Intel's president, and threatened to go to the press with his gambling story unless he was given the job.

The letters were sometimes signed by name, and sometimes simply with the words "Silver Bullet." It might have been tempting to dismiss the writer as a harmless nutcase—but Andy Grove believed the engineer had been trying to follow him around. He wanted Intel's security people to put a stop to this alleged harassment. Hudock's boss, Steve Kopp, took Grove's demand for action as an indication that his job at Intel depended on getting rid of the renegade engineer at almost any cost.

An initial attempt was made to make contact with the letter writer, and he agreed to meet an Intel representative in a park in the prosperous seaside town of Carmel, an hour or so south of Santa Clara. Rob Miller was sent to meet him, wired up with a microphone and a tape recorder so that the conversation could if necessary be used as evidence against him. But the engineer never showed up, and Miller

spent an entire week sitting in the park in the vain hope that the letter writer would appear.

When a second meeting was set up at the Stanford Shopping Center in Palo Alto during the last week of September 1986, Steve Kopp
decided to meet the correspondent himself. This time, the engineer
did show up. He met Kopp in a restaurant close to Neiman Marcus
and talked to him for some time. Miller and Hudock, listening to the
conversation at a distance via a radio-microphone, could not stop
themselves laughing. It was clear that the engineer was simply crazy.

For Kopp, however, this was not enough. Before walking into the
restaurant, he had arranged to have an entire team of people waiting
for the engineer's arrival. He ordered Hudock to wait until the engineer was safely involved in the conversation with Kopp, and then to
break into his car in order to find out where he was staying and what
else he was up to. Hudock refused point-blank; so did Leonard Balli,
a former police officer who was another member of the security department. Later on, Kopp told the two over his radio to drop the
idea, because he had just seen a sheriff's patrol driving into the parking lot of the shopping mall.

After the meeting, the engineer climbed back into his car and
started to drive south to Scotts Valley, a small community outside
Santa Cruz. Five Intel investigators followed in hot pursuit. When the
engineer drew up outside a Best Western Hotel, Kopp ordered Miller
to check into the hotel and to try to obtain the room immediately below the engineer's.

Later that day, Kopp instructed Miller to get into the room by
bribing a hotel chambermaid, and then to plant a bug in the room
and go through the engineer's papers in search of his bank details.
Miller, younger than Hudock and without the experience in official
investigative work that would have alerted him to the illegality of
what he was being asked to do, agreed. He started by approaching
the manager of the motel, showing her his Intel ID, and telling her
that they believed the engineer was concealing a firearm in his room.
That was a blind: His true purpose was not to search for weapons but
to take a general look around and to find out what he could about the
engineer. But the story, with the help of a $50 bill, helped persuade
the motel manager that she should cooperate. Later on, Miller approached a chambermaid as Kopp had originally suggested—but because she stood by the door as he looked around, he was unable to
plant the bug in the room.

Eventually, the crisis blew over. The engineer, who was an Indian citizen, had overstayed his U.S. visa, and it was a simple matter for Intel to forward information to the authorities that led to his being deported. The correspondence ended, and no more complaints about being followed were heard from Andy Grove. After the engineer had left, his car somehow fell into the hands of Steve Kopp, who put it to his own use.

But Terry Hudock was still not happy with the way the department was being run—and his complaints began to make both Steve Kopp and Howard Hunter uneasy. In January 1987, Hunter called Hudock into a conference room and told him that his work performance was either "does not meet" or "marginally meets", under the company's rating system. He also complained that Hudock had failed to follow through on a security incident report and was doing work on the side in his spare time. Hudock was incensed; he interpreted Hunter's action as retaliation for his earlier refusal to conduct break-ins on the company's behalf. He became even angrier when Hunter then put him on "corrective action"—an arrangement under Intel's employment policies when an underperforming employee was given a fixed period of time in which to mend his ways, with the threat of being fired if he did not meet a set of agreed objectives. Hunter gave Hudock a few days to sign a letter agreeing to the basis of the corrective action, and threatened to fire him immediately if he refused.

On January 31, Hudock hit back. He drafted a memo to Andy Grove and Gordon Moore, with copies to Dick Boucher, the Intel vice-president who oversaw the security department, and Sandy Price, in Intel's legal department. In the memo, he rebutted the complaints of bad job performance made against him and raised a series of new allegations against members of the Intel security department.

Among Hudock's claims were allegations that he and his colleagues had been ordered to take police and law enforcement officials out to free lunches in order to obtain unauthorized criminal-record checks. That Intel carried out license-plate checks through the Department of Motor Vehicles, repeatedly circumventing the usual legal procedures that ensured a driver would be notified automatically when a check had been made. That Intel also performed illicit checks on both employees and outsiders by using a computer terminal belonging to the Intel Credit Union (an internal financing arm that delivered services to its staff) to find out how much money people under investigation had, and where they spent it.

Hudock ended his memo by proposing that he take some holiday time immediately while tempers cooled, and then be relocated to a different department within Intel.

Before sending the memo, Hudock asked for a meeting with Sandy Price. He handed her the memo as he sat down.

"Who else knows of this?" she asked.

Hudock replied that the memo was being hand-delivered as they spoke to the offices of Grove and Moore.

The memo produced immediate results. Hudock was sent off on paid leave for the next seven weeks while the company investigated his allegations. During the investigation, the lawyer whom Hudock had consulted received a call from the company offering to pay Hudock off with a year and a half's salary if he would leave quietly. Hudock, who wanted his job back rather than compensation, said he wouldn't take less than ten years' pay.

On March 25, Sandy Price wrote back to Hudock. On the complaint made by Hudock's boss that he was doing work on the side, she said that the investigation had found "no evidence to require any disciplinary action." On his job performance, she said, the corrective action plan appeared to be "justified, since there was objective evidence of a difference between your expected and actual performance. However, it appears that there may not have been sufficient communication/direction from your supervisor. To ensure fairness to all parties, we will withdraw the corrective action plan." On the allegations of illegality that had formed the bulk of Hudock's memo, she made no comment. Grove and Moore failed to reply at all to the memo, even though it had been primarily addressed to them.

The result of the exchange between Hudock and Price was that Hudock was reassigned to a new job in the company's internal audit department—but only after he sent a further letter reiterating that the charges made against him "were commenced as a deliberate plan to get rid of me because of my refusal to perform certain functions which in my belief constitute wrongful, improper and potentially illegal conduct."

Although Hudock performed well in the new audit job, and Price had assured him that Hunter and Kopp had been ordered to have no further contact with him, it was not long before Hudock began to worry that he was being harassed again by his former supervisors from the security department. In October 1987, he discovered that the ribbon of his IBM typewriter had been removed by Intel security and confiscated. This immediately alarmed him: IBM typewriter ribbons at the time were made of a long plastic tape covered with carbon, which moved along gradually from one end to the other as letters were typed. Because the tape was not reusable like a traditional fabric ribbon, the words that had been typed could be read back from it.

Rob Miller, still in the security department, knew exactly what had happened, and lost no time in warning Hudock. "They were trying to substantiate again that he was working for someone else or doing work on the side," Miller recalled. "They took . . . the tapes from his typewriters, and a guy from Oregon took them back to . . . have them transcribed."

Once again, Hudock complained angrily to Intel. In the end, however, his problem was resolved only when he received a job offer from another company, Business Risks International. Bob Westervelt, now out of Intel and suing the company for wrongful dismissal, believed that the new job had been arranged by Intel as a neat way to get an inconvenient whistle-blower to leave. He warned Hudock that he was being bought off. But Hudock thought the new job seemed exciting, so he left Intel without taking the company to court.

And Hunter, Kopp, and Zietzke? Six months after leaving Intel for National Semiconductor, Zietzke quit and became a security consultant in partnership with a former colleague. He continues to work for Intel on a consultancy basis to this day. So, according to a source close to the company, do Kopp and Hunter.

29

Davidian's Bonus

The decision inside Intel to jettison all the company's second sources for its coming 386 chip, including AMD, was a victory for Andy Grove. Fifteen years earlier, Grove had argued vociferously against licensing the company's technology to other businesses. But he had been overruled by Bob Noyce and Gordon Moore on the twin grounds of Intel's need for short-term cash and the impossibility of convincing customers to buy from a start-up Intel's size without a second source. By the time Intel's 1982 technology-sharing agreement with AMD began to crumble, both of these pressures had disappeared. The microprocessor business was booming, and Intel had no need to raise any money in a hurry. It was now the world's largest supplier of microprocessors, so the idea of taking a stand against the industry practice of second sourcing was at least plausible.

To turn the idea of being a sole source into reality, however, Intel had to do two things. First, it had to increase both the quantity and quality of its production. The 80186 chip had proved that there was still far to go on this front, because Intel had proven unable to deliver shipments in the required quantities, let alone on schedule. In March 1984, Intel's customers in the personal computer industry became so angry about this that they went to the press. A story in the *San Jose Mercury-News* quoted analysts as estimating that Intel was able to supply only between one-fifth and one-third of current demand for the chip. To make matters worse still, the company raised its price for the chip to $79. The official explanation for the increase was that Intel wanted "to cover the costs of its energetic manufacturing effort"; furious customers interpreted the price hike as a naked attempt to cash in on a shortage. It was clear to Andy Grove that Intel would have to become a great deal more reliable before it was ready to make its move.

Even after the company had sharpened up its act, ending its existing second-source arrangements would not be easy. Intel had issued no fewer than twelve different licenses for the 8086 and 8088 chips, so the world was full of companies that owned mask sets to Intel processors and knew many of the manufacturing secrets of the company's hottest-selling products. These earlier Intel products were still big sellers even in 1984. Statistics from Dataquest, a research firm, showed that a total of 75 million 8-bit processors were shipped in 1984, compared with only 10 million of the 16-bit processors that Intel had developed since the second-source deals were signed. The licenses that Intel had issued, together with wider cross-licenses exchanged between Intel and other leading companies in the industry, required time and attention to unwind.

But there was more to removing second sources than simply ending the company's licensing program. Intel also had to become more aggressive in pursuing unlicensed users of its chip standards. The company's crown jewel was the instruction set of the 8086 processor: Software companies all over the world had invested billions of dollars in designing programs that used the chip's 133 instructions. But Intel could not stop anyone else from designing a chip that accepted the same instructions—for doing so was a breach neither of copyright nor of patent law.

There was some consolation: American copyright law, traditionally used only to protect works of art like novels, plays, and movies, had been extended in 1980 to cover computer software. So copyright might well be taken to cover the "microcode"—the set of one hundred or so miniature programs stored on the chip itself and used by the processor to interpret complex instructions and break them down into much simpler steps.

Andy Grove realized as early as 1979 that the company would in future need a stronger form of protection for its intellectual property. He raised the issue in one of his regular one-on-ones with Roger Borovoy, then still the company's general counsel.

"I've got an idea," said Grove. "I think there should be copyright protection for masks. You have patents on the circuits, but they're all cross-licensed to everyone else. That's fine, but so much time and effort goes into the layout of these chips, and the photolithography is getting better and better. . . . We're going to have situations where someone knocks off a chip by peeling off layer after layer and photographing it."

Borovoy looked at him. Both men knew that U.S. law did not at the time provide any way of protecting the intellectual effort that went into designing masks. What was Grove suggesting—that the company should single-handedly try to change the law?

"Go do it," said Grove.

Borovoy went away and started talking to the congressmen who represented the districts where Intel had facilities. In 1980, he took a group of congressmen on a tour through the company's computer-aided design (CAD) department to show them how much effort was involved in designing masks and how helpful it would be for American industry to protect that effort against foreign knockoffs. Naturally enough, they asked him to come up with a draft of what the bill should say—so Borovoy, who had never before gone anywhere near the drafting of laws, began to spend time in his one-on-ones with Andy Grove discussing the key points they should try to get into a piece of upcoming federal legislation.

The bill took some time to get through Congress, and matters were not helped when the congressmen discovered that Borovoy had not been telling them the whole truth when he asserted that the entire industry was behind the Intel draft. Hearings were held in San Jose in 1981; to the dismay of the legislators, lawyers from both National Semiconductor and Fairchild Semiconductor said they did not like Borovoy's bill. It was not until 1984 that a modified version of the bill became law. All the same, the Semiconductor Protection Act was a striking example of how successfully Grove's ideas had been enshrined directly in the statute book.

"The bill got a lot bigger, with all kinds of exceptions and tie-ins," recalled Borovoy. "But I'd say at least a third to a half of what I had done was retained."

As it turned out, the strategic legal battle for exclusive control of the x86 architecture was fought over microcode.

The opponent was the Nippon Electric Company (NEC). In typical Japanese style, NEC had bought a license to Intel's 8086 and 8088, and then gone away and quietly made some changes and improvements to the chip—which it then launched in Japan, with some fanfare, as its own. Adding injury to insult, NEC refused to pay any royalties to Intel on the sale of the new processors. By late 1984, Grove had taken enough. Already angry at the Japanese incursion into the memory market, he was in no mood to compromise over microprocessors. Tom Dunlap, who had succeeded Borovoy as head of the Intel legal department and had now been awarded the title of general counsel, warned the nascent computer industry, which had sprung up to make "clones" of IBM machines, that any firm using the NEC chips in machines sold in the United States might find itself in court facing a lawsuit from Intel.

But NEC was no Seeq. Far from being a thinly funded start-up that needed every penny it had for developing new products, the Japanese firm was a $7 billion giant, four times Intel's size, that could easily afford to spend a few million dollars on a court case of such strategic importance. Using a U.S. law firm, NEC promptly sued Intel for restraint of trade and sought a declaration from the federal district court in northern California that its processors did not, in fact, infringe on Intel's microcode copyright.

The weak point in Intel's case was that the U.S. courts had never before addressed the question of whether microcode could be copyrighted. Even if it could, owners of copyrights were supposed to substantiate their claims by making sure that all licensed copies of the copyrighted material had clear copyright notices attached to them. Yet Intel's license to NEC, and similar licenses it had sold to Fujitsu and Mitsubishi between 1981 and 1984, did not require the licensees to print microcode copyright notices on the chips. Earlier 8086 licenses had given Intel a right to ask for copyright notices, but the company had never bothered to exercise that right. Intel had even allowed AMD to print '© AMD 1982' on a chip containing Intel microcode. As a result, over 10 percent of the twenty-eight million microprocessors containing the 8086 microcode that were distributed carried no copyright notice. To win its case, Intel would have to convince the court that the unlabeled chips, numbering nearly three million, counted as only a "relatively small number" of copies.

When the court case opened, NEC began with the obvious claims that microcode was not entitled to copyright at all—and that even if it were, Intel had forfeited its copyright by breaking the rule about copyright notices. But the Japanese company added an argument that initially took Intel by surprise: It claimed that the microcode for its series of processors, known as the V20, V30, and V40, had not in fact been copied from Intel's microcode at all. Although NEC admitted that it had full access to the Intel microcode, it maintained that the microcode in its own chips had in fact been written quite independently from scratch by a young Japanese software engineer named Hiroaki Kaneko. Given the dubious intellectual-property record of so many Japanese companies, it was not surprising that Intel viewed this defense with contempt.

The microcode consisted of ninety different mini-programs, and many of them appeared at first sight to be substantially similar to Intel's. Dunlap made sure that the court knew every detail of the blatant copying that NEC and other companies had carried out in the past, and had in front of it all the evidence that NEC had easy access to the Intel microcode. The implied question answered itself: Could the leopard change its spots so easily?

The judge seemed set to side with Intel. But before the case could be concluded, NEC's American lawyers raised a procedural objection. They pointed out that the judge had disclosed an interest in an investment club of old war buddies that he belonged to—but had failed to mention that through this investment club, he owned Intel stock worth about $80. Accordingly, the law firm asked the judge to "recuse" himself from the case—to withdraw, call a retrial, and hand over control to someone else. The judge, furious at the implied accusation that he might sell his good name for the sake of a few dollars of profit on a couple of Intel shares he had forgotten that he even owned, refused. The NEC lawyers appealed; the judge who heard the appeal passed the matter on to a third judge; and the third judge came to the conclusion that Judge Ingram, the owner of the Intel stock, need not pull out. NEC appealed again. This time, Judge Ingram gave in. The entire case had to begin again.

As the second trial opened, NEC already knew in advance where its weakest point was. It would have to convince a skeptical new judge that the circumstantial evidence supporting Intel's allegation of copying should be set aside. NEC's chances of success seemed remote. So the company's lawyers, a prominent San Jose firm called Skjerven, Morrill, MacPherson, Franklin and Friel, decided to prepare an insurance policy for NEC in case Intel won. To allow NEC to continue to sell its V-series processors, the law firm advised it to write the microcode again—but this time, to do it in a way that would be provably free from copying. That way, even if the judge decided that microcode was copyrightable and that Intel's copyright was valid, NEC would be able to show that it now had a new set of microcode that was immune from legal challenge.

In proposing this strategy, the lawyers were relying on the fact that copyright law draws a clear distinction between an idea and the way it is expressed. The law doesn't allow ideas to be copyrighted; the proper way to protect an idea is by patenting it. Only the expression of an idea is copyrightable. Courts have also come up with a doctrine called "merger," which says that when the idea and its expression cannot be separated, the law does not allow a copyright holder to pursue an infringer. (Otherwise, said Judge Browning in an important case in 1971, "protecting the 'expression' would confer a copyright of the 'idea' upon the copyright owner free of the conditions and limitations imposed by the patent law.") So NEC's lawyers planned to rely on the merger doctrine to produce new microcode that would be immune from attack.

Here's how it was going to work. While the legal maneuvering over the recusal of the first judge was being concluded, NEC authorized Skjerven, Morrill to go off and commission a new set of microcode. Dan Siegal, a young lawyer at the firm, came up with a neat way to prove that no copying had taken place. One consultant would be hired to study the 8086 chip, and draw up a specification for the microcode—a set of instructions based on the chip design and the way it was supposed to behave. Another consultant would then be hired to use that specification to write the microcode. The two consultants, however, would never be allowed to communicate. Siegal would act as a "firewall" between them, and all communications between the two consultants would be in writing, with Siegal checking that nothing passed between them that could compromise the purity of the new microcode. The result would be that only by proving Siegal and his firm liars could Intel challenge NEC's new microcode.

Siegal's brief was to find a pair of extremely bright software engineers. His first hire was Richard Belgard, one of the smartest consulting microprocessor experts on the market. Belgard's job was to "reverse-engineer" the 8086 microcode and write the spec. The second hire was more difficult; Siegel had to find someone who was an expert on microcode but had no knowledge of the most popular microprocessor architecture on the market. After making a few inquiries, Siegal identified a young engineer called Gary Davidian who had been writing microcode since he was in college. Davidian had worked for Data General, and then for a Californian company called Rational, and he was willing to sign an affidavit saying that he had never seen the inside of an 8086.

Time was of the essence. NEC needed to have a working set of microcode ready in case it lost the case and had to stop selling its existing processor line. Yet it was obvious that imposing the firewall between the two consultants and preventing them from ever knowing who the other was, let alone meeting face-to-face, would dramatically slow down the process of producing the microcode. Siegal's estimate was that it could take six months or more for Davidian to do the job. So with NEC's permission, Siegal offered the young engineer a choice of two contracts—each including a flat rate, and incentives for early completion. Since Davidian had not yet been told anything substantive about the project, he found it impossible to choose between them. So he told NEC he would be happy with either; his only stipulation was that the total contract had to be valuable enough to compensate him for throwing in his job at Rational and forfeiting his stock options. Given the choice, NEC picked the contract with a lower flat rate and higher incentives.

In August 1986, Davidian quit his job, took delivery from Siegal of a computer and a binder of documentation that Belgard had produced, and set up to work on the dining-room table of his home in Mountain View. His working methods put even the most dedicated computer geek to shame.

"I was just working at home the entire time," he recalled. "I didn't leave the house, really. I ate microwaved dinners. I'd start working at seven in the morning, and work until midnight or two." His approach was to switch from a twenty-four-hour cycle to a twenty-eight-hour cycle, and to work all his waking hours for six days on the trot, and then take a day off to go shopping and do his laundry.

Davidian's target was to implement the microcode for the NEC processor in such a way that it would pass a set of verification tests supplied by Belgard and forwarded to him by Siegal. At the end of each day's work, he would send off a set of questions to Siegal. Siegal would then forward the questions to Belgard. By the time Davidian woke up again, Siegal had the answers ready to forward to him.

"The fact that it was all going back and forth made it tough," Davidian recalled. "[To save time,] I'd put details into my questions that could anticipate their answers and ask follow-ups."

A week into the project, Siegal sent him a message to say that he was going away for a vacation but that he would take a modem with him. Since the Internet wasn't in mass use in 1986 and there were no low-cost portable fax machines either, Davidian dialed in from his modem directly into Siegal's computer at his office in Sunnyvale. Siegal—who was on a driving trip down the Pacific coast of Washington State—then dialed into the same machine from a portable he had with him to pick up messages.

To the astonishment of both Siegal and his masters at NEC, Davidian delivered a complete set of microcode that passed all the verification tests after only fifteen days. As a result, he earned himself $250,000 for just over two weeks' work. To be fair, there were lots of little bits to do over the succeeding months—the simulator that Belgard was using contained some errors, and the documentation he had written wasn't absolutely right—but Davidian needed to put in only a few days each month after that until the job was finally finished in early 1987. One day in January 1987, delighted at the idea that he had earned enough money to supply his wants for several years to come, Davidian saw on CNN that the Voyager space shuttle had landed at an airport in the Mojave Desert an hour and a half inland from Los Angeles. Spontaneously, he pulled out a map to identify the location of the airport, walked out of his house to his car, and drove down to the desert to see the landed shuttle.

NEC got their money's worth from Davidian, but not in the way they expected. To the engineer's great disappointment, his microcode was never implemented in any NEC processors. But it was used as the trump card in the new trial, and it helped NEC to win its case in a most unexpected way.

The new judge concluded that microcode *was* copyrightable, but that Intel had in fact forfeited its copyright by failing to take reasonable steps to ensure the right notices were fixed to its chips after discovering that the chips were not properly labeled. So Intel lost its claim against NEC. But it was on the question of "merger" that the most interesting discussion took place. The lawyers from Skjerven, Morrill argued in the courtroom that the design of the 8086 imposed very tight constraints on how the microcode could be designed—and that these constraints, rather than any copying, were the real explanation behind the strong similarities that both sides agreed existed between the NEC and Intel microcodes.

Siegal gave the example of two people driving from San Jose to San Francisco. "It was true that there were a number of different ways to go, probably an infinite number, but for the most part, you'd either take [Highway] 101 or 280," he said. "Those were the two reasonable ways to get to San Francisco—and the fact that both people went via 280 doesn't mean one was following the other."

To prove the point, NEC produced the code that Davidian had produced in the "clean-room" experiment. That code, which Siegal could prove had been written entirely independently and without any copying, was impossible for Intel to discredit—yet it was in many ways *more* similar to the original Intel microcode than the work of Hiroaki Kaneko, the Japanese engineer whom Intel had accused of nakedly stealing its code.

By the time the trial had finished, Gary Davidian had already found a new job at Apple Computer. His quarter-million dollars could therefore be put aside as a little nest egg for some future use. NEC had the right to carry on selling its V-series processors, without paying a penny in royalties to Intel. But Intel had won a victory of sorts, too. Although NEC had made a ritual objection to the claim that microcode could be copyrighted, it had never made this objection an important plank in its case. By concluding that microcode could be copyrighted, the judge had given Intel a prize of great value. Other rivals who were willing to go to the same trouble as NEC would be able to replicate its 8086 microcode. But those who just copied it, bit for bit, would be attacked by Intel with the full force of the law.

30

The New CEO

"We're pleased to report 1986 is over. It was, without question, the toughest year in Intel's history, filled with plant closings, layoffs and deep losses."

The news that Andy Grove and Gordon Moore delivered to Intel's shareholders early in 1987 was indeed grim. The company's sales had shrunk for the second successive year, leaving Intel's net revenues for 1986 at $1.27 billion compared with the $1.6 billion peak of 1984. Over the same two-year period, annual profits of $198 million had turned into losses of $173 million. In their management report, Grove and Moore admitted that after the 1984 boom, the company had found itself with an overhead structure "appropriate to the $2–3 billion company we wanted to be rather than the $1.0–1.5 billion company we were becoming." As a result of the turmoil in the industry, the competition from Japan, and their own slow response to the DRAM problem, Moore and Grove were forced to lay off 7,200 Intel staffers that year, close Intel's plants in Barbados and Puerto Rico, sell its bubble memory business, and take a $60 million restructuring charge against earnings.

But the light was already visible at the end of the tunnel, and Intel was fully ready to take advantage of the upturn. Having spent $388 million on new plant and equipment in 1984, and another $391 million in 1984 and 1986, it had plenty of spare manufacturing capacity. Having invested unflinchingly on R&D throughout the recession—

spending actually rose from \$180 million in 1984 to \$195 million in 1985 and \$228 million in 1986—the company also had a string of new products ready for release and in development. One of them was the 386—a new processor, many times faster than the current 286 standard, that handled data 32 bits at a time.

Intel had been trying for over a year to persuade IBM to market a new model that used its 386 chip. Yet to their frustration, the Intel engineers discovered that IBM just didn't seem to be interested. The larger company wasn't committing its best computer scientists to the job, and made it clear to Intel that it was actually frightened by the idea of a 32-bit microprocessor, which would bring the PC alarmingly close in power and flexibility to minicomputers that IBM was profitably selling for nearly ten times the price. From IBM's point of view, therefore, it made perfect sense to keep 32-bit PCs off the market for as long as possible.

But the strategy raised a worrying threat for Intel. Even though nothing could challenge the x86 architecture's position in the IBM machine and its clones, there was now another player in town. In 1984, Apple Computer had launched its Macintosh computer. The MAC made the IBM PC look Neanderthal. Instead of a nasty green-on-black screen, it displayed the words you were typing exactly as they would appear on paper—in black on white. Instead of requiring you to learn a string of incomprehensible codes to control the computer, the Mac gave you a mouse and a set of little pictures on the screen called icons. It was a thousand times more intuitive and convenient. Built around a Motorola processor, the Mac accounted for fewer than one in seven computers sold. But Intel knew that the Mac's usability advantages posed a long-term threat to the PC architecture, and by extension to Intel itself. It was bad enough for the company to be forced to wait for outsiders to develop a graphical interface like the Mac's for its x86 chips. It was quite another to allow IBM to halt the development process altogether and prevent Intel's best new technology from getting out to the customer.

Luckily, Intel had a potential ally. Compaq Computer, the first and arguably the leading manufacturer of what were known as "IBM clones," had a track record of innovation. It had reverse-engineered IBM's Basic Input-Output System (BIOS) by taking a pile of the most popular software packages on the market and analyzing the signals that the programs sent to the PC hardware and the signals they expected back in response. The company was then able to create its own version of the BIOS, without using any IBM code, and use it to build the first successful portable version of the PC. This achievement had earned Compaq sales of $111 million in its first year of operation, making it the fastest growing company in history. The company's engineers therefore had all the intellectual confidence to become a partner for Intel and develop a computer of their own based on the 386 processor. In October 1986, Compaq's new machine was unveiled at the Comdex trade show. To Grove's delight, it led to a rush of other computer manufacturers approaching Intel for supplies of the new chip so they could make their own versions. Computer users were willing to pay handsomely for the extra performance that a 386 chip gave them—and Intel was the sole source for the device. The company's average selling price on 286 chips, for which there were competitors, was $40. The 386, by contrast, brought in revenue of $150 a time.

The launch of Compaq's new machines had a wider significance. It marked a turning point in the history of the computer industry, because the company had gone ahead without waiting to see what IBM would do. Although IBM's share of the market for personal computers had declined steadily since the introduction of its first PC model, this was the first time that one of the clones had challenged IBM's technical leadership of the industry. From now on, Big Blue would simply be one of many computer makers—the most important, but still just one of many. The guardianship of the standards that defined a personal computer was no longer in the hands of any single player. And the destiny of the computer business would be steered jointly by the owner of the underlying processor technology, and the owner of the computer operating system. That meant Intel and Microsoft.

Given that IBM's abdication of its leadership role in 1986 had made the two companies joint captains of the industry, it was surprising how little they understood each other. To Andy Grove, Microsoft was still the company that had hit it lucky by selling a lousy operating system to IBM, and what was more, an operating system that it had to buy in from another company. Microsoft had gotten bigger and more powerful since then—Bill Gates took the company public in March 1986, earning himself a paper profit of over $300 million—but to Intel's eyes, little had changed. Founded by a guy who was twenty years younger than Andy Grove, Microsoft seemed to take a teenage approach to developing software.

A striking demonstration of the difference between the outlook of the two companies was the work they did on developing compilers—programs that take code written in a high-level, easy-to-use computer language and convert it into the basic nuts-and-bolts assembly language that can be fed directly to the microprocessor. Intel's compilers were simply better. This wasn't a matter of opinion: the compiler writers inside Intel had software tools that made it a snap to measure how quickly a program compiled and how many bugs it turned—and you could look at the size of the compiler itself to see how successful the person who wrote it had been in turning out a small and elegantly simple program. "The compilers we wrote at Intel would typically be half as big physically," recalled John Novitsky, one of the Intel compiler team, "and when you had only 16 or 32K [of memory] on the system, that mattered a lot. The Microsoft compiler code was typically bug-filled, and in its execution speed two to three times slower than the code the Intel compilers produced."

In Andy Grove's eyes, this was more than incompetence. It was immorality. If Intel was putting teams of people to work for two years at a time on wringing a 15 percent improvement in the performance of its processors, it was horrific that Microsoft would throw away an opportunity to deliver a fivefold increase in the effective speed delivered to the user simply because it was so stupid in the way it wrote compilers.

Gradually, the view took shape inside Intel that the guys at Microsoft simply didn't care that their programs ran so slowly on Intel processors. Intel set up a team of three or four people inside the group developing its 386 microprocessor and gave them the job of making sure that all the key applications developers and computer companies who would be writing software for the 386 knew how to take advantage of the chip's new features. Yet Microsoft, in stark contrast to the programmers working on the Lotus 1-2-3 spreadsheet, or the UNIX operating system, didn't seem to be listening. "They were completely uninterested in the kind of working relationship we were trying to establish. They didn't care. They just thought Intel was irrelevant."

The contempt was mutual. Up in Seattle, the design compromise that Intel had made in its 8086 chip—arranging the computer's memory in segments of 16 bytes each—looked like the stupidest decision ever made in computing history. From Microsoft's point of view, it made no difference that the original rationale for the arrangement was to maintain backward compatibility; Bill Gates wasn't interested in Intel's concern for customers who had designed products on its earlier 8-bit processors and wanted a quick and easy way to get some of the benefits of 16-bit computing. The cost of the segmentation decision, in Microsoft's eyes, had been to cause untold trouble and inconvenience: It had been a pain in the neck for thousands of applications software writers—so much so that programmers who wrote for the Mac sometimes declared that it was actually "impossible" to write code for x86 machines—and, as a result, a pain in the neck for millions of computer users around the world.

As a result, programmers at Microsoft were less than receptive when Intel's crack software engineers would call up with suggestions on how Microsoft could improve its programs. One Intel engineer recalled the reaction. "We'd go to the applications guys, and say, 'We studied the code in Excel, and we found this loop that if you change it you can speed the whole thing up by a factor of eight,' " he said. "They'd say, 'We don't care. We're going to add this new feature.' We'd debate this, and we'd say, 'The version [of Excel] running on the Mac runs eight times faster. Can't you make a release for the PC?' 'No,' they said. 'People buy our applications because of new features.' "

With this mistrust between the two companies lying in the background, it was no wonder that the fading of IBM as a force in the PC industry coincided with the beginnings of out-and-out hostility between Microsoft and Intel. From Bill Gates's point of view, the PC business was now a zero-sum game between the two firms. Every dollar that Intel could extract from the buyer of a PC would be a dollar out of Microsoft's pocket—and vice versa.

The war between the two companies would be waged on many fronts, but ultimately it boiled down to a single issue. From 1986 onwards, Intel had a near-monopoly of the processor while Microsoft had a near-monopoly of the operating system. Each one had a clear incentive to dismantle the other's monopoly.

But it was to be some time before any signs of struggle between Intel and Microsoft became public. Meanwhile, Andy Grove could claim success in turning his company around from the nightmare days of the 1985–86 slump. In April 1987, Intel reported net income of $25 million for the most recent quarter—hardly impressive on sales of nearly $400 million for the period, but nevertheless a clear turn into profit. To celebrate the change, it held a number of parties for employees, all based on the theme of "back in the black." Another significant change happened during the same month: Intel's board of directors appointed Grove the company's CEO, leaving Gordon Moore still holding the title of chairman. Intel's public face now finally reflected its internal realities.

The handover from Moore to Grove was perfectly timed. From that quarter onwards, Intel's sales exploded. By the end of 1987, they had grown to $1.9 billion, and within another year they were at $2.9 billion—close to the top end of the range that Grove had hoped to achieve before the company was hit by the downturn of 1985.

Part of the sharp increase in Intel's sales, and correspondingly in its profitability, came from the growth of the computer market and of demand for 386-class microprocessors. Part of it came from improvements in manufacturing efficiency; in 1986 alone, for instance, the company could boast that it had cut defects per million parts shipped from 8,500 to just 100 in six years; manufacturing cost per step of fabrication by 30 percent in three years; and chip fabrication time by 20 percent in just one year. And part of the increase was due simply to the fact that the ill effects that Ed Gelbach and Gordon Moore had predicted would result from Intel's withdrawal from the DRAM business didn't materialize.

Gelbach's worry had been that customers would be less keen to buy from a semiconductor supplier that did not offer a full lineup of products. This had been dealt with easily by signing a highly profitable long-term supply agreement with Samsung, the leading chipmaker in Korea, which was trying to do to the Japanese what they had just done to the Americans. Moore's worry had been that DRAM was necessary as a "technology driver"—that without millions of DRAM wafers to practice on, Intel would be unable to develop new manufacturing processes and improve the efficiency of its existing processes. This, too, proved mistaken.

"You don't learn quickly when you increase volume by brute force," said Sun Lin Chou, one of the company's senior technologists, to researchers from Stanford Business School in 1990. "You have to learn by examining wafers. Learning is based on the number of wafers looked at, analyzed, and the number of effective corrective actions taken. Even if you have processed 1,000 wafers, the technical learning probably only came from the 10 wafers you analyzed. Technical learning is time- and engineering-constrained, not number-of-wafers-constrained."

"A great deal of the know-how is now generated at the equipment suppliers," added Gerry Parker, the company's vice-president of technology development. "The Japanese really have taught us something. They expect excellence from equipment vendors, and make *them* develop the expertise to provide the best possible equipment. If a piece of equipment has a problem, the vendor is right there in the fab area fixing it and he can make appropriate changes on the next generation."

But the overwhelming reason for the long-term turnaround in Intel's fortunes was the decision to end the practice of second sourcing its microprocessors. From the 386 onwards, Intel was determined to be the only supplier in the world of its architecture—and to use every legal means to stop Jerry Sanders, or anyone else, from getting a share of the profits from what was formally called the "iAPX architecture," short for Intel Advanced Processor Architecture, but was now commonly referred to in the industry simply as "x86."

The financial significance of this was revealed in the figures that Intel provided to the writers of a case study in the business school of Stanford University. In 1984, the company was selling 286 processors, which cost $34 to make, for $250, and was selling samples of the upcoming 386 processors, which cost $141 to make, for $900. Intel's margins on the two products were 86 percent and 84 percent respectively. By comparison, a standard 8-bit processor was fetching only $4.06 in the same year. Intel's ownership of the chip architecture that every computer company in the world wanted to use was immensely valuable—and the most important way to preserve the profitability of that ownership was keeping competitors out. Like every other business in the world, Intel would always be keen to look for ways to cut its costs. But anything that kept competitors away from its market just for a short time could have a disproportionately positive effect on Intel's bottom line. Give Grove the choice between investing money and time to shave 10 percent off the manufacturing cost of a microprocessor and investing the same money and time in keeping a competitor out of the market for a year who would otherwise have built a 10 percent market share, and there was no contest. The fight to protect Intel's intellectual property would take priority every time. It was no wonder that Grove, during internal presentations to other Intel managers, liked to put up a slide showing Intel as a castle, beset by invaders from all sides, each invader after one thing: the jewel of the kingdom, the 386 chip.

It was with this imperative in mind that Intel resisted AMD's request for arbitration of the 1982 technology-sharing agreement.

AMD had to go to court in 1987 to get an arbitrator appointed, and Intel kept the case going so long that the arbitrator, a retired superior court judge named Barton Phelps, was unable to deliver his conclusions until 1990. In his decision, Judge Phelps damned AMD for being starry-eyed about the agreement to begin with, incompetent in delivering low-quality chips to Intel in fulfilment of its side of the bargain, and imprudent in failing to start development of its own 386 chip until long after it had become clear that Intel would never hand over the 386 to AMD voluntarily. But he accused Intel of acting in cold-blooded bad faith by frustrating the working of the agreement and trying to make AMD cooperate with Intel in the belief that it would get the 386, even though Intel had already secretly decided not to hand it over.

The key point of the award was that Judge Phelps ordered Intel to give AMD a "permanent, nonexclusive and royalty-free license" to the 386. But even after three years of arbitration, Intel had still not had enough. It went to the courts for a declaration that the arbitrator had overstepped his authority in ordering Intel to grant AMD the license—and the case went all the way to the State Supreme Court before the arbitrator's decision was finally upheld in 1994. From a commercial point of view, the costs of the case that Intel incurred each year was money well spent. It had kept Jerry Sanders out of the 386 market for another year.

31

An Anonymous Caller

On December 8, 1987, one of Intel's senior patent lawyers took a call that gave the company the first clue that a new competitor was raising its head above the parapet. The lawyer was Carl Silverman, and he reported to Tom Dunlap in a department that had recently grown from a small in-house legal practice of five people to a full-fledged "document factory" staffed by no fewer than twenty lawyers. The factory was a typical piece of Andy Grove management. Intel's new CEO was willing to spend heavily on legal costs, but he saw no reason to spend a penny more than was really necessary. Beefing up the company's legal department allowed Intel to bring in-house much of the work that it had previously given to outside firms. When the company did send more specialist work to outside firms, the existence of the factory gave Intel a useful reality check against invoices from its outside counsel.

The caller would not tell Silverman who he was. But he told the Intel lawyer that he had information on a company that was building a clone of Intel's 387 math coprocessor chip—and for $400,000, he was willing to hand over that information to Intel. Silverman tried to get the informant to talk but was unable to get any important further details—or to stop him from hanging up.

Nearly a month later, the phone rang again. This time, Silverman was prepared and had a tape-recorder attached to the phone line in his office cubicle. Once again, the caller talked about the mystery competitor; once again, he demanded money for his information. But Silverman would not commit there and then to a payment, and tried to persuade the mystery caller to meet an Intel representative so they could discuss the matter further. The call ended inconclusively—and once again, Silverman was left at a loose end. There was nothing to do but report the conversation to Tom Dunlap and Intel's security department and wait by the phone.

In April, the mist began to lift. A letter arrived on Dunlap's desk from Alan MacPherson, a partner in Skjerven, Morrill, the law firm that represented NEC against Intel in the microcode case. MacPherson's letter explained that one of his corporate clients had recently discovered some proprietary Intel documents on its premises. The client, MacPherson continued, was a start-up company called ULSI Systems, and was developing a competing product to Intel's 387. ULSI had passed the documents to MacPherson for advice, and MacPherson had sequestered them, keeping only one copy for its records. The lawyer was now writing to reassure Intel that "ULSI has taken all reasonable steps to ensure that its development effort is free from the use of Intel's trade secrets. ULSI will continue its development effort in a manner free from any such use." His letter ended with an offer to meet an Intel representative and counsel to discuss the question further.

ULSI's founder was a wiry, energetic immigrant from Taiwan named George Hwang. After studying electrical engineering at San Jose State University, Hwang had joined Hewlett-Packard; in 1980, he had been one of the founders of Integrated Device Technology, a company dedicated to developing a new high-performance CMOS process. By coincidence, one of IDT's leading investors was John Carey, recently retired from AMD. Carey later became the company's chairman and CEO, and took the company public.

Hwang collected over $1 million from the company's IPO—but he was determined not to retire at the age of forty-five. Instead, he decided to start a new business, combining his own expertise in process technology and manufacturing with the talents of Bob Woo, a friend who had an expert command of floating-point logic design. Woo did not have any money to invest, but Hwang was happy to give him a share of the equity in return for the intellectual capital that he would contribute.

Intel's 386 had been launched shortly before Hwang left IDT, and the spectacular profits it was earning for Intel had not passed him by unnoticed. On the contrary, he saw that the 386 created an opening for someone to start up a new semiconductor business.

In order to keep the size of the 386 chip to a minimum, Intel had followed its usual practice of not including any specialist hardware inside the unit to carry out floating-point operations such as long division. This made sense for the majority of customers, who would never need to do heavy-duty number crunching. But for financial analysts, engineers, and people using computer graphics for design, a floating-point unit, or FPU, was essential: It could do arithmetic ten or a hundred times as fast as a standard chip. Ever since the 8086 generation, Intel had sold this unit as a separate "math coprocessor." Installed next to the main processor, the device would keep tabs on the main processor and step in to perform the arithmetic whenever needed.

The argument for selling the coprocessor as a separate unit was part commercial and part technological. The commercial argument was that excluding the floating-point unit from the standard 386 allowed Intel to keep the price down, and thus to speed up the chip's acceptance in the computer marketplace. The technological argument concerned the size of the die that contained the 386's circuits. As we've seen, it was one of the rules of the chip business that die size was closely related to yield—the bigger the die, the smaller the proportion of usable chips on each wafer that came out of the fab.

As soon as the 386 began shipping in volume, it was clear that the coprocessor that accompanied it—to be known as the 80387, or simply "387"—was certain to be a big seller. Hwang did a little market research and concluded that his new company could make a lot of money if it could develop a competitor to the Intel coprocessor. "Intel was the only supplier, and theirs was not a very high performance part," he said afterwards. "It was very easy to design parts that outperform the Intel part manyfold. [The 387] was selling for $600–$700 apiece, yet most integrated circuits cost only $20 to build."

Studying analysts' reports, Hwang came to the conclusion that if he and Woo could design a competing coprocessor that did the job as well as Intel's or better, and could price it at $400, then that one product alone over a three-year lifetime could sell one million units, and thus bring in $400 million of revenue—more than enough to kick-start a serious semiconductor business. The development budget need not be high. Hwang thought it would cost under $1 million to develop the part—and once he had samples of a working coprocessor, he expected to be able to raise money from venture capitalists to pay for manufacturing and marketing. Hwang knew his manufacturing costs would be higher than Intel's, because he would have to go to a "chip foundry," a company that built chips on a contract basis for other firms. But since there was so much margin to play with, manufacturing cost was not an issue.

ULSI started up in spring 1987. One of the company's first hires was an engineer named Richard Yau, who had worked some years earlier at Intel. Hwang felt Yau was "very young, dynamic, aggressive, had some entrepreneurial spirit." His technical credentials left a little to be desired, but Hwang and Woo were convinced that Yau would soon learn—particularly since the young engineer declared that he was very excited by the idea of building a high-performance coprocessor to beat the 387.

To make sure its own design could be fully compatible with the 386, ULSI had to find out precisely how Intel's coprocessor communicated with the main processor chip. But Yau, who had been given responsibility for this aspect of the project, soon proved unable to do the job on his own. At his suggestion, ULSI hired a friend of his, Yee Wong, to work as a contractor to help put together a clear specification. Wong proposed to follow the traditional first step of a reverse-engineer job—to "pop the top" of the 386 and 387 and take a look at the circuits inside using high-powered photography. This, combined with analysis of the signals going in and out of the chip, ought to help ULSI pin down exactly how the two parts interfaced together. By July, however, Wong had got little further than Yau. ULSI decided to pay him off, settling his bill with a check for $5,000, compared with the $20,000 he would have been paid for completing the job. In his place, the company hired Alfred Chen, another Chinese-born engineer who had worked at Intel on the 386. Then things began to look up: In August, Intel published a detailed guide to the workings of its coprocessor in *IEEE Micro*, a respected industry magazine. This answered most of the outstanding questions, and allowed ULSI to make some progress designing its own coprocessor to do the job five to ten times faster than Intel's.

In December, Alfred Chen gave ULSI's chief executive a shock. He showed Hwang a copy of a document called a "target specification" for the 387, marked "Intel proprietary." The "T-spec," as the document was known for short, was only an early outline of how the chip would work. It had been superseded by the version that went into manufacturing, and the key information that it contained had now been published by Intel in a trade magazine anyway. But Hwang, realizing that he could not condone the holding of Intel documents on

ULSI's premises, immediately called his lawyer. Alan MacPherson's response was swift: He took possession of the document immediately and made sure there was nothing else belonging to Intel on the premises. He then began to investigate the circumstances surrounding the appearance of the document.

It certainly didn't look good. Unknown to ULSI, Wong had in fact been working at Intel while he was moonlighting on the abortive consultancy project. And Yau, who by now had been fired by ULSI, was threatening to go to Intel and accuse Hwang of complicity in the appearance of the T-spec unless he was paid off in ULSI stock

MacPherson proposed to Hwang that ULSI should do exactly what NEC had done with its microcode. To make the coprocessor totally immune from legal attack by Intel, he suggested that the chip should be redesigned using a "clean-room" technique. That way, he would be able to demonstrate that no matter how many incriminating documents may have been brought into the office, and no matter what accusations Yau might make against ULSI, the coprocessor was provably free of Intel trade secrets.

The clean-room process was already well under way when Tom Dunlap and two other Intel representatives received MacPherson's letter and came to visit ULSI. In a tense meeting, Hwang offered to open his laboratories to Intel lawyers in order to prove that everything was above board.

"We told them, 'Our part is totally different from yours, and we'll open our database [to prove it]. We've done the architecture, we've done the algorithm, but we haven't gone far into the implementation,' " recalled Hwang.

Intel's response was cautious. Dunlap thanked Hwang for his openness, but suggested that the best way to resolve the issue would be for ULSI to drop the project completely.

"No. The object of this meeting is to assure you that we're not using your trade secrets," replied Hwang.

And there the matter was left to rest. Hearing nothing further from Intel, and receiving no substantive further response to MacPherson's follow-up letters, the ULSI development team went on with the design of their 387-killer. As the chip neared completion, Hwang started talking to venture capitalists—and to AMD, which had no equivalent of the 387 of its own, and was the company that could most obviously benefit by manufacturing and marketing ULSI's design. By then, AMD had acquired a new vice-chairman, Irwin Federman of Monolithic Memories, a company that AMD had taken over earlier in the year. Federman offered to clear the air with Intel by having a chat with Andy Grove about ULSI.

"Let me go talk to Andy and convince him that there's nothing to it," said Federman. He also made an imaginative suggestion: Why not have Intel take an equity position in ULSI?

With Hwang's agreement, Federman set up a breakfast with Andy Grove. He said his piece about ULSI; the Intel CEO, declining to make an instant decision, promised to get back to him within two weeks. Two weeks later, Grove sent back a message to say that Intel was not interested. But by then, it didn't matter; Hwang's ship seemed close to home anyway. AMD had made a convertible loan of a half million dollars to ULSI, and had sent Hwang a draft technical agreement covering the terms under which it would market the ULSI coprocessor through AMD. The product would be called the "US101"; and AMD would take responsibility for defending any legal action from Intel over the chip.

Then disaster struck. On the very day that Hwang received the AMD agreement for signature, seven officers from the Santa Clara Police Department arrived at ULSI's premises, armed with a search warrant entitling them to scour the premises for evidence that the company had stolen Intel's trade secrets. Echoing the hostile trade relations between the United States and Japan, the police officers angrily ordered all the engineers in the building with Oriental looks to stay in one place, while allowing the Caucasians to walk about as they pleased during the search.

The next day's edition of the *San Jose Mercury-News*, Silicon Valley's leading business paper, contained a front-page story about the search. It quoted a police sergeant as saying that ULSI was a front organization funded from Taiwan or Hong Kong, whose purpose was to sell Intel trade secrets; the district attorney claimed to have evidence that would be sufficient to put Hwang away for three to five years. On his attorney's advice, Hwang kept silent, making no attempt to tell his side of the story.

Five days later, Intel filed its own civil suit against ULSI. Tom Dunlap used the same tactic with ULSI as Roger Borovoy had with Seeq. He proposed that the company should agree, in a "stipulated preliminary injunction" lodged formally at the court, not to transfer its technology to anywhere other than Hewlett-Packard, the chip foundry where Hwang had already made arrangements to fabricate the coprocessors.

Hwang asked his lawyer how long the injunction was likely to remain in force.

"At worst, the case will take six months to go away," Hwang's lawyer told him. Since Hwang thought it would take more than six months getting the chip into production anyway, they decided there would be no harm in agreeing to the injunction.

But Hwang and his lawyers had never fought Intel before. Dunlap fully appreciated that every extra month he could keep ULSI and Hwang in court would be one extra month that Intel had a monopoly over the 387, and one extra month during which venture capitalists would be unwilling to put any money into Hwang's operation.

To make matters worse for Hwang, Intel had friends in the team responsible for the parallel criminal investigation. The leader of the team that had busted ULSI was Sergeant Nels Pearson; Leonard Balli, a former colleague of his, now worked in Intel's security department. Pearson, who later did some private consulting for Intel while on the police payroll, made no objection to allowing Balli to be present at the interrogation of Richard Yau, the anonymous caller who had provoked the entire incident. A day after the search, Pearson also allowed Pat Gelsinger, the designer manager for Intel's next-generation processor, to see documents on ULSI's coprocessor that had been seized during the search. When Pearson went to interview Richard Lovgren, AMD's deputy general counsel, on the affair, it was after receiving a briefing from Tom Dunlap at Intel on the key issues he should raise.

Intel also had good connections in the DA's office. The criminal case against Hwang was handled there by Kenneth Rosenblatt, a prosecutor who had formerly worked in a firm retained by Intel for work that the company's in-house paper factory could not handle. Rosenblatt was quoted in a profile of Tom Dunlap published in the *San Francisco Chronicle* that testified to the closeness of their relationship: "Do I hate Tom Dunlap?" he asked rhetorically. "No, I don't hate him. I have a very nice house and he paid for it. I hope Tom Dunlap stays around for a long time doing what he's doing."

To encourage the DA's office to take the case seriously, Intel officials emphasized the importance of the T-spec that had shown up on ULSI's premises. Charles Quarton, one of Intel's senior intellectual-property attorneys, told Rosenblatt in September 1988 that the document could probably have saved ULSI $2 million in research costs. But Intel did not make clear to the prosecutors that much of the information contained in the T-spec had been published by Intel in *IEEE Micro*, a prominent industry magazine, six months before the search was carried out. Not surprisingly, the prosecutors launched a criminal case against Hwang.

The stress of the search and the civil lawsuit led to strains between Hwang and his business partner, which finally culminated in an acrimonious parting. Woo resigned his seat on the company's board in late 1988, forcing Hwang to put in more and more of his own money to keep ULSI afloat. It was not until January 1991, when two other later entrants had already started selling their own 387 clones, and the ULSI coprocessor had been sitting on the shelf for a year and a half, that Hwang was able at last to put a product on the market. Despite pricing his chip at a bargain-basement $220, Hwang still faced suspicion from customers who had heard about the lawsuits and wanted ULSI to give them legal guarantees of protection against Intel before they would buy any parts.

In July 1991, following up the civil suit and criminal prosecution that were still in progress, Intel opened a third front against Hwang. It sued him for infringing a patent covering a method of making floating-point calculations accurately. At first, Hwang thought the case, and indeed the underlying patent, was laughable: The method for carrying out the calculations proposed in the patent was one that had been adopted as an industry standard by a twenty-strong committee on which Intel had a member. But Intel was able to refile the patent to remove the controversial issues, and use it to sue ULSI. Instead of choosing Santa Clara as the venue for the case, Intel took it before a judge in Oregon, where the company was a prominent local employer. Intel won; ULSI appealed and won; Intel appealed again. Not until 1994 was the patent infringement claim finally thrown out.

But by then, it did not matter. The civil case had gone on for so long that Hwang had run into a new problem: Hewlett-Packard, the company manufacturing coprocessors for him on a contracting basis, notified Hwang that it was getting out of the "chip foundry" business altogether. Since Hwang had agreed to the injunction banning any transfer of his technology elsewhere, he was now faced with the risk of being unable to build any more chips while the trial continued. This proved to be the straw that broke the camel's back. Hwang gave in and settled with Intel, agreeing to pay it a royalty of 3 percent on all the revenue ULSI received from its coprocessor. The settlement, finalized in May 1993, also included an agreement that Intel would be allowed to say in public that the ULSI device was not 100 percent compatible with the 387, while Hwang would be allowed to assert that his chip was compatible with the 386. Technically speaking, this distinction was nonsense; the chip that the ULSI device would be installed next to was the 386, and there was no need for it to be compatible with the 387. But the distinction allowed Intel to sow a doubt in the minds of computer users about whether a ULSI coprocessor would work with their machines if they bought it. This was of considerable commercial value. It would make ULSI's processor just that little bit harder to sell.

Intel, then, had managed to take ULSI to court nearly a year after it first became aware of the appearance of the T-spec on ULSI premises, and after ULSI had offered it access to its records to prove that there had been no foul play. No judge ever had a chance to assess the merits of Dunlap's accusation or Hwang's defense, yet Intel had kept ULSI busy with the proceedings for nearly five years. Hwang calculated afterwards that developing his coprocessor had cost $2.5 million; fighting Intel had cost $3.5 million.

But the nightmare was not yet over. After three and a half years of preparation, the prosecutors were at last ready to put Hwang on criminal trial. His trial lasted four months, with the possibility hanging over him every night that he might be sent to jail if found guilty. One of the key moments in the trial was when John Crawford, an Intel Fellow who was on the stand as an expert witness, testified to the secrecy of the information contained in the T-spec. When asked to account for the fact that much of the information he claimed was secret had in fact been published by Intel in the magazine article, he disclaimed responsibility for the article. Intel's attorney interrupted the proceedings to demand an immediate recess, during which Crawford was later seen talking anxiously on the phone to another Intel lawyer, who wanted to ensure that he said nothing that would prejudice Intel's case in the civil action. Crawford then returned to the stand and changed his testimony.

At the end of the trial, it took the jury just one day to throw out the case.

Hwang was a free man. But he was not willing just to pick up the pieces of his former life. So incensed was he by Intel's behavior, and so convinced that the company had taken him to court in bad faith simply in order to pursue its own commercial advantage, that he approached a prominent firm of antitrust lawyers to look into the question of whether it might be possible to make a claim for damages against Intel.

The case looked promising at first. Hwang could show that Intel's action had broken up a $25 million marketing arrangement with AMD, and had resulted in reducing ULSI's annual sales from $25–30 million to between $10 million and $12 million. In a confidential memo to the senior partner of the antitrust firm, one of the lawyers studying the case described Crawford's about-face as an "astounding example" of the hand-in glove partnership between Intel and the prosecutors.

"It is our position that Intel knowingly provided false and fraudulent information to the Deputy District Attorney's Office of Santa Clara County," said another internal paper, "which served as a basis for pursuing its claim and for the court binding over Hwang and Chan as a result of the preliminary hearing." The paper also charged that Intel had prepared many witnesses for testimony, withheld key documents from the prosecution authorities, sponsored an expert witness to claim that the information found was a trade secret when 95 percent of it was not, and had been present during the questioning of every witness interviewed by the DA's office.

Asked for his opinion by the anti-trust specialists, Hwang's civil attorney took a similarly dim view of the case. "I believe a review of Intel's preliminary injunction motions and all their other efforts in the trade secret case could lead a jury to conclude that they had no interest in assessing fairly whether ULSI had conducted an effective clean-room, but were engaged solely in an effort to attack the clean-room effort regardless of its apparent merits. The legal and financial incentives for doing so, especially the potential relationship with AMD, supply the motive for bad faith litigation."

The case was never mounted. Hwang had hoped to be able to produce as witnesses customers who had been threatened by Intel after deciding to buy ULSI's coprocessor chips. But such was Intel's power in the market that none of the PC companies that had reported Intel's behavior to Hwang was willing to take the stand in court against their most important supplier. After paying another $100,000 in legal fees for the abandoned antitrust case, Hwang gave up the fight. He still runs ULSI today; at present, Hwang is working on a new chip.

32

Lagging the Koreans

One of the effects of Intel's increasingly sharp focus on micro-processors was to make some of the company's senior employees working in other areas feel left out. An early casualty was Tim May, the astrophysicist whose solution to the alpha-particle radiation problem had saved Intel's memory-chip business millions of dollars. By 1986, May, one of the few long-serving engineers who had resisted promotion to management, had been promoted to a salary and seniority point known inside Intel as Level 10. For the past two years, as the company's financial difficulties deepened in the face of Japanese competition and the computer recession, May had been doing research into LISP software and artificial intelligence.

"I hated walking through hallways in this gloomy atmosphere and have people like Les Vadasz give me sneering looks because he thought I was an ivory-tower scientist," May recalled. "Always at Intel there was a strong feeling that you were either working on important projects, or you were dead weight."

Then May's boss, Gene Meieran, gave him a bad performance review. Meieran explained that he felt bad doing so, but the company had put out the word to give a higher quota of bad reviews. It needed to lose some staff, and a bad review was an essential first step in firing someone without paying compensation.

"I'm a researcher," replied May. "I've worked long and hard for this company."

"We're not reducing anything," replied Meieran. "Your salary is the same. Your options are the same."

But May, incensed, would not accept his bad review without a fight. He crossed out large portions of it, writing comments in the margins like *THIS IS BULLSHIT* and *THIS IS NONSENSE.*

"I've never had a bad review," he insisted. "Just because times are tight, I refuse to accept this."

May was in an unusual position. While most Intel employees had families, mortgages, and responsibilities to keep them loyal, he did not. He had exercised his stock options, but never cashed in any of the stock. Since his first day at Intel, he had regularly invested another 20 percent of his basic pay in Intel shares bought through a separate stock purchase scheme offered by the company. He had also invested in both Sun and Apple when they went public.

Immediately after receiving his review, May told Meieran that he was going to take the next two days off, a Thursday and a Friday.

"I said to myself, *This is an insult. This is a fucking insult. I'm not going to take this shit.*" With these thoughts going through his head, May went off to Santa Cruz on Friday and bought himself a new house. On Monday, he returned to the office and handed in his notice.

Before he cleared his desk, May received a message that Andy Grove wanted to see him. This was an "exit interview"—the standard process that Grove had introduced sometimes to try to persuade a leaver to change his mind, sometimes to learn whatever lessons were appropriate from his departure.

"So I hear you're leaving," Grove began.

"Yup," May replied.

"Can we talk you out of it?"

"You can go back in a time machine and give me a good review," said May bitterly. "I'm superfluous here. I'm supercargo. My path has diverged from your path. Nothing I'm working on is interesting to you. There's a lot of hostility, a lot of morale problems."

After five minutes of trying to persuade him, Grove spent the remaining thirty-five minutes of the interview taking notes on May's criticisms of Intel.

Gordon Moore was sadder; he had been in contact with May a lot over recent years. He asked May for some suggestions on ultra-long-range research that the company should be doing. He told May he was sorry to see him go, and asked him if there was anything that the company could have done differently.

Craig Barrett, the former Stanford professor who had been May's boss, was now a senior vice-president. When May came in for his exit interview, he sat there, with a finger on one side of his face and smirked as only he knew how.

"So you're finally making the big move," he said. "I hope you have a good life."

Barrett's promotion to senior VP resulted in another casualty: Will Kauffman, the fab manager who had risen gradually through Intel's ranks during his career. Kauffman found that his growing respect for Japanese manufacturing techniques did not endear him to the Intel top brass.

"My last mission to myself while I was VP of [quality assurance] was . . . to get the management of the company, including Andy, to accept some of the methods that were needed to be competitive. It fell on deaf ears," he recalled. "Internally, throughout the manufacturing organization, we started to believe in things like JIT,"—just-in-time management, the principle of keeping inventories as close to zero as possible, and making sure that every step of the production process was defect-free before passing product on to the next step—"and taking specific manufacturing areas and trying to get teams of people together to figure out how they could do their jobs better than before. Unless that's driven from the top, it has a very difficult time flourishing. People hear different messages, and they're not sure what the right thing to do is. I went on a campaign to try to convince Andy that he should be doing things a little differently from what he was doing. He didn't have time; he didn't believe in it."

It was not long before Grove promoted Barrett over Kauffman's head. In theory, Kauffman would then be responsible for quality under Barrett's overall direction of the company's manufacturing efforts; in practice, it soon became clear that Barrett was not willing to tolerate Kauffman's continued presence even if his former equal was now reporting to him.

The result was that Kauffman was told, in the gentlest possible way, that he was fired. "Andy, Craig and I agreed that I wasn't going to be in the running. . . . I was kinda getting off the track at Intel. For my own good, I probably ought to go someplace else."

Before he left Intel, Kauffman made one last attempt to convince Grove to take manufacturing quality more seriously. He put together a careful memo outlining a program in which Grove could assemble the essentials of a companywide quality program, and a punchy set of arguments. Knowing Grove's belief that there was more hype than reality in quality programs, he headed his memo: "A 4-hour (or less) Time Investment To Find The Substance In Total Quality Control." Kauffman's proselytizing on the issue did nothing to advance his own cause at Intel; he was soon gone, first to a start-up and then onwards to the job of chief operating officer at a successful maker of magnetic disk drives. But he did, at least, have the satisfaction of watching Barrett put some of his prescriptions into effect.

One of the new objectives that Andy Grove set for Intel after he took over as chief executive was to make the company a more exciting and rewarding place to work. The first step toward achieving this goal was to remove the austerity measures that Grove himself had put in place. The Late List, for example, was withdrawn in June 1988 after nearly seventeen years of continuous operation. A few old-timers were nostalgic for it—the kind of people who worried for Intel's future when they realized that the company parking lots at Santa Clara seemed to be so much emptier on weekends these days. Everyone else greeted its departure with enthusiasm.

In the same month, Andy Grove withdrew another of his favorite company rules. For twenty years, he had believed strongly that Intel should be a place to work and not to play—and that while the company should encourage staff to kick a ball around on weekends at an Intel outing or picnic, it should specifically not do anything to provide recreational facilities on its sites. Terry Opdendyk, the manager of the 8086 design project, had received a terrible dressing down from Grove on one occasion in the late 1970s when he used company money to rent a bowling alley for an evening.

"The schedule was for an off-site meeting so we could go and talk out the problems," Opdendyk explained when Grove found out. "If I'd had a hotel and an open bar, would that have been a problem?"

"No," replied Grove.

"Well, look at these guys," Opdendyk said. "They're talking now." He explained that he had been trying unsuccessfully for a while to encourage a group of software engineers and a group of hardware engineers to cooperate. At the bowling alley, he had paired off one from each team, and the communications barriers had melted away.

"That's sport," snapped Grove. "That's play. I don't *ever* want you to spend one minute of people's time on something that isn't work."

So seriously had Grove taken this principle that he refused to allow even showers installed at Intel sites. In 1988, however, he relented—and the first Intel showers were opened in the very month that the Late List went.

As Andy Grove became more accustomed to holding the title of chief executive officer, he began to talk of retirement. At first, the idea seemed shocking to his colleagues. Not only had Grove been at Intel from the very beginning; he had also been in effective control of the company's internal operations from its very earliest days. The only people in the company who had never reported to him and were still around were Gordon Moore and his secretary, Jean Jones. Eventually, however, the executive staff began to buzz with gossip about who was in and out of the running. The leading candidate had already ruled himself out. Ed Gelbach, after Grove and Moore the third most powerful executive in the company and the only one other than Grove with a seat on the board of directors, had declared in 1987 that he was tired of putting in the hours and wanted to retire.

One candidate was Larry Hootnick, who had come in as chief financial officer, and had gradually taken on more responsibilities around the business. He had got the company's computer systems working properly, tried to stem the losses of the Microma digital watch business, and moved around from corporate sales and marketing to managing operations in the fabs. Hootnick was a brilliant analyst and a powerful leader who knew where he wanted to go and left the people who reported to him in no doubt about what he wanted them to do. He was not a great listener, but then neither was Grove. His shortcoming was that he was not a semiconductor man. Hootnick had a degree from MIT, but hadn't come up through the ranks of running fabs. Intel's culture was so much suffused with the attitudes of engineers that it was hard to see him at its helm, no matter how good he might be at setting strategies.

There had been a time when Andy Grove had hinted to Hootnick that he was next in line. In 1984, Grove had taken the initiative to call Bettie Hootnick at home to tell her to "try to convince him to be president."

Caught unawares in her own kitchen by a call from her husband's boss, she didn't know what to reply.

"Andy, you know he doesn't want to do that," she said.

"Not now," Grove replied. "But I want to retire in five years. Try and talk to him. Try and talk to him."

The house joke was that Hootnick was just one of a half-dozen people to whom Andy Grove had held out the promise of succeeding him. Another was Jack Carsten, the fiery sales and marketing man Gelbach had brought in from Texas Instruments. Talented, quick, and aggressive, Carsten was the obvious figure to step into Gelbach's shoes, but he suffered from a disability. While Gelbach had succeeded in charming people as he exerted his power over them, Carsten had acquired a reputation as a bully. "Jack had all the attributes of being the next guy except one," recalled one of his colleagues. "He didn't treat people real well." There were tales of how Carsten would terrify his subordinates into submission by shouting at them, and then restore them to favor almost on a whim. And his part in Casey Powell's departure had made Carsten too many vocal enemies inside Intel for him to have a serious chance of winning the top job.

In the end, it was to Craig Barrett, former university professor, that the job of executive vice president, and later chief operating officer, finally went. The key to understanding Barrett, explained his former subordinate Tim May, is that "he's a jock. He's an athlete who is extremely bright." Winner of the 1969 Stanford pentathlon, Barrett could intimidate people by his hulking size. He was also a consummate palace politician, who could sense exactly whose star was in the ascendant and who was out of favor. Barrett's strong point was that he could demonstrate considerable improvements in quality and reductions in cost inside Intel since Kauffman's departure. He was now known as the company's Mr. Quality.

The trouble was that Larry Hootnick, who still kept a close eye on the numbers even though he had long been promoted out of the chief financial officer's job, knew that although Intel was closer to its Japanese competitors in 1988 than it had been in 1980, the company was still a second-rate manufacturer by world-class standards. And Hootnick did not mince his words.

"If you're throwing away 15–17 percent of your wafers before you start, and the Japanese are throwing away 2 percent, how are you going to beat them?" he would ask Grove.

To press his argument, Hootnick would point out that even after a decade of the "McIntel" campaign to standardize production between sites, there were still sharp differences in manufacturing efficiency between different fabs. Some of the newer fabs never managed to achieve first-class yields; Fab 4, at Aloha, Oregon, by contrast, somehow managed to deliver line yields with percentages in the high nineties using the oldest equipment in the company.

The turning point for Hootnick was when Intel decided in 1989 to withdraw from EPROMs, the only mass-market memory product the company was still making, and concentrate instead on a higher-margin new technology called "flash," which allowed the circuits to be erased swiftly using electric currents instead of ultraviolet light.

"EPROM was losing a ton of money," recalled Hootnick. "We had the wafer fabs segregated, so we couldn't switch them over easily from memory to processors."

To keep its existing EPROM customers happy, Intel signed an OEM deal with Samsung, Korea's biggest semiconductor company, whereby Intel would sell Samsung EPROMs under its own name. In the course of negotiating the deal, Hootnick discovered something astounding: Samsung was actually building EPROMs at barely half Intel's costs. The difference was not because of labor costs, since labor accounts for only a small percentage of total cost in semiconductor manufacturing; nor was it because of experience, since Samsung was new to the game and Intel had been playing it since the beginning. Nor was it to do with the size of the wafers, which allowed you to get more good die from each process step; Samsung was using smaller wafers than Intel. It was simply that the Koreans knew how to run the wafer fabs better than Intel did.

"If Andy really cared, he would have got his ass over there and walked through that factory," recalled Hootnick. "He never walked through Samsung, and never walked through NMB [a Japanese ball-bearing manufacturer that diversified with considerable success into DRAMs in the 1980s]. Gordon went through NMB and saw it; he didn't want to hear it either. That's when I got very frustrated."

When Hootnick told Grove about the cost differences he had discovered at Samsung, Grove went nuclear.

"It can't be," he said. "Their wafers are just too small."

Hootnick replied that he made no claim to being a fab expert. He was merely reporting what the Koreans had told him.

Grove started shouting.

"They can't do it! They can't do it!" he yelled.

In March 1991, after Intel had been promoting manufacturing quality and cost as one of its key corporate objectives for six years, the company participated in a "benchmarking" exercise where it shared confidential data from its chip fabrication activities with other big semiconductor companies around the world. The results showed that on overall manufacturing costs, the top two tiers of participants consisted of Japanese companies, the Koreans came next, and Intel last, on a par with Taiwan.

Intel was also slower at building factories than average, and slower to ramp production of a new product up to the desired level. On each new process, Intel took more than two years to achieve or approach the same yields as the competition. And on indirect staffing—the number of people in the fab site who were not actually working on the lines—Intel's head count was "dramatically higher" than all the other vendors surveyed.

When you paused for thought, it wasn't hard to see why this was. With its dominance of the x86 processor market, Intel was making so much money that it didn't *need* to be an efficient producer.

33

Raising the Tax

While Intel was milking profits from its 386 processor—the *New York Times* described the chip in 1988 as "one of the most lucrative monopolies in America"—Microsoft was beginning to look increasingly like the company's most important enemy.

Bill Gates did a lot of talking in public about a new microprocessor technology, known as RISC, that was being championed by the makers of processors for high-end engineering workstations. The acronym stood for "reduced instruction-set computing," and the insight behind it was that most of the instructions in the lexicon of a processor like Intel's 386 weren't used very often. If you could identify a subset of very commonly used instructions, you could design a processor around executing those at blistering speed. Even though there would be a penalty every time it came across one of the rarer instructions that a traditional processor could manage in one go, the overall result would be a dramatic increase in performance and a dramatic simplification of the chip's architecture.

Andy Grove was smart enough to recognize the technical attractions of RISC. But Intel was a prisoner of its history and its customers. Making sure that its new products were as compatible as possible with its current range was always a high priority with the company—and this backward compatibility made it well-nigh impossible for Intel to build a RISC machine. The company had an advanced processor already in preparation, which would follow the successor to the 386, that incorporated some of the features of RISC. But that was a long way away, and the processor would still have to carry much of the x86 baggage that irritated the programmers at Microsoft so mightily.

This vulnerability meant that Intel was very sensitive to any hint that Microsoft might be encouraging a general switch in the industry to RISC. For if such a switch began to take place, Intel's hold on the market—and its ability to charge hundreds of dollars for processors that cost only ten or twenty bucks to make—would be in jeopardy.

The technical meetings that took place between Intel and Microsoft soon became soured by discussion of this issue. Nathan Myhrvold, one of the Redmond company's top technology strategists, got into the habit of lecturing Intel on the inevitability of the replacement of standard processors with RISC every time the two companies held a technical meeting. To the extreme irritation of the Intel team, he would also throw in some unsolicited advice on programming practice, microprocessor design, and business organization—despite claiming without embarrassment that he'd never written a line of code in his life.

Myhrvold became a hated figure inside Intel. What the Intel engineers particularly disliked about him was his habit of talking from hunches. One of them remembered: "Myhrvold would say, 'I had a beer last night, and it occurred to me that such-and-such.' We'd say, 'Yeah, Nathan, it could be true, but if you measure it you'll find out that it's not the case.' There was no scientific rigor in the way he approached this. There was gut feel, intuition, wild guesses." The Intel scientists believed that you ought to link the strength of your opinion to the strength of your data. Microsoft's top technology strategist, in their view, didn't pass this test.

With so much valuable intellectual property on both sides, it was no wonder that both Microsoft and Intel appointed a link person to manage the relationship with the other company and keep track of what information was flowing in each direction. But the RISC debate began to poison this link, too. The two representatives, Carl Stork at Microsoft and John Novitsky at Intel, lost trust in each other to such a degree that accusations began to fly that the simple job of carrying mail—forwarding information or requests for help to the appropriate person in the organization—wasn't being done properly. Dave House, the senior VP at Intel responsible for the issue, called Gates directly and suggested that the personal animosity that had developed was harming both sides. Stork and Novitsky were assigned to new jobs immediately after the call.

But Bill Gates and his colleagues at Microsoft were doing more than just talking about RISC. In 1988, Gates launched a development program for a new operating system that would offer a graphical interface better than Microsoft Windows, and with the added advantage of being "portable" from one microprocessor to another. This operating system, known as Windows NT (for New Technology) represented the ultimate doomsday scenario for Intel. Mere talk wouldn't persuade millions of computer users all over the world to junk their x86-based machines. But if Gates could give them an operating system that would run all their existing software without a flaw, and also run a whole load of new software at ten times the speed . . . well, that was a business proposition that could turn the entire computer industry upside down.

Evidence that Gates was serious came in 1991, when Microsoft announced the formation of an industry grouping called ACE, or Advanced Computing Environment. The group included twenty-one different companies. The presence in the consortium of MIPS and DEC, both makers of RISC processors, wasn't a surprise to Intel; these companies' architectures were already in Andy Grove's gunsights. Much more frightening was the fact that two computer companies that Intel believed to be among its closest allies—Compaq and Dell—were also on the list.

"Guys like me were devastated when [we found] Compaq was doing that ACE thing," recalled John Novitsky. "They were in it up to their eyeballs. I felt like I'd caught my wife in bed with my best friend. The sense of betrayal, the sense of disgust . . . nearly all of us were walking with our heads down, almost shell-shocked that Microsoft and Compaq would behave like this. We weren't trying to kill them, but they were trying to kill us."

It took Andy Grove to inject a sense of realism. At an internal meeting in which Intel's processor architects were bemoaning the betrayal, repeating their fury and disbelief at what they saw as Microsoft's duplicity, Grove offered an alternative view.

"You guys should think about it differently," he said. "They're not your wives. They're in business for their own vested interests, and we should never assume that their interests match ours. We have to give them room to be different. Think of Microsoft more like a fellow traveler in a train. The guy gets on, and he's going in the same direction as you. When you're in the train, you're going to be civil. But you're not going to give him the keys to your house, and you're not going to give him your credit cards. You know that your paths will diverge at some point. It doesn't pay to put too much trust in him."

In October 1989, Intel employees across the United States opened their newspapers to find an astounding new full-page ad. Plastered across the page was the number 286, the designation of the processor that was still Intel's biggest selling product. On top of it, a huge X had been spray-painted in vivid red.

At first sight, the ad looked like a piece of "knocking copy" from a competitor. When you looked more closely, though, you noticed that the logo at the bottom of the page was Intel's—and when you turned the page to carry on reading the paper, you found another Intel ad taking up the whole of the next right-hand page. This advertisement showed the number 386 at the top of the page, with the red spray can used this time to inscribe the letters SX at maximum size below it.

It was not only in newspapers that the ad was published. Intel also bought outdoor sites—billboards—in eleven major cities across the United States. The "Red X" campaign, as the series of ads came to be known, was the company's first serious piece of consumer advertising since the abortive TV spot for the ailing Microma watch business over a decade earlier. Costing $4 million, it represented one of the most significant changes of corporate focus in the company's history—and one of the activities that was most controversial among Intel's customers.

The official explanation behind Red X was that it was a simple matter of consumer education. "The Intel386 chip was a successful product, but it was mired in the high end of the market," recalled Dennis Carter, director of the company's new Corporate Marketing Group. "The market was stagnant, and people perceived that the Intel 286 CPU was all that they would ever need. The Windows operating system was coming, giving people a compelling reason to move to 32-bit processors, but that message wasn't getting across. We wanted a dramatic way to convey that the Intel386 SX CPU was an affordable way to enter the 32-bit world."

Ron Whittier, Intel's marketing director, explained the issue in more detail. "We researched the marketplace, and there is a considerable amount of confusion about the benefits of technology to the consumer. They are swamped with alternatives and information, and they're clearly not absorbing it well."

But there were opponents of the idea inside the company. Dave House, who had achieved his senior vice-president's title after coming up through the company's marketing ranks, described the campaign as "eating our own babies."

There was more to it than that. Intel was beginning to realize that it had moved into an unusual no-man's-land between the industrial and consumer markets. On the one hand, its microprocessors were largely sold to computer companies. On the other, the microprocessor had become such an important part of the personal computer, such a key determinant of the computer's price and performance, that consumers were beginning to make buying decisions based on what kind of processor was inside the machine. The trouble was that Intel was still in part a prisoner of the PC industry. Compaq's first 386-based machines had incorporated the Intel part number into their product names to emphasize a performance edge over the rest of the market, and they had been hot sellers since late 1986. But not enough other manufacturers had chosen to follow Compaq's lead. The industry as a whole preferred to take fat margins on the old 286 technology rather than stimulate sales of the 386 machines by discounting them until they were competitive with the 286s.

The Red X campaign was the first evidence of Intel's realization that it could escape from the tyranny imposed on it collectively by a thousand PC manufacturers. Instead of turning out new processors and just hoping that computer companies would build them into systems that consumers would then buy, the company could take the initiative. It could go direct to the consumer with its pitch for a new processor. If the pitch was convincing, the consumer would go down to the local computer store asking for a machine, any machine, containing the new processor—and this pressure would force PC makers to start designing systems incorporating the new chip.

But there was another strategy behind Red X that Intel was less keen to talk about. The company's 286 chips, still its biggest sellers by volume, were licensed to AMD, Siemens, and Harris, and also to IBM, which had the right to make 286s for its own consumption. With four competing processor manufacturers on the market, there was considerable pressure on prices—and in the 286 generation, Intel was forced to compete. There was always a certain amount it could do to protect its position—such as making licensees agree to flat-rate license fees per processor sold, which created an effective floor below which they could not sell it profitably. But the pressure from Kauffman and Hootnick had not yet made Intel a world-class manufacturer, so the company would always be fighting at a disadvantage against its licensees when it made 286s.

With the 386 chip, however, everything was different. Ditching its technology-sharing agreement with AMD, Intel had forged ahead with its single-source policy. There was now only one maker of 386 chips in the world—Intel itself. Consequently, the margins on 386 processors were considerably higher than the company's 286 margins. Wafer for wafer, it made more sense to be building the new chip. So anything that Intel could do to steer customers away from the competitive 286 and toward the monopolistic 386 would have a big effect on its bottom line.

The industry was not slow to see what was going on. First to complain were the computer retailers, who had piles of 286 computers sitting in boxes waiting for buyers. The last thing they needed was an ad campaign from Intel that would make their inventory redundant overnight. One leading retailer, Matt Fitzsimmons, president of Computerland, argued that the ads might confuse or discourage PC buyers. He put the point succinctly: "These ads are sheer foolishness." One of his managers went further. Quoted in a newspaper article at the time, she poured scorn on the body copy of the Red X ad, which had described the 386SX chip as "a zillion percent better" than the 286. " 'A zillion percent better' sounds like false advertising to me," she complained.

Jerry Sanders also caught on quickly to what Intel had in mind. AMD's Los Angeles ad agency was instructed to draw up a quick-fire advertisement to run across an entire page of the *New York Times* attacking Intel's policy. The advertisement, headed "How to tell a chip from a computer," accused Intel of "using the strategic insights it acquires as a healthy part of the vendor process for an unhealthy advantage in the competing process." Unfortunately for Sanders, however, there was nothing illegal about the Red X campaign—and ultimately, nothing he could do about it. Realizing this, Intel's Ron Whittier could not resist crowing that AMD had wasted its money by buying the ad: "It's an expensive way to vent your frustration."

Other 286 vendors tried different tacks. Chips & Technologies, the company that Gordie Campbell had founded after leaving Intel for Seeq, had a 286 chip of its own that had been designed without a license from Intel. Chips ran a series of ads that tried to capitalize on the familiarity of the image of the red spray paint across the 286 with a more subtle dig at Intel. "While some companies try to limit your options, Chips provides complete choices for all processors."

The real test of Red X was in the market. According to Shafer and Shafer, the ad agency that created Intel's campaign, it was pushing at an open door. "Our analysis of the research said we should be positioned at the entry level of a new family of processors. So we've got to kill off the old standard," argued Chip Shafer, the agency's president. "We knew we had a potentially explosive message, but the target audience all nodded their heads and said it was true. We confirmed that they all understand the industry is moving to 32-bit, and based on that we went ahead. . . . When we launched this campaign in September, you couldn't find a retail or product ad that identified the 386SX. By December, you couldn't find a single retail ad in which the SX was not prominently displayed with its price."

Eventually, the significance of Red X began to dawn on the PC industry: If it increased demand for new computers, then the sales of the entire industry would be stimulated. In the end, therefore, Red X proved to be good news even for the retailers who had bad-mouthed it at the outset.

34

The Two Webbs

In 1989, while the arbitration arising from AMD's technology-sharing agreement with Intel was still in progress, Jerry Sanders had belatedly ordered a team of young AMD engineers to start developing the company's own 386 chip, fully compatible with the Intel original but designed from scratch using only publicly available information.

There was a great deal more to the job than merely making a fast processor that was compatible with the x86 instruction set. With 270,000 transistors, the 386 was one of the most complex logic chips ever built—and to match it in performance while maintaining 100 percent compatibility would be no mean feat. There were voices inside AMD who believed the project, codenamed "Longhorn," was actually impossible.

Sanders refused to be discouraged. The team in Austin, Texas, were brought together in a sealed-off area of AMD's facility and told that they had two years to build a working processor. The company switched off the overhead lights, locked the doors, and made it clear that it expected them to work as many hours as it took to get the job done.

In August 1990, eighteen six-inch wafers, each imprinted with several hundred samples of the new Am386 processor, emerged from AMD's Austin fab for testing after being rushed through in the record time of eight days. The team found just one defect. Four days later, the entire Longhorn team, now thirty members, gathered around a PC into which a sample Am386 chip, the bug fixed, had been installed. They switched on the machine and ran a series of popular programs: Windows 3.0, Excel, Lotus 1-2-3, dBase, Xenix, Auto CAD . . . all of them worked.

"By early afternoon," wrote Jerry Sanders triumphantly in the company's next annual report, "most of the Longhorn team was 30 miles outside of Austin sitting at no-frills picnic tables in a joint called the Salt Lick, in a town named Dripping Springs, washing down some of the best barbecue in the State of Texas with a few well-earned beers."

Shortly before Sanders was ready to unveil the Am386, a senior AMD marketing man named Mike Webb came from the Austin facility to the company's headquarters to make a presentation on the plans for advertising the new part. While Webb was in California he arranged for his secretary back in Texas to FedEx to his hotel an extra set of overhead project foils relating to the launch. By coincidence, an Intel employee with exactly the same name who ran sales in the Portland area was staying in the same hotel. By the time the package arrived, though, the Intel Mike Webb had already gone back to Oregon. Unaware that two guests with the same name had stayed in the hotel the night before, the hotel receptionist who received the package pulled up the details of the wrong Mike Webb. On discovering that he had already checked out, the receptionist dialed the home phone number on the reservations record and got through to his wife in Portland.

The sharp-eyed receptionist pointed out to Mrs. Webb that there was a discrepancy between the package and the hotel's computer system. Mike Webb's reservation record said he worked for Intel, but the waybill said "Mike Webb, AMD."

"Oh, you know I think Intel and AMD do a lot of things together," replied Mrs. Webb.

As the package winged its way to the wrong Mike Webb in Portland, the right Mike Webb finished his presentations at AMD's headquarters and flew back to Texas, forgetting about the set of foils that his secretary had sent him.

A few days later, Rich Lovgren, AMD's deputy general counsel, received a call from Tom Dunlap at Intel.

"Hey, Rich," said Dunlap. "Are you coming out with a part called the Am386?"

"Gee, Tom, I can't answer you that. Any new products plans are proprietary, so don't take that as a yes or no."

"Well, I think you're coming out with something called a 386," said Dunlap.

"I'm not admitting it, Tom, it's proprietary information."

"That's a violation of Intel's trademark. The term 386 belongs to Intel. I'm gonna sue you."

"Well, Tom," replied Lovgren, "you do what you want to do."

An hour after he got home from work, Lovgren received a call from John Greenagle, the company's press chief, saying that a trade reporter had called saying that Dunlap had faxed him what looked like the front page of a set of overhead project foils relating to AMD's new part. *Boy, that's strange*, thought Lovgren. He pulled out his company phone book and dialed AMD's Mike Webb at home in Texas. It was 11:30 P.M. local time.

"Hey, Mike, just gotta weird call," said Lovgren. "Have you been missing something? Have you distributed a set of foils to anyone? Have you misplaced any foils, left something behind somewhere?"

Webb replied that he remembered his secretary sending him something in Sunnyvale that had never arrived. The next day, he chased up the waybill number with Federal Express, and discovered through the FedEx tracking system how the package had found its way to Intel, via the home address of Webb's namesake in Oregon. Lovgren was furious: He had put Dunlap on notice that the documents were proprietary, and he believed that Dunlap had deliberately leaked AMD's upcoming product name to the press after being warned.

What made Lovgren particularly angry was that some months earlier, a midlevel Intel employee had left a package of confidential company papers under the counter of a sushi bar in San Jose. The papers were discovered after his departure—and by coincidence, the *itamae-san* of the sushi bar had handed them to an AMD employee who happened to be eating in the same restaurant. The AMD man had passed the papers to Marvin Burkett, the company's chief financial officer, who thought it would be unethical to read them. He had passed them on to Tom Armstrong, AMD's general counsel, who had similar qualms and passed them on to his deputy. Lovgren, who was not an electrical engineer and had no technical background, counted the pages and the sections, wrote some notes on the document's size and nature for his file to guard against the risk of being accused later of having returned only part of it, but took care not to read it. Instead, he asked his paralegal to walk it over to Dunlap's office, together with a cover note explaining what had happened and ending with a quip that Intel should widen its confidentiality warning at the top of each page to remind members of its staff not to leave documents in sushi bars.

Lovgren felt that Dunlap's behavior in the Webb case was a strange reward for his honesty in the case of the sushi-bar papers. Calling back Intel's general counsel, Lovgren challenged him to deny that the foils had been sent to the wrong Mike Webb and had gotten into Intel's hands by mistake. Dunlap only repeated his complaint about the use of the 386 name. He offered no defense against the allegation that he had knowingly publicized AMD's proprietary information.

"I'm gonna sue you, Tom," said Lovgren.

Both men were as good as their word. But while AMD later withdrew its complaint against Intel for anticompetitive behavior, Intel pushed its trademark infringement case against AMD all the way to trial. Once again, Intel lost. In March 1991, the judge in the case ruled that the number 386 had become so prevalent in the industry—Intel had positively encouraged computer companies all over the world to include the 386 designation in their product names—that it had effectively become a generic name. So AMD, and all the other makers of 386 clones, would be entitled to use 386 in their product marketing—and to piggyback on the $4 million Intel had invested in its Red X campaign.

In an attempt to limit the damage, Intel belatedly changed its naming system for the 386, calling it the Intel386 and appending a ™ symbol to assert the company's claim that the name was a trademark. But the underlying problem remained: Simply by using the name 386, any competitor could tell its customers which Intel product a new chip was being marketed against.

Intel was going to have to change tack if it wanted to stop its trademarks from being helpful to competitors. A crucial first step was to depart from the four-digit numbers that the company had used throughout its history as product names. Instead, the company's corporate marketing team suggested to Andy Grove that Intel should switch to using words for its processors. It was too late for this new tactic to affect the 486, a new processor with 1.2 million transistors that had been launched in April 1989. The 486's successor, however, was due in 1993—less than two years away. Trade journals and specialists outside Intel were already referring to the upcoming chip as the 586, assuming that the company would stick to its old naming system. But a year before the processor's launch, Intel registered a new name for it: Pentium. Not only would the name sound more friendly to the average home computer user who was becoming an increasingly important Intel customer. Also, and more importantly, the name would provide much greater protection against competing processors. With a number, AMD and the rest of the clone makers would only need to make a small change—inserting an x, perhaps—to distinguish their mark enough to avoid legal problems, while remaining similar enough for consumers to see exactly what their product was. But with the name Pentium, the matter was more clearcut: Either a processor was a Pentium, or it wasn't. If AMD wanted to market a competing product, it would have to invest its own money in brand marketing. Sanders tried to make a joke out of it—he told friendly journalists that the word "Pentium" sounded like a toothpaste—but the piggyback days were over.

Before this change of policy was unveiled to the outside world, however, Intel began a companywide initiative whose effect would be to change the rules of battle in the microprocessor business. Until now, with the focus on marketing to engineers inside computer companies, branding had been almost the last thing on the minds of Intel and its competitors. In the 1970s and 1980s the best competitive edge came from good processor performance, measured by benchmark tests designed by independent outsiders. And the next most important advantage came from having a good set of technical marketing aids, ranging from emulators and development systems to data sheets, application notes, and technical manuals. By the 1990s, end users were in the loop, making purchasing decisions inside computer superstores or over the telephone to direct-mail PC makers like Dell. They now had some influence on the process. Intel would have to find a way of getting its message through to consumers like the makers of any other consumer product—in thirty seconds.

Thus was born the "Intel Inside" campaign. Starting in May 1991, the company began to spend heavily on a nationwide advertising campaign telling consumers that buying a computer with an Intel chip inside would guarantee advanced technology and compatibility with the huge range of software written for the Intel x86 processor family. The opening shot of the campaign was a stunning, minute-long journey through the insides of a PC, borrowing from the styles of *Star Wars* and *Star Trek*. Intel's ad budget for year one was $20 million, and there was much more to follow.

The paradox behind the campaign was that it was advertising a range of products that almost no consumers were expected to buy themselves. Unless you were a technology-savvy computer jock who knew how to open up the box of a PC and upgrade the motherboard, the chance that you would ever buy an Intel product was minimal. Instead, the focus was entirely on putting customers in a frame of mind so that when they were next buying a computer, it would be the Intel name, and the Intel Inside logo, that would provoke the spark of recognition and relief that often precedes a buying decision.

Intel Inside had its precedents: Dolby noise reduction systems, which could not be bought separately but were installed inside cassette decks; Teflon nonstick material, which could only be bought with a frying-pan attached; NutraSweet, the sweetener that came in many soft drinks. But Intel added a twist of its own. The company launched a partnership marketing campaign, agreeing to share the cost of computer companies' own advertisements if they included the Intel Inside logo in their ad copy with appropriate prominence. The terms of the deal were that each customer would be assigned a "marketing development fund" equivalent to 3 percent of its spending on microprocessors. Assuming that the ads themselves and the magazine or newspaper in which they appeared were approved by Intel, the company would then use this fund to pay up to half the cost of the ads. Once the fund was exhausted, the computer maker would have to buy more processors from Intel before receiving further contributions to its advertising budget. There were separate programs for using the Intel Inside logo on the front of the computer itself, and on packaging materials.

The partnership campaign, which was given a budget of $125 million over its first eighteen months, was an extraordinarily clever way of letting the computer industry itself choose the best place for Intel's advertising.

Once again, though, the initiative had its detractors. "I think it's money down the drain because manufacturers don't think Intel gives them a great selling advantage," said Michael Murphy, editor of the *California Technology Newsletter*, to the *Los Angeles Times*. "The public, unfortunately, is either too unsophisticated to listen, or it listens to what trade journals say, not ads," he continued.

Murphy was wrong. After some initial hesitation, manufacturers signed up for the program in the hundreds; by 1994, 1,200 companies, almost the entire PC industry, had joined in. Intel's worldwide sales rose 63 percent in 1992, the first full year of the campaign, and its brand came to be listed by marketing analysts as the third most valuable name on earth after Coca-Cola and Marlboro. The campaign had the effect of making the Intel name almost ubiquitous—and the Intel Inside logo so attractive that some PC makers wanted to include it in their ads even without any contribution from Intel.

In his speech at Intel's 1993 annual meeting, Andy Grove was able to boast that the company's "brand preference"—the percentage of people who said they preferred to buy computers with Intel processors—had risen from 60 percent to nearly 80 percent in the course of the previous year. The result was that to get PC makers to buy their parts, Intel's competitors would now have to make their processors less expensive and measurably higher in performance.

The Intel Inside campaign was particularly popular with original equipment manufacturers, or OEMs—the companies that built PCs for resale via other companies that put their own brand on the box. But the campaign had compromised one of the cardinal rules that Intel had adhered to most closely over the past decade in its marketing policies. From the first emergence of the "clone" market competing with IBM in the manufacturing of PCs, Intel had decided that its best stance would be to "let the leaders lead." This meant that the company would make no attempt to influence the competitive balance between makers of computers. Intel would give its biggest customers—Compaq, IBM, Gateway, Dell—longer advance notice of new products, because experience had shown that these companies had the muscle needed to diffuse a new Intel technology swiftly through the market. Given that the company could devote only limited resources to technical liaison, it made sense to help the makers who would ship the largest number of boxes. But Intel did not go out of its way to give the big guys breaks. Under Andy Grove's orders, the sales department stuck rigorously to the company's official price list. Even the largest customer could not expect a discount of more than 20 percent or 30 percent off the 1,000-part price that was quoted over the phone to casual callers from no-name OEMs.

Intel Inside changed all that. From a position of neutrality between big and small companies, Intel now seemed to be using its marketing dollars to help the smaller OEMs gain market share at the expense of the larger companies with bigger overheads and bigger advertising budgets. There were no two ways about it: Either Intel was trying to encourage customers to make buying decisions on the basis of the processor, or it was not. If it was, then the campaign would reduce the value of the money that Compaq, IBM, and others had put into building up their brands. To make matters worse, it looked to some in the computer industry as though Intel had an ulterior motive, too: By reducing the pressure for concentration in the PC industry, the company was keeping its customers smaller, more divided, and less able to resist its leadership.

The first big PC maker to rebel was Compaq. The Houston-based PC assembler, fully recovered from its loss-making days thanks to the leadership of Eckhard Pfeiffer, formerly head of its European operations, was particularly sensitive to the encroaching power of the Intel brand. As its own rating among consumers improved, Compaq fired a warning shot across Andy Grove's bow by buying a few microprocessors from AMD and opening negotiations with other chipmakers to assess the quality and compatibility of their products. Then the company went public. At a trade show and conference in Europe, Pfeiffer launched an outspoken attack on Intel and its new marketing campaign, making headlines in the computer press all over the world. The battle lines for consumers' loyalty had been drawn: Intel versus the giants of the computer industry.

35

Departures

Long before he became Intel's chief executive, Andy Grove made an illuminating comment to Terry Opdendyk, the manager who had looked after the rush job of designing the 8086 chip. "Terry," he said, "fundamentally, you believe that people left to their own volition will do good and not bad. I believe they'll do bad and not good."

By the end of the 1980s, the attitude that he revealed in this observation could be seen in everything that Intel did. Grove was not a leader in the sense of someone who inspires the troops from the front and relies on his own charisma to persuade them to follow. Instead, he was more like a shepherd—signaling with his crook where he wanted the flock to go, but keeping a team of dogs to bite the ankles of any sheep that strayed off in the wrong direction.

Grove had avoided the most obvious temptation. In the fast-moving computer business, any attempt from the center to second-guess people in the field would be doomed to fail. Not only did Intel's senior managers lack the technical knowledge to decide what functionality should go on which chip; they also lacked the market knowledge to know what terms should be offered to which customer. Breaking the golden rule of devolving decisions down to the lowest possible level would make the company slower and less responsive— and was the quickest way to oblivion. Grove knew this.

He did not believe, however, that devolved decision making should result in loss of control. Although managers at Intel were required to take the initiative—dealing with most issues themselves rather than passing them upwards, and forming a short-term committee of peers chaired by a "czar" to solve single-issue, companywide problems— Intel still had a rigorous budgeting process that required everyone from the members of the executive staff downward to produce regularly updated forecasts of costs and sales, and to account immediately for inaccuracies and divergences from plan. Even before the days of client-server computing, Intel's finance function was so efficient that a detailed set of monthly management accounts was always available three days after the end of each month.

But the most powerful tools of Grove's system of control were the personal incentives that rewarded success and punished failure. The key incentive for success was stock options. Intel's option scheme covered one of the largest number of employees in U.S. industry— over five thousand as early as 1984. Because the company's stock price had risen so spectacularly—from $23.50 a share at the IPO in 1971 to $4,385 in June 1993 when you adjusted for stock splits— options were recognized by everyone as the key motivator. An engineer who had been given a thousand stock options at the IPO and held on to the stock for twenty-two years would have made $5 million. Dozens of employees had received more than twice that number over their careers; around a thousand more Intel employees could have made more than $1 million each from their options. The effect of this munificence was that thousands of Intel employees with options were willing to put up with more regimentation, more inconvenience, more indignity than people in other companies. Tim May, the wayward scientist who discovered the alpha-particle problem, had an aphorism that expressed the situation neatly. "A rising stock price," he liked to say, "heals all wounds."

The option scheme also allowed Intel to implement a policy that few other companies have ever attempted: "recycling." When Andy Grove felt that a manager had performed badly in a job, he had no compunction in arranging an instant demotion to a different and less important job. In most companies, few people would be able to deal with the humiliation of seeing their status reduced. At Intel, where staying on for a couple more years could be worth a half-million dollars, managers would not only put up with it but also work hard to try to regain their former status. The practice became a standard part of Intel's management system.

Intel also had a sabbatical program, allowing employees to take eight weeks' paid holiday every seven years. Like the option scheme, which gave staff an incentive to stay because each grant of options took three years to work its way through to stock in hand, the sabbatical scheme had been specifically designed to keep talented people in the company just at the point when they might otherwise decide to move on. Grove had opposed the idea when it was first mooted; by the end of the 1980s, when a growing number of burned-out people had taken sabbaticals, it had emerged as a low-cost way to keep morale high.

The company's system of "ranking and rating," known internally as "ranting and raving," created intense internal competition. Every employee was still given a rating—though the system had been amended to three simple categories, "outstanding," "successful," and "improvement required," because the human resource department complained that the old system had been eroded by inflation, with many managers marking the majority of their staff as exceeding expectations. There was also a measure of progress relative to peers. Employees were told each year whether their rate of improvement was faster or slower than the average. Absolute rankings were never revealed to employees themselves, but Intel kept records so that when layoffs were required the laggards could be easily identified and picked off. The information was used ruthlessly. If your performance began to slip, no quantity of past successes, no history of loyal service would be enough to allow you to coast along. Your rating would swiftly change to "improvement required," you would be put on a sixty-day or ninety-day program of "corrective action," or "CA"— and if you failed to deliver the improvements required by the CA plan, you would be out for good.

The trouble with this system was that its operation was left mostly in the hands of the employee's own supervisor, putting Intel people at high risk of losing their jobs if they fell out of favor with their immediate boss. One of its saddest victims was Bill Handel, the field sales engineer who had won the Operation Crush competition for the largest number of design wins in 1980. Eight years on, Handel had matured into one of Intel's best salesmen. He sold $62 million worth of Intel goods in 1988, persuading six customers to design the 386 processor into new products. Handel's coup in persuading Olivetti to base a new minicomputer on an Intel chip won him the Intel Achievement Award for 1988. His performance review described him as a "master of account management for large customers," praised his ability to work in teams and without managerial supervision, and described his "amazing patience" in dealing with Intel employees from other countries. The following year, Handel was given the standard rating of "successful," with his rate of improvement reported as equal to his peers. He was given the Hewlett-Packard account, which his supervisor reported he handled with "intensity and a lot of hard work." He was praised for having "perfected the art of detail" in "another exceptional year," for working "efficiently with credit applications and administration," and for exhibiting "leadership in the office" and a "corporate commitment to Intel and an attitude that is admired in the office." Under "improvements," he was warned to "pay attention to the smaller and less glamorous devices that Intel has to offer," making a special effort to "get C+T [Chips & Technologies] out for good" from Hewlett-Packard, and to "become more aware of the importance of the distribution channel."

Then things began to go wrong. By 1990, Handel had come under a new boss who took him off the Hewlett-Packard account, complaining that he did not get "the confidence of Intel management and the customer that would enable him to proceed." He was accused of "a lack of attention to detail" and blamed for letting one client see information on a new Intel chip without signing a nondisclosure agreement. Handel found himself immediately put on ninety-day corrective action.

The veteran salesman completed the corrective action plan, but was then fired anyway.

"I did fine. I did everything they asked. I knew I would," he recalled. "The problem was that there wasn't a problem." He believed that the real reason for his reported slip in performance from second quartile to fourth quartile was not because he had done anything differently, but simply because of his age. As a forty-year-old sales engineer earning over $100,000 a year, he was a great deal more expensive to keep than a newcomer only a few years out of college. People inside the company had already begun to talk about "bumping"—the practice, suggested to Intel by management consultants who feared that the company was aging too fast, of easing older employees out of the company and replacing them with younger ones.

Incensed by his treatment after a decade's loyalty to his employer, Handel sued Intel, claiming that it had fired him out of age discrimination. His lawyer took depositions from twelve Intel managers, focusing on the issue of bumping. But Intel would not give in without a fight. It filed a motion for summary judgment, trying to persuade the court that there was no discrimination case to answer; when the motion was denied, it appealed. Handel and his attorney soon realized that fighting the case to the end would cost several hundred thousand dollars. In the end, they settled, and Handel took a job at AMD.

Bill Handel was not the only Intel employee who started to get bad reviews as he reached his forties. The same dilemma faced Henry Gregor, the sales engineer who had worked so hard to get Intel chips designed into Hewlett-Packard products earlier in the 1980s when there were so many problems with quality and delivery. After working on the Hewlett-Packard account, Gregor had achieved some notable successes with Tektronix, the printer manufacturer. But in mid-1991, Intel announced that it was reorganizing its sales force in order to focus more on the PC industry. Distribution had become less important as a way of selling parts; the big manufacturers and mail-order houses tended to do more business direct on a national basis.

"They closed thirty sales offices," Gregor recalled. "They trimmed the sales force down so if you did not have a key PC account, you were either let go or asked to go take another job [inside Intel]." Gregor was one of the lucky ones; there was no instant dismissal in his case.

So he began to stumble around inside the company looking for various jobs. What he found, however, was that the only places available were inside the regimented atmosphere of Intel factories—which salesmen always hated after spending a few years independently in the field.

"Instead of greasing the skids to make it easy for people to find jobs, they were making it hard. They were drying up all help-wanted requests. You'd find a lot of people competing for the same jobs. I perceived that obviously these people wanted us out of the company."

Gregor decided to give in to the pressure. Shortly after leaving Intel, he received a call from the lawyer representing Bill Handel that made him wonder whether his departure from Intel was part of a bigger plan to rid the company of its older staff. On reflection, he came to the firm conclusion that he had been a victim of age discrimination—and decided to sue.

Once his case was filed, though, Gregor was warned by his lawyer that he should expect Intel to play dirty.

"You'll find people you previously worked with, your friends and allies, will suddenly form ranks against you because you're attacking what they feel is justifiably theirs," the lawyer predicted.

What Gregor found was worse still. As Intel delivered documents to his lawyer under the pretrial discovery process, he realized that new papers had appeared in his personnel record since his departure.

"I was finding a lot of things in my file that I knew weren't there, because I had got my file copied when I left the company—I called up the archive people and asked them if they'd send me a copy."

The most startling discovery Gregor made was that Intel was now alleging he had been put on corrective action before being fired.

"Usually there's a process: a verbal warning, then a written warning, then CA. But none of this stuff occurred. Suddenly a written letter of warning showed up in my file long after I'd left, signed by some person in personnel that I'd never heard of."

Gregor also discovered after leaving Intel that he had been the object of snooping. "There was a lady that was in our office . . . she didn't particularly like me, and she'd been sending E-mails to the personnel lady. . . . This lady was keeping a calendar of things I was supposed to have done in the office, and sending E-mails and had kept the records of this. These records were not in my personnel file, and they appeared subsequently."

While taking depositions, Gregor's lawyer discovered that the informant in the sales office had carried out an exactly similar operation against a sales engineer in Bellevue, Washington, the Intel office closest to the Microsoft headquarters.

"She was sales support, acting as a secret agent for human resources," Gregor concluded.

But there was worse to come. Soon, an accusation emerged that Gregor had sexually harassed an office receptionist. Gregor told his lawyer that the accusation was ludicrous.

"We used to chat," he explained. "All the guys in the office would talk with her. She taught aerobics, I was involved in aerobics, and we talked about that."

"I understand that you disclaim all this stuff," Gregor's lawyer told him. "But the fact is, it's there—and if we went to court, it would be a toss-up whether we'd win."

Gregor gave up his complaint.

Another Intel employee who found the company a formidable opponent after his departure was Pat Roboostoff, a senior executive in Intel's human resources department.

Roboostoff had joined Intel in 1978, and was one of the company's few senior women employees. She was beaten to the distinction of becoming the company's first woman vice-president by Carlene Ellis, a systems and administrative expert whose name first appeared in the list of VPs in the 1986 annual report. But by 1990, Roboostoff had become an influential figure not only in terms of her personnel work but also more widely in the company. She was known to have Andy Grove's ear, and her human resources job at Intel's Folsom facility, near the California state capital of Sacramento, stretched across engineering and manufacturing.

It was an accident entirely beyond her control that cut short Roboostoff's career at Intel. One morning, she received an unexpected visit in her office from the wife of Ron Whittier, Intel's marketing director. Lucy Whittier burst into her office and started screaming that Roboostoff had been having an affair with her husband. When Roboostoff tried to deny the charge, her accuser responded by insisting that her husband had admitted his infidelity—and had already named Pat Roboostoff as his lover. She then stormed out of the office, but not before threatening to attack Roboostoff physically to avenge the injury that had been done to her.

Discreet inquiries revealed that Ron Whittier, in common with a number of other senior executives at Intel, had indeed been having an office romance. But he had not been able to bring himself to admit his lover's real name—and his wife, living only fifteen minutes away from Roboostoff and already aware of her attractions and her prominent position inside the company, had drawn the conclusion that Roboostoff was the culprit.

Worried that Whittier's wife, unbalanced by the shock of her husband's affair, might somehow make good on her threat of violence, Roboostoff alerted her superiors at Intel to the problem. She was told that the company would tighten up admission checks in the building where she worked and would arrange some discreet private security around her house in case Lucy Whittier should try to approach her there. But the security was less discreet than promised. The following weekend, when Roboostoff was in her backyard with her children and her mother, and her husband was puttering in the garage at the front, a pair of vans drew up outside Roboostoff's home and a gang of men jumped out. They grabbed her husband, pinned him against the wall, ignoring his angry complaints, and demanded to know who he was and the nature of his business in the house.

The incident provoked a domestic disaster in the Roboostoff

household. Partly because of the pressure of Pat Roboostoff's work at Intel, the couple had been gradually moving apart for some time, and had recently decided amicably that a separation followed by a divorce would probably be the best solution for them and their children. But Roboostoff's husband's anger at being maltreated in his own home by the security people hired by Intel soon turned to suspicion. If his wife was *not* having an affair with Ron Whittier, he demanded angrily, why on earth did she need protection from Whittier's wife? As the discussion in the kitchen turned into a full-blown argument in front of their children, the phone rang. Roboostoff's husband picked up; it was Ron Whittier, cálling to apologize. Seeing the call as further evidence of Roboostoff's guilt, her husband immediately stormed out of the house. Within a matter of days, he had found a new home and demanded that his wife and her "rich boyfriend" Whittier should contribute $100,000 to the cost of buying it.

Since the problem had arisen entirely from the behavior of an Intel officer, from threats made against Roboostoff on Intel property, and from the blunderings of the Intel security people at her house, Roboostoff was offered a loan from the company to help her pay the $100,000 demanded by her husband. Over the coming year, as her divorce went through, Roboostoff tried to carry on with her job as if nothing had happened—though it was galling to have to do so when Whittier himself, far from being disciplined by the company, was promoted to senior vice-president.

As she tried to assemble the shattered pieces of her life after the divorce, Roboostoff began to date Mike Splinter, a systems executive who had joined Intel eight years earlier and had become general manager of components manufacturing. She kept her relationship secret at work, because she knew that top Intel executives frowned on public dating by company employees, despite the prevalence of office romance and the fact that Paul Otellini, another senior vice-president of the company, was married to one of Intel's top labor lawyers. One day, however, she decided that her relationship with Splinter had progressed to the point where they could "come out"—and she asked Andy Grove whether he had any objection to her accompanying Splinter to an Intel party.

"Not at all," replied Grove.

The morning after the occasion, however, Intel's executive staff was abuzz with the scandal. Craig Barrett, Intel's chief operating officer, called Roboostoff into his office for a dressing down; so did Gerry

Parker, another senior vice-president. Roboostoff first told them it was none of their business. Then, when greater pressure was applied, she told them that they had better make sure they had the CEO's backing for their complaints. When Barrett hinted to her that the company would not tolerate two of its top employees going out in such a visible way, she retorted that he had better ask Splinter to resign if he had a problem, since she certainly had no intention of leaving.

Some weeks later, the company's human resources function was reorganized. Two days after it was complete, Roboostoff was left with an empty desk and no job—despite the fact that the slot intended for her, human resources across the whole company's engineering and manufacturing departments, was clearly vacant. She interpreted the delay as an attempt to intimidate her into ending her relationship with Splinter. Furious, she stormed into Grove's office.

"I'm going to give you guys until tomorrow morning to come up with a job for me," she told him, "otherwise you'll have some tough questions to answer. This is discrimination."

The next day, Roboostoff was given the job she had wanted. But over the coming two months, she found that Splinter, whom she was now preparing to marry, was being put in an increasingly difficult position at work by her continued presence inside Intel. Reluctantly and a little resentfully, Roboostoff decided to leave—and to go work for Larry Hootnick, the company's former senior vice-president, who was now running a company making disk drives Before quitting Intel, Roboostoff had a meeting with Carlene Ellis, her boss. Her $100,000 loan from Intel, formally due for repayment when she left, was extended for six months—but Roboostoff was left with the clear impression that the company would forgive the loan as informal compensation for the disruption that the company had caused to her career and her family life.

Six months later, now happily married to Mike Splinter, Roboostoff received a letter from the Intel legal department calling in the company's $100,000. She wrote a friendly note to Ellis, with a copy to Grove, reminding her gently of the circumstances and asking for the loan now to be formally forgiven. Ellis's reply reiterated that the loan was due for repayment, and threatened to foreclose on Roboostoff's house unless it was repaid. A formal notice of foreclosure followed shortly after.

Hot with resentment, Roboostoff wrote a stinging letter to Grove and then consulted a lawyer. Within weeks, the lawyer prepared documents for a discrimination suit against Intel and sent the company a demand for compensation. But Roboostoff had forgotten that Intel still had an indirect hold on her through her husband. Splinter began to receive discreet warnings at work that his own career would suffer if his wife persisted in her complaint against the company.

In the end, Roboostoff realized that going through with the lawsuit would be counterproductive. It might well bring her some fair compensation for the way the company had behaved to her. But it would undoubtedly put an end to her husband's career—and the resulting publicity would make it hard for either of them to move on to jobs in the Valley in the future. So the papers were never filed.

Despite their long friendship during the years she had been inside the company, Roboostoff found that Grove—along with most of her former colleagues—now refused to acknowledge her. Only one person came out of the episode with some credit: Larry Hootnick, the former senior vice-president who had hired Roboostoff when he moved on. Aware of all the circumstances and the way in which Intel had behaved, Hootnick arranged for Roboostoff's new employer to help repay the $100,000 loan so she could keep her house.

36

A Question of Drafting

Not many company CEOs would have the patience to pursue a contractual dispute through a three-year arbitration process. Fewer still would have the stomach to take the arbitrator to court if they disliked his finding. But it was a symptom of Andy Grove's attitude to the dispute between Intel and AMD that he grasped every opportunity to open up new fronts in the war between the two companies.

The last reported event in the Intel-AMD rivalry was the bigger company's failure in its attempt to overturn the arbitrator's ruling that AMD should be given a royalty-free license to the 386 chip. But there was a separate issue that the arbitrator had not addressed. This was the earlier agreement struck between Intel and AMD in 1976—in which Intel won the support of AMD as a valuable second source for its 8085 chip in the battle against Motorola, and AMD in return got a bundle of different benefits including wide-ranging rights to Intel microcode.

More than ten years had passed since that agreement, and the microcode in Intel's 8080 and 8086 chips was no longer of much commercial value. Not only were both chips outdated, and selling as commodity products for razor-thin margins. Also, Gary Davidian's work in reverse-engineering the 8086 microcode for NEC meant that there was an alternative source of supply for 8086 microcode that was safe from challenge by Grove's legal bloodhounds.

But Intel had kept writing new and more complex microcode every time it developed a new product. These later sets of microcode would be more difficult to reverse-engineer than the 8086 version. It certainly wouldn't be possible to do the job in two weeks, as Davidian had done—and it might not be possible to do it at all.

The 286 chip was the last product that Intel willingly second-sourced to AMD. As the relationship between the companies deteriorated, Grove decided not to give AMD second-source rights over anything else—starting with a device named the 287, a coprocessor that went with the 286.

Jerry Sanders may have been slow in developing an independent 386, but he was much quicker off the mark with the 287. As soon as it became clear that Grove wasn't handing over Intel's version of the coprocessor to AMD, Sanders set up an independent effort to build a 287 of his own. Everything would be developed by AMD using its own engineering resources and information from Intel that was already publicly available—with one exception. Under the 1976 agreement, Intel had given AMD certain rights to use its microcode until the end of 1995. So Sanders decided he would copy the 286 microcode, bit for bit, into the 287 coprocessor. This shortcut, he thought, would be legally unassailable and would save a considerable amount of effort in the 287 development process.

It was only when another writ arrived from Intel that Sanders realized he had miscalculated. Intel took a different view of the 1976 agreement. According to Tom Dunlap, the company's general counsel, the microcode to which Intel had awarded AMD rights until the end of 1995 was only microcode *in microcomputers*. In Dunlap's view, that meant the microcode in complete systems designed by Intel, such as the development systems used by engineers to develop new applications for chips. It didn't mean the microcode inside Intel microprocessors.

In the late 1980s, the word *microcomputer* meant pretty much what it means today: a desktop computer, containing a microprocessor and various other devices, that is small enough not to qualify as a minicomputer or a mainframe. But in the early 1970s, when Intel had introduced its first microprocessors, the company had sometimes used the word *microcomputer* almost interchangeably with the word *microprocessor*.

It was quite true that the 1976 agreement, which had been drafted by Intel, used the word *microcomputer*. But in Jerry Sanders's view, both sides had known exactly what they meant when they struck the microcode deal. It was rights to the microcode in the processors that AMD had been awarded—not rights to the much less valuable microcode elsewhere in Intel's development systems.

The issue of the microcode was now a second front in the war between the two companies. Although it may have sounded academic to the casual outsider, it was of great commercial importance. If AMD's interpretation of the 1976 agreement was right, then Jerry Sanders had a valuable head start in developing competing processors to Intel's 386 and 486 machines, and the designs that would follow them. If not, he would have to stop using Intel's 286 microcode, give up any claim on the microcode in its successors, and pay damages to the company for having wrongly made use of its microcode in the 287 coprocessor. Since there was no arbitration clause in the 1976 deal, the issue could not be settled informally. Sanders realized that he was in for a full-blown court case, certain to take even longer and cost even more than the earlier dispute.

There was one possible escape route, but it closed swiftly. AMD set up an attempt to reverse-engineer the 286 code in a clean-room environment, just as Davidian had done. But the effort did not succeed. Many months and many hundreds of thousands of dollars later, Sanders realized with a heavy heart that the reverse-engineering effort was not going to succeed. He had no choice: Since Intel had issued its writ, he must fight it. And since Tom Dunlap wanted damages for patent infringement on the 287, and an undertaking that AMD wouldn't use Intel microcode in 386 or 486 class chips, Sanders was betting the company on the outcome.

The microcode dispute added a new degree of personal animosity to the relations between Intel and AMD. While the senior figures at Intel who had negotiated the microcode deal in 1976 took the view in court that the meaning of the word *microcomputer* could have been the subject of an honest misunderstanding, their AMD counterparts didn't agree. Sven Simonsen, Jerry Sanders, and a number of other key AMD executives swore that Intel had known exactly what it was signing when it struck the deal. The only explanation for Intel's new interpretation of the word *microcomputer*, they believed, was bad faith. Andy Grove, they were convinced, was trying to screw AMD.

AMD was fighting an uphill battle. It proved impossible to convince the jury hearing the case to accept that the use of the word *microcomputer* in the agreement didn't have the meaning in 1976 that most reasonable people would have accepted it had in 1988. The verdict went against Sanders, and to his great disappointment and worry the AMD chairman was forced to face the fact that he would go down to the tune of tens or even hundreds of millions of dollars.

But the intertwined tales of Intel and AMD had always been subject to coincidences, and this case was to be no exception. After the verdict was given, the court gave each side a chance to present arguments on how big the award in Intel's favor should be. True to form, Intel wasn't making the process easy. It sent box after box of documents to AMD's lawyers, who believed that an attempt was being made to snow them with information that would be expensive and time-consuming to read and process.

Late one evening, an associate at Skjerven, Morrill, the law firm handling the case on AMD's behalf, was flipping disconsolately through the thousandth page of the thousandth box of papers when he suddenly stopped. He stared at the page before him, and then began searching feverishly through his index of Intel papers that AMD and its lawyers had already assembled in the case.

Half an hour later, the associate had two documents before him. One of them, the paper that had attracted his attention, was an internal paper from a "slurp"—a strategic long-range planning session at Intel. The other, which he had dug out of the copious files on the case, was a second copy of the same paper, but with two crucial differences. This version, which AMD had been sent by Intel many months earlier as part of the discovery process, carried a different date—and was missing some text. Whited out from the earlier version were a few words, written by an Intel executive, that came perilously close to supporting AMD's view of what the word *microcomputer* meant.

Intel, or someone working for Intel, had altered the date on a crucial document and had removed some incriminating text that weakened its case before the court.

In April 1993, four months after the original verdict against AMD had been handed down, the company persuaded the judge to issue a new judgment *non obstentio verdicto*, meaning notwithstanding the verdict. Overruling the jury's original verdict, the judge declared that Intel's breach of the rules of fair play entitled AMD to an entirely new trial. And in the meantime, the injunctions that had prevented AMD from releasing the 486 processor it had developed using Intel's microcode would be lifted.

The news reached Rich Lovgren, AMD's deputy general counsel, when he was sitting in a meeting room with Jerry Sanders in San Francisco. "Look," he explained to Sanders, "what it means is, it's as if the first trial never happened. There's not a prohibition on this planet that exists to stop us from making a part called the 486 that relies on our license to their microcode."

Sanders looked at him in amazement.

"You mean I can sell [the 486s] now?" AMD had a stockpile of 486s, which it had built during the trial but was waiting for legal clearance to release.

"You betcha."

Sanders picked up the phone to the head of the AMD division that was building the 486 devices. "How many parts you got?" he asked.

"Coupla thousand."

"Let's ship 'em," said Sanders.

With the aid of the document that Intel had accidentally given Sanders, AMD won the second microcode trial. But by then, Tom Dunlap and his legal team had found a new means of attack. They had looked at one of the microprocessor patents that had been won for Intel by John Crawford, one if its leading scientists, and found a nugget that had never before been used as a weapon in the fight against AMD.

The patent, known in the industry for short as '338 because of the last three digits of the number it was given by the U.S. Patent and Trademark Office, was one of the scores of pieces of intellectual property that Intel used to protect itself from interlopers and to maintain good relations with the other titans of the computer business. Rather than paying royalties to each other, a pair of powerful companies often made wide-ranging agreements covering free use of each other's entire patent portfolio.

The '338 patent asserted two claims. One covered the microprocessor itself; the other covered the use of a microprocessor in a computer system—and in particular the conjunction of a microprocessor with a memory device.

The point at issue was not whether AMD was entitled to use this patent; both sides accepted that '338 fell into the basket of patents that AMD did have rights to. Instead, the question was whether AMD's *customers* were allowed to make use of it. Intel accepted that AMD customers were covered on the first claim of the patent, by virtue of a principle known as "exhaustion," which meant that once the holder of a patent had been paid something by the first purchaser, he wasn't allowed to pursue that purchaser's customers for a second bite. But were AMD's customers allowed to put those microprocessors inside computers, as opposed to using them as paperweights or key chains? According to Intel, they weren't. If computer companies wanted to buy microprocessors from AMD and then actually use them as intended, then they would need to pay a royalty to Intel.

This was a daring and clever piece of legal reasoning, and at least in abstract terms it made sense. But AMD had a counterargument. Under U.S. patent law, a device that could only be used in combination with something else had special status, because a patent license covering the device alone wasn't worth anything. If the holder of the patent granted someone a license, then that license was taken to be an "implied license" allowing the licensee not just to use the device, but also to use it in the expected combination. That, according to AMD, was exactly where things stood with the microprocessor. Since people bought AMD microprocessors only for one thing—to put them in computers—its license from Intel should be taken to cover its customers too by implication.

AMD had another piece of ammunition against Intel. If Intel was right that the '338 patent prevented anyone from using a microprocessor inside a computer system without a license from Intel, then what had Intel's own customers been doing all these years? Compaq and Dell and the rest of the PC industry didn't have '338 licenses— and if Tom Dunlap had ever tried to sell them one, said AMD, they would have laughed in his face. Intel wasn't joking, however. The company actually began a program of approaching its own customers and offering them free licenses to the second claim of the '338 patent.

Had this tactic worked, Intel would then have been on stronger ground in asserting that AMD customers needed a '338 license too. But to the great relief of AMD, the computer industry reacted strongly against Intel's new licensing initiative. Even though Intel's license looked like a free offer, it was actually nothing of the kind— because once a PC manufacturer signed the license, it was effectively acknowledging Intel's claim and giving up any right to buy an x86 processor from AMD or anyone else and put it in a computer.

The latest twist in the debate gave AMD a further opening, too. When Intel started offering "free" licenses to the controversial use of

'338, it wasn't offering them for nothing to everyone—only to its own customers. So the company was "tying" the distribution of one product (free licenses) to the distribution of a less attractive product (Intel processors that customers had to pay for). This tying, asserted AMD, was an abuse of antitrust law. A company in the dominant position that Intel held in the computer industry wasn't allowed to use this tactic.

Tom Dunlap wasn't beaten yet. He picked a victim from among the hordes of Taiwanese clone makers, a company called Twinhead that exported its products to the United States, and he went to the U.S. International Trade Commission with a complaint that Twinhead was making illicit use of the '338 patent by selling computers in the United States that contained a chip made by Cyrix, a maker of x86 clones based in Texas. While the ITC deliberated the issue, the PC industry held its breath. Things had come to quite a pass when Intel took its battle with the x86 clone makers into the wider computer business. Was there any limit to Dunlap's legal aggressiveness? Or might Intel actually end up litigating against dozens of other PC manufacturers that were also its own customers?

37

The Traitorous Two

Intel's twenty-fifth birthday was coming up in July 1993. As the company approached the anniversary, its fortunes had never looked better. Sales for 1992 were nudging up toward $6 billion; income topped $1 billion for the first time. In December, the board authorized the payment of the first cash dividend in Intel's history—ten cents a share out of $4.97 per share earnings for the year. "We feel that the company has matured to the point where we can return a small percentage of our earnings directly to stockholders and still meet our capital needs," wrote Andy Grove and Gordon Moore in the annual report, "thus making it possible for our stockholders to realize some income without having to sell the stock. In this way, we believe that we will increase holdings of Intel stock by long-term investors."

A pair of important new technical marketing ideas had helped increase the company's profitability for 1992. One was "clock doubling": a system of making changes to the innards of a microprocessor that allowed it to perform many of its internal operations in double time, while continuing to communicate with the rest of the computer at normal speed. This allowed PC manufacturers to use an existing computer design and simply drop a new chip into it, delivering performance up to 70 percent higher, without suffering the delay or expense of rearranging the rest of the design of the machine. For the manufacturer, the innovation meant swifter product introductions and lower development costs; for Intel, it meant an opportunity to get a new chip out to consumers in a matter of weeks, not months, after the processor went into manufacturing.

The other innovation was the "OverDrive" processor. The idea here was that the manufacturer would ship a computer with a spare slot left empty on the motherboard that housed the microprocessor and other key components. When Intel was ready with a faster processor, the customer could buy it as a spare part from the retailer and snap it in the motherboard in an upgrade operation that took about as long as changing a disk drive.

For the manufacturer, the OverDrive concept helped persuade customers to buy a computer now instead of waiting for something more advanced six months down the line. For Intel, OverDrive provided an opportunity to sell a second processor for each computer shipped—and to increase the percentage of the PC industry's sales that dropped straight to the Intel bottom line.

What was striking about both of these innovations was that they represented a new trend in Intel's strategic thinking. Instead of looking at the computer business as a cake of fixed size, with Intel's slice tied to the ebb and flow of world PC sales, the company had now begun to realize that it was powerful enough in the industry to influence the size of the cake itself. The extra revenue to be gained by using techniques such as clock doubling and OverDrive processors to make the cake bigger might in the long term be more important for Intel than wringing another percentage point away from the market share of AMD and the other x86 chip manufacturers.

Despite this broader focus, Intel was still intensifying its battle against competitors. One new weapon was capital investment. The 386 chip, and its successor the 486, had proven such cash cows that Intel was able to spend $2 billion in 1992 on new manufacturing capacity and R&D, and to plan spending of $2.5 billion for the coming anniversary year. With two entirely new fabs coming on line, one in Ireland and the other in Santa Clara, this was the largest capital investment of any company in the chip industry. Intel was now the only company that could plausibly claim to be able to meet the processor demands of the world computer industry. So expensive had new fabs become that even the best-designed processor from another company would have difficulty building market share—simply because of lack of spare manufacturing capacity.

To make its capacity advantage more valuable, Intel began to issue suits for patent infringement against the chip foundries owned by companies such as Hewlett-Packard and SGS Thomson that built microprocessors for smaller competitors. It was a commonly accepted view in the industry that if your product was fabricated in a foundry that had the right to use Intel's device technologies, then Intel's rights were "exhausted" by the royalty that it received from the foundry owner. Tom Dunlap, however, insisted that the licenses to HP and SGS were part of wider patent-sharing agreements that had been struck between Intel and those of its peers that owned valuable technology of their own—and that when small companies piggybacked on the foundry licenses, they were merely trying to get around the fact that they had no technology to offer Intel in return for its patents. His argument was that since the foundries were really just "printing" circuitry designed by tiny firms like Cyrix onto wafers, they couldn't claim to be carrying out the design work themselves.

In the end, the courts found against Intel—because it could have specified that the foundries weren't allowed to use their licenses to Intel patents to fabricate chips for others, but had not taken the opportunity to do so. But the litigation costs were a good investment for Intel. If the company won, then newcomers to the semiconductor business could never become serious competitors unless they were able to spend billions of dollars developing their own fabs and inventing their own process technologies. If it lost—well, the delay and confusion caused to Intel's competitors was worth a few million dollars, and Tom Dunlap was never a guy to turn down a gamble.

Another weapon against the competition was to crank up the pace of new product introductions. To derive maximum benefit from the Pentium, the flagship processor due to succeed the 486, Intel needed to do two things. It needed to make sure that information on the new processor that would be valuable to competitors was kept secret until the very last moment before its launch; and it needed to make the Pentium "ramp"—the rate at which it took over from the 486 as the technology standard of the industry—as fast as possible. "There are only two kinds of companies," said Andy Grove in the company's annual report. "The quick and the dead."

Albert Mu was a typical example of the new breed of engineer inside Intel at the beginning of the 1990s. Born in Taiwan, he had emigrated to the United States after completing his military service and his studies at Taipei University, and had spent another eighteen months earning a master's in electrical engineering at the University of Texas at Austin. At thirty-two years old, he was shy, recently married, and not yet fully relaxed speaking English. But he was an excellent circuit designer. Joining AMD in Sunnyvale immediately after graduation, Mu had moved to IDT for the promise of a stimulating job working on a new large-capacity static RAM chip. But IDT hadn't worked out; Mu found the company culture uncooperative, and got a strong feeling that IDT engineers were unwilling to share their ideas with each other. When the call came in from an Intel recruiter in late 1989, he did not take much persuading to come and talk to the industry's leading microprocessor company about a new job.

After a couple of lunchtime meetings, Mu had been hooked. He left IDT for Intel and joined the hundred-strong team of engineers who were developing the Pentium. It was a monster team for a monster product. With over three million transistors, the Pentium would be by far the most complex processor Intel had ever built. It would also be the fastest, running at 100 million instructions per second (MIPS), twenty times as fast as the 286. In keeping with Intel's principle of trying to break down the job into smaller chunks, Mu's responsibility would be for only a tiny part of the processor—the design of part of the input-output portions of the device.

Mu's first performance evaluation was excellent. But by 1991, he was getting restless. Although he had only been in Silicon Valley a few years, he had already realized the basic principle—that the way for a truly ambitious engineer to build a successful career was to start up a new business. Working with another Taiwanese-born colleague at Intel named Frank Chen, Mu began preparing a business plan for a company building multichip modules—single packages containing more than one silicon chip. Unfortunately, Mu forgot the discretion that is an essential part of start-ups. One Sunday, he invited a friend from work who knew nothing of his plans and mistakenly left the business plan around in his sitting room where its cover could be seen.

The following Tuesday, Mu received an unexpected visitor in his cubicle: Vinod Dham, the Indian-born engineer who was czar of the entire Pentium project and a vice-president of the company. Dham, accompanied by two other people the young engineer didn't know, ordered him to come out of his working area and sit down with them in a conference room. As soon as the door was closed, Mu found himself subject to a hostile interrogation about his plans. Dham wanted to know every detail of the business that Mu and Chen were planning to start. As Mu tried to explain, Dham made it clear that he did not believe a word of what Mu was telling him. Instead, he accused the two men of planning to jump ship to AMD, taking key secrets from the Pentium project with them.

"Intel can put you in jail just like that," he told the young Taiwanese engineer. Under threats from Dham and the representatives from security and human resources who were the other two people present in the meeting, Mu agreed to allow his house to be searched. After thirty minutes of grilling, in which Mu was unable to convince Dham that his plan for a new business was unrelated to Intel, the meeting was adjourned, and Mu was ordered to drive one Intel security man to his home while another followed in a second car. When they arrived home, the security man carried out a thorough search of the entire house, looking not only at his business plan and all the documents it was based on but also the annual reports of public companies that Mu had acquired to keep track of his investments in the stock market. When Mu protested, the security man told him he would be liable to immediate arrest and imprisonment by the police and the FBI if he objected to the search.

The behavior of the security men was particularly humiliating because Mu's wife and a friend visiting them were forced to watch while Mu submitted to interrogation and search like a common criminal. When the ordeal was over, the security man repossessed two hundred pages of documents marked "Intel Confidential," which Mu had signed out from the office to use at home while working on the Pentium project weekends and in the evenings, and left with three boxes of materials in his colleague's car.

Mu spent the next two days at home, suspended from his job and in a state of misery and uncertainty. All he knew was that Frank Chen had been forced to submit to a similar interrogation and search. Then the call came from Intel: He was summoned back to Santa Clara. The meeting, called for 11:00 A.M. was brief and businesslike. A representative of the company's human resources department told Mu he had been summarily fired, and presented him with a number of papers to sign. Mu refused; in response, the company refused to return the personal belongings that were in his desk. When his salary check appeared at the end of the month, Mu found that Intel had stopped his pay from the day of the search onwards.

A week after the abrupt termination of his job at Intel, Mu's shock turned to anger. Talking to Chen, he came to the conclusion that he had been fired unfairly—and also that the threats that had been used to persuade him to permit the search of his house were improper. The two men later filed suit against Intel for invasion of privacy, but lost confidence in the attorney they hired to fight the case after they felt he became too keen to settle the case contrary to their interests. The case was dropped. Today, both men work at Hal Computer Systems, a Silicon Valley company owned by Fujitsu.

Looking back on his experiences, Mu attributed what had happened to him more to internal politics than to rationality. Vin Dham, the overall head of the Pentium project, was keen to make his mark at the company. Dham had already helped arrange for a rival Intel star, Pat Gelsinger, to be moved to Oregon, where the plans for the company's 686-generation chip were being worked on. "I believe Vin Dham [thought] his position was in danger because Intel also started a 686 group in Oregon. He found our case, he thought that we were joining a competitor. Before he even [thought] deeply about the case, he just jumped in. He later found out he made a mistake, but it was too late. He basically [needed] to defend himself."

"If we wanted to sell the information [on Pentium] to AMD or any [other] competitor, Vin Dham would think this was very helpful to his career," Mu speculated. "[He could] show Intel executives that he found a spy from AMD for example, [and] stopped leakage to the competitor." But Mu was clear on one thing. "Vin is a very political person. . . . Vin is a kind of person that if you become an enemy of his, you are in deep trouble."

The computer industry awaited the Pentium with mixed feelings. On the one hand, there was quiet bemusement that the 8086 standard of which the Pentium was the latest manifestation had survived as long as it had. It was now fifteen years since the first 8086 chips had hit the market as a stopgap to keep customers loyal until Intel's new standard would be ready. Since then, microprocessor performance had increased five hundredfold, and the x86 standard and its accumulated baggage had become a technical inconvenience. A measure of how much more complex and difficult the x86 standard had made the job of the Pentium team could be seen by comparing their part with the state-of-the-art designs that were free of the x86 constraint. The new generation of RISC chips were simpler in architecture than Intel's, quicker and easier to design, smaller in size, higher in performance, and considerably lower in price. Yet Intel had played its hand brilliantly since 1978. With every year that went by, the weight of software packages available for the x86 standard had grown, and with it the price-performance advantage that competing architectures would require in order to unseat Intel from its throne.

The new element in the puzzle at the turn of the 1990s was that Windows NT seemed set to give Microsoft a new chance to knock out the competing operating systems that kept it out of high-end computing—and to force a redivision of the PC industry pie. Once Microsoft could deliver a fully portable OS and persuade the market to accept it, Intel faced the risk of becoming just one of a number of processor vendors, competing on equal terms on price and performance. There were some high-end chips that Microsoft wasn't likely to develop. One was the PowerPC, born of an alliance between IBM and Apple; another was Sun's SPARC, because the same company's Solaris operating system was a competitor to Microsoft. But Gates could easily imagine offering Windows NT on the MIPS 4000 processor, used by Silicon Graphics, and Digital Equipment's Alpha processor.

NT was due to ship almost at the same time as Pentium. But Intel had been lucky. The company's inability to stop AMD from shipping a 386 clone, irritating though it was, had helped accelerate the decline in selling prices of the 386 processor. In the first quarter of 1992 alone, AMD shipped two million units, equivalent to a 40 percent market share. So PC makers were less conscious than usual of the "tax" they were paying Intel for the x86 architecture, subsidizing its high margins from their own pockets. Intel had also managed to cloud the technical debate in the industry on the relative advantages of RISC chips versus its own "complex instruction set computing," or CISC, devices. By constantly referring to RISC-like features in the 486 and the coming Pentium, Intel had persuaded many potential RISC buyers that the competition offered little that Intel would not itself be able to deliver in a few months' time.

As the Pentium launch approached, excitement in the industry began to grow. Experience had taught PC makers that "early adopters" would always pay premium prices to get their hands on the new product. The suppliers who were able to meet that demand quickest could profit handsomely. With every new processor generation, the PC industry had grown, and the stakes had risen. The pace of change had increased too. It had taken four and a half years for the 386 to achieve a 25 percent share of the x86 market, but only three and a half for the 486 to do so. Everyone knew that with Intel's new focus on speeding up the "ramp" of its new processor, the Pentium's rise to domination would probably be quicker still.

Since IBM had lost control of the PC industry, three tiers had emerged in the business. In the first tier were firms like Compaq, Dell, and IBM itself, each of which carried out a significant quantity of technology development, looking for ways to tweak the best possible performance from the different components in the box before building its machines. Then came companies like Gateway 2000, Packard Bell, and Acer, all of them large companies with international marketing reach and formidable managements, but companies that did little to push out the envelope of emerging PC technology. Finally came the rest of the clones, the no-name mom-and-pop outfits in the third category, assembling computers from components with few tools more complex than a screwdriver. These firms relied on other companies to integrate the hundreds of components that made up a PC into a dozen or so larger modules. Most important among the integrators were the "motherboard" manufacturers, which designed the circuit board putting the new processor in place with the computer's other key components. It was the motherboard that made the difference between a good and a bad implementation of a new processor. But the motherboard makers, ranging from a handful of $50 million companies in America to hundreds of smaller firms in Taiwan, had only a small window of opportunity. If they failed to deliver a low-cost, high-performance board within a few weeks or months of receiving the new generation chip from Intel, they missed out on the fattest part of the product cycle.

The most striking new partnership that had emerged in the industry over recent years was between Micronics, a motherboard maker in Fremont, on the east side of the San Francisco Bay, and Gateway 2000 in North Sioux City, South Dakota. Started by a cattle rancher's son out of a barn, Gateway was almost the paradigm of the new computer industry. It didn't build any parts at all; instead, the company scoured the landscape for the best and cheapest in new PC components, sold by mail order off the back of eccentric home-brewed ads in the computer press. Gateway bolted PCs together in a huge shed set in the wheatfields. The secret of its competitive advantage was the "BOM"—the bill of materials. Every supplier had to supply Gateway with a bill of materials revealing exactly what its own component costs were, together with its overhead and its "requested profit." Gateway would then beat the supplier down to what it considered a fair margin and pass its savings on to the end consumer.

Only one supplier didn't give Gateway its BOM. Micronics had been Gateway's motherboard supplier almost from the beginning, and the excellent performance of its boards had won Gateway a number of key magazine awards that had put the fledgling company on the map and kept it in front of consumers. Given that Gateway had no presence at all in computer stores, performance awards were its lifeblood, for they gave its ads in the computer press real credibility. Micronics was Gateway's most important supplier, and Gateway was Micronics' most important and most loyal customer, accounting for over half the motherboard maker's sales.

In July 1993, however, something strange happened. Robert Gunn, the marketing chief at Micronics, received an unexpected call from Gateway, asking for sample motherboards suitable for the new Pentium chip to be shipped to South Dakota by the twenty-eighth of the month. Gunn protested; Micronics had only just received its first Pentium samples from Intel. There was no way that the company would be able to complete its design and testing in time to have sample motherboards with Gateway before the end of the month. After some negotiation, it was agreed that Micronics would ship the sample boards to Gateway by August 17. As he hung up the phone, Gunn began to muse on what was up with Gateway. *They've been in the business long enough to know we couldn't deliver the boards that fast. It's physically impossible. Why did they ask, then? What's goin' on?*

Over the next few weeks, Micronics drove its engineers hard to meet the deadline imposed by Gateway. Working the design teams in shifts, twenty-four hours a day, the company succeeded in sending its motherboard samples a few days earlier than the date agreed. Yet Gateway didn't seem to appreciate the gesture. Impressed though the guys at North Sioux City were at the speed of Micronics' operation, they started to drive a much harder bargain than ever before on price. Micronics came in asking $320 for the boards; Gateway demanded to see its BOM. When Micronics refused, offended that Gateway was treating it like any other supplier instead of like the long-term partner it believed itself to be, the PC company took a different tack. *You need to hit a price of $260*, Micronics was told.

By the end of the month, the fog suddenly lifted. Gunn and his colleagues realized that the competitor they were pricing against was Intel itself—and the reason that Gateway had demanded the evaluation boards so much earlier than usual was that Intel had promised to send Gateway its own evaluation boards by July 28. To make matters worse, it became clear that Ted Waitt, Gateway's thirty-year-old CEO, wasn't really interested in buying Pentium boards from Micronics anymore—at any price. He expected that Intel would run short of production capacity on the Pentium later in the cycle, and he was convinced that Gateway's best chance of getting the allocation of chips it wanted when the crunch came was to demonstrate loyalty now by buying Intel's motherboards.

With more than half the company's entire sales going to Gateway, the contract was almost a matter of life and death to Micronics. Steve Kitrosser, the company's president, flew out to South Dakota a couple of times over the succeeding weeks. So did Gunn. So did Larry Barber, Micronic's VP of sales. They ran the entire gamut of Gateway management.

"We'd talk to engineering to make sure there were no engineering differences," recalled Gunn, "[and we] also dealt with purchasing to see if there was a pricing delta. There wasn't. We also had some negotiations with the chief operating officer of Gateway, Rick Snyder, trying to make sure there weren't any operational issues we were dealing with."

Finally, the Micronics team made a powerful pitch to Waitt himself. "We tried to show him that we will be able to match or beat Intel's introduction timing of their board. We will meet their pricing, and we will guarantee that our board will outperform their board, so he'd be able to win more awards [than if he] based on their board." But nothing worked. Intel had not threatened Gateway if it refused to buy Pentium boards, but it had clearly provided a mixture of carrots and sticks that was irresistible.

What made the move so galling to Micronics was that Intel's motherboard manufacturing division, based in Hillsboro, Oregon, had an apparently unfair advantage over Micronics. Not only would customers believe that buying motherboards directly from Intel would give them favored status when chips were on allocation; worse, the Hillsboro operation would get advance knowledge of information on processor bugs and design changes. Even working faster and smarter, it would be tough for Micronics to match Intel's delivery dates.

Kitrosser and his lieutenants therefore decided on a change of tack. They called a meeting with Earl Whetstone, the Intel VP who was director of sales and marketing in the United States. When Whetstone arrived at Micronics' office in Fremont, the team started by reminding him that their company bought $40 million of parts from Intel every year. They explained that a major customer of the company's had just switched to using Hillsboro boards, and complained that Intel had put Micronics at an unfair disadvantage by sending technical information to Hillsboro that allowed the in-house board operation to develop its product quicker than an outside company. No threats of legal action were made, but Micronics made it clear that it had consulted its outside counsel and believed that Intel had acted anticompetitively.

Asked what he proposed to do to help ease the pain, Whetstone promised to help Micronics find some other customers for its Pentium boards to replace the lost Gateway account. On Whetstone's instructions, Gunn arranged for some data sheets on the Micronics Pentium board to be sent to Intel for distribution to its sales force. The idea was that when Hillsboro was sold out of boards to capacity, Intel would still have plenty of Pentiums to sell, and customers who wanted to buy the processors already installed in motherboards could be discreetly steered over to Micronics.

Meanwhile, Micronics had to decide what to tell the stock market. In an attempt to salvage the relationship, Waitt had promised that Gateway would double its purchases of 486 boards for the last quarter of 1993. This meant that Micronics could truthfully report an acceleration of sales to Gateway, while warning Wall Street in mid-December that the first quarter of 1994 would see a dip because of delays in introducing the Pentium board and slower than expected demand. When the moment came, the harm that Micronics sustained was mitigated by the fact that the first Pentium configuration on the market was a 5-volt, 60 MHz processor that offered only a modest performance advantage over the fastest 486 chip Intel was sampling at the same time. By the time a new lower-powered 3.3-volt version was on the market, Micronics had recovered its position enough to scoop many of the major magazine awards, including the top slots for fastest 90MHz and 100MHz Pentium box. But Micronics never sold another Pentium board to Gateway—and never bought another processor from Intel. Since Intel no longer offered significant price breaks for bulk purchases, it did not make sense for Micronics to take on the inventory risk of buying tens of thousands of Intel processors that might suddenly lose 20 percent or more of their value if Intel brought forward a price cut. Instead, the company got its customers to buy boards directly from Intel and have Intel ship them directly to Micronics for assembly.

Intel's sudden entry into the manufacturing of motherboards caused a great deal more pain in Taiwan than in Fremont. After building fewer than a million boards in 1993, Intel shipped two million in 1994, and between ten million and twelve million in 1995. By the end of the year, when Intel was already talking of shipping 20 to 25 million boards in 1996, 280 of the 300 motherboard manufacturers in Taiwan had disappeared. One purpose of the initiative was expanding into a new downstream business. Also, by building millions of motherboards and selling them at low margin, Intel could force down the margins of other motherboard makers, which would help it to increase the profitability of its processors.

Most important of all, though, was the question of "ramp." By making its own motherboards, Intel could help manufacturers get the new Pentium chip into computers around the world much faster than ever before. This reduced the competitive advantage of companies like Compaq and IBM, which built their own boards and were generally able to get to market well before the smaller players and win high margins for the first few months. But it still made sense for Intel. While it had taken four and a half years to get the 386 up to 25 percent of the x86 market, and three and a half years with the 486, it took only one and a half years to achieve the same milestone with the Pentium. The swifter introduction of the new processor added several hundred million dollars to Intel's bottom line. And if some of those dollars came from companies such as Micronics, could Intel really be blamed?

38

A Hacker Inside

At the end of the 1980s, outsiders used to joke that Intel had become so ordered, so focused, so rigorous that a young Bob Noyce who applied to work there wouldn't get a job. This may have been true at Santa Clara, where the talk was all of margins, product cycles, lawsuits, and corporate marketing. Farther afield, it was not. The atmosphere at Intel's Oregon site, where work was being done on a joint venture with the German electrical conglomerate Siemens, was very different. With nine time zones and a language between the Oregon researchers and their counterparts in Germany, it was surprising that anything got done at all. Nobody could remember what the official name of the joint venture, BiiN, really stood for; it was commonly referred to as Billions Invested In Nothing. This wasn't entirely fair: after long years in which Intel had bad-mouthed the technology of RISC processing, using the derogatory acronym YARP inside the company to refer to "Yet Another RISC Processor," the company had at last decided to build one of its own—and the BiiN technology led directly to the i960, a processor that became the biggest selling RISC device by units shipped ever. Another division based at the Oregon site was SSD, the Intel "superscalar" division, which worked on advanced supercomputing projects that were still further from the company's mainstream PC business.

Like other technology companies, Intel employed contractors to work alongside its staffers; also like other technology companies, Intel sometimes allowed them to stay working on a contract basis long after it could have saved money by bringing them on to the payroll. But informal arrangements sometimes suited both sides. For a hard-pressed Intel manager, continuing a subcontracting arrangement was less hassle than the process of arguing for a new position and dealing with all the formalities of advertising the position and interviewing candidates. For the contractor, remaining off the Intel payroll meant less security—but it also meant more freedom and more money. In some ways, contracting at Intel was the sort of job that would have perfectly suited a young Bob Noyce.

One of the Oregon contractors was a young software specialist called Randal Schwartz. Not only did Schwartz lack the Ph.D. that was standard issue in the Oregon labs; he also hadn't even been to college. He had joined Tektronix immediately after leaving high school, and had acquired an encyclopedic knowledge of the UNIX operating system on the job. By 1993, Schwartz had been working for Intel in Oregon for five years. He started out as a writer, putting together the technical manual, but also worked for more than one department as a systems administrator. "Sysadmin" was a job that was often hard to fill, because people who knew enough software to do it properly were usually unwilling to spend their time doing what really amounted to a midlevel maintenance job. But the job suited Schwartz perfectly. It allowed him to spend time on other projects—notably to consult and lecture on the side, and to write a best-selling book on Perl, a scripting language often used under UNIX. Schwartz lived very much for the short term. He enjoyed what he did and was well paid for it, but he didn't save any money—and lived entirely off his wits. Knowing that Intel had a strong financial incentive to fire him the moment it no longer needed his services, he saw it as his job to make himself indispensable. Instead of going to his supervisor with problems, Schwartz's objective was to go with solutions to problems that nobody had even thought of yet.

What Schwartz saw inside Intel was quite different from the standard Santa Clara company experience. Talking to friends outside the company, he explained that he rated the company as a 7 on the *Dilbert* scale, meaning that it was pretty similar to the famous cartoon-strip story of disempowered engineers working in cubicles. He also liked to poke fun at the meetings that Andy Grove considered the most important part of an executive's job. Schwartz saw a sharp distinction between the grunts—the "individual contributors," as Intel called them—who actually did the work, and the managers who went to the meetings. The more senior you were, he observed, the more meetings you went to. And because they all spent their days at meetings, managers could never get hold of each other. They played voice-mail tag all the time. E-mail made more sense because it was higher bandwidth, but generally the more senior people didn't know how to use E-mail. So they'd return to their desks at 6:00 P.M. after the day of meetings and start returning calls. By contrast, Schwartz's life was a great deal more free. As a contractor, he worked on the basis that the company would specify what it wanted him to do, but he would be allowed within reason to choose the means of doing it—including the hours. If he wanted to come into the office late, play around with the computers for a bit, and then work until midnight, that was his affair.

One day in early October 1993, Schwartz got word that the Internet service provider he used to read his E-mail from home had been broken into by hackers. Realizing that the ISP, a small company called Techbook, didn't have the technical resources to protect itself against hacker attack, Schwartz decided to offer some of his own expertise gratis and do something about it. He downloaded from the Internet a utility called Crack and started using it to check the security of the passwords of Techbook's customers.

Like other ISPs, Techbook required its customers to log in with a user name and password, and kept a file of user names and passwords for corroboration. To keep hackers out, the passwords were encrypted so that you could not tell what the password was just by looking in the file. When someone logged in and typed a password, the computer would encrypt the letters typed in and see if the resulting string of characters matched what was in the password file. If it did, then the log-in would be allowed; if not, it would be rejected. The trouble with this system was that although it provided basic protection against someone just reading passwords straight out of the file, it created a security chink: Hackers could download the password file and try out thousands of letter and number combinations one after the other until they got a match. What made the job easier for hackers was that too many users liked to use easy-to-remember passwords instead of just randomly chosen letters and numbers.

The Crack program was a weapon that could be used in two ways. In the hands of a hacker, it provided a way to find a password that would provide admittance to someone else's system. In the hands of the good guys, it provided a helpful check that users were being responsible about passwords. When you ran Crack on your password file, it tried all the words in the directory one by one; then in various combinations, such as with the letter *I* replaced with a number 1 or with the letter *s* replaced with a $; then it tried all the words again with single digits put at the beginning or the end. When it had finished, it would deliver a list of passwords that it could break, allowing the system administrator to contact the users and tell them to choose something more secure.

Schwartz ran Crack on the Techbook password file and found that over thirty of the company's customers had insecure passwords. A day and a half later, he sent his findings off to the owner of the ISP with a recommendation to tell the offending customers to change their passwords. Then, out of curiosity, Schwartz tried out Crack on the password file of O'Reilly & Associates, the publisher of his book on Perl. Here it was clear that precautions were already being taken; only one password out of six hundred failed the test.

But what about Intel itself? Schwartz pulled the password file for his own group of thirty users—and to his surprise, he found that the program could crack two of them. Further research showed something more alarming still: One user, whose log-in was "RonB," used the same password to get into the wider cluster of Intel company servers as he used for the local machine. This meant that an outsider who discovered his password could break into the heart of the company's computer system. Using RonB's log-in to pull the password file from the superscalar division's cluster file, Schwartz now set Crack to work again on a much longer list of Intel employee log-ins. A few days later—the checking process required serious number crunching, and took a long time—the program came back with forty-eight dud passwords, a frighteningly high figure. Schwartz then went off for a couple of weeks to teach some classes on Perl. When he returned, Schwartz decided to run Crack just one more time so he could present up-to-date results to his supervisor. Setting the program running on Thursday, Schwartz went back to his regular Intel duties.

Unknown to Schwartz, however, a senior systems administrator on Intel's staff noticed that Crack was running. Since Schwartz had made no attempt to hide the fact that he was running the program, there was no mystery about who had set it off. Yet the colleague, instead of asking Schwartz why he was trying to crack a company password file, picked up the phone to talk to Intel security. Together, the administrators and the security men spent Friday secretly looking through Schwartz's files, checking his computer activities, and downloading everything onto magnetic tape so the company would have a record of what he had been up to. They called the police in, and the following Monday obtained a search warrant for Schwartz's house.

Oblivious to what was going on, Schwartz finished his day's work on Monday and went home to change before going on to the local health club for a workout. Just before he was ready to leave his house, there was a knock at the door. A pair of police officers, brandishing their warrant from the court, demanded to come in. Two hours later, after tearing out every piece of computer equipment in the building, they left. Astonished by what had happened, Schwartz had tried to convince them that he had meant no harm, but without success. The police offers told him flatly that they didn't believe him—and said they would only take him seriously if he was willing to undergo a lie-detector test.

The next morning, Schwartz talked to Mike Godwin, counsel for the Electronic Frontier Foundation, an organization that lobbies on behalf of Internet users. With Godwin's help, he found a competent local attorney. On his behalf, the lawyer approached the police and conveyed his offer to take the lie-detector test. But the police were no longer interested. Schwartz could do nothing but wait to see what the next move from Intel and the local prosecutor would be. Since he kept everything from his address book to his financial records on an Apple PowerBook confiscated during the search, Schwartz was also left in a strange state of uncommunicative limbo. Only after a few days did he realize that he might well have to face a criminal trial—and since he had no savings, he had better start working in order to earn the money to pay his lawyer.

Four months later, Schwartz was in Phoenix doing some contract work for Motorola when his lawyer called. With Intel's cooperation, the lawyer explained, Schwartz had been indicted by the prosecutors on three separate felonies. The court would likely grant him bail, but he would have to go down to the local jail with his bail money in cash and spend an hour or so behind bars waiting for the paperwork to be filled out.

Because his lawyer was doing his best to stop the case from going to trial, Schwartz appeared in court nine times before the trial itself began. When it opened, Schwartz's lawyer offered a spirited defense. He explained that Schwartz knew so much about the Intel computer system and how it worked that he could easily have hidden the Crack program under someone else's user name if his purpose in running it had been malevolent. Intel had put forward no evidence that Schwartz had ever done any harm with the information he had obtained by running Crack, nor that he had intended to do any. In any case, continued his attorney, Schwartz had already had all the chances he'd ever need to break the rules. The previous year, he had held "system administrator" privileges on the entire Intel SSD computer cluster, which meant that he didn't need Crack if he wanted to read the private files of other company employees. The accusation made against Schwartz, his lawyer argued, was the equivalent of accusing a janitor whose job gave him access to every room in the building of copying keys for the purpose of a break-in.

Although a number of his Intel colleagues came to vouch for Schwartz, and his supervisor at Motorola appeared also in his support, the case was open and shut. Under Oregon state law, it was a felony to alter a computer without authorization—and although Schwartz claimed that his contract with Intel generally authorized him to "perform system administration tasks" on the company network, his lawyer was unable to convince the jury that running Crack came under this heading. To make matters worse, the Oregon law that criminalized unauthorized alteration of a computer did not specify in detail what counted as proper authorization; in every other one of the 613 instances in the state's laws where authorization was mentioned, it was defined more precisely.

The jury, only one of whose members used a computer regularly, found Schwartz guilty on all three charges. He was sentenced in 1994 to five months' probation, a three-month jail sentence suspended until 1998, and 480 hours of community service, which he was allowed to spend helping set up Web pages for not-for-profit organizations. He was also ordered to pay damages to Intel for the harm he had caused. Arguing that it had been forced to reload the operating systems of all the machines affected by his use of Crack and reconfigure every piece of software on them, the company came up with a figure of $69,000. Schwartz's defense cost him a further $170,000.

The case was prominently covered in the U.S. technology press, and a Web page was set up to solicit donations to Schwartz's defense fund. Opinion on his case was divided. Some thought he had behaved in a wholly unpardonable way. Others said he should just have been fired, or should have been required to compensate the company but spared the humiliation of a criminal prosecution. Nobody, however, drew a parallel between Schwartz's action and the case of the pig that Bob Noyce stole for a campus barbecue when he was a freshman at Grinnell College in Iowa. Noyce had been lucky; the angry farmer was persuaded to drop his demand for a prosecution, and Noyce had got off with a summer's suspension, which he spent working in New York City as an actuary for an insurance company. Schwartz had been less lucky. But this was 1993, not 1948. The rules were different now—and Bob Noyce, dead after suffering a massive heart attack in June 1989, was no more than a memory at Intel.

39

Tech Support Screws Up

The name of the guy who took the call has never been made public. But one day in October 1994, a technical support specialist at Intel's call center in Folsom, California, mishandled a call from a customer so badly that a chain of events was set in motion that ended two months later costing the company nearly a half-billion dollars.

Here's how it happened.

The caller identified himself as Thomas Nicely, of the department of mathematics at Lynchburg College, Virginia. He explained that he was doing some number crunching on a set of computers—working on prime numbers—and that he'd come across some anomalous results. To be precise, one of his computers had given an error in a long-division sum. Asked to divide one by 824,633,702,441, it had come up with the wrong answer.

Nicely was soft-spoken but absolutely confident. He explained that he'd checked the program he had written, the data he had started from, the off-the-shelf software that he'd used. He'd rebooted his computer no end of times. He'd wiped a load of unnecessary programs off his hard disk in case they were messing things up. He'd even tried out the calculation on a different machine in a local computer store. The results all pointed to one thing. The culprit, said Nicely nicely, was the Pentium chip. It wasn't doing the math properly.

Intel organizes its tech support people in three layers. The frontline staff, numbering around one thousand, deal with common or garden-variety questions from members of the public. Most of the time, the questions aren't anything to do with Intel's processors; they're issues that arise from applications software, from the operating system, or from some other part of the computer's hardware. But the company offers free help anyway as a matter of goodwill. Behind these frontline staff are another 250 or so people who serve the Intel sales force and the computer industry. They deal with issues that are directly focused on Intel products—but once again, they are not the focus of the company's technical expertise. To get an answer to a really difficult question, you have to go to an engineer in one of the product divisions.

What seems to have happened to Nicely is that his call should have been routed immediately to a specialist inside the Pentium team. All the warning signs were there. He was a math professor, not a teenager playing computer games. He identified his problem clearly as being related to the processor itself. And he had done enough corroborative testing to support, at least initially, the view that there was a bug inside Intel's flagship chip.

Yet instead of treating Nicely's call as a high priority that required careful handling, the Intel staff member who spoke to him gave him the brush-off. He was told that there wasn't a problem with the chip, that it must be some other part of his computer system that was responsible, and that the company would get back to him. It didn't. The tech support person who spoke to Nicely didn't even have access to an up-to-date bug list for the new microprocessor—and being unaware of the seriousness of the issue that Nicely was raising, simply let his complaint fall through the cracks.

If Nicely had been made aware then of how much Intel really knew about his problem, he would probably have been astounded. For not only did the company know that its chip was flawed. It had also known for around five months—longer than Nicely himself had spent checking the initial hypothesis that something was wrong with the processor.

When the Pentium design program had begun, Intel had recognized that the complexity of the chip design and the size of the team working on it posed an increasing risk of introducing errors. In the old days of "one man, one chip, one year," there had been plenty of straight human errors in processor design—but the projects were small enough for one engineer, or at least a handful, to keep an overall grip on the design. With three million transistors in the Pentium, this was clearly not going to be possible: The danger was that two parts of the chip layout, each working correctly on its own, might fail to work together.

This had already been a big problem on the 486. An analysis afterwards discovered that most of the bugs on the chip had come from the interfaces between the functional blocks in the processor rather than inside the blocks themselves. One of these bugs, discovered by a customer after the 486 went into production, was so severe that the company had to turn fifty thousand 486s into souvenir key chains. So with typical Intel thoroughness, Vin Dham, the Pentium czar, set up a team which had no responsibility for any single block, but was responsible just for looking after the interfaces between the blocks. Dham also tried a new technique to winkle out errors in the design at the last minute.

"As the project was nearing completion, after each of my teams assured me there were no bugs, I offered to pay anyone $100 on the spot if they found a bug," he recalled. To Dham's surprise, there were takers for his offer, and he was forced to pay out a few hundred dollars. But the discovery of the bugs was excellent news.

"This was a lot cheaper than finding the bug later or having a customer find the bug for us," he told researchers working on a business-school case study shortly after the launch. "With Pentium processors, no bugs have gone to customers."

Unfortunately, Dham was wrong. In May 1994, a full year after the first Pentium samples completed their twelve-week journeys through Intel's fabs, the reliability tests that continued after the new chip's launch threw up a problem—the Pentium was producing wrong answers on long-division sums. With three million transistors of silicon real estate to scour for the source of the problem, finding out what was going on took several more weeks—so it was late June or early July before Dham was ready to brief Intel's executive staff on the results of the bug search. His report was depressing evidence that the new approach of creating an "interface team" had not lived up to expectations.

The method the Pentium chip used for long division had been described exactly twenty-five years earlier in an academic computing journal published by the Institute of Electrical and Electronics Engineers. To work out the answer to x divided by y, you picked the first four binary digits of y and the first seven binary digits of x and produced a guess by looking up the approximate answer in a multiplication table. Then you multiplied the guess by y to see how close you were. If the remainder was nil, that meant the guess was accurate; if not, then you divided y into the remainder by making another guess based on the numbers in the table. Step by step, the guess would get more accurate and the remainder would get smaller, until in the end you had an answer that was accurate to fifteen figures after the decimal point.

To speed up the division process, the lookup table was actually laid out in silicon on the Pentium chip. Unfortunately, five of the table's 2,048 entries were wrong. The error wasn't obvious, because the way that the long division worked usually meant that a mistake would correct itself. But a very small number of combinations of binary numbers would yield a final answer to the division sum that was actually wrong.

Calculating how many combinations would produce the wrong result was a relatively simple matter: The engineers who carried out an analysis for the team that had been swiftly assembled to assess the problem estimated the figure was about one calculation in nine billion. The more difficult question was how much it would matter to Pentium users to get a wrong answer once every nine billion times the chip carried out a division. For most users, who didn't use the processor's floating-point unit very often, and didn't need accuracy to fifteen significant figures when they did, the answer was almost never. At the rate that the average Pentium owner used the floating-point unit, the Intel engineers calculated, wrong answers would come up about once every twenty-seven thousand years. The vast majority of PCs containing the flawed Pentium chips would be scrapped long before then. Memory chips had a mean time between failure, or MTBF, of about seven hundred years, and the Pentium chip itself had an MTBF of only about two hundred years.

But what about people who took real advantage of the Pentium's floating-point calculation facilities? Some of these were graphic designers and typographers using software packages like PhotoShop; for them, the bug would only be likely to produce one pixel wrong out of hundreds of thousands or even millions. The result would be no worse than a single misplaced dot in a photo or page of text. If they could even see the dot on the page, most people would attribute it to a speck of dust on a printing plate and forget it. But graphic designers weren't the chip's only heavy-duty users. Engineers, economists, and financial analysts also used the Pentium. Fifteen significant figures of accuracy could make an important difference by putting the blue-print for a new rocket design a few millimeters out of kilter, or by miscalculating the present value of a stream of future cash flows in-correctly by a few dollars on a billion-dollar transaction. Then there was a third set of users: theoretical mathematicians and other scien-tists, who would be using their Pentium-powered computers to crunch numbers all day long. For a user in this category, the bug could turn in a wrong answer as often as once a day.

These intensive users represented a tiny minority of the 2 million or more Pentium chips that Intel was hoping to pump out by the end of 1994; the engineers and analysts whose work was heavy-duty enough to count would number at most a few hundred, and the math-ematicians might number only a few dozen. Yet the cost of fixing the bug just for them would be high. Simply changing the masks to rein-state the five table entries correctly would run to tens of thousands of dollars. Then there would be work in progress—the thousands of chips, each worth $900 because of Intel's policy of pricing new parts very dear at the beginning of the product cycle—that would have to be junked. And what about the chips already shipped? The Pentium ramp was proceeding according to plan: Many hundreds of thousands of the new chips were already on customers' desks or in the retail channel—and retrieving them would be prohibitively expensive. Each machine would have to be opened by an expert technician so the old processor could be eased out and a new one put in its place. It was clear that Intel was looking at millions of dollars—perhaps even tens of millions—if it decided to do what it had done with the bug-ridden 486 chips, and turn them into key chains.

The easy option for the company was to say nothing to the outside world but work out a set of mask changes that would fix the bug. Intel already had a standard "stepping" process, in which new chip designs went through a succession of changes and "shrinks" to re-move errors, reduce the chip size, or cut its manufacturing cost. The floating-point bug could be easily removed in the next stepping, and doing this would allow the problem to be solved unobtrusively with-out doing anything to harm the new chip's image in the market.

What made this option more attractive was that it was already standard practice in the chip industry. Insiders knew that no chip was ever perfect the first time around—that like a new car model with a sticky window or ill-fitting door panel, it would always take a few months to iron out the bugs. Those who were bothered by such small defects should wait until a new product was established before taking out their credit cards. Coincidentally, Intel's tiny rival, Cyrix, had just experienced precisely this problem with one of its 486 chips. A reporter at *Windows* magazine had discovered a bug in the floating-point Cyrix 486DX, but the Texas company flatly refused either to replace any of the few thousand chips containing the bug or to notify customers of its existence. Instead, it had just corrected the bug in the next revision of the chip design and continued with business as usual.

But Cyrix wasn't Intel. Cyrix hadn't spend nearly $100 million the previous year advertising its chip. Cyrix wasn't running a corporate marketing campaign to persuade consumers all over the world that buying a computer containing one of its chips was a solid guarantee of quality and reliability. And Cyrix wasn't trying to transform itself from a component company selling primarily to engineers into a global consumer brand. Intel, by contrast, was doing all of these things. It was not only advertisements that carried the Intel Inside logo, but also computers themselves, packaging materials, and even— in an inspired piece of marketing for the world's most populous market—bicycle reflectors in China. In many respects, Intel was trying to change the rules of the game. Could the company continue to play by the old rules in others?

Six months later, Andy Grove would discover, personally, that the answer to this question was a firm no. But in summer 1994, he and his colleagues still looked at the world from an engineering rather than a marketing point of view. Branding, image, consumer psychology— all the factors that argued for taking a short-term cost in order to maintain the value of the Intel name in customers' minds were just beginning to appear on the Intel horizon. The disciplines that had been central to Intel's past successes—technology, measurement, estimating failure probabilities, cost-benefit analysis on process changes—all these argued in favor of secrecy. So the decision was taken, inside the task force, to keep the bug secret.

40

The 10X Force

Six days after his call to Intel's tech support line, Professor Thomas Nicely gave up waiting for someone to call him back. Instead, he started sending E-mails to fellow mathematicians in other institutions, alerting them to the problem he had detected and asking whether they could reproduce it. Someone posted his message on the Internet, in a news group called "comp.sys.intel" that serves as an electronic hangout for processor freaks, technical people, and Intel customers. Within a week, over a hundred people had tried out Nicely's calculation on their Pentium computers—and had also discovered that their own copy of the much-vaunted new chip couldn't divide properly.

As the volume of postings grew, Intel gave in and shipped a couple of new Pentiums to Nicely. But now the genie was out of the bottle; being nice to the guy holding the cork wasn't going to get it back in. A rising chorus on comp.sys.intel was demanding to know what the company proposed to do about this flaw in its top-of-the-line processor, whether it had known of the problem beforehand, and if so why it had kept quiet about it. On November 7, *Electrical Engineering Times* ran a front-page story on the bug, quoting Intel as saying that the problem had been discovered "in the summer" but corrected in a routine upgrade of the chip's production process. An Intel spokesman said that the company would replace chips for the tiny minority of people whose work would be affected by the very slight inaccuracies caused by the bug.

The people on comp.sys.intel hooted with laughter at the company's arrogance when they heard this. They began posting jokes about the company—so much so that a new Usenet group was set up, called alt.jokes.pentium.

Q. Have you heard about Intel's new salary plan for its workers?
A. You can pick up your paycheck every other Friday, but only if you can prove you really NEED it.

Q. Why didn't Intel call the Pentium the 586?
A. Because they added 486 and 100 on the first Pentium and got 585.99999.

Q. What does Pentium stand for?
A. Perfect Enough for Nine out of Ten Instructors at the University of Montana. Or: Practically Everyone Now Thinks It's Useless for Math.

Seen on the tee-shirt of an in-line skater in Mountain View: *I asked for a refund on my Pentium, and all I got was this lousy T-shirt.*

And, best of all:

An Intel Pentium engineer goes into a bar and orders a drink. The bartender serves him and says, "That'll be five dollars." The engineer slaps a five-dollar bill on the counter and says, "Keep the change!"

Unfortunately, not all the comments on comp.sys.intel were so lighthearted. Many people were genuinely outraged that the company should acknowledge that its product was flawed (Intel refused to use the word *bug*) but refuse to provide a perfect version except for a minority of customers. Hell, the people who bought Pentium computers to play games on at home had paid the same price as the mathematicians; why did they have any less right to a working chip? And who was Intel to tell them that they didn't need accurate math? People began to post details of what happened when they called the Intel help line. They described horror stories of long waits; aggressive and overbearing engineers at the other end; long interrogations of innocent customers as if it was they who were in the wrong; and failures to call back or respond within agreed deadlines. They also reported that Intel was demanding a credit-card number from people who called in for a replacement Pentium to guarantee payment in case they failed to send in the old one.

It was a classic big-company story. Problem surfaces with product; maker keeps problem secret; outsider uncovers problem; maker insists problem is unimportant; maker grudgingly agrees to compensate losers; maker's internal bureaucracy makes customers have to run a gauntlet to get fair treatment. It was Tylenol, Perrier, whatever you liked, all over again.

The inevitable happened on November 22, 1994, the Tuesday before Thanksgiving. The number of daily postings on comp.sys.intel had begun to fall and the company firefighters thought the problem was at last about to go away. Andy Grove was at the Stanford University Graduate School of Business where he taught a regular class, going through the roster with a Stanford professor to grade the performance of the MBA students who had been present.

"The process was taking a little longer than usual," Grove recalled, "and I was about to excuse myself to call my office when the phone rang. It was my office calling me. Our head of communications wanted to talk to me—urgently. She wanted to let me know that a CNN crew was coming to Intel. They had heard of the floating-point flaw in the Pentium processor and the story was about to blow up."

The report aired that evening.

JAN HOPKINS, ANCHOR: Intel's stock finishing the day down one and three eighths to sixty-four and three quarters. The company telling CNN Business News today that its state-of-the-art Pentium chip has a bug in it. For the first time, Intel acknowledged that it's known about the defect since last summer. Steve Young has been covering the story. Steve, if Intel's known for months, what about its customers?

STEVE YOUNG, SENIOR BUSINESS NEWS CORRESPONDENT: Well, Jan, word began spreading about two weeks ago among high-end Pentium users. Intel says its typical customers will never notice the problem, but a growing number of Intel customers are upset by the way Intel is handling the situation. Intel acknowledges its Pentium microprocessors have contained a subtle mistake ever since the chip was shipped in March 1993. The Pentium defect, in rare cases, can cause sophisticated mathematical calculations to go wrong. Intel says it found the problem earlier this summer and removed it, starting about two months ago. That means the bug is in at least two million chips. But Intel says the typical user will run into the problem once in 27,000 years, barely a speck in the solar system.

STEPHEN SMITH, PENTIUM ENGINEERING MANAGER, INTEL: If you measure the distance from the earth to the sun, the one part is on the order of feet, a few feet of difference relative to the measured distance between the earth and the sun.

YOUNG: Intel says it's had just a single complaint, but CNN Business News has spoken with a dozen Pentium customers, from scientists to government, who say they've lost confidence, and there are hundreds of worried messages on the Internet—one posted by a software company, Mathworks in Nadick, Massachusetts, which sells math-intensive software used to design cars, aircraft, even parts for PCs themselves.

CLEVE MOLAR, CHAIRMAN AND CHIEF SCIENTIST, MATHWORKS: The concern I have is just the reliability of the results. I'd like to compare it with a dead battery in a smoke detector at home. Chances are your smoke detector is never going to go off, but you sure want to know that it's working.

YOUNG: Intel is issuing no Pentium recall. It says if a worried customer wants a replacement chip, Intel will decide if the customer really needs one. The Jet Propulsion Laboratory in Pasadena, California, which runs unmanned spacecraft missions, is discussing whether to continue relying on Pentium PCs after complaints from staff scientists. Intel has spent tens of millions of dollars on its brand loyalty campaign. It faces PR problems now on the Internet and in trade magazines, which could spill into the mainstream. The episode may undermine Intel's ability to position Pentium as its first chip suitable for scientific workstations, but it's being widely adopted in the much bigger consumer market, for multimedia machines—and there, the bug is a non-issue. Jan?

The story was correct in every detail except one: In claiming that Intel had acknowledged "for the first time" that it had known about the bug since the summer, CNN was trying to make its story seem a bit more up-to-the-minute. In fact Intel had given that information to the trade press several weeks earlier. But this was a forgivable journalistic foible. Otherwise, the channel conveyed all the key points of the issue fairly. It pointed out the rarity of the bug, and the fact that it wouldn't affect most users—and it had focused, correctly, on the greater importance in the market of perception than reality and on the loss of confidence that discovery of the bug had provoked among the specialist scientists who were a tiny minority of users. And the story's key prediction—that Intel's PR problems "may spill into the mainstream"—proved self-fulfilling. Within two days, the *New York Times*, *Wall Street Journal*, and *Boston Globe* had all run long stories that treated the issue responsibly and put it into context. Within another week, David Letterman had included a Pentium joke in his monolog.

At the technical support center in Folsom, the lights on the phones began blinking minutes after the CNN broadcast. A day later, the center was working to capacity. Its daily volume had shot up from 1,500 incoming calls to nearly 7,000—and the result of the flood of angry customers was to block incoming and outgoing calls from the entire Folsom facility.

Now, surely, the time had come for Andy Grove to change his mind. If only Intel would give up the "qualification process" and state that anyone who wanted a replacement Pentium would get one, then most of the anger on comp.sys.intel would subside and the media would lose interest in the story. But Grove and his colleagues, now meeting daily in conference room 528, twenty feet from the CEO's cubicle, could not bring themselves to take a step which they knew made no sense at all in engineering terms: to replace, free of charge, tens of thousands of chips for customers whose work would hardly be affected. The policy became to brazen it out: to keep repeating, as often as possible and with support from as many PC companies and other chipmakers as possible, that every processor had a few tiny flaws, and that this one didn't matter.

Although Intel's stock dipped 2 percent the day after the *Wall Street Journal* story hit the streets, and other newspapers across the world followed suit in reporting the flaw, the policy looked for a while as though it might work.

"Users started to call us asking for replacement chips," recalled Grove in *Only the Paranoid Survive*. "People whose use pattern suggested that they might do a lot of divisions got their chips replaced. Other users we tried to reassure by walking them through our studies and our analyses, offering to send them a white paper that we wrote on this subject. After the first week or so, this dual approach seemed to be working reasonably well. The daily call volumes were decreasing, we were gearing up to refine our replacement procedures, and, although the press was still pillorying us, all tangible indicators—from computer sales to replacement requests—showed that we were managing to work our way through this problem.

"Then came Monday, December 12. I walked into my office at eight o'clock that morning and in the little clip where my assistant leaves phone messages, there was a folded computer printout. It was a wire service report. And as so often happens with breaking news it consisted only of the title. It said something to this effect: IBM stops shipments of all Pentium-based computers. . . . The phones started ringing furiously from all quarters. The call volume to our hotline skyrocketed. Our other customers wanted to know what was going on. And their tone, which had been quite constructive the week before, became confused and anxious. We were back on the defensive in a major way."

IBM's intervention in the Pentium affair was not an example of the company on its finest behavior. A decision had been taken that IBM should no longer pursue the policy of protecting Intel for its own sake. Instead, its first loyalty should be to its customers—which required taking a thoroughly conservative view of the Pentium bug until it was absolutely clear how extensively it would affect computer use. Relying on some rough estimates of computer usage provided by a writer from a trade magazine, and on some analysis of whether numbers in spreadsheets tend to be randomly distributed or not, IBM suggested that in fact some mainstream users might find that the Pentium would cause errors in their spreadsheets more often than once a month. The company therefore announced that it would stop shipping Pentiums to its customers until the matter was resolved, unless customers specifically said they wanted a Pentium computer, bug and all.

In the event, the IBM analysis was quite wrong. It was based on the assumption that the chip would carry out 5,000 divides a second when recalculating spreadsheets, and that a spreadsheet user might spend fifteen minutes a day on recalculations—resulting in 4.2 million divides each day. But these numbers ignored the fact that most of the divides would simply be recalculations based on the same spreadsheet numbers. To recalculate 4.2 million divides, the spreadsheet would need to have hundreds of thousands of new numbers typed into it every day—something that almost never happened on the average desktop PC.

"IBM's ban on Pentium sales has little technical merit," argued the editor of *Microprocessor Report*, a leading industry newsletter, two weeks later. "If errors were as probable as IBM claims, many more users would have noticed the problem; in fact, Intel probably would have caught the bug in prerelease testing. . . . The ban appears to be a marketing ploy to make IBM look good and kick Intel when it's down. Although IBM is a major Intel customer, it markets X86 and PowerPC processors that compete directly with Intel's chips. Few users are likely to switch from a Pentium to an IBM processor today, but it is in IBM's long-term interest to sully both Intel and the Pentium brand name."

Intel had partly itself to blame. Its Intel Inside campaign, and its efforts to market the Pentium as a brand in its own right were a direct attack on the brands of the PC industry that Intel had known from the outset would cause anger inside not only IBM but also Compaq, Dell, and other companies. Compaq was the only firm that had so far allowed its enmity to become visible in public—partly because the PC makers who were most hurt by the new marketing policies were also such big customers that they could not afford to offend Intel for fear of jeopardizing their supply of processors. It was no surprise that IBM, having bided its time, should look for a chance to strike. Grove was spitting mad with IBM. But now was not the time to vent his anger. Intel was now facing a full-fledged crisis.

On Monday, December 19, 1994, Intel's directors held an emergency board meeting by telephone and decided to reverse the old policy. From now on, the company would replace Pentium processors for any customer who wanted an exchange—"whether they were doing statistical analysis or playing computer games," as Andy Grove put it. They agreed to announce the decision after the markets had closed that evening, and to schedule a conference call for stock analysts early the next morning. Intel would take a charge of $475 million—just over half the company's income for the quarter—to cover the cost.

Andy Grove made sure not to repeat the disastrously slow execution of the withdrawal from the DRAM business, where the company's belated recognition that it was going in the wrong direction was compounded by wasting a further year between the decision to change course and the change itself. The press release was put out at 5:00 A.M. Pacific standard time the next morning; by six, 415 financial analysts and editors were hooked up to the conference call. Within a couple of hours of the market's opening in New York, the stock price had begun to recover and things began to return to normal.

But the work had only just begun. The night before the announcement was made, the largest conference room at Intel's Folsom site was filled with hastily assembled tables and chairs, plus 135 new phones and several miles of tape.

"By 2:00 A.M., we had the phones installed, tested, connected and taped," recalled Ken Hendren, the application support manager at Folsom. "By 3:30 A.M., AT&T had flown T1 lines from San Diego. . . . At 6:30 A.M., our first crew of volunteers came in. Since we hadn't had time to set up computers, we supplied them with paper, pencil and scripts." The plan was that every employee on the site would come in to work on telephone support for a two-hour slot, preceded by half an hour of training. The phones went live at 7:30 A.M. "We had twenty-six thousand calls that first day. . . . The average hold time was less than five seconds. We lost only seventy-nine callers that day; the first forty-nine we lost during our first half-hour, when we were still working out the phone system. The longest hold for a lost caller was only seventy-six seconds." Within a few days, the volume began to fall—first to twenty thousand and then to seventeen thousand—and the company had time to hire agency workers to handle the phones.

Over the succeeding months, it became clear that the decision to capitulate and offer the lifetime replacement guarantee had marked a turning point. Although the Pentium jokes on the Internet continued to proliferate, the bad publicity in print and on TV ceased almost immediately. Analysts suggested that the figure of $475 million was based on scrapping 500,000 Pentiums from inventory, and another 1.5 million returns from the field—raising the possibility that Intel would be able to benefit later on if it turned out that the actual number of chips returned was fewer than the 30 percent of the installed base that this figure implied.

The crisis also strikingly demonstrated Intel's financial strength compared with the rest of the manufacturers serving the market. Of all microprocessor vendors, it was the only one that could remotely afford to pay for an error in a product that had shipped to the mass market on this scale. The guarantee that Intel eventually came up with—grudgingly, belatedly, and against its better judgment—was the strongest proof it could give that there was meaning behind the phrase "Intel Inside." That proof might easily have been given at one tenth of the cost or even less, if only Andy Grove had been willing to change his mind a few weeks earlier. But the point was made all the same.

Intel also learned a lesson from the Pentium that had been self-evident to analysts of the industry for some years. The practice of keeping bugs secret and revealing their existence only to a handful of large and particularly valued customers was self-defeating. It clearly made more sense to put all the information in the public domain and allow customers and software houses to decide which were important enough to worry about. So early in 1995, Intel published, for the first time ever, a full list of the known bugs in one of its key processors. The errata list showed that the floating-point divide problem was just one of dozens of bugs present in the millions of Pentiums shipped during 1993 and 1994. Publishing the list helped Intel in two ways: It raised the pressure on the competition, notably Motorola and AMD, to publish their own bug lists; and it provided a constant, low-key reminder to computer users that a microprocessor without any bugs at all was not a realistic thing to expect. But one aspect of the decision revealed that Intel still had some distance to go in realizing that the customer who mattered most was the final consumer, not the computer company. The circulation plan for the errata list involved sending it out to system makers and software houses thirty days before end-users had their first access to it.

EPILOGUE

Winning the Platform Wars

Even after getting the Pentium chip back on track, Andy Grove and his colleagues knew that 1995 was set to be a difficult year. Not only was Jerry Sanders promising an AMD competitor to the Pentium for 1995; also, the long-running concern was returning that another microprocessor using an entirely different architecture from Intel's x86 might sweep the market. The alliance of IBM, Motorola, and Apple had led to the creation of the PowerPC 601, a chip that offered Pentium-class performance at half of Intel prices. With Motorola's proven expertise in chip fabrication, IBM's marketing clout in the PC industry, and Apple's reputation for elegant design and ease of use, the PowerPC consortium was a more serious competitor to Intel than all the other vendors of reduced instruction set computing (RISC) chips combined.

But the 601's potential was never realized. When the PowerPC consortium tried to build a new chip offering 60 percent better performance than the Pentium, known as the PowerPC 604, its efforts began to unravel. The new chip was plagued with bugs—ironic, given the bruising experience that Intel had suffered in 1994. By the time it was finally shipped, the 604 delivered only a 15 percent performance improvement over Pentium chips of the same clock speed.

The PowerPC threat was reduced still further by Apple's inability to come to terms with the realities of the PC market. The Cupertino-based company had recognized that its refusal to allow other manufacturers to build Mac-compatible hardware had made its own computers more expensive than comparable PCs. But the company's top management could not bring itself to accept what most commentators believed was the only way to remedy the problem: an aggressive licensing program, allowing any hardware maker in the world to build Mac-compatible equipment. Instead, Apple tried to have it both ways. After agonizing soul-searching, it did license its intellectual property; but the only companies it would do business with were a handful of small makers that posed no threat to the preeminence of its own manufacturing operations. Apple's customers remained as loyal as ever, particularly in publishing and graphic design. But it was becoming clear that the company would never break out of its 10 percent market share ghetto. The lion's share of the market was left to Intel and Microsoft.

Meanwhile, great things were happening at Intel. The excitement over RISC in the late 1980s and early 1990s had shaken the company to its roots. With a chorus of outsiders telling them that their own CISC architecture was doomed to fall behind RISC as chips grew more advanced, the Intel engineering teams had begun to feel vulnerable for the first time since the fat days of the 386. To increase the sense of urgency, Andy Grove had reinstated the Late List in 1994, tightened up the company's policy on telecommuting and flexible working hours, and instituted a "back to basics" campaign to focus the minds of Intel people on the issue.

The fruit of these initiatives ripened in 1995. The company introduced a new manufacturing process, which reduced the gate length of its chips (a measure of miniaturization) to only 0.35 microns, or millionths of a meter. This gave Intel a double advantage. By shrinking a chip's layout to smaller size, Intel's designers reduced the distance that electrons had to travel as they made their way around the circuits. This increased the speed of the device, allowing it to crunch numbers faster once it was inside a PC. Other things being equal, the new device was also cheaper to manufacture: you got more chips off a wafer of fixed size if the chips were smaller, and also higher yields for a given number of defects per wafer. In the course of 1995, Intel was able to cut the prices of its existing Pentium product lines repeatedly, and also to crank up the clock speeds of the highest-specification parts from 100 MHz to 120MHz and then 133MHz. Not content with introducing a new process, cutting prices, and bringing out new variants of the Pentium, Intel also began shipping the successor to the Pentium chip: the device originally known as the P6 but introduced to the market as the Pentium Pro. (By 1995, Intel had invested too much money in the Pentium name just to throw it away; adding the suffix "Pro" told customers this was a more expensive, "professional" chip than the Pentium.) The new device, whose development had begun long before the Pentium design was complete, took the transistor count on a single Intel chip above five million for the first time. It was positioned as a high-end product intended to go inside power servers and engineering workstations, and priced to deliver the fat 80-percent-plus margins that were by now traditional for newly introduced Intel technology. The most startling achievement of the Pentium Pro was to steal from the RISC processors the crown of fastest chip in the world. As evidence of its success, Intel signed up Data General, the minicomputer company that was considered a strategic account by most RISC vendors, to the Pentium Pro architecture.

The launch of the Pentium Pro signed the commercial death warrant of RISC technology in the mainstream PC market. Although Intel's new chip was soon superseded by a faster RISC device in the raw performance stakes, it was clear by the end of 1995 that RISC had failed to deliver enough of a performance edge to get most computer users to look seriously at moving away from the x86 architecture. The same advantages that had brought Intel victory in the battle with Motorola more than a decade earlier were once again in play. The gigantic installed base of software for the x86, and Intel's proven ability to deliver products on time with consistent cuts in price and improvements in performance, simply made the x86 architecture compelling for PC manufacturers. And the economies achieved by cutthroat competition between a thousand makers to produce an Intel-powered box at the lowest possible price made it impossible for RISC vendors to compete. One study carried out by a former RISC architect from AMD, who was one of the last people one could accuse of prejudice in Intel's favor, made the point succinctly: "What is so disappointing to me is not only are RISC boxes not cheaper, but they do not, in general, deliver higher performance than comparable x86 machines." The result was that RISC machines remained in the market, but were unable to break out of a high-priced, small-volume niche.

An even more striking symptom of Intel's success could be seen outside the computer industry. One industry analyst was astounded to discover how many engineers using microprocessors in other applications, ranging from vacuum cleaners to mobile phones and cars, were buying Intel chips. These engineers weren't running DOS or

Windows software, so they were free to choose any other architecture they wanted. Didn't they know that Intel's "ownership" of the x86 standard meant that its chips cost considerably more than devices offering comparable performance from other vendors? The answers boiled down to one thing. Of course it cost more to buy an Intel x86 chip, and the higher cost couldn't be justified in pure engineering terms. But chips themselves were only a small part of the cost of developing a new product. Skilled labor was more significant. And while it might be hard to find developers specializing in a rare RISC chip, you couldn't swing a cat in Silicon Valley without hitting someone who knew how to program an x86. There were also scores of free or cheap technical tools available for the x86 world that were expensive or unobtainable for other devices. Taking everything together, Intel had made sure that opting for x86 rather than a superior competing technology saved the customer money in the long run.

Meanwhile, Intel's x86 competitors had a miserable year. Although AMD managed to ship well over 9 million processors in 1995, the vast majority of them were 486-class devices. The company's K5 chip, originally expected for summer 1995, was postponed after the company found it impossible to meet its public goal of offering 30 percent better performance than the Pentium at the same clock rates. Difficulties with its P6-killer, known as the K6, prompted AMD to buy NexGen, a start-up that had been working for years on an advanced design to compete with the Pentium Pro. NexGen had the distinction of actually having shipped a Pentium-class chip in 1995, but had not achieved significant sales because its "pinout"—the layout of metal pins connecting the chip to the PC's motherboard—was unique, requiring customers to redesign their computers if they wanted to buy a NexGen chip. Cyrix, the Texas-based x86 chip company, had its own 5x86 and 6x86 designs, but sales were constrained by a shortage of fab capacity. By comparison with Intel's flawless execution and the billions that it was able to invest in new plant and R&D, its clones were floundering and under financial pressure.

But Intel itself was changing. After the company's years of focus on keeping interlopers away from its x86 monopoly, the recognition was beginning to permeate through the company that the key to its future growth would lie less in pushing its x86 competitors further and further into their corners than in increasing the growth rate of the entire computer market.

In January 1995, Intel suddenly announced a resolution to its long-running battle with AMD. The two sparring chipmakers agreed to drop all pending cases against each other, and promised not to start any new lawsuits based on anything that had happened up to the signing of the agreement. They agreed to exchange a new patent cross-license to replace one originally signed in 1976, and they settled the various disputes between them that were still working their way through the courts.

The question that excited the Silicon Valley press was which company had blinked. Analysts looked for answers in the financial settlement attached to the deal—in which Intel paid AMD $18 million as required by the arbitrator in the old 386 case, while AMD paid Intel $58 million in damages for infringing its patents on an in-circuit emulator used in the 486 chip. But the checks were not what was most important. Fighting Intel in the courts was costing AMD nearly $40 million a year, and had taken up an alarming proportion of its top management time. In one crucial case, Jerry Sanders had spent all day in the courtroom in an attempt to convey to the jury how much he cared about the outcome. The settlement allowed the company to return to business as usual.

For Intel, the settlement was a tacit admission that its strategy of legal harassment, while useful from month to month in keeping competitors at bay, wasn't working in the long term. The in-circuit emulator issue was Intel's most prominent victory against AMD; in almost all the other cases, its ingenious and expensively prepared arguments had been found by judges and juries to be unconvincing. The latest rebuff to Tom Dunlap and his document factory came only a few days before the AMD settlement, when the California Supreme Court restored an arbitrator's ruling favorable to AMD, overturning a lower court judgment won by Intel that the arbitrator had overstepped his powers. So the decision to make peace with AMD was well timed.

The striking thing about the settlement was that Andy Grove and Jerry Sanders had not been part of it. So embittered had the personal rivalry between the two men become that the general counsels of the two companies who took the first steps toward reconciliation decided that they would have a better chance of achieving a compromise if they kept the two chief executives away from the negotiations, and instead went one rung down the latter to the chief operating officer level. When the deal was done and publicized, Jerry Sanders expressed his willingness to shake hands with his old enemy and let bygones be bygones. Journalists asked Andy Grove for his response; he refused to comment.

This settlement wasn't the only sign that Intel now took a broader view of its mission. Intel's architecture lab, employing hundreds of talented scientists to work on technologies that would make the PC more attractive as a product, had grown to become the biggest PC research and development center in the world—evidence that Intel now saw itself as a leader whose job was to lead the computer industry toward its destiny. Few of the technologies that came out of the lab turned into products that made money for Intel, but that wasn't what mattered. If the lab's work could help the industry as a whole to create new hardware and software that encouraged consumers to upgrade their machines, then Intel's objectives were still satisfied. The most startling case in point was the lab's work on videoconferencing and Internet's telephony. Intel's ProShare videoconferencing system never became a big money-earner for the company; its Internet Phone product, never even intended to be commercial, was actually given away on the company web site. But both products fed the demand for high-specification processors, and made the PC a more attractive product in general.

Relations with Microsoft were dramatically affected by this change of emphasis. In 1996, Bill Gates explained that "there's been more time spent on Intel–Microsoft collaboration in the last couple of years than in the preceding decade put together." But the road to détente had not been smooth. During the 1980s, the quick tempers of Gates and Andy Grove had often exacerbated, rather than smoothed, tensions between the two companies. When Grove invited Gates to his house for dinner in an attempt to cool things down, tempers ran so high that the food lay uneaten on the table in front of Gates, and the caterers rushed into the room from the kitchen to find out what all the shouting was about.

To avoid the recurrence of such problems, the companies set up an informal system a little like the high-level summits that take place between heads of state. Formal Grove–Gates meetings would be scheduled quarterly—though the two men's calendars rarely coincided more often than twice or three times a year—and executives from the two companies would meet, like political "sherpas," to negotiate the agenda of the meeting beforehand in painstaking detail.

Part of the reason for the new cordiality was that Intel made it clear to Microsoft for the first time that it was willing to assume a subordinate role in the relationship. Evidence of this could be seen in Intel's attempts to develop a new standard for "native signal processing." NSP allowed much of the manipulation of audio and video traditionally carried out on specialized chips on the computer's motherboard to be built into the microprocessor itself.

In principle, NSP was in both companies' interests: Intel wanted to absorb more of the value-added of each computer into its microprocessors, and Microsoft wanted there to be a standard platform that made multimedia applications easier to develop and faster to run. But Intel made a mistake. Just as Microsoft was gearing up for the launch of Windows 95, the graphic operating system that belatedly caught up most of the remaining advantages of the Apple Macintosh, Intel began to take its new technical standards and protocols around to hardware manufacturers, trying to persuade them to commit to designing for NSP in the future. The problem was that the NSP technology Intel had developed didn't slot into DOS or Windows. It stood alone, and by doing so, it appeared to challenge Microsoft's hegemony over software standards.

The response from Redmond was swift and vicious. Without saying anything to Intel, Microsoft warned the PC manufacturers that it had no intention of supporting NSP in future releases of Windows, effectively forcing them to sacrifice 100 percent compatibility with Microsoft's standards if they went along with Intel's initiative. Realizing that he faced an unwinnable battle, Andy Grove blinked. Intel repackaged NSP so that it was less threatening to Microsoft, and the two companies suddenly began to find it easy to talk to one another.

When *Fortune* magazine got the two leaders together for a double interview, they put a careful gloss on this incident. "I admit we were dumb enough not to understand that the software we had developed was actually contrary to some of the features of Windows 95," said Grove. "And hence came all that crap." Gates suggested that it was only at a summer 1995 dinner with Grove in San Jose that he'd understood what was going on. "For the first time, really, I was able to articulate the problem. I was able to say, 'Look, we don't disagree with your guys. We think they're smart. But this stuff does not work well with Windows 95.' So we said, 'Given that we agree on goals, can we share in the development of things?' "

In short, the two men positioned the dispute in public as a misunderstanding over technology, not a struggle for power in the industry. Yet somehow, it seems hard to believe that Intel could have developed NSP and taken it on the road without realizing what compatibility issues its technology raised with Microsoft's software. A more likely interpretation is that Intel knew exactly what it was doing when it began to evangelize NSP; its change of approach later was a tactical withdrawal, not the clarification of a misunderstanding. Whatever the cause, Grove at least was frank about Intel's response to the Microsoft attack. "We didn't have much of a choice. We basically caved," he admitted.

There is still tension in the relationship. Microsoft's launch of Windows CE, a stripped-down version of its operating system for handheld portable devices like personal digital assistants (PDAs) is another irritation at Intel. If the handheld market takes off, then Microsoft will for the first time have an operating system that runs on a number of different processor architectures, none of which is controlled by Intel. So far, it has not had much impact, but Intel is watching developments carefully. CE apart, the two companies are probably on better terms now than ever before. With a succession of small announcements, they have revealed that their technical teams have not only given up working against one another; they're actually cooperating.

In November 1996, Andy Grove delivered a keynote speech at Comdex, the computer industry's leading trade show. His speech—more of an all-singing, all-dancing multimedia presentation than a mere speech—combined a celebration of the quarter century that had passed since the launch of Intel's first microprocessor with a set of predictions of where Grove believed computer technology was heading.

With TV-quality video and movie-theater sound, the presentation was a powerful illustration of how far the technology had progressed since the days of the 4004. More interestingly, it illustrated the distance that Grove himself had traveled. Gone were the thick glasses, gold chains, and Art Garfunkel hairstyle of his 1970s persona. In their place was the 1996-vintage Andy Grove: clipped, tanned, mountain-bike-lean, and with an accent that was more a reminder of an exotic past than a barrier to comprehension. Speaking without any sign of an autocue, Grove delivered his pitch with high speed and fluency. The presentation was designed like a segment from a chat show: it included movie clips, a conversation with a "special guest" from Starbucks Coffee Company on a set gussied up to look like the café of the future, and a computer demo with a technology marketing guy from Intel who had a ponytail.

Andy Grove had arrived. No longer was he the earnest, socially inept physicist who knew exactly how to get a semiconductor fab working smoothly but was at a loss when his secretary burst into tears. Now he was a celebrity—celebrated on the covers of business magazines, adored by the Intel shareholders to whom he had delivered 40 percent annual returns over his decade at the company's helm, and rich beyond most people's dreams. It was true that Gordon Moore, with the benefit of a large stake in Intel from the company's inception, was worth twenty times what Andy Grove was. But his Intel stock options allowed Grove to clear nearly $95 million in 1996 alone. By most people's standards, that was rich. Sweetest of all, Grove was now out of the shadow of Intel's two founders. There had never been rivalry or tension with Gordon Moore. But it was nice, after years of being the back-office guy who did all the unpleasant jobs while Bob Noyce basked in the sun, to be so widely recognized as the principal architect of Intel's glory.

There were drawbacks to being a public figure. When Terry Gross of National Public Radio's Fresh Air invited Grove on to her program to discuss what he'd said about management in his new book *Only the Paranoid Survive*, the Intel CEO found himself being asked about his family background—and hated it.

GROSS: You grew up in World War II, and I'm wondering how your family was affected.
(Pause)
GROSS [again]: Are you Jewish?
GROVE: Unn-hmm. Yes.
GROSS: Did you have to hide during the war?
GROVE: Unn-hmm. Yes.
GROSS: Was your whole family successful in hiding, or did you have family that was unsuccessful?
GROVE: Well, I don't want to get into the details of it. But some of my family survived and others didn't.
GROSS: You were one of the people who—after managing to survive the Nazis, then Stalin invaded Hungary—you were stuck with communism.
(Pause)
GROVE: Unn-hmm.

But fame had its little pleasures, too. When *Fortune* magazine discovered in 1996 that Grove had recently been treated for prostate cancer, it invited him to write a blow-by-blow account of how he discovered the existence of the tumor, tracked down the latest academic papers and the greatest experts on the subject, and then took control of his own treatment. In an article headed "Our Reluctant Author Comes Forward," which accompanied Grove's seven-thousand-word opus, the managing editor wrote: "We at *Fortune* are honored that he selected our magazine as the forum for his findings."

To be fair, the transformation from statistician and detail merchant to media star and high-tech visionary was incomplete. During his Comdex presentation, the Intel CEO looked uncomfortable amidst the glitz. His delivery was oddly flat—almost as if a slightly cocky lighting engineer had been asked to take over from David Letterman for the evening. But Andy Grove was clearly learning, just as he always had. It wouldn't take him too long to pick up the skills needed for his new role.

At the height of the Pentium incident, it had been hard to imagine Intel without Grove—or Grove without Intel. After the Comdex speech, the world began to look different. Grove, now sixty, succeeded Gordon Moore as Intel's chairman in May 1997, handing over the presidency of the company to Craig Barrett. In the press release announcing the change, Grove was quoted as saying: "Craig is the guy who keeps the Intel machine running. He is the architect of our manufacturing system, and the principal driver behind our management methods and culture." Significantly, however, Grove retained the title of CEO. But the day was clearly drawing closer when he could retire from Intel and devote himself to skiing, teaching his business school students at Stanford, riding his mountain bike, and spending time with his friends and family in carefully programmed one-on-ones.

Inside St. Paul's Cathedral in London lies the tomb of Sir Christopher Wren, the man who built not only the cathedral itself but also much of the rest of the London skyline after the Great Fire of 1666. Instead of trying to compete with the spectacular sculptures on other tombs nearby, those who were responsible for commemorating Wren, the greatest English architect of the seventeenth century, chose a simple tombstone. On the stone is carved the Latin motto *si monumentum requiris, circumspice*—"If you seek a monument, look around you."

Andy Grove is in a similar situation. The legacy that he leaves behind him is visible throughout the world, in hundreds of millions of personal computers powered by Intel processors. Intel may be second to Microsoft in its power in the industry, but it is considerably more profitable and more profitable than all its customers put together. As well as delivering spectacular returns to shareholders, Intel has also done well by its employees. The company does not publish figures of how many millionaires it has created, but the doubling of the Intel stock price that began in mid-1996 has meant that scores of middle managers inside the company, and possibly hundreds, have made more than enough money to retire on. The decision to extend the company's stock option scheme to all its employees in 1997 came after a spectacular year in which Intel paid out profit-sharing and retirement contributions of $820 million to its staff.

Not all Intel employees could stand the pace. In March 1997, the company's long-standing policy of trying to weed out the least productive 10 percent of its workforce by means of ranking and rating and corrective action plans produced an unprecedented public backlash. A group of disgruntled Intel people based in Folsom, California, formed a lobby group called FACE Intel (Former and Current Employees of). They published a web site providing details of the numerous pending unfair dismissal lawsuits against the company from its employees, and quoting an unfortunate comment by Craig Barrett that "the half-life of an engineer is only a few years." The web site alleged that the company's continuous weeding policy provoked stress and made Intel an unpleasant place to work, and offered support and information to employees who wanted to sue the company. Intel responded by blocking access to the site from computers on its sites.

The rigor of Intel's approach to human resources is only one of Grove's legacies. Another symptom of his thoroughness is the seasoned top management team he will leave behind on his retirement, with a solid corporate culture and rigorous processes in place to ensure that the machine continues to move forward after his departure. With over 80 percent of the market for microprocessors in desktop computers, Intel is also overwhelmingly dominant in the sector in which it operates.

How much of its success the company has given back to the community is a different question. Like a prosperous entrepreneur who retires to a country estate to do good works, Intel has over recent years sharply increased the scale—and the publicizing—of its corporate donation program. In 1996, the company was able to claim gifts of some $55 million to the community. The list included some glittering projects: support for the 150th anniversary of the Smithsonian Institution, including a traveling exhibit on the history of the personal computer; donations of computer laboratories to Irish universities; and programs to facilitate the use of technology by Native Americans in Arizona and New Mexico. But closer examination of the numbers revealed that nearly $40 million of the total was equipment, much of it used semiconductor manufacturing machinery from Intel fabs, and a further $6 million was in grants supporting electrical engineering and computer science in universities and colleges. The programs brought the company clear advantages in terms of either reduced taxes or long-term improvement in the availability of skilled workforces. Only $2.5 million of the total budget—about 0.05 percent of Intel's profits for the year—went to nonprofit organizations in the communities where Intel sites were located.

It is hard to assess how generous Intel's founders have been in contributing to society from their own personal fortunes. A foundation in memory of Robert Noyce has been set up by Noyce's second wife, Ann Bowers, and his children; its endowment, according to the last public document made available by the foundation for the researching of this book, was around $100 million—less than one-twentieth of the value of Noyce's Intel stock. Friends of Moore, who spent around $10 million on acquiring a large estate in the San Francisco Bay Area, say that he has established his own charitable trust, which is administered by one of his sons. No public information on the assets of the trust, or the use to which it puts them, is available. By comparison, other Silicon Valley entrepreneurs have been more visibly lavish with gifts from their fortunes. For example, the name of David Packard, one of the founders of Hewlett-Packard, is associated with a hospital in Palo Alto, an innovative aquarium at Monterey Bay, and numerous other projects in the Bay Area.

In December 1996, almost a year after Intel and AMD settled their differences, the two companies signed a new patent license agreement to replace the old agreement expiring on December 31. It was a sign of how far the balance of power between the companies had shifted in Intel's favor that the new agreement, negotiated right up to the line and only announced five days after the old one had expired, ran for just five years compared with the previous agreement's twenty. Even the agreed text of the press release announcing the deal showed a tilt in Intel's favor. Gone was the old Sanders braggadocio about an "alliance of peers"; in its place was a form of words that left no doubt who held the technological whip hand. The release quoted Craig Barrett as describing licensing as "one way of ensuring others respect our intellectual property," and it referred to the "massive investments" Intel made. Sanders's only quoted comment in the release was to say lamely that the deal "ensures that AMD has legal rights to all the enabling intellectual property necessary to continue providing our customers with competitive products that are fully software-compatible with the Intel instruction set."

The agreement had two important exclusions. One was that AMD was forbidden under its terms to use Intel's microcode beyond the 486 generation—meaning that it would have to write its own microcode for all future chip generations, a job that had proven difficult enough in the Pentium generation and would get harder still as processors grew larger and more complex. Given the long history of microcode litigation between the two companies, this was hardly unexpected.

More seriously, AMD was forbidden to "socket steal" beyond the Pentium generation. This meant that even if Sanders's engineers could design processors that were fully compatible with Intel's without breaching any of Intel's patents, AMD was still forbidden to design them so they could be slotted into the sockets in the PC's motherboard that fitted the competing Intel device. So PC manufacturers in future would not be able to make a straight choice between an Intel processor and a cheaper AMD equivalent. Instead, AMD would have to devote more resources to designing chipsets or "daughter boards" of its own, and its customers would face greater inconvenience and greater risk in transferring business away from Intel.

The socket-steal clause in the 1996 agreement was a symptom of a greater change that was taking place in Intel's business. Not content with building a big chipset and motherboard business, the company was moving toward a position in which the majority of all its chips were sold as part of larger modules instead of on their own. This had short-term advantages for Intel: as well as raising the bar for competitors like AMD and Cyrix, the module policy increased the portion of the computer as a whole that came from Intel and allowed the company to take a bigger slice of the industry's profits. In the long term, the policy had even more significant results. By setting the cost and specification of these all-important modules, Intel had a strong influence over price points and configurations for the entire computer industry. Also, the modules reduced the design work that PC manufacturers needed to do, so Intel could now roll out new generations of processors across the industry more swiftly and easily than ever before.

The new agreement did contain a small plum for AMD: it covered an important new technology called multimedia extensions. With the PC increasingly being used to handle video and audio, industry engineers had noticed that dramatic performance improvements could be achieved by adding some new instructions to the standard x86 instruction set. The new instructions could handle audio and video data in bulk, and number-crunch up to eight results in parallel.

Intel engineers came up with fifty-seven new instructions, and some corresponding changes to the microprocessor—including new circuitry and microcode, and an enlarged on-chip cache memory. Contrary to the expectations of the outside world, Intel decided to put this new intellectual property, known as MMX, on the negotiating table instead of forcing AMD to develop its own. "The old Intel surely would have seen [excluding MMX from the deal] as a benefit," wrote Slater in *Microprocessor Report* a month after the 1996 agreement was made public. "The new Intel realizes that, one way or another, AMD and others are going to be there—and as long as they are, having a single instruction-set architecture will benefit software developers and ultimately lead to faster-growth."

But the kinder, gentler Intel was far from becoming a pussycat. In March 1997, just days before AMD was scheduled to launch its new K6 chip against Intel's Pentium Pro, Tom Dunlap's avenging angels struck again. They filed a complaint in federal court in Delaware, accusing AMD and Cyrix of "adopting a strategy designed to leverage off of [sic] Intel's enormous investment in the MMX™ branding and performance message, and to appropriate that investment to themselves." The two companies, Intel complained, "have misled and intend to mislead the public by suggesting that their respective microprocessors have MMX™ media enhancement technology" and had "announced their intention to use Intel's MMX™ trademark to promote their microprocessors, without any acknowledgment that MMX™ is a trademark of Intel." The suit explained that "several months of negotiations" had ended in impasse. "Accordingly, with defendants' infringing products about to be launched, Intel must now seek judicial relief to prevent defendants from misappropriating its valuable MMX™ trademark and misleading and deceiving the consuming public." Intel's complaint comprised seven counts: false designation of origin, false advertising, trademark infringement, trademark dilution, deceptive trade practices, common law trademark infringement, and unfair competition.

At first sight, the lawsuit may seem incomprehensible. Hadn't Intel licensed the MMX extensions to AMD? Yes, it had. But Dunlap's argument was that Intel had not licensed the circuitry and microcode changes to either AMD or Cyrix, nor had it granted the two companies the right to use the acronym MMX to promote their own products. The fact that MMX sounded like an abbreviation for "multimedia extension," Intel contended, was purely a coincidence. The letters belonged to Intel just as much as the phrase "Intel Inside" or the Pentium name. The company had spent heavily on an MMX advertising campaign showing fab operators in colored bunny suits performing gymnastic feats to illustrate how much better an MMX chip was than a standard Pentium, and it wasn't fair that AMD and Cyrix should benefit from its ad dollars. For good measure, Intel also applied for a temporary restraining order from the court, an order that would have prevented AMD and Cyrix from selling their K6 and M2 chips until the issue had been tried before a jury many months later.

The two defendants took different approaches to the lawsuit. Cyrix, the smaller company of the two, settled almost immediately, agreeing to credit Intel with ownership of an MMX trademark. AMD fought back. In a hearing convened at short notice, it pointed out to a federal judge that Intel had not registered the MMX mark, and it produced opinion poll evidence suggesting that in most people's minds, MMX referred to a technology in the computer industry, not to a product from a single company. The judge turned down Intel's request for a restraining order, and the case went forward to trial.

From AMD's point of view, the new lawsuit was strangely reminiscent of the old Intel. It looked like an attempt to reawaken doubt in the minds of PC manufacturers that they might face legal problems if they bought chips from AMD—a move that would have the effect of slowing down the erosion of Intel's market share by the K6 and M2 chips. Looking back to the 1995 settlement, it seemed no wonder that Andy Grove hadn't wanted to shake Jerry Sanders's hand.

"This case is really about advertising and marketing," said Thomas McCoy, AMD's general counsel, "which no doubt explains the timing of Intel's lawsuit, right before AMD's scheduled product launch.

There is no dispute about product intellectual property or technology rights."

To the surprise of many veterans of the microprocessor business, the trademark suit between Intel and AMD was settled quietly a matter of weeks later. The two companies agreed that AMD would accept the validity of Intel's trademark over MMX, while Intel would in return allow AMD the right to use the trademark free of charge.

Meanwhile, however, a new and more dramatic battle had begun. Digital Equipment, the computer maker behind the Alpha chip, which had been such a threat to Intel at the turn of the 1990s, filed a surprise lawsuit against the company in May 1997. The complaint alleged that Intel had "willfully" based key parts of its Pentium and Pentium Pro designs on technologies patented by Digital. According to Robert Palmer, Digital's chairman, his company had offered Intel a license to its Alpha technology in 1990, and shown Intel scientists blueprints from the chips. Intel had rejected the offer.

When Intel's Pentium Pro later hit the market, Digital's engineers were astounded by how well it performed. "It gradually became apparent that there were substantial similarities between Pentium Pro and Alpha," claimed Palmer. The suspicions inside Digital were heightened by a story in the *Wall Street Journal* on Intel's plans to strengthen its R&D. The story had quoted Craig Barrett as saying, "There's nothing left to copy," and Andy Grove as saying, "We can't rely on others to do our research and development for us."

The guts of the Digital case was that Intel had filched three of its most important innovations. One was a cache management technique, which Intel processors used to put frequently used data in a high-speed storage area, avoiding the delay of writing the data into the slower main memory of the PC. A second was branch prediction—guessing which commands the processor would be asked to carry out in the future. A third was a technique for executing several commands simultaneously instead of one after another. Because Digital's allegation was that its patents had been willfully infringed, the billions of dollars that Intel might be liable for if it lost the case would be tripled.

It was the biggest patent infringement claim in history.

Because Digital feared that Intel might delay and maneuver if it tried to negotiate the issue, it filed the suit without warning. After an initial period of confusion, Intel hit back just two weeks later with a countersuit of its own, claiming that Digital had failed to return to

Intel confidential documents it had received in the course of the Alpha negotiations. Intel also warned Digital of its intention to cut off supplies of microprocessors once the current contract between the two companies expired later in 1997.

Digital retorted that the documents were no more than the standard technical information that Intel shares with its computer-industry customers—and as this book went to press, the company was considering making an anti-trust complaint against Intel.

In *Only the Paranoid Survive*, Andy Grove acknowledges the arrival of the Internet as a "10x force" facing Intel.

But there is another tidal wave approaching the Intel shore that is entirely of the company's own making. Its code name is Merced. Named after a river whose source is in California's Yosemite National Park, Merced is the successor to the Pentium Pro. But it is a successor with a difference. With Merced, Intel proposes to overhaul the x86 instruction set for the first time in twenty years. The change represents a recognition inside Intel that it needs to redesign its chip architecture, from the basic instructions upwards, in order to continue to deliver the kind of performance improvements in the future that it has achieved in the past. Significantly, the new instruction set has been developed in cooperation with engineers at Hewlett-Packard. There's just one drawback to the plan: in doing so, the company puts at risk the backward compatibility—the ability to run every program ever written for any of its predecessors—that helped its x86 architecture to win the processor wars.

The Merced project approaches the problem with a thoroughness that is characteristic of Intel. The company recognizes that not even its own daunting market power will be enough to persuade the entire computer universe—hardware makers, software companies and consumers—to throw away all the programs ever written for the PC. So the jump to the new instruction set, known inside the company as IA-64 because it is a 64-bit Intel architecture, will take place in two stages. The Merced chip is stage one. A portion of its real estate will be devoted to circuitry that delivers full backward compatibility with x86 software. The rest of it will be based on an entirely new architecture that implements much of the recent research into microprocessor design. Stage two will be a future Intel device, not necessarily the immediate successor to Merced, that junks x86 compatibility once and for all and migrates the computing world to Intel's new architecture.

Clearly, Intel's strategy has to be to do everything it can to encourage the software industry to write new code for its new instruction set, and to postpone the introduction of "son of Merced" until the company is confident that the switch can be made. The evangelizing job may be easier than it first appears: Microsoft's introduction of Windows 95 demonstrated that software companies have a financial interest in persuading all their customers to upgrade to a new version of the project, and that if handled right, an industry-wide switch can take place.

But Intel's new chip brings more dangers with it than Microsoft's new operating system. If Intel introduces son of Merced too early, it risks provoking a split inside the computer industry—a sort of Protestants versus Catholics of the technology world—with some computer companies and software developers resisting the shift while others accept it. AMD, Cyrix and the other x86 clones, and also the proponents of different RISC architectures would pounce on such a schism with great enthusiasm, for it would give them the best chance they have ever had to dislodge Intel from its leading position in the industry.

There are equal risks if Intel is too conservative. If the company introduces Merced but then hesitates for too long before introducing son of Merced, its own products will be placed at a considerable disadvantage to the competition. Merced and its successor chips will effectively be two processors in one: evidently a more expensive prospect than a straight device that handles either x86 or the new 64-bit instruction set but not both. While Intel remains hobbled in this way, competitors will have an opportunity to pick whichever of the two architectures looks more profitable, and concentrate on that one. Of course, different competitors could choose different strategies, and Intel could then find itself faced with more effective low-cost competitors than at any time since the beginning of the 1980s.

Despite these risks, only brave souls will be ready to bet against Intel. With its dominant position in the industry, its massive investments in manufacturing capacity, and a management system that helps it to respond to change faster than many companies of its size, Intel doesn't look vulnerable.

NOTES

Page 3 **Rock's office:** Arthur Rock interview, 16 September 1995.
When Arthur Rock invested: Interview with Arthur Rock in *Harvard Business Review*, November–December 1987, p. 63.
Incoming phone call: Arthur Rock interview, 16 September 1995.
Soft-spoken voice: Jean Jones interview, 13 September 1995.
4 *New York Times:* See, for example, the front pages of the *New York Times* of 24 November 1994 and the *Wall Street Journal* of 25 November 1994.
known about the flaw: Andrew S. Grove, *Only the Paranoid Survive*, p. 16.
damaging report on CNN: *Moneyline*, 22 November 1994. Cable News Network, Inc.
Andy Grove . . . insisted: Grove Usenet posting, 27 November 1994.
5 **IBM . . . had broken ranks:** See final chapter.
[post-IBM] pandemonium: *Only the Paranoid Survive*, p. 14.
half a billion: Intel annual report 1994, p1.
6 **Class-action lawsuits:** In case 745729 filed in the Santa Clara District Superior Court, Intel agreed to pay some $6 million in lawyers' fees to settle the case.
Ornamental tie-pins: The company has never formally disclosed what it did with the Pentium chips that were returned from the distribution channel and customers or removed from its own inventories.
Share price . . . quadrupled: See www.yahoo.com for historic quotes of Intel stock.
Towering among its achievements: The microprocessor was patented by Texas Instruments, not by Intel, despite the fact that TI's device was not manufactured for the mass market. The patent has given rise to a great deal of expensive litigation and provided a handsome living for some of the engi-

neers who were around at the time and now work as consultants to the parties in litigation.

Page 8 **Acknowledged even by its own:** See William H. Davidow, *Marketing High Technology: An Insider's View* (Free Press, 1986), p. 6.

Intel resolved secretly: See the detailed account, given later in this book, of the breakdown of Intel's partnership with Advanced Micro Devices.

A string of . . . lawsuits: Among the legal disputes covered in this book are those between Intel and AMD, Intel and NEC, Intel and ULSI, Intel and Seeq, Intel and Kleiner, Perkins, Caufield & Byers, and Intel and Sequent. Among the cases that I have not found space to cover are Intel's disputes with Cyrix, and with other Japanese and Taiwanese technology companies.

9 **the company switched:** This too gave rise to lawsuits. Intel's attempts in 1997 to prevent AMD and Cyrix from using the MMX label on their microprocessors is discussed at the end of this book.

10 **House joke:** A senior official of AMD told me that an internal Intel document produced during the discovery process of one of the company's many legal tussles with AMD demonstrated that this "joke" is factually correct, but I have been unable to substantiate the claim.

tool of management: See *Only the Paranoid Survive*, passim.

11 **two of its best:** Federico Faggin and Ralph Ungermann. The creation of Zilog and its competition against Intel is described in detail in this book.

Gary Kildall: Brian Halla interview.

analyzed exhaustively: See, for example, Bruce Graham, *Intel Corporation (B): Implementing the DRAM Decision*, Graduate School of Business, Stanford University case PS-BP-256B.

13 **The company . . . refused to cooperate:** See Acknowledgments for a detailed account of the author's relations with Intel and the company's involvement in this project.

18 **One of the sketchiest:** The document itself is held at Intel's corporate museum in its Santa Clara headquarters.

If one of the Fairchild team can claim most credit for inventing the integrated circuit, it is Jean Hoerni. See Michael Malone, *The Microprocessor: A Biography* (Springer-Verlag, 1995), pp. 56–57.

19 **the Quiz Kid:** This paragraph and the one following draw heavily on Tom Wolfe's profile, "The Tinkerings of Dr. Noyce," *Esquire*, December 1983, p. 346ff. The fact that this is the only major magazine profile of Noyce written in his lifetime is an indication of how recently the leading figures of the computer business have received prominent coverage in the U.S. media.

local hardware store: Bruce MacKay interview, 10 January 1996.

20 **Gordon Moore:** Material on this page is drawn from interviews with Gene Flath, H. T. Chua, Jean Jones, Tim May, and others.

21 I am grateful to Joel Shurkin, author of a forthcoming biography of Shockley, for his help in checking the details of the departure of the "Traitorous Eight."

If it was a success: Arthur Rock interview, 16 September 1995.

The account given here of the problems of Fairchild draws on interviews with Arthur Rock, who helped the Shockley renegades come to terms with Sherman Fairchild, and with a number of former Fairchild employees who joined Intel, including Federico Faggin, Roger Borovoy, Joe Friedrich, and others. It also draws on the detailed accounts of Fairchild's history that appear in Clyde Prestowitz, *Trading Places* (Charles E. Tuttle, 1988), pp. 20–22; Dirk Hansen, *The New Alchemists* (Avon, 1982), pp. 92-115; Michael S. Malone, *The Big Score: The Billion Dollar Story of Silicon Valley* (Doubleday, 1985), p. 57ff.

Page 22 **Sunny weekend afternoon:** By the account given by Moore and published in the company's *Defining Intel: 25 Years/25 Events* (order number 241730; Intel Corp 1993), this meeting was the first time that Moore and Noyce discussed the possibility of leaving Fairchild. It is understandable that the two men would not wish to admit that they had planned their departure earlier. The Moore chronology is contradicted in the account given by Bob Graham, in interviews with the author, of his own involvement with the creation of Intel.

scale back the contributions: One of the consequences of the policy on equity at Intel that was adopted by Noyce, Moore, and Rock was that the company's two first hires, Bob Graham and Andy Grove, were given no opportunity at the company's foundation to buy equity in the business. They did of course receive options later on, which have in Grove's case netted him close to $100 million; but the close holding of equity at the outset is the key reason for the twentyfold disparity between the financial rewards that Moore and Grove derived from their involvement with Intel. See Intel's IPO prospectus, published by C. E. Unterberg, Towbin Co., 13 October 1971, pp. 13–17.

23 **the Intel name:** See *A Revolution in Progress: A History of Intel to Date* (Intel Corp., 1984) (Order number 231295), p. 8.

Two . . . leave Fairchild: *Palo Alto Times*, 2 August 1968, p. 6. See also "Two found new firm," *San Jose Mercury-News*, 6 August 1968, p. 2.

25 **Exactly what we were predicting:** Joe Friedrich interview.

magnetic core: I am grateful to Stan Mazor and Rich Belgard for helping me put the significance of magnetic core in context.

26 **Silicon gate:** Federico Faggin, Joe Friedrich, Gene Flath interviews.

Goldilocks strategy: See *Defining Intel*, p. 7.

27 **Founded to steal:** Stan Mazor interview, 17 September 1995.

Scientists were happy: Histories of Silicon Valley have placed considerable emphasis on this point. See, for example, *The Big Score: The Billion Dollar Story of Silicon Valley*, Michael S. Malone, (Doubleday, 1985), p. 91ff.

the Wagon Wheel: See Wolfe, "The Tinkerings of Robert Noyce."

Selection process: This paragraph draws on interviews with Ted Hoff, Gene Flath, Joe Friedrich, Hal Feeney, Stan Mazor, Tom Rowe, and others.

28 **Even if we don't succeed:** Ted Hoff interview, 12 September 1995.

put in an order: Gene Flath interview; also see *A Revolution in Progress: A History of Intel To Date*, Intel Corp 1984 (Order number 231295), p. 6, for a slightly different account of the same incident.

Page 29 **Barbie combs:** H. T. Chua interview. 4 January 1996.

30 **two thousand wafer starts:** Tom Rowe interview.

32 **Holland Tunnel by bus:** See Constance Casey, "Manager Puts Practical Advice in Print", *San Jose Mercury-News*, 18 October 1983; also see Grove's interview with Terry Gross on "Fresh Air," National Public Radio, **date?** 1996.

working as a busboy: Background interview.

33 **To one . . . to another . . . to a third:** Background interviews. The close friends and associates of Grove who provided this information did so on condition of not being identified.

34 One of Silicon Valley's leading PR men told me on condition of not being identified that Andy Grove once sent back to him a draft text he had prepared on Intel's early history for a company document, which Grove considered gave him insufficient credit by failing to describe him as one of the company's founders. The PR man was more amused than annoyed, but thought it would be impolitic to argue the toss.

A fourth man: Bob Graham interview.

36 **Organization chart:** background interview.

37 **Doctor[s] Noyce, Moore, Grove:** Bruce MacKay interview. See also *A Revolution in Progress*, p. 7. The company's official history claims that the idea of paging members of staff who had Ph.D.s as "Doctor" was "another [short-lived] attempt to impress customers," and suggests that "the Ph.D.s soon put a stop to it themselves." Grove is unusual among CEOs of U.S. industrial companies, however, in having himself referred to even today as "Dr. Grove" in a wide range of corporate materials, including press releases.

Flath confronted Grove: Gene Flath interview.

38 **first engineering hires:** Ibid.

friendly rivalry: This paragraph is based on interviews with Hal Feeney, Stan Mazor, H. T. Chua, Bruce MacKay, John Reed.

39 **Honeywell wanted . . . to ship:** Phil Spiegel interview.

40 **Toasted . . . with champagne:** For more details on Intel's champagne tradition, see *A Revolution in Progress*, p. 8.

Willy Wonka's factory: Grove quoted in *Defining Intel*, p. 7.

41 **I want to see every wafer:** Joel Karp interview.

42 **reflow . . . referred to . . . using "anneal":** Ibid.

Setting his alarm clock: Bob Graham interview.

44 **C. Lester Hogan:** There are conflicting accounts of Hogan's arrival at Fairchild and the dispute with Motorola in *The Big Score*, Everett M. Rogers and Judith K. Larsen, *Silicon Valley Fever* (Basic Books, 1984), *The New Alchemists*, and *Trading Places*. This paragraph draws on those accounts and on interviews with Ed Turney, Sven Simonsen, Elliot Sopkin, and Tom Skornia.

45 **Gang of local toughs:** I am grateful to Tom Skornia for giving me access to "American Dream," his unpublished manuscript memoir, which covers this incident. The account here also draws on *The Big Score*, pp. 100–103.

46 **Turney . . . was holed up:** Ed Turney interview.

Page 47 **Sanders's first port of call:** Tom Skornia, Arthur Rock interviews.

Turney and Carey began to chafe: Ed Turney interview.

48 **incorporated in Delaware:** Tom Skornia interview.

The man who walked: Tom Skornia interview.

49 **It was June 20, 1969:** Ibid.

50 **We are . . . revolutionaries:** *Fortune*, November 1975, p. 134ff.

Karp displayed a wonderful ability: Material in this and the three succeeding paragraphs from Stan Mazor, John Reed, Joel Karp interviews.

51 **It's lucky:** Bruce MacKay interview.

52 **How can you do this?:** Ibid.

53 **carried them in a leather carpetbag:** Ibid.

Grove asked him: John Reed interview.

54 **Reed, you screwed up:** Ibid.

55 **when Noyce . . . began to speak:** Ibid.

his boss was a terrifying driver: Ibid.

56 **One of the clichés:** The quotations here are taken from a copy of Vadasz's review of Reed shown to the author.

57 **Here is a . . . report:** The quotation is taken from a copy of Reed's reply shown to the author.

happy with ninety-five: John Reed interview.

58 **The latest . . . *Electronics*:** Hoff's article appeared 3 August 1970.

as long as I am in this company: Joel Karp interview.

The bipolar engineers began to find it harder to book time on the testing equipment. H. T. Chua interview; also unattributable background interview.

the most diehard enthusiasts: H. T. Chua interview.

59 **He had a knack:** material on the bipolar/MOS tensions is drawn from interviews with H. T. Chua, Federico Faggin, Stan Mazor, John Reed, Joel Karp, and others.

the pressure became too much: H. T. Chua, John Reed interviews.

Grove would confide: Unattributable background interview.

60 **A downturn:** See "Business," Intel IPO prospectus, p. 8, and "Consolidated Statements of Income," p. 6.

twenty-six acres: See also *A Revolution in Progress*, p. 8.

The term "Silicon Valley" was coined by Don Hoefler, a prominent industry reporter at the time.

61 **Ann Bowers . . . went:** Ann Bowers interview.

What is the meaning of this: Ibid.

Bowers would have to warn: Sue McFarland interview.

62 **I am Andy Grove:** The account of this incident is based on an interview with Sue McFarland.

64 Work at Intel starts at 8:00. Sue McFarland interview; see also "Intel Delivers Promptness," in *A Revolution in Progress*, p. 45, and *What Makes Intel Int$_e$l?*, November 1984, Intel order number 231193-001, unnumbered third page.

65 **No interruptions:** Sue McFarland interview. On one occasion, McFarland recalled that Larry Hootnick, Intel's CFO, asked her to interrupt Grove

during a meeting to ask him an urgent question. McFarland explained that Grove disliked being interrupted; Hootnick insisted. When she went in to put the question, Grove was as furious as she had expected. He shouted "Fuck Larry Hootnick!" McFarland replied: "Do I really have to?"
He threw the dictionary: Sue McFarland interview.
eat yellow snow: Ibid.

Page 68   **You should have thought:** Ibid.
Memo in reply: The account given here is drawn on a copy of the memo shown to the author.

69   **news of Intel's breakthrough:** Federico Faggin interview.

70   A good and very detailed account of the creation of Intel's first microprocessor appears in Michael Malone's *The Microprocessor: A Biography*, pp. 10–15. The version here is primarily based on the author's interviews with Ted Hoff, Federico Faggin, Hal Feeney, and Stan Mazor, and on correspondence between Intel and Nippon Calculating Machine Corporation. Where these primary sources conflict with Malone, I have preferred the primary source of the interviews.

74   **Intel's marketing people:** Stan Mazor, Ted Hoff interviews.
For more information on the adventures of the Microsoft founders with Intel's early microprocessors, see Stephen Manes and Paul Andrews, *Gates* (Doubleday, 1993), where this incident is described.

76   **Intel's first development system:** I am grateful to John Doerr for his insights into the significance of the developments systems in Intel's history.
a neat way of hooking customers: Jim Lally interview.
The kind of business: Ed Gelbach interview.

77   **Andy Grove published a book:** *High-Output Management* by Andrew S. Grove (Vintage Books, 1986).

78   **Grove's determination:** Mike Gullard, Gene Flath, Joe Friedrich interviews.
We embarked: See Robert Burgelman, ed., *Strategic Management of Technology*, pp. 314–51.
Grove's sleepless nights: See "The Rocky Road to a RAM," in *A Revolution in Progress*, p. 11.
going out on the line: Keith Thomson, quoted from ibid.

79   **turd polishing:** Bill Lattin interview.
Betty or Jane: Gene Flath interview; see also "Clean Rooms and Bunny Suits," in *A Revolution in Progress*, p. 31.

80   **He was damned:** Bob Graham interview.
HAVE RECEIVED MUSKETS: Ibid.
Graham resented: Ibid.
I'm not that kind: Ibid.

81   **Huh? Huh?:** Bill Jordan interview.
I could not get Andy to understand: Bob Graham interview.

82   **Bob, we can't do this:** Ibid.

84   The sales and income figures in this newsflash and those that follow it are based on the annual reports from the corresponding years, not on the restated figures used by Intel in retrospect.

Page 88 **found himself pounding the streets:** Ed Turney interview.
    89 **Fairchild took the threat . . . seriously:** Ibid.
        most customers had no . . . need: I am grateful to Tom Skornia for giving me access to the discussion of AMD's marketing of Mil Spec parts in his unpublished memoir.
        just a marketing ploy?: Sven Simonsen interview.
    90 **We'll do it in six weeks:** Ibid.
        The goodwill . . . earned: Ibid.
    91 As noted above, the consolidated statement of operations in Intel's 1971 annual report (pages unnumbered) included an extraordinary item of $1,427,504 in income from MIL. Without the extraordinary item, the company would have reported losses of $412,424 for 1971.
    92 **not as emotionally satisfying:** Grove's quotation appears in Burgelman, *Strategic Management of Technology and Innovation*, p. 336.
        AMD's public relations: Elliot Sopkin interview.
    93 **always six months ahead:** Ed Turney interview.
        Others thought Sanders's clothes: Background interview.
        let's go and have a drink: Elliot Sopkin interview.
    94 **Noyce and Moore . . . sit back:** *Defining Intel*, p. 8.
        gave his colleagues little opportunity: Sven Simonsen, Ed Turney, Elliot Sopkin interviews.
        Elliot, do we have security guards: Elliot Sopkin interview.
    95 **Botte had sued:** AMD prospectus for IPO, Donaldson, Lufkin & Jenrette, Inc., 27 September 1972, p. 19.
        Four of Sanders's partners: Background interview.
    96 **Sanders was . . . paying himself:** AMD prospectus for IPO, p. 20.
        Sanders set to work: Tom Skornia interview; *American Dream*.
    97 **the most difficult-to-use:** Moore quoted in *Strategic Management of Technology and Innovation*, p. 317.
    99 **"turd polishing":** Bill Jordan interview.
        a company that never had a product: Ibid.
   101 **Memory systems might be:** Bill Jordan, Larry Hootnick interviews.
        We put together a 16-bit array: Dov Frohman quotation from *A Revolution in Progress*, p. 21.
   102 **The movie showed a pattern:** Gordon Moore quotation from *Defining Intel*, p. 11.
   103 **Watch out for Dov:** Joe Friedrich interview.
   105 **the first set of wafers:** Ibid.
   107 **Within seven years:** Intel Corp. *Annual Report* 1973, p. 3.
        issuing nearly 70,000 new shares: Ibid., p. 20.
        Vadasz called Friedrich: Joe Friedrich interview.
   108 **Vadasz refused to sanction:** Federico Faggin interview.
   109 **No more, he begged:** Stan Mazor interview.
        Ed Gelbach decided: As head of Intel's sales and marketing operation, Gelbach had the final operational say over product pricing.
   110 **That got his attention:** Unattributable background interview.
        Grove was yelling: Joel Karp interview.

Page 111 **Every employee was required:** Roger Nordby interview.

A manager's work: Quotation from *High-Output Management* by Andrew S. Grove, p. 71.

112 **Grove was always . . . taking notes:** This account of Grove's management techniques is drawn from discussions with a number of interviewees, including Ed Gelbach, Jack Carsten, Casey Powell, Larry Hootnick, and Roger Borovoy. **I thought I told you:** Terry Opdendyk interview.

114 **Andy pounded on the table:** Thomson quote from *A Revolution in Progress*, p. 45.

The idea was . . . opposed: Ann Bowers, Roger Nordby, Pat Roboostoff interviews. An interesting feature of the Late List's introduction was that it was confined to the parts of the company that reported to Andy Grove, only becoming universal when his operational responsibilities spread to cover the entire business.

115 **the Late List was a symbol:** Federico Faggin interview.

116 **A chance remark:** Ibid.

Let's go see Grove: Ibid.

117 **To his great chagrin:** Ralph Ungermann interview.

He knew where the industry was going: Ibid.

118 **this would break down . . . communication:** See interview with Robert Noyce in "Creativity by the Numbers," *Harvard Business Review*, May–June 1980, pp. 122–32. It is worth noting that Noyce had long ceased to have day-to-day involvement in decision making at Intel when he gave the interview, so the idealized view he had of the company's inner workings was not surprising.

120 **Your name will be forgotten:** Federico Faggin interview. Many years later, Faggin was surprised to discover that an exhibit on the history of the microprocessor at the Intel museum failed to give appropriate prominence to his role in the development of the 4004 chip. When he remonstrated with Grove, the Intel CEO's response was to say: "PR is an asset. Do you want us to be promoting you?"

124 **I want you to fire Ted:** Roger Borovoy interview.

Andy was president: Ibid.

126 **Here you are:** Ibid.

127 **we give you a five-year license:** Ibid.

128 **Do you want the good news:** Ibid.

130 **picked up a rumor:** See *Electronics News*, 4 November 1974, p. 1; also *Electronics News*, 21 October 1974, p. 1.

131 **Borovoy . . . issued blood-curdling threats:** Ralph Ungermann interview. **It will increase the die size:** Ibid.

133 **We need to start work:** Federico Faggin interview.

135 **Go to the airport:** Paul Engel interview.

139 **Where's your copy of the memo:** Ibid.

Just give it to me: Interviewed for this book, Meieran maintained that the area of the Penang plant where Engel had noticed faulty wiring was different from the area where the fire started.

140 **Only because of the zeal:** Phil Spiegel interview.

Meieran briefed Engel: Paul Engel interview.

Page 141 **I need some help:** Ibid.

146 **Intel has experienced no stoppages:** See Intel's IPO prospectus, p. 12.
10,000 wafer starts a week: Howard Gopen, Roger Nordby, Will Kauffman interviews.

147 **Will, it's Howard:** Howard Gopen interview.

149 **I've just had a call:** Ibid.

153 **Grove had a very abrasive style:** Bill Lattin interview.

154 **Lattin's background . . . different:** Ibid.

155 **you want me to be program manager:** Ibid.

156 **work on the . . . new processor:** Bill Davidow interview; also see *Marketing High Technology*, pp. 1–12.

157 **Morse shared with Grove:** Steve Morse interview.

158 **he had learned the ropes . . . at Hewlett-Packard:** Terry Opdendyk interview.

162 **What Morse produced:** In accordance with Intel's long-running policy of treating the authorship of inventions partly as public relations, the patent over the 20-bit addressing system in the 8086 processor assigned to Intel was credited to the authorship of William Pohlman, Bruce Ravenel, James McKevitt, and Stephen Morse. Morse claims that "the design and instruction set was all mine." Ravenel did not join the project until the last design document was drafted; McKevitt wrote the microcode. Morse said: "What I did was the instruction set, the address base, the interrupt mechanism, everything describing the processor as a black box." Morse was not responsible for the implementation in hardware, including the circuit design, details of logic gates and pinouts. Morse also claimed that after Ravenel's departure, the company tried to remove Ravenel's name from an academic paper to which he had contributed.

163 **Would you please stop calling me that:** Ann Bowers interview.

164 **Tom Wolfe, "The Tinkerings of Robert Noyce,"** *Esquire*, December 1983.

165 **actually I'm Betty Noyce:** Background interview.
Betty Noyce . . . a large shareholder: See *Electronics News*, 24 June 1974, p. 79.
Turney had a reputation: Background interview.

166 **Some personal things:** Ed Turney interview.

168 **On the other side:** Sven Simonsen interview.
Jerry is very self-assured: Background interview.

170 **AMD took out double-page spreads:** Tom Skornia interview.
And a consortium: *American Dream*, p. 120.

172 **Jerry? Joe here:** Tom Skornia interview.

173 **I was told:** Sven Simonsen interview.

175 **Andy Grove circulated a memo:** The account given here and the quotations from the memorandum are based on a copy shown to the author.

176 **he . . . included a table:** *High-Output Management*, p. 18.

177 **One potential hire:** John Wharton interview.
Tell you what: Roger Nordby interview.

179 **This is a profit-making organization:** *A Revolution in Progress*, p. 46.
the wheels went . . . into action: John Wharton interview.

Page 181 **What is zis bullsheet:** Tim May interview.

184 **We just blew them away:** Ibid.

186 **return figures showed that 80 percent:** Jim Lally interview.

188 **Bob could stand up:** Background interview.

189 **He once forced Powell:** Casey Powell interview.
Grove paid a courtesy call: Ibid.

190 **People used to say:** Joe Friedrich interview.

192 **clues . . . harder to close your eyes to:** Jim Lally, Bill Davidow, Casey Powell, Ed Gelbach interviews.

193 **These guys are beating us:** see *Marketing High Technology*, pp. 1–12.

194 **to fucking kill Motorola:** Jim Lally interview.
Intel had five advantages: *Marketing High Technology*, p. 6.

195 **To make Intel's claim . . . plausible:** This account of Crush draws on Davidow's account in *Marketing High Technology* and on Jim Lally, John Doerr, Bill Davidow, Casey Powell, Jack Carsten, Ed Gelbach interviews.

196 **Handel wasn't a star salesman:** Bill Handel interview.

198 **All's fair in love, war, and sales:** Ibid.
Faggin and Ungermann had fallen prey: Ralph Ungermann, Federico Faggin interviews.

199 **I'm making the wrong part:** Tom Skornia interview.

201 **a young marketing planner:** Rich Melmon interview.
What's it good for?: Ted Hoff, Stan Mazor, Terry Opdendyk interviews; Moore quotation from *Defining Intel*, p. 13.

202 **Markkula put $91,000 of his fortune into Apple:** See John Sculley with John A. Byrne, *Odyssey: Pepsi to Apple*, (HarperCollins, 1987), 1994 edition, p. 93.

203 **Grove tried to have him fired:** Casey Powell interview.

204 **With only partial approval from above:** Terry Opdendyk interview.
When we went to provide technical support: Whetstone quote from *Defining Intel*, p. 16.

205 **Intel wasn't interested:** Brian Halla interview.
Kildall was out: Since Kildall is now dead, my account of this incident is not based on primary sources but on a reading of the coverage of it in various books and newspaper and magazine articles. The nub of the controversy is whether Kildall's absence when IBM came to call was evidence of arrogance and failure to grasp a big commercial opportunity, or whether it was simply because he had another important engagement out of town that day to which he happened to travel on his private aircraft. It is also acknowledged by many commentators that the agreement IBM presented to Kildall's wife and lawyer was so one-sided as to be almost unfair. By contrast, Bill Gates was willing to accept unreasonable demands from IBM; a slogan inside Microsoft as the company's relationship with IBM developed was "BOGU"—Bend Over, Grease Up. For further information, see Joel Shurkin, *Engines of The Mind* (W. W. Norton, 1984). A paticularly comprehensive account appears in Charles H. Ferguson and Charles R. Morris, *Computer Wars: How the West Can Win in a Post-IBM World* (Random House, 1993).

Page 206 **an unqualified no:** John Wharton interview.

IBM approached him: Sven Simonsen interview.

207 **Zilog ... was already done for:** Federico Faggin, Ralph Ungermann interviews.

211 **Shortly before Christmas 1980:** Gordie Campbell interview.

212 **guys showing up with suitcases of cash:** Ibid.

Ed, we need to see you: Ibid.

213 **The company was also incensed:** Roger Borovoy interview.

214 **Andy Grove was much less sanguine:** Ibid.

215 **Suing the VCs ... Rock's idea:** Ibid.

217 **Gee, Gordie:** Davidow quote from Gordie Campbell interview.

218 **John's firm had invested:** Ann Doerr interview.

220 **Grove had instituted:** See *A Revolution in Progress*, p. 47. To assuage employees' feelings at the end of the program, Intel gave out commemorative mugs bearing the legend "I Survived the 125," which were 25 percent larger than the standard twelve-ounce size. Intel was big on mugs, pins, badges, and commemorative ashtrays.

221 **Carsten hated his guts:** Casey Powell interview.

222 **Well, aren't you the problem:** My account of this meeting draws on interviews with many of the members of the executive staff, including Casey Powell, Larry Hootnick, Ed Gelbach, Bill Davidow, Gene Flath, Will Kauffman, and Bill Lattin—half of the officers of Intel other than the three founders named in the company's 1982 annual report. Many of those present still have extremely vivid recollections of the occasion. Jack Carsten refused to discuss the incident with the author, but said: "I want to be on record that I disagree strongly with your characterization of me as the instigator of the incident."

224 **On that fateful day:** I have not seen this note. My account of it is drawn from an interview with Powell.

225 **Andy, that's an also-ran:** Roger Borovoy interview.

These guys want to sue: Casey Powell interview.

227 **Linda Sanders, his first wife:** Tom Skornia interview.

228 **he hired Bruce Springsteen:** See *San Jose Mercury-News*, 19 December 1983, p. 1ff.

He gave away $240,000: "What Silicon Valley Firms Do to Motivate Their Employees," *New York Times*, 5 August 1980, p. 3E.

to finance my rather lavish lifestyle: Bruce Entin, "Why Sanders Sold Some of His AMD Stock," *San Jose Mercury-News*, 11 March 1981, p. 14D.

Sanders held a sheet of paper: Bruce Entin, "Sanders Leaves 'em Laughing," *San Jose Mercury-News*, 7 October 1981, p. 17D.

229 **he concocted:** Tom Skornia interview.

230 **It's fine with me:** Roger Borovoy interview.

231 **Simonsen had tried:** Sven Simonsen interview.

The look on Grove's face: Tom Skornia interview.

232 **Ten days later:** Rich Lovgren interview.

233 **Assure AMD they are our primary source:** See judgment in AMD–Intel arbitration, p. 10. The same arbitrator's judgment criticizes Intel for stalling on the transfer of some information to AMD which it had

promised under the agreement. "The information . . . was deliberately incomplete, deliberately indecipherable, and deliberately unusable by AMD engineers," wrote Judge Barton Phelps. "I need not at this point recite all the shabby facts concerning this failure. Suffice it to say that Intel's conduct in this regard was inexcusable and unworthy of a company whose announced standards . . . in respect of responsibility and good faith are as high as those at Intel. . . . I find that this delay in transfer and the transfer of erroneous information was the result of policies put into place and approved by Intel's senior management. There is no explanation for the Intel conduct other than to conclude that Intel was deliberately trying to shackle AMD's progress," ibid. p. 40. The text of the judgment appears as an exhibit in the Superior Court of the State of California in Santa Clara County courthouse, San Jose; the case number is 626879.

Page 234 **another internal Intel memo:** See Ibid., p. 55.

235 **The ad in the paper:** Rob Miller interview.

236 **someone's personal details:** Ibid.; unattributable background interview.
a year after he started: Rob Miller interview.

239 **Miller hit paydirt:** Ibid.
A few weeks later: Ibid.

240 **at the first high-level meeting:** Scott Gibson interview.
company legend had it: Unattributable background interview.

242 **Revenues from DRAMs had risen:** See tables on pp. 319–20 in *Strategic Management of Technology and Innovation.*

243 **An alert Intel engineer:** Dan Morgan, "Battling to Innovate and Emulate: Intel vs. Nippon Electric," *Washington Post*, 2 May 1983, p. 1; cited in *Trading Places*, p. 46.
the chips won't come back to us: see *Palo Alto Times*, 4 September 1979, p. 2.
The description here of the history of operating methods of Japanese semiconductor companies is partly based on the author's coverage of the Japanese semiconductor industry out of Tokyo between 1988 and 1991.

244 **didn't . . . let the vendors into our fabs:** Unattributable background interview.

245 **When . . . executives were taken around:** Larry Hootnick interview.
I had actually obtained leases: Quote from *Strategic Management of Technology and Innovation*, p. 329.

246 **The first Intel employee to see:** Henry Gregor interview.

247 **the issue became public:** My account of this meeting is based on *Trading Places*. Although I disagree with a fundamental premise of Prestowitz's analysis—namely, that the difficulties that the U.S. semiconductor companies had in competing with Japanese industry during the 1980s were overwhelmingly more due to unfair trading practices by the Japanese than to bad management by the Americans—his book is well researched and argued, and an essential introduction for anyone seeking to understand the topic of U.S.–Japan high-tech trade relations.
Hootnick took great pride: Larry Hootnick interview.
When he had finance responsibility: Will Kauffman interview.

Page 248 **a shocking new development:** see Burgelman, *Strategic Management of Technology and Innovation*, p. 331.

249 **a row-and-column addressing system:** Whittier quote appears in ibid., p. 333.

Gibson came to the conclusion: Scott Gibson interview.

251 **later published by the *Wall Street Journal*:** See *Trading Places*, p. 54.

Intel's own IPO document, published by C. E. Unterberg, Towbin Co., 13 October 1971, p. 3.

252 **the . . . U.S. Trade Representative:** See *Trading Places*, pp. 55–61.

253 **Moore and I were discussing:** Grove quoted in his own *Only the Paranoid Survive*, p. 89.

254 **Grove devoted a section to . . ."The Blast":** *High-Output Management*, p. 193–97.

255 **middlemen would board the morning buses:** Larry Hootnick, Rob Miller, Terry Hudock interviews.

256 **Zietzke, the former probation officer:** Unattributable background interview.

His name was Robert Westervelt: The account in this book of Westervelt's career with Intel is based on unattributable background interviews, an interview with Mike Fehr, and on court records held at the Santa Clara District Superior Court, San Jose. The case number is 617125.

259 **thick file of documents:** Mike Fehr interview.

261 **Another was Terry Hudock:** Terry Hudock interview.

262 **things we don't discuss with Price:** Hunter quote from ibid.

264 **He drafted a memo:** The description of the memo is based on a copy shown to the author by Terry Hudock.

265 **he discovered that the ribbon of his IBM typewriter had been removed:** Terry Hudock, Rob Miller interviews.

267 **A story in the *San Jose Mercury-News*:** "Chip Shortage Slows Progress," 11 March 1984, p. 1.

I've got an idea: Grove quotation from Roger Borovoy interview.

270 **Intel's license to NEC:** *NEC Corporation and NEC Electronics Inc. v. Intel*, judgment, case no. C-84-20799-WPG, Judge William P. Gray, United States District Court, Northern District of California, p. 11.

271 **The judge seemed to side with Intel:** Dan Siegal, Doug Derwin, Rich Belgard, Roger Borovoy interviews.

273 **Siegal offered the . . . engineer a choice:** Gary Davidian interview.

276 **We're pleased to report:** Intel *Annual Report* 1986, p. 3.

277 **the 386—a new processor:** Formally, the device was known as the Intel 80386. Since the launch of the 386, the names of Intel processors have become a rich source of income for lawyers, as explained later in the book.

278 **Compaq sales of $111 million:** See Compaq Computer Corporation *Annual Report* 1983, p. 3.

279 **The compilers we wrote:** John Novitsky interview.

280 **We'd go to the applications guys:** Unattributable background interview.

Intel reported net income of $25 million: See Intel Corporation *Annual Report* 1987, p. 3.

Page 281 **Gelbach's worry:** see Burgelman, *Strategic Management of Technology and Innovation*, p. 313ff.

282 **case study in the business school:** Grove continues to provide lecture courses to students at Stanford's Graduate School of Business.

the jewel of the kingdom: see *New York Times*, 3 April 1988, p. B1.

284 **one of Intel's senior patent lawyers:** The account of Intel's dealings with ULSI is based on the extensive court records of the cases involved.

285 **a wiry, energetic immigrant:** George Hwang interview.

286 **the only supplier:** Ibid.

287 **Intel published a detailed guide:** See *IEEE Micro*, August 1987.

288 **Dunlap thanked Hwang:** *Intel v. ULSI* case notes; George Hwang interview.

290 **Pearson went to interview Lovgren:** Lovgren interview, *Intel v. ULSI* court papers.

293 **It is our position:** *Intel v. ULSI* court papers.

294 **I hated walking through hallways:** Tim May interview.

295 **So I hear you're leaving:** Grove quote from ibid.

296 **finally making the big move:** Barrett quote from ibid.

My last mission to myself: Will Kauffman interview.

297 **prescriptions into effect:** When Grove handed over the presidency of Intel to Craig Barrett in 1997, he credited Barrett as "the architect of our manufacturing system."

No, replied Grove: Terry Opdendyk interview.

298 **the third most powerful executive:** Unattributable background interview; Ed Gelbach interview.

299 **Not now, Grove replied:** Bettie Hootnick interview.

300 **EPROM was losing:** Larry Hootnick interview.

301 **They can't do it!:** Grove quoted in ibid.

participated in a "benchmarking" exercise: The account of the project given here is based on a summary of the survey results shown to the author.

302 *New York Times:* "An 'Awesome' Intel Corners Its Market," 3 April 1988, p. B1.

303 **Nathan Myhrvold:** Unattributable background briefing.

304 **Stork and Novitsky were assigned:** John Novitsky interview.

305 **Costing $4 million:** See *Defining Intel*, p. 27; also see Cathy Madison, "Intel Ads Provoke Rivals' Wrath," *Adweek*, 26 February 1990; John Hillkirk, "Intel Ads Called 'Sheer Foolishness,' " *USA Today*, 6 November 1989.

The Intel386 chip . . . successful: Dennis Carter quoted in Hillkirk.

Ron Whittier, marketing director: quote from Madison.

307 **an expensive way to vent:** Ibid.

309 **The company switched off:** See AMD *Annual Report* 1991, p. 4.

310 **Mike Webb came from Austin:** Rich Lovgren interview.

311 **Hey, Rich, said Dunlap:** Ibid.

passed them on to Armstrong: Ibid.

313 **Sanders tried to make a joke:** See Russell Blinch, "Intel in Tough Battle

Marketing Pentium," Reuters Financial Services, San Francisco, 14 July 1994.

Page 314   **The partnership campaign:** See Shelly Garcia, "Agencies Split over Wisdom of Intel Effort to Brand Its Microprocessor Chips," *Adweek*, 11 November 1991.

     money down the drain: Michael Murphy quote on Intel Inside campaign from Associated Press report, "Intel Launches a Huge Advertising Campaign," published in *Los Angeles Times*, 2 November 1991, p. D3.

315   **Let the leaders lead:** Will Kauffman, Larry Hootnick interviews; unattributable background interviews.

317   **they'll do bad and not good:** Grove quote from Terry Opdendyk interview.

318   **over five thousand as early as 1984:** See Intel Corporation *Annual Report* 1984, p. 25.

     Intel also had a sabbatical program: Roger Nordby interview.

319   **Handel had matured:** As described later in this section, Handel sued Intel following his departure from the company. The details here are drawn from the papers on the lawsuit in the Santa Clara District Superior Court in San Jose, California. The case number is 719434.

320   **His lawyer took depositions:** Bill Handel interview.

321   **The same dilemma faced Gregor:** The account of Gregor's case given here is based on the documents held in the Santa Clara District Superior Court and on an interview with Henry Gregor.

322   **Roboostoff had joined Intel in 1978:** The details of Roboostoff's early career with Intel are based on an interview with Pat Roboostoff.

323   **It was an accident:** The account given here of Roboostoff's departure from the company is based on unattributable background interviews.

326   **Hootnick arranged for Roboostoff's new employer:** Unattributable background interviews.

328   **It didn't mean:** In order to avoid confusion, the word "microcomputer" has been used in the early parts of this book to refer only to the complete computer system including processor, memory, and peripheral devices, and not in the narrower usage that AMD argued for in the dispute. This choice was based on the fact that in current 1990s usage "microcomputer" is almost never used to describe a processor. But it should not be taken as an endorsement of Intel's position in the dispute, which centered on the usage of the word two decades earlier.

331   **The patent:** I am grateful to Rich Belgard and Roger Borovoy for their advice on the subject of the '338 patent and semiconductor patents in general. The technical issues surrounding the patent are covered with great clarity in the *Microprocessor Report* newsletter, which I drew on in producing this account.

334   **its fortunes had never looked better:** Intel Corporation *Annual Report* 1992, p. 3 and passim.

336   **the foundries were really just "printing":** Rich Belgard, Roger Borovoy, Michael Slater interviews.

     Albert Mu was a typical example: The account of Mu's case in this book is derived from the documents in the Santa Clara District Superior Court in San Jose, California, and on unattributable background interviews. Vinod Dham, who now works for AMD, was contacted in order to obtain a comment but failed to return calls. The case number is 718315.

Page 341 **The most striking new partnership:** An excellent account of Gateway's history appears in Charles Platt, "Beats Skinning Hogs," *Wired* 3.05, May 1995, and at www.wired.com.

342 **Gunn began to muse:** Robert Gunn interview.

347 **One of the Oregon contractors:** Randal Schwartz interview. The account of Schwartz's prosecution given here is also derived from court papers filed in Oregon and from material posted on the World Wide Web.

353 **The caller identified himself:** Numerous newspapers and magazines have published stories on Nicely's dealings with Intel. The account here draws on Martha Slud, "Chipping Pentium's Reputation," Associated Press, 25 December 1994; Peter Baker, "Math Prof Wasn't Counting on Bringing Down Pentium," *Washington Post*, 18 December 1994; "Marketing and Technology: Intel's Chip of Worms?" *The Economist*, 17 December 1994; Aaron Zitner, "Sorry, Wrong Number: Intel Computer Chip Sometimes Makes Inaccurate Math," *Boston Globe*, 24 November 1994; John Markoff, "Flaw Undermines Accuracy of Pentium Chips," *New York Times*, 24 November 1994; "Floating Point Flaw Makes Headlines," *Intel Leads*, January 1995, p. 4.

Intel organizes its tech support: John Novitsky interview.

355 **As the project was nearing completion:** Burgelman, *Strategic Management of Technology and Innovation*, pp. 462–63.

356 **To speed up division:** The best technical description of the Pentium bug appears in Linley Gwennap, "How Bad Is the Pentium FPU Bug?" *Microprocessor Report*, 26 December 1994.

357 **it was already standard practice:** Michael Slater had campaigned for some time in his newsletter to get the industry to change its approach to the issue. See Michael Slater, "Intel's Handling of Bug Is the Real Problem," *Microprocessor Report*, 26 December 1994.

360 **Intel's new salary plan for its workers:** The jokes reprinted here were downloaded from alt.jokes.pentium.

361 **The process was taking . . . longer:** Grove quote from *Only the Paranoid Survive*, p.11.

Intel's stock finishing the day: Quotations from CNN printed by kind permission of Cable News Network, Inc., *Moneyline*, 22 November 1994.

363 **Users started calling:** Grove quote in *Only the Paranoid Survive*, p. 13.

364 **the IBM analysis was quite wrong:** See also Intel's rebuttal of IBM's analysis on www.intel.com.

365 **IBM's ban on Pentium sales:** See "How Bad Is the Pentium FPU Bug?"

366 **By 2:00 A.M.:** Ken Hendren quote from Mark Ivey, "Surviving the Flaw," *Intel Leads*, February 1995.

368 **The 604 delivered only 15 percent:** For detailed performance comparisons, see Linley Gwennap, "PowerPC Delivers Beef, but No Sizzle," *Microprocessor Report*, 19 June 1995.

Page 369   **most commentators believed:** The suggestion was first made publicly in an article in the *Harvard Business Review*; by 1996, the idea had become almost received wisdom in the computer industry

       tightened up the ... policy: The decision for the change was presumably based on the belief that Intel employees were using telecommuting and flexible working as a way of delivering lower productivity. If this were the case, it is hard to see why the company's procedures were not changed earlier.

       Intel was able to cut: A good summary of the important technical developments inside Intel appears in Linley Gwennap, "RISC Ambushed by Pentium Pro," *Microprocessor Report*, 22 January 1996.

  370   **What is so disappointing:** Quotation from Brian Case, "The x86 Is Here to Stay—Get Used to It," *Microprocessor Report*, 16 February 1995.

  373   **he refused to comment:** "Asked whether he would shake hands with Jerry Sanders, chief executive officer of AMD, Grove said, 'I have nothing to say about that.'" "A Few Words with Andrew S. Grove," *San Jose Mercury-News*, 1 February 1995.

       Intel's architecture lab: See James F. Moore, *The Death of Competition* (HarperCollins Business, 1996), pp. 216–22, for a detailed description of the lab's activities.

       more time spent on Intel–Microsoft collaboration: Gates quote appears in "A Conversation with the Lords of Wintel," *Fortune* 8 July 1996, p. 42.

  374   **response from Redmond was swift:** Unattributable background interviews.

       they put a careful gloss: Gates and Grove quotes are from "A Conversation with the Lords of Wintel," *Fortune* 8 July 1996, p. 42.

  375   **Grove delivered a keynote speech:** Part of the text of the speech appears at www.intel.com; Intel distributes free copies of a videotape of the presentation to members of the public who order from its website.

  378   **the company was able to claim:** See "Intel's Corporate Donations Hit New Record: Donations Increase 83 Percent from 1995," press release dated March 19, 1997.

  381   The account of the MMX dispute that appears here is drawn from court documents filed by Intel and AMD, together with a transcript of the hearing. I am also grateful to Rich Belgard for his advice on the significance of the dispute.

       The old Intel: Michael Slater, "Intel's New World View: Market Growth, Not Competition, Is the Top Concern," *Microprocessor Report*, 12 February 1996.

  382   **Thomas McCoy:** Quote from Thomas McCoy appears in an AMD press release issued the day after the filing of the suit, which appears on the Web at www.amd.com.

ACKNOWLEDGMENTS

Thanks for the idea, Howard.

It was in the spring of 1995, and we were sitting in a cafeteria at Intel's headquarters in Santa Clara. Across the table from me was Howard High, one of the company's most senior PR people.

I was supposed to be on vacation at the time. Having just quit a job as technology-page editor of one newspaper, I'd decided to take a couple of weeks off with my family in California before starting another job writing a weekly technology column for another newspaper. Since we were almost driving past Intel's door, it seemed to make sense to spend a couple of hours getting a little more familiar with the world's most powerful chip manufacturer. So here I was, trying not to grimace at the bitterness of the evil-tasting Intel coffee, chatting with the PR man after a pair of useful background briefings. It was already clear that Intel was more than just an important company. It was a fascinating company, too, and one that I needed to learn more about.

"Tell me, Howard," I asked. "Which of the books on Intel do you think I ought to read?" I'd assumed there must be at least three. By most measures—stature, profitability, market influence—Intel was more important than companies like IBM, Apple, Dell, and Compaq, all of whose stories had already been told at length in books. The only company that surpassed Intel's dominance of the computer business was Microsoft, and a new crop of titles on Bill Gates and his empire seemed to come every season.

But my assumption that Intel must already have been studied in depth by an outside writer was wrong. "There aren't any books," said High.

It was six months later before I began to realize why.

As soon as that vacation was over, I set to work on the preliminary research for this book. In the summer of 1995, I sent faxes to Andy Grove and Gordon Moore, telling them that I'd been commissioned by publishers in New York and London to write a book on the company, and offering to fly over and brief Intel people on the project. "My aim is to write a book that is fair, serious, and accurate," I wrote, "a task that will be easier with your participation than without."

The initial reactions were positive. At Intel's suggestion, I sent over a preliminary list of people inside the company I hoped to interview and started talking to the company's PR department about access to the Intel archives. I then moved over to Silicon Valley with my family to start work in earnest on the project. That was when things at Intel began to change. None of the interview requests yielded fruit. The copies of archive materials that I'd been offered didn't arrive. Calls to the company went unreturned.

At first, there seemed nothing surprising about this. The research for my last book, about Richard Branson, the billionaire founder of Britain's Virgin airline conglomerate, had followed a similar pattern. I'd approached Branson at the outset to let him know that I would be writing a book and that he would be welcome to take part if he chose. Initially he decided not to; then, when word began to filter back to him of the extensive research and interviewing I was doing, he changed his mind. Three months into the project, Branson's PR man called out of the blue: "Richard wants to know when you want to come and interview him," he said.

My hope was that when Grove and Moore realized that the project was serious, Intel might reconsider. I started my interviewing outside the company, talking to Intel suppliers, partners, and clients, and tracking down scores of former employees across the United States. The process was fascinating; it demonstrated the high caliber of the company's hiring. A high proportion of people who had joined Intel and then left had gone on to stellar careers elsewhere in America's high-tech industries—as engineers and inventors, managers and leaders, lawyers and accountants, venture capitalists and professional investors.

In February 1996, I received the expected out-of-the-blue call from an Intel vice-president, with the news that an interview with Andy Grove was about to be set up. At last, it seemed, the work was paying off. Two days later, the same VP called back and told me, with some embarrassment, that the interview had been canceled for reasons that she could not explain.

Over the following weeks, I received indirect messages from Intel managers and other people close to Grove, each offering conflicting reasons for the company's decision to pull out. One suggested that my faxes to Grove and Moore had offended people in the PR department, who liked to know about upcoming projects before their supervisors did. Another suggested that the company was worried that it would be seen as endorsing the book if it offered any cooperation at all. A third suggested that Grove was simply unable to come to terms with the idea of Intel's being the subject of a book over which he didn't have editorial control and explained that earlier attempts by outsiders to write the company's history had foundered over this very issue.

I never found out which of those reasons, if any, was the right one. But the outcome was clear. Aside from a conference call I had with Gordon Moore, a brief meeting and a few E-mail exchanges with Andy Grove, Intel's participation was limited to an offer to send me any documents on the company I wanted, provided they were already available from other public sources.

That was the company's official stance. Unofficially, Intel was doing a great deal more than just staying aloof from the project. After I told the company the names of some of the most prominent people in its history whom I had already spoken to at length, senior Intel executives contacted them, demanding they talk no further. A message was sent out from the top of the company to Intel managers all over the world, warning them that they might be approached in connection with this book and instructing them to say nothing and report all calls immediately to the company's press office. Current employees of the company who spoke to me knew that they were risking their jobs by doing so. Business partners were left with the clear impression that their relationship with Intel might suffer if they participated.

In one case, I tracked down an Intel consultant who had been named in a lawsuit against the company, asking for a comment on the allegation made against him in court papers that he had broken the law while carrying out an operation for Intel. In response, the frightened consultant made it clear that the company had put pressure on him. He had a lucrative contract with Intel, he explained, which made up a substantial proportion of his income, and the company had threatened to terminate the deal immediately if he said anything at all on the record. I urged him to think again: Since he was accused in the court papers of breaking the law on the company's behalf, it would be his own reputation as well as the company's that would be at risk if he chose to let the allegations against him go unanswered. He replied, through a Silicon Valley lawyer, in a strongly worded letter accusing me of bias.

Why did a company as prominent and respected as Intel respond in this way to a straightforward business book? I concluded that there were probably two reasons. One was that Intel and its top management have not yet fully adjusted to their new public role. As this book describes, Intel until the late 1980s saw itself as a component company whose key customers were engineers in other big companies. Only since the early 1990s has the company begun to market to consumers in earnest and to appreciate the consequences that flow from that change in emphasis.

The second factor behind Intel's attitude to this book may be the culture of secrecy that Andy Grove has created inside the organization. This culture is summed up in the slogan "Only the paranoid survive," and Grove has intellectualized it into a principle of management that requires even his very successful company to worry about threats that may be just around the corner.

But Intel is paranoid in its day-to-day business practices as well as its long-term strategies. AMD discovered, in one of its many court battles against the company during the 1980s, that Intel routinely kept stacks of paper next to its photocopiers preprinted with the legend "Intel Confidential." Midlevel Intel managers twice a year receive a standard three hours of legal training warning them among other things never to say that the company *dominates* the world's microprocessor business but only that it *leads*. To make sure its managers exercise proper caution, the company stages mock investigations and trials in which teams of Intel staff pretending to be law enforcement officials burst unannounced into an executive's office, seal it off, and cart away documents from the filing cabinets to check for any careless words that might put Intel at risk.

My belief is that this culture helps to explain why the company has become what it is today. That is why the later chapters of this book devote less attention to the details of how Intel designs and manufactures new products—activities that have developed in an evolutionary rather than a revolutionary way during the past decade—and more attention to the company's marketing, management, and competitive tactics.

Intel's attempts to frustrate the project mean that this book cannot claim to be more than an imperfect first draft of the company's history. It would have been illuminating to hear detailed responses from Andy Grove and Gordon Moore to many of the incidents described here by their colleagues, partners, and competitors. But the lack of input from Intel does not by any means invalidate the project, for the Grove and Moore view of Intel's history is largely available from other sources. Intel has published several extensive essays on its own history and culture, and the company's top management have put their views on record in the thousands of news clippings, technical articles, interviews, reports, and business-school case studies examined in the researching of this book. Public court documents and government papers, obtained under the Freedom of Information Act, provided further information.

None of these outside sources gave much clue as to what the world inside Intel really looks like. For that, I relied on hundreds of hours of interviews with Intel's partners, customers, suppliers, advisers, competitors, and of course its employees, officers, and directors, and their families. The Intel people I spoke to—whose periods of service with the company began at its founding in 1968 and before, and run right up to the publication of this book—have a combined experience at Intel of many hundreds of years.

I am particularly grateful to the current Intel employees and their families who spoke to me in defiance of the company's instructions; for obvious reasons, they cannot be named here. The same is true of a number of people working for companies that have commercial relations with Intel who helped me but feared that they or their employers might suffer if they were identified.

Among those who gave interviews without requesting anonymity, there were many who were generous enough to spend long hours with me, talking in several separate sessions. I would like to thank Tom Armstrong, Richard Belgard, Brenda Borovoy, Roger Borovoy, Ann Bowers, Lee Boysel, Robert Burgelman, Gordie Campbell, Jack Carsten, H. T. Chua, Cathy Cook, Barry Cox, Jack Cundari, Gary Davidian, Bill Davidow, Doug Derwin, Vin Dham, Gerry Diamond, Ann Doerr, John Doerr, Paul Engel, David Epstein, Elvia Faggin, Federico Faggin, Hal Feeney, Mike Fehr, Skip Fehr, Gene Flath, Joe

Friedrich, Ed Gelbach, Scott Gibson, Howard Gopen, Bob Graham, Henry Gregor, Ron Grindstaff, Mike Gullard, Robert Gunn, Brian Halla, Bill Handel, Ted Hoff, Bette Hootnick, Larry Hootnick, Terry Hudock, George Hwang, Jean Jones, Bill Jordan, Joel Karp, Will Kauffman, Jim Lally, Bill Lattin, Tom Lawrence, Richard Lovgren, Tor Lund, Bruce MacKay, Mike Malik, Tim May, Stan Mazor, Sue McFarland, Rich Melmon, Rob Miller, Steve Morse, Albert Mu, Terry Mudrock, Nick Nichols, Jan Nielsen, Roger Nordby, Terry Opdendyk, Kim Parrish, Mike Peak, Casey Powell, John Reed, Dave Rickey, Arthur Rock, Tom Rowe, Randal Schwartz, Dan Siegal, Sven Simonsen, Tom Skornia, Michael Slater, Elliot Sopkin, Phil Spiegel, Gary Summers, Tim Thurgate, Ed Turney, Ralph Ungermann, Rob Walker, John Wharton, Jack Yelverton.

The most useful secondary source I found was *Microprocessor Report*, the excellent newsletter published by the team of analysts and writers at MicroDesign Resources. Tom Skornia was particularly generous in allowing me access to his unpublished memoir covering his long association with Advanced Micro Devices and his dealings with Intel.

I am also grateful to Henry Lowood, history of science curator at Stanford University, for his help with videotaped archive material from the university's Silicon Valley project. Library staff and researchers at Stanford University, the University of California at Berkeley, Peter Cheek and his colleagues at the library of the *Financial Times*, and the Berkeley and San Francisco public libraries were also helpful beyond the call of duty. I would also like to thank the staff at the U.S. Department of Justice and the Federal Trade Commission who deal with requests for information under the Freedom of Information Act.

Joel Shurkin, Rich Belgard, Joel Karp, Richard Dale, Michael Jackson, Mike Peak, Bill Jordan, Gian Pablo Villamil, Tom Skornia, John Wharton, Larry Hootnick, Richard Lander, Stan Mazor, and Daniel Jackson were all very generous with their time in reading part or all of the manuscript, and alerted me to many mistakes both large and small. Al Zuckerman, my agent at Writers House in New York, shepherded the project from outline to finished book and was a wise adviser and tireless advocate throughout. I am also particularly grateful for the work done by Arnold Dolin and Matthew Carnicelli at Dutton and by Michael Fishwick at HarperCollins Publishers in championing the project and seeing it through to publication.

Emily Marbach's contributions as inspiration, guide, supporter, and confidante are beyond measure. I owe her more than thanks.

INDEX